The Story of the Interior

The Story of the Interior

How We Have Shaped Rooms and How They Shape Us

Graeme Brooker

With over 500 illustrations

Contents

Introduction 8

The Room

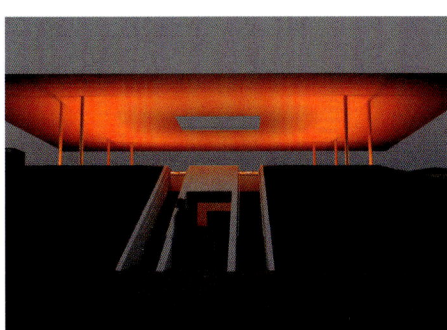

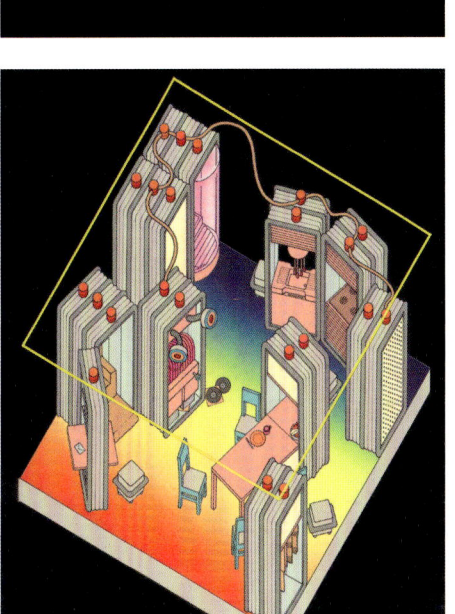

The Unified and the Autonomous Interior	18
Enclosures	24
Atmospheres	46
Passages	66
Objects	88
Technologies	106

The Private Interior

Rooms and the Home	126
Living Room	132
Kitchen	158
Dining Room	174
Bathroom	196
Bedroom	222

The Public Interior

The City and the Room	242
Social	248
Shop	276
Work	304
Infrastructures	324
Culture	350
Notes	382
Further Reading	384
Acknowledgments	386
Author Biography	387
Sources of Illustrations	388
Index	394

Introduction

We spend between 90 to 98 per cent of our existence indoors.[1] That means all but half a day a week is spent *inside*. Have you ever stopped to ask yourself why, how or from where the forms of interiors that you occupy have emerged? This book will help you answer these questions. *The Story of the Interior* reveals how concepts and elements found in ancient spaces are still in evidence in even the most contemporary rooms of today. From the cave to the castle, the palazzo to the palace, the airport terminal to the fashion boutique, through the interiors of history's most powerful people to the humble spaces within which you and I spend our days, this book will explore the ideas and realities of a vast and diverse array of inside spaces.

Why are interiors important? The twenty-first century is characterized as a time of responses to the challenges posed by a warming planet. The future of architecture is set to render new-build and single-use processes obsolete. Interior

01 Forming an ambiguous threshold between inside and out, the curved walls of Temporary Museum (Lake) in Amsterdam by Studio Anne Holtrop, 2010, exemplify how enclosure is fundamental to interiors.

INTRODUCTION

02　Light filtered by the vertical slit of the *mihrab* orientates prayer and creates atmosphere in Bait ur Rouf Jame mosque by Marina Tabassum Architects, 2012.
03　Furniture defines working and socializing in the office landscape by Kinzo, 2019, on the twenty-first floor of the Amorepacific headquarters in Seoul.
04　The pool room of Philip Johnson's iconic Four Seasons restaurant in the Seagram Building, New York, 1959, is inextricably linked to the idea of the 'power lunch'.

architects, designers and decorators are tasked with making existing buildings adapt to our new needs. This puts them and the interior front and centre of the future of the built environment. Interiors have always provided shelter (increasingly so in air-polluted, post-pandemic and climatically challenging times). The interiors that surround our lives are the constant companions to the obstacles we face, and their designers actively shape the ways in which we work, learn, love, travel and take our leisure.

Why a *story*? The stories that we hear and tell define us; we have relayed stories to each other since time began. These are narratives that are painted on cave walls, written in books or expressed in songs and through dance. Our understanding of history changes not because of the passage of time, but because of the way we interpret it and then how we tell stories about it to each other. Therefore, this book is not a linear chronologically focused history, but instead it is a retelling of stories that narrate the past, present and future of inside spaces. Both facts and fictions are hardwired into the DNA of the interior. The facts are the tangible interior elements: the walls, the materials and the objects of a room. The fictions are images, drawings, films – the portrayals of the way in which we live, work and play within interior spaces. The combination of fact and fiction makes for a rich and fluid narrative of both the solid

05 Objects displayed in *zidaka*, recessed niches, in a house in Lamu, Kenya, enliven the cool interior and enrich it with the life of its occupants.

06 Reusing existing structures to contain new interiors creates unique identities, as in the Capsule Hotel and Bookstore by Atelier Tao+C in Zheijiang, China, 2019.

and the ephemeral, issues and concerns that are fundamental when we consider interiors enclose the source of permanently shifting change – *us*.

What is new about *this* story? It was as recently as the nineteenth century that the word 'interior' was aligned with the specific meaning of the inside of a building.[2] Before then, it was used to refer to the non-coastal regions of a continent or an internal mode of thinking. For instance, in the US, the Department of the Interior (DOI), which is responsible for managing the nation's natural resources, landscapes and heritages, retains this older sense. Following this designation, the interior emerged as a distinct territory with its own activities and agents, shifting away from older traditions of upholsterers

INTRODUCTION

07 The Croft Lodge Studio, UK, 2017, by Kate Darby and David Connor, epitomizes the integration of old and new.

and furniture makers, and thereby questioning its associations with other built environment practices – namely, architecture. This separation accelerated in and throughout the twentieth century, giving rise to the professionalization of a subject that was often aligned to domesticity and the gender of its practitioners. It is an independent tradition and, in contrast to other spatial and built environment practices, constitutes a new story to be told.

The vast majority of history books on inside spaces utilize both architecture and linear chronologies as their methods of organization – in my view, unsatisfactory ways in which to describe the story of the interior. This story is not linear nor always tied to the same timelines as the building envelopes within which the interiors are contained. The chronologies of architecture are not relevant when significant aspects of the practices, processes, ideas and histories of the interior involve the reworking of existing buildings to be adapted for new uses. Chronology is not a helpful device when describing the complex changes of use, say, from an old power station or warehouse to a new art gallery, a banking building to a swish restaurant and so on. The stories of the interior are not the same as the histories of the architecture that surrounds them.

This book contests that the story of the interior is based on thematics: the enduring ideas, elements and types of spaces seen in both ancient and modern examples. This approach suits the fluid narratives of inner space and how flexibility between what is inside and outside, and what is interchangeable in both private and public interiors is fundamental to its particular stories.

The Story of the Interior is structured into three parts. 'The Room' describes how all interiors are formed from one or more of these spaces. Each room is formed from enclosures, atmospheres, passages, objects and technologies; all of which are constantly evolving entities. 'The Private Interior' charts how domestic interiors represent the archetype of inside spaces. These rooms encapsulate many ideas, experiments, stories and hence convey the lives of their inhabitants. 'The Public Interior' documents the great inside spaces of the city. It explores how cultural, work, display, infrastructural and social interiors enclose our daily public lives. From the scale of the city to the room, it explores how these spaces also contain elements and ideas borrowed from their domestic counterparts.

The story of the interior engenders numerous voices, narratives and ideas about inside spaces and their uses. The multiplicity of ways in which interiors can be thought about, created and then used provides a broad spatial geography of the many ways of understanding patterns of human presence and behaviour.

INTRODUCTION

The Room

The Unified and
the Autonomous Interior

01 Batu Aoqier and his wife, AoYong Qimuge, in front of their yurt in Inner Mongolia, from the series 'Family Stuff' by Qingjun Huang, 2007; externalized possessions form an autonomous 'room'.

For over twenty years the photographer Qingjun Huang has been taking pictures across the world of people and their homes and the possessions that are in them. But this has been undertaken in a very unorthodox manner. Entitled 'Family Stuff', for each of the 150 projects he asked a family to stand outside their home with all their worldly goods, their clothes, cooking utensils, food and even their pets laid out with them. He started photographing in China, during a time of rapid economic development. Each family picture documented the possessions of both rural and urban families as their fortunes changed in the economic upturn. Then he started to photograph American families, showing how their accumulated goods represented a different kind of wealth and lifestyle. One of the most compelling images was a picture of a family in Inner Mongolia. Two family members stand proudly outside their yurt surrounded by their possessions in a large featureless desert landscape. The yurt has an open door, inviting a view into the interior. Their pets roam among the television set and sewing machine, the generator, satellite dish and pots, pans and shoes.

  This and the other images in the series are captivating for many reasons, not least for provoking wonder at how all of the

02 *Saint Jerome in his Study* by Antonello da Messina, c. 1474, unifies furniture and objects to define enclosure.

goods fit into the different homes. As the photographs are deliberately staged, with all the possessions neatly arranged outside the homes, they form an imaginary room, made up of the extracted possessions. The images beguile as they reverse the normal relations between inside and out. In each photograph, the inner lives of the occupants are laid bare – brought outside and exposed for scrutiny. This enables comparison with other families' stuff across the collection of photographs. Rather than acting as the container of the objects, the house becomes a stage set, the backdrop to the family and their goods. Each image acts as a record of the relations between people and their possessions.

This photographic series exemplifies what I describe as two underlying principles of the story of all inside spaces: the unified and the autonomous interior. These principles refer to the enduring interplay between the assimilation of the interior into the envelope that defines it, and, conversely, the autonomy of the interior from that within which it is contained. Put simply, an interior is either conceived and built in chronological unity with the building that contains it, or it is not. This extends to possessions, which can be built-in or free-standing. Huang's photographs play on this relationship by deliberately putting what is normally inside out.

An interior made by redesigning an existing building can be described as autonomous in that it is conceived and constructed at an entirely different time from the building in which it is situated. A unified interior is developed and made chronologically, and often aesthetically, in accord with its enclosure. Whether unified or autonomous, inside spaces are inherently programmed to contain lived experiences and thus will always represent the shifting of time. Whether those interiors and their elements are placed inside or outside an enclosure, as Huang's photographs demonstrate, the interior is a space that is built for change.

If the story of art is told through paintings and sculptures, and the story of fashion is told through dress, then the story of the interior can be told through the room. It is the space that structures and materializes the lives, the power and the ambitions of its inhabitants. Every room conveys a vision that encapsulates the spirit of the age. While undesirable, we can live without that favourite dress or painting, but we cannot live without rooms. The room represents the story of the interior through the formation of a series of ideas and types that are evident in both the ancient and the most contemporary of inside spaces.

Whether unified or autonomous, the envelope delimiting the inside will, to a varying degree affect the interior. *Saint Jerome in his Study* was painted by Antonello da Messina in

02

Europe c. 1474. In the painting, Saint Jerome is reading at his study: an elegant piece of furniture that is elevated from the ground on a series of vaulted arches, which appear to take some of their formal qualities from the space the study was placed into. Saint Jerome is clearly the centre of the viewer's attentions, framed numerous times through an arched opening, his furniture and by the arches and columns deeper in the building. Distant views through the interior to a landscape beyond reinforce the perspectival qualities of the image. Symbols of his life and work – a peacock, a partridge and a brass bowl – are placed on the ledge of the first opening. The peacock symbolized immortality; the partridge referred to truth and deceit. The image projects a harmonious composition, one in which inhabitant and furniture are conceived together and are both unified while also autonomous from their surrounds.

The Korean artist Do Ho Suh has for many years created works of art that explore questions of home, displacement and memory. He has made numerous reconstructions of various domestic spaces in Korea, London, Berlin and New York that he and his family have lived in. The works are made from fabric and are representations of what he has called acts 'of

03   The unified and yet autonomous ghost-like structure of *Home Within Home Within Home Within Home Within Home* by Do Ho Suh, 2013.

memorialization'.[1] The installations are usually facsimiles of spaces that have been important or of interest to the artist. *Home Within Home Within Home Within Home Within Home*, exhibited for the first time in Seoul in 2013, was a reconstruction of the housing block he inhabited in Rhode Island, USA, when studying as an art student. Inside the structure was another house, a representation of his Korean childhood home. The latter was suspended from the ceiling and hovered inside the semi-opaque mesh-veiled exterior, like an inner ghost. At precisely 15.30 × 12.83 × 12.97 metres (50 feet 2 inches × 42 feet 1 inch × 42 feet 6 inches) the work was a full-scale house, large enough for visitors to walk into.

    Though created over five hundred years apart, both painting and installation emulate their precedents and yet express autonomy from their referents. They both show how rooms can be conceived sometimes with and sometimes without their building 'envelope' in mind, influencing how they are made and how people occupy them. The painting is regarded by historians to portray a fictional space, with the inspiration for the furniture and inhabitant drawn from the context. Suh's installation is closely drawn from existing referents, two houses, yet their transportation to another site leaves the visitor ambivalent as to where they have come from (despite remaining unequivocal about what they are).

    This section of the book sets out the stories of the unified and autonomous room through five thematics:

Enclosures
Enclosing – that is, separating inside from out – is a fundamental part of how interiors are created. The size of an enclosure can range in scale from a city to a piece of furniture. Whatever scale is used, to enclose space is to make the *room*.

Atmospheres
Atmospheres describes the intoxicating effect of materials, blended with the softer characteristics of light, sound, smell and mood in order to create the intangible yet significant effects of ambience and the sensations of the interior.

Passages
Circulation can be understood as an act of movement that facilitates flow in an interior. Halls, corridors, courtyards and stairs are all means of journeying between rooms.

Objects
The tangible things that reinforce the material qualities of people and spaces. Objects are also a prime example of how reuse is an integral part of making interior spaces.

THE ROOM | THE UNIFIED AND THE AUTONOMOUS INTERIOR

02

Europe c. 1474. In the painting, Saint Jerome is reading at his study: an elegant piece of furniture that is elevated from the ground on a series of vaulted arches, which appear to take some of their formal qualities from the space the study was placed into. Saint Jerome is clearly the centre of the viewer's attentions, framed numerous times through an arched opening, his furniture and by the arches and columns deeper in the building. Distant views through the interior to a landscape beyond reinforce the perspectival qualities of the image. Symbols of his life and work – a peacock, a partridge and a brass bowl – are placed on the ledge of the first opening. The peacock symbolized immortality; the partridge referred to truth and deceit. The image projects a harmonious composition, one in which inhabitant and furniture are conceived together and are both unified while also autonomous from their surrounds.

The Korean artist Do Ho Suh has for many years created works of art that explore questions of home, displacement and memory. He has made numerous reconstructions of various domestic spaces in Korea, London, Berlin and New York that he and his family have lived in. The works are made from fabric and are representations of what he has called acts 'of

03 The unified and yet autonomous ghost-like structure of *Home Within Home Within Home Within Home Within Home* by Do Ho Suh, 2013.

memorialization'.[1] The installations are usually facsimiles of spaces that have been important or of interest to the artist. *Home Within Home Within Home Within Home Within Home*, exhibited for the first time in Seoul in 2013, was a reconstruction of the housing block he inhabited in Rhode Island, USA, when studying as an art student. Inside the structure was another house, a representation of his Korean childhood home. The latter was suspended from the ceiling and hovered inside the semi-opaque mesh-veiled exterior, like an inner ghost. At precisely 15.30 × 12.83 × 12.97 metres (50 feet 2 inches × 42 feet 1 inch × 42 feet 6 inches) the work was a full-scale house, large enough for visitors to walk into.

Though created over five hundred years apart, both painting and installation emulate their precedents and yet express autonomy from their referents. They both show how rooms can be conceived sometimes with and sometimes without their building 'envelope' in mind, influencing how they are made and how people occupy them. The painting is regarded by historians to portray a fictional space, with the inspiration for the furniture and inhabitant drawn from the context. Suh's installation is closely drawn from existing referents, two houses, yet their transportation to another site leaves the visitor ambivalent as to where they have come from (despite remaining unequivocal about what they are).

This section of the book sets out the stories of the unified and autonomous room through five thematics:

Enclosures
Enclosing – that is, separating inside from out – is a fundamental part of how interiors are created. The size of an enclosure can range in scale from a city to a piece of furniture. Whatever scale is used, to enclose space is to make the *room*.

Atmospheres
Atmospheres describes the intoxicating effect of materials, blended with the softer characteristics of light, sound, smell and mood in order to create the intangible yet significant effects of ambience and the sensations of the interior.

Passages
Circulation can be understood as an act of movement that facilitates flow in an interior. Halls, corridors, courtyards and stairs are all means of journeying between rooms.

Objects
The tangible things that reinforce the material qualities of people and spaces. Objects are also a prime example of how reuse is an integral part of making interior spaces.

Technologies
Air movement, water, plumbing, wiring, heating and lighting, televisions, radios, Wi-Fi and even revolving doors are technologies that have all significantly impacted interior spaces and how people use and find comfort within them.

Enclosures, atmospheres, passages, objects and technologies are ever present, but their manifestation from rudimentary beginnings becomes a far more sophisticated affair in the ongoing evolution of the room.

Enclosures

04 Ajlan Gharem, *Paradise Has Many Gates*, 2015. Enclosures enact separations that encourage numerous interpretations.

Sitting in the desert one hour from Riyadh in Saudi Arabia, just for one day in 2015, was a wire-frame enclosure measuring 10 × 6.5 metres (33 × 21 feet). It was shaped like a mosque, topped by a dome and a minaret that was lit with green light and emitted recordings of the call to prayer. Ajlan Gharem's *Paradise Has Many Gates* reimagined a mosque as an enclosure that recalled, through its material languages, refugee detention centres and border fences as a nod to concerns about migration. The transparency of the installation also indicated the potential to demystify and challenge authoritarian politics and the privacies associated with all types of religious buildings. The temporary structure has since been installed in the US, Canada and Bahrain, and it is always accompanied by performances, prayer and poetry readings, seeking to unpack anxieties regarding Islamophobia through interaction and discussion around religion. The project, by demonstrating the arbitrary and ambiguous nature of separations, typifies enclosure.

All enclosed spaces, created through the nuances of separating inside and out, result in partitions – which require further exploration as to why they have been made and what they mean.

The wall is the primary element of enclosure. Whether the Great Wall of China or a humble internal partition inside a domestic space, both do exactly the same job: they are constructed to separate and delineate space. Walls might be portable and made from sticks and covered with textiles; they may be immovable, made from mud, brick or stone. Whatever they are made of, they provide shelter, regulate temperature, moderate views through openings such as doors and windows, and distinguish between who is in and who is outside of them.

Portable constructions such as tents, wigwams, yurts and tepees are movable enclosures often made out of materials from the immediate vicinity of the settlement. The San people of Southern Africa traditionally constructed lightweight environments made from branches and twigs from the surrounding bushes, which would then be covered with grass or leaves. *Sansevieria*, a genus of abundant thick-leafed plants, were pulled up, beaten out with rocks or sticks and joined together to form lengths of rope. This was then wrapped around the circular tent enclosures to bind the cladding and structure together. These enclosures could be made without the use of any particular tools, just hands, rocks and sticks. This approach to enclosing – using materials to hand – is both ancient and modern. In China, many hilltop regions are covered in *mao zhu*, a type

05 San women outside their homestead constructed from grass extracted from the landscape, Northern Cape, South Africa.
06 The bent-bamboo enclosure centralizes the performer in the theatre by DnA_Design and Architecture in Hengkeng village, China, 2015.
07 Before and after drawings of the theatre structure formation.

of bamboo renowned for its tensile strength. Its roots grow horizontally in the ground as opposed to vertically, linking with other plants to make extremely strong foundations. DnA_Design and Architecture utilized this innate strength to make a small bamboo theatre just outside of Hengkeng village in Songyang, eastern China. Bending the trees into a vault-like structure they then tied the tops together with a bamboo ring. Along with a circular arrangement of stones for seats, the structure created a light-dappled enclosed space for performance. One that, when finished with, could be untied so the bamboo walls could spring back into their original positions, dissolving once again into the forest of trees. The traditional dwellings of the San people and the Bamboo Theatre are both examples of enclosures made manifest from materials close at hand, making site-specific yet temporary spaces that could contain all kinds of life within them.

All forms of itinerant lifestyles reinforce the importance of sheltering from the outside. Nomadic enclosures are environments that are based on portability and formed from materials that can sustain a transient lifestyle. The Bedouin, from the Arabic *badawi*, 'dweller in the desert', have historically inhabited the Arabian Peninsula, North Africa, the Levant and Mesopotamia. Their enclosures, or 'black tents' are a symbol of both the migratory synergies of many nomadic tribes and their resistance to the vagaries of their environments, but they also represent the enclosing and encouragement of communality. Black tents traditionally consist of several narrow strips of heavy cloth, 23 metres (75 feet) long, woven from black (or sometimes brown) goat's hair or sheep's wool. These strips are sewn together to form a large rectangle which is then raised on four poles to become the roof of the shelter. Another long narrow strip, the *ruaq*, is pinned to three sides of the roof and draped to the ground. The open side, which always faces away from the wind, is further divided by a number of *qata*, vertical curtains of intricate design that separate the various sections of the tent. These generally

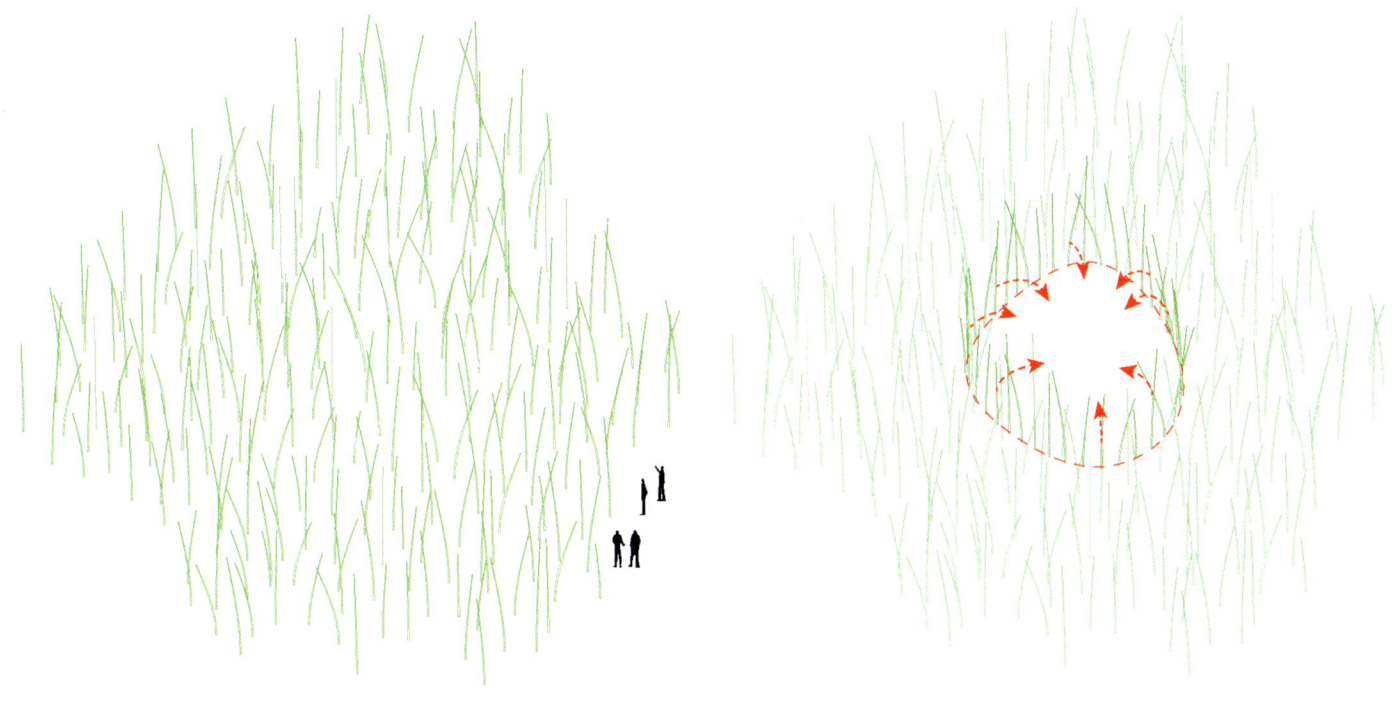

THE ROOM | ENCLOSURES

consisted of a men's section, which doubled as a guest room, a kitchen and women's quarters. The tent floor is often covered by woven rugs or with carpets. In hot weather the *ruaq* shielding the sides can be rolled up to allow the free circulation of air without admitting sunlight. During cold nights the long *qata* are drawn across the open end of the tent, completely enclosing it so that the fire keeps the occupants warm. The communal purpose of the black tents was reiterated in a project by Decolonizing Art Architecture Research (DAAR). The Concrete Tent was a gathering space formed for communal learning, hosting cultural activities and for social meetings. Its first iteration was in Dheisheh refugee camp in Palestine in 2015. This camp was set up in 1949 for families expelled from around Jerusalem and Hebron. The Concrete Tent was made to invite discussion around the political conditions of exile. Its concrete form represented temporariness and permanency, movement and stillness. In the camp it was a place for gathering and debates and was even used by newlyweds to celebrate their union. Negotiators from

08 A Bedouin tent creates a nomadic enclosure by joining strips of heavy cloth elevated on poles.
09 Permanent temporariness symbolized by the Concrete Tent, a solidified mobile structure in Dheisheh, Palestine, by DAAR, 2015.
10 Instead of outdoors, Toyo Ito's *Pao II* floated in the atrium of a department store, 1986.
11 Essential provisions for the urban nomad in the *Pao I* interior, 1985.

the camp used it for peace resolution meetings among families. The success of the tent meant it was recreated several times in Abu Dhabi, UAE (2018), Rabat, Morocco (2019) and Sharjah, UAE (2023). The Bedouin black tents and the Concrete Tent both symbolize nomadic movement and enclose the rituals and needs of the daily lives of their communities and occupants.

In contrast to rural or camp settlements, urban nomadism is a result of itinerant modern city lifestyles. This was illustrated in the late 1980s by the Japanese architect Toyo Ito who designed two temporary installations entitled *Pao: Dwellings for the Tokyo Nomad Woman*. In this work the urban nomad was the hunter-gatherer of information and experiences as opposed to their traditional counterpart focused on sustenance. The urban nomad's existence was distributed among the existing locales of the city. The need to hunt for food was satisfied in the local restaurants and cafés. The gymnasium became not merely a space for morning exercise but also a dressing room, with the locker as the nomad's personal wardrobe. The evening's entertainment took place in bars, theatres and clubs. All that was needed in the *pao* (the Japanese word for a yurt) was a bed, a table and a seat. The *pao* was akin to the black tent and other forms of temporary enclosure. But instead of being in the savannah or the desert, it was located in the atrium of a department store, sheltering and protecting its occupant from quite

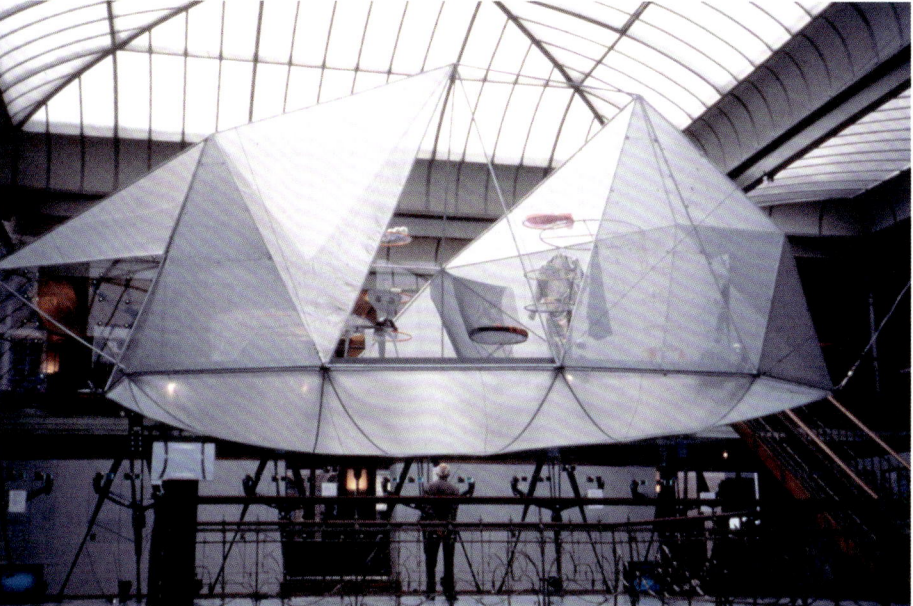

a different landscape to its traditional counterparts.

In contrast to the temporary walls of a tent or a *pao*, static or fortified walls reinforce a fixed type of enclosure through their capacity to keep people in or out. They can enclose and protect life as well as ritualizing death – as in the case of dolmen. Dating from around 7000 BCE and found in western Europe, the Middle East and Korea, dolmen were made from huge boulders stacked to create a chamber, which was then covered in earth and stones. Over time the mounds of soil and stones were eroded by the weather to reveal the structure underneath: two or more upright megaliths supporting a capstone, giving the appearance of a table (dolmen is said to derive from the Breton words for stone and table). It is thought that the structures were tombs and therefore constitute enclosures that were built to ritualize social, ceremonial and religious activities through confining people, whether alive or dead, under one roof.

Static fortified walls manifest the anxieties of people and the ideologies of nations. Although, as in the Teeter-Totter Wall project by Virginia San Fratello and Ronald Rael, which inserted see-saws into the Mexico-US border wall, they can also be the sites of activities that highlight the absurdities of such divisions – really we are all the same people on either side of the barriers. The feudalist early Middle Ages were defined by the walled enclosure known as the castle. Castles were fortified villages or houses that were often elevated on a hill or mound to anticipate attacks and protect their occupants. Over time, wooden fences were replaced with stone, creating thick masonry walls punctuated with minimal openings. The addition of water-filled moats around the walls, with a single bridged entrance and a defensive tower or keep, made a construction that could be retreated to were the walls ever breached. Travellers were attracted to the protected environs of the castle and, as they settled in and around them, more walls were constructed to protect them. Many early cities across the world grew around this pattern of repeated enclosing-wall building.

THE ROOM | ENCLOSURES

Another protected enclosure that dominated the Middle Ages across the world was the monastery. While the castle evolved through years of warfare, the monastery united its inhabitants through the pursuit of education and religious devotion. The European model of a monastery was inspired by the Plan of Saint Gall, a drawing that was traced onto parchment between 820 and 830 CE. It is widely believed to have acted much like an architectural blueprint that formed the guide for all forms of Benedictine monastic planning. Like a city, it accommodated the needs of all aspects of the inhabitants' religious and secular lives arranged around a central church (reinforcing the importance of the monks' devotions). There were houses for physicians, an infirmary to care for the sick, and spaces for coopers and wheelwrights, brewers and bakers. Combined with orchards, vegetable and herb gardens and adjacent to a cemetery, the masterplan of the monastery prescribed an ideal self-sustaining community – a model for cities to come. The requirements of non-western monasteries similarly revolved around the protection afforded by an external wall. The Monastery of Anba Hatre (also known as the Monastery of Saint Simeon) on the western bank of the Nile in Egypt originated in the sixth century CE. Anba Hatre was a saint whose religious devotion formed a community that became a centre of pilgrimage. The enclosure of chapels, living and dining areas, as well as cells for hermits carved into an adjacent rock formation, all took place within gated walls, like its European counterpart, it safely enclosed the devoted inhabitants within them.

Enclosures can be created from naturally occurring features within the landscape – often for religious purposes. Rock-cut architecture appears all across India and has an established tradition in Buddhist architecture, for which isolated places and remote sites were sought in order to construct edifices for worship. The caves at Karla (or Karli) are open volumes unencumbered by internal structures; their structural integrity derives from the fact they are carved out of solid rock and therefore require no free-standing columns. Thus, all

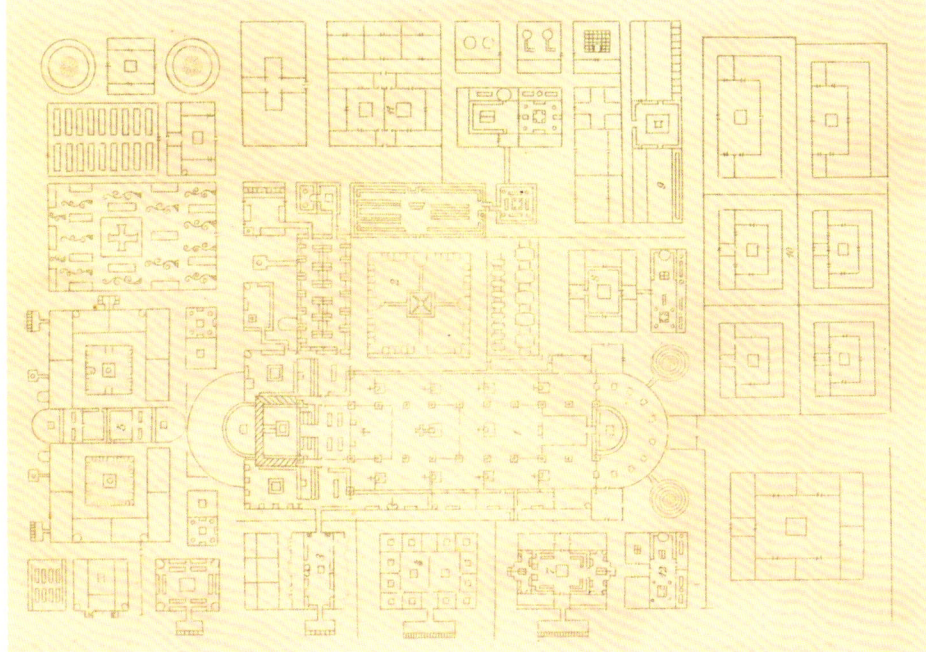

14

15

12 The exposed and elevated structure of Lanyon Quoit, a dolmen in Cornwall, UK.
13 Teeter-Totter Wall at the Mexico–US border dissolved the barrier between countries and united participants in play. Rael San Fratello with Colectivo Chopeke, 2019.
14 Plan of Saint Gall monastery, c. 820 CE.
15 The ruined walls of the sixth-century CE Monastery of Anba Hatre in Aswan, Egypt.

16 The rock-carved chambers of Karla, Maharashtra, India.
17 Light is admitted via carefully ordered formal patterns in the walls of the prayer hall of the Mosque of Mohamed Abdulkhaliq Gargash in Dubai, by Sumaya Dabbagh.
18 The naturally illuminated *mihrab* of the prayer room in the Sancaklar Mosque in Istanbul, Türkiye.

the walls are embellished with non-load-bearing decorative elements. The temples at Karla, Bhaja and Ajanta are notable examples of this kind of open, carved enclosure. The Barabar caves, dating from the third century BCE, are possibly the oldest rock-carved chambers. Other complexes, such as Bamiyan in Afghanistan, where two huge Buddha statues were carved into the rock faces, exemplified the adroitness with which masons could excise the landscape. The statues were unfortunately destroyed in 2001 by acts of religious intolerance.

Walls don't always have to fortify and protect. They can be illustrative, representing something other than just division. Islamic design uses the wall as an element of separation but more so as one of representation. Walls were conceived in a completely different fashion compared to Western thinking.[2] In part to ensure that idolatry is not practised, traditional Arab-Islamic design often avoids the use of figures, in particular any imagery associated with the prophet Muhammad. Mosque designs are therefore examples of sophisticated symbolic design vocabularies. They are interiors that are organized through the distribution of rooms of exacting geometries combined with calligraphic elements, often filled with intricate lacing patterns. As Islamic architecture evolved primarily in hot and dry climates, enclosures also had to control the temperature of the interior. Combined together, the religious and climatic requirements of a mosque's walls ensure that they are some of the most highly sophisticated constructions used to enclose space. The Mosque of Mohamed Abdulkhaliq Gargash in Dubai, designed by Sumaya Dabbagh, was the first mosque in the UAE to be designed by a woman and named in honour of the late patriarch of the family who commissioned the project. Its design unites walls with light, geometry and climate control to form

a prayer space of calm and reflection, removed from the hustle and bustle of the city outside. The building is formed from two blocks linked by a courtyard. The walls are covered with a geometric pattern of triangles, some of which are cut into the walls to allow light into the interior prayer hall. The hall has a verse of the Qur'an inscribed calligraphically onto its walls.

As well as a climatic and religious role, the wall in a mosque is deployed to guide orientation. Set into the wall is the *mihrab*, the ornamented niche indicating the direction of Mecca (*qibla*) towards which Muslims pray. The *mihrab* of a mosque is based on its roots as the description for a special room in a house or palace. It was adopted by the prophet Muhammad to denote the place of prayer and subsequently became the main architectural feature of all mosque wall designs. The Sancaklar Mosque in Istanbul was built on a sloping landscape that orientates the interior towards Mecca. The *qibla* wall of the prayer room was designed to be raw and simple, illuminated by natural light as it moves around the building throughout the day. The mosque also broke with prayer and gender traditions by having women occupy the same spaces and pray in the same rows as the men – instead of placing them at the back or on another level of the hall.

Enclosing walls can be flexible even when permanent. From the fourteenth century onwards the word 'curtain' was used to describe the hanging cloth that surrounded a bed. One possible derivation is from the Latin *cohors*, meaning courtyard or enclosure. Curtains as we now understand them were not generally present in the European interior until the early seventeenth century; the French became the leading exponents of interior textile hangings and upholstery by the middle of the century. Curtains necessitated their own design language of pelmets, swags, braids, fringes and rods with which to hold them up or to pull them together for privacy.

A 'curtain wall' is a non-load-bearing façade so called for its propensity, like its interior counterpart, to be hung from the structure of the building it is enclosing. They are often glazed. Dar Al Jinaa, a music

THE ROOM | ENCLOSURES

19 The traditional fixed curtain-wall façade system is reinvented by Inside Outside with diaphanous fabric that moves in the breeze in OMA's Maison à Bordeaux, 2011–12.
20 Transparent portholes in the curtain enhance its effect in rendering inside/outside boundaries ambiguous.
21 When hitched up, the curtain wall of Dar Al Jinaa in Muharraq, Bahrain, by Office Kersten Geers David Van Severen dissolves the external threshold.

centre by Office Kersten Geers David Van Severen in Muharraq, Bahrain, is covered by an exterior steel-mesh veil that protects the interior from the climate. Like all curtains, when they are 'twitched' or pulled back, they increase the anticipation towards the reveal of the performances taking place behind them. But façades are not always so fixed. The curtain-wall system designed by Inside Outside for the Maison à Bordeaux house by OMA symbolizes – like its interior counterpart – a much more fluid relationship between a building's interior and exterior. The hanging fabric denotes what is inside and out, but as it moves in the breeze this boundary became very flexible.

Other forms of interior enclosures can regulate view and temperature. In Islamic architecture, *jali* describes the perforated ornamentation or carved patterns, usually in wood or stone, that are used as screens and dividers between rooms. *Jali* originated from Mughal architecture and is primarily used to dissolve the boundaries between inside spaces. It is an extremely practical enclosing idea in hot climates, as it facilitates cooling via fresh air moving through its openings. In Japanese architecture, the use of the screen wall emphasizes flexibility and how partitions can create links between the interior and other spaces such as gardens. Both ancient and modern Japanese houses are often conceived as a series of courtyards with verandas protected by the overhang of the roof. The Katsura Imperial Villa, on the western outskirts of Kyoto, was begun in the early seventeenth century and is arranged as a series of pavilions set in a carefully organized landscape. The arrangement of buildings and gardens epitomizes the intimate relationships expressed in Japanese architecture between inside and out and the public and the private through the deployment of a combination of screens, walls and gardens.

The dissolution of any barriers between inside and out is nothing new, but the technologies for achieving this transparency have changed. Before the widespread use of glass, it was not unusual to utilize the walls of a room to depict what was outside and beyond them. Japanese houses and temples, enclosed by sliding screens or *fusuma*,

22 Paolo Veronese's allegorical paintings in the Villa Barbaro, Italy, 1560–61, create the illusion of walls dissolving into the surrounding landscape.
23 The considered alignment of openings and gardens orders the views in and through the Shokintei teahouse at the Katsura Imperial Villa, Kyoto.
24 Exquisitely painted sliding screens (*fusuma*) in the interior reception room at Konchi-in temple, Kyoto.

were often painted as landscapes. The *fusuma* of the Konchi-in temple in Kyoto were painted to resemble the landscapes beyond them with the real gardens to be revealed when they were slid back. In the Sala delle Prospettive in the Villa Farnesina in Rome, Baldassare Peruzzi painted the walls to appear as though a loggia, framing what appeared to be the city beyond. The interior of the Villa Barbaro by Andrea Palladio was painted by Paolo Veronese with allegorical landscapes, the ages of man and even images of astrology and the four seasons adorning the walls. Being inside these rooms was not just to be transported into the landscapes outside and beyond their walls but also to be placed among the stars.

All of these rooms have in common the desire to perpetuate the illusion of their disappearance into the surrounding landscape through embellishment. Twentieth-century European Modernism strove to dissolve the enclosure through making the walls between inside and out transparent, 'universal' and seamless. Schröder House, designed by Gerrit Rietveld, who trained as a cabinetmaker, was conceived much like a piece of

THE ROOM | ENCLOSURES

25

25 Sliding partition walls on the upper level of Gerrit Rietveld's Schröder House, Utrecht, the Netherlands, 1925, enabled one large room to become four separate ones.
26 The occupants of Sou Fujimoto's twenty-one-level House NA in Tokyo, 2012, live like nomads in an urban treehouse.

furniture. It is a space where in and out are conflated through the use of walls that appear to be on both the inside and the outside of the building. The interior was designed as though a box of tricks; rooms are created through the movement of partitions and screens. For instance, by moving three screens on the upper level of the building, the space can be transformed from one into four separate rooms. Sou Fujimoto's House NA in Tokyo furthered the ideas of seamlessness between inside and out. The house confounds any straightforward understanding of what might be enclosed and inside, and what might be external space. Unlike Schröder House, it is not designed to be reconfigured with flexible partitions. Instead, its porosity is emphasized by a thin frame structure containing numerous levels of occupation. The resultant house appears permanently open to the city it is in.

If walls are the lead characters, then floors and ceilings are the supporting actors in the play of enclosure. The ground is where early civilizations staked their claim to enclosure. In the Chinese Loess Plateau, encompassing parts of the provinces of Henan, Shanxi, Shaanxi and Gansu, millions of people live below ground in apartments (known as *dikengyuan*) carved out of the land. Loess is a soft silt that is porous and easily excavated. The dwellings give their inhabitants a close affinity with the earth and still today provide a highly sustainable environment, one that can be cool in the hot summers and warm in the harsher winters. Significant constructions based around

THE ROOM | ENCLOSURES

the excavation of the ground include those built for the provision of natural resources. Indian step wells were constructed in places where reliable sources of ground water could be located and extracted. Excavations were often lined with huge flights of stairs in order to facilitate access to the deep-lying water tables. Chand Baori, in Abhaneri in Rajasthan, extends more than 30 metres (98 feet) into the ground and its thirteen-storey depth consists of 3,500 narrow steps down to the water. Step wells provided not only water but also relief from the hot sun. Thus, they were often meeting places, important social hubs and sometimes even places of worship.

Because of gravity you will always be in contact with the ground – principally with some kind of a floor. Floors unite their users. The floor of a mosque is the unifying surface for prayer. The Qur'an describes the earth as a smooth carpet, represented in a mosque interior as a floor covered in prayer rugs. The colours of mosque carpets are symbolic: green is sacred, symbolizing life, renewal, fertility and paradise; white is purity; black for mourning; blue for protection, spirituality and heaven; and red symbolizes attention and sacrifice. Standing or kneeling in a mosque interior means that your body is in contact with dimensions that are beyond your very consciousness. Floors do this, they organize and delineate, powerful and exciting ones will raise your awareness of another dimension. The floor of Saint Mark's Basilica in Venice is a watery carpet of marble, terrazzo and mosaic. Its layout and plan suggest rooms – but without walls. Its complete opposite is the pavilion by Mies van der Rohe for the 1929 International Exposition in Barcelona. It has a continuous unbroken floor within which, in plan, the walls are merely directing people to glide seamlessly through the space. Both basilica and pavilion represent, in entirely different ways, expansive landscapes that reinforce the relationship between interior and exterior and its potential to be limitless. Yet, as we see in the mosque, the basilica and in the pavilion, the floor is the element that articulates the boundaries of enclosure. Its

27 Traditional sunken *dikengyuan* residences in Henan province, China.
28 The upside-down ziggurat of the Chand Baori step well in Rajasthan, India, consists of 3,500 steps down to the water.
29 The carpeted floor in Al-Azhar Mosque, Cairo, orientates and orders devotees amid a sea of red, symbolizing attention and sacrifice.
30 This drawing by Mary Griep, 2013–15, shows the tessellated 'marble carpet' of the floor of Saint Mark's Basilica.
31 In contrast to the basilica floor, the plan of Mies van der Rohe's 1929 Barcelona Pavilion is expressed through a minimal arrangement of vertical and horizontal lines.

30

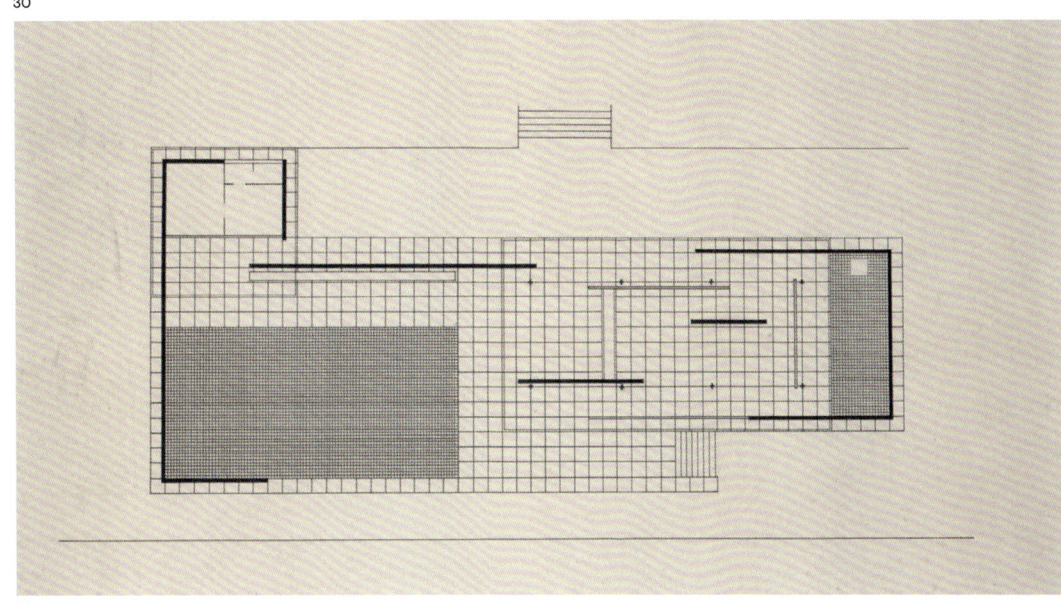

31

THE ROOM | ENCLOSURES

32 The most famous ceiling in the world, telling the story of God's creation of Earth and humanity's fall from grace. Michelangelo, Sistine Chapel, the Vatican, 1508–12.

fundamental quality is its ability to give both comfort and direction. Along with walls and floors an interior is always enclosed beneath a ceiling. Derived from the Middle English *ceil* (to line or to cover) it is possibly related to the Latin *caelum* and French *ciel*, meaning 'sky'. In an interior it is the lining or panelling of the inside of the roof, but its lofty position above our heads gives us the opportunity to make and embellish our very own interior sky. It is a place for simple paintings, a light fixture – or it might be for frescoes, mosaics, the expressions of our dreams. In Italian *soffitto* described the attaching of panels to the structural frame of the underside of the roof, a lining that could be used for a wide variety of very expressive designs. In the Vatican's Sistine Chapel, Michelangelo organized the ceiling decoration around nine scenes from the book of Genesis, the account of the creation of the world. The central panels depict the narratives of Noah and the flood, Adam and Eve and the divisions of water and earth, light and dark. The 35-metre (118-foot) long, 14-metre (46-foot) wide ceiling is 20 metres (66 feet) above the floor of the chapel. Though Michelangelo was initially reluctant to accept the commission, because he considered

33 Hikma Community Complex, Dandaji, Niger, by Mariam Issoufou Architects with Studio Chahar, 2018.
34 The mosque turned library and community centre highlighted the link between study and devoutness beneath a vaulted ceiling of compressed earth brick.
35 The gigantic multi-purpose New Century Global Center, Chengdu, China, symbolizes the future of enclosures as climate change creates an increasingly unstable exterior environment.

35

himself a sculptor rather than a painter, it has continued to dazzle visitors since the chapel first opened to the public in 1512. A soffit describes the underside of any roof, the Sistine Chapel ceiling elevates it to extraordinary dimensions.

Ceilings can be expressive in a manner that exemplifies the activities that are taking place below them. Mariam Issoufou Kamara, in collaboration with Yasaman Esmaili of Studio Chahar, adapted a disused mosque into a library and community centre alongside a new religious building in the village of Dandaji, Niger. The library reflected one of the important aspects of Islam – the pursuit of knowledge. Therefore, the insertion of the new library into the old mosque initiated a dialogue regarding the connections between secular and religious spaces. The new ceiling was constructed from compressed earth bricks, with each vault containing a light sourced cheaply from the local market. The ceiling unified the worship and library spaces under one expansive plane. Whichever way ceilings are designed and made, their power lies in encouraging the people underneath them to think of the realms beyond.

From small tents to big buildings, walls, floors and ceilings are the elements for making enclosures. The biggest enclosures can even contain whole cities. At over thirty storeys high and 1.7 million square metres (18.3 million square feet) of enclosed space, the New Century Global Center in Chengdu, China is the equivalent of eight Louvres or almost three times the size of Shanghai Pudong Airport. Under this huge roof are shops, hotels, cinemas, a conference centre and a university. It's a thousand kilometres from the coastline but the space is organized around a 400-metre (1,300-foot) long beach, leading onto a gigantic sea-like swimming pool. The view from the beach consists of a 150 × 40-metre (490 × 130-foot) screen, showing the horizon complete with sunrise and sunset. The centre encloses its visitors in one large space, protecting them from the weather and any other inclemency that might disrupt the routines of their day. The urge to enclose and to make interior space satisfies a primary instinct in us all.

Atmospheres

36 Thoughtful manipulation of surfaces, materials, light and mood can create atmospheres that provoke awe. Olafur Eliasson, *The weather project*, installation view, Tate Modern, London, 2003.

The unforgettable images of people luxuriating underneath the acclaimed *The weather project* by Olafur Eliasson, a five-month installation in the Turbine Hall of the Tate Modern in London, showed how atmospheres affect us all. The light, smoke and mirrors drew over two million viewers into the space to sit and watch the misty sun piercing through the reflective plane of the ceiling: a transcendental interior experience. Once enclosed, the story of an interior can be told through its surfaces and their materials – the generators of atmospheres. The qualities of atmosphere are epitomized by the word's etymological roots: the Greek *atmos* is a vapour, a breath of air, while *sphaira* is a sphere. The conjoining of both words is literally used to describe the ether surrounding a planet, but when used figuratively in relation to the built environment it illustrates the resultant ambience of a room. It is what the Italian art critic Mario Praz referred to as the *Stimmung*, the particular and unique ambience of a space.[3] In essence, 'atmospheres' describes the intoxicating effects of materials and surfaces blended with the intangible qualities of light, character and mood.

In some moments of history, surfaces have been stereotyped as insubstantial and one-dimensional. European Modernism contested them, particularly in relation to their ornamentation. The tone was set by the Viennese architect Adolf Loos in 1910 when he determined that to ornament was to commit 'a crime'.[4] One of the most well-known architects of the twentieth century, Le Corbusier, expressed a similar distaste for decoration calling it an 'abominable perversion'.[5] Modernists' eschewing of ornamentation merely masked their closeted desires to embrace and utilize surface embellishments. Loos's Villa Müller and Villa Moller (Prague and Vienna respectively) were exalted precisely because of their elaborately decorated interiors. Conceived via his spatial system known as the Raumplan, both were highly detailed concoctions of stairs, landings and rooms decorated in rich surfaces of oak, polished lemonwood, lacquered mahogany, Persian rugs, leather upholstery and numerous planes of highly veined cipollino marble. Le Corbusier's

37

38

fondness for unadorned exterior and interior whiteness was in itself arguably a highly decorated surface. Their absurd position with regards to ornament was detrimental to the idea and story of the interior not only because it led to the downgrading of surface as an important intellectual consideration but also because, when at its most pernicious (and often misogynistic), it denigrated the status and agency of the interior designers and decorators undertaking it.[6]

The irrationality of being repulsed by surface decoration was laid bare by a project in 2018 by Anna and Eugeni Bach. They covered the surfaces of the iconic Modernist classic the Barcelona Pavilion by Mies van der Rohe in numerous sheets of white card. The resurfacing made a clever comment on the archetypal white Modernist surfaces, and it also showed just how much the beautiful travertine, green Alpine marble and golden onyx walls were missed when they disappeared. The real crime was the fact of ever considering that surface elaborations and the designers who undertook them were irrelevant.

37 Adolf Loos deployed rich surfaces of timber and marble with geometric precision in Villa Müller, Prague, 1928–30.
38 The importance of surface embellishment was demonstrated through its absence in Anna and Eugeni Bach's *Mies Missing Materiality* installation, Barcelona, 2018.
39 Human embellishment of surfaces began with rock paintings, as in the Tsodilo Hills in Botswana.
40 The Cave of Hands in Argentina is decorated with outlines of the hands of the ancestors of the Tehuelche people of Patagonia.
41 The paintings and the acoustic and environmental conditions of the Lascaux Caves, France, were meticulously replicated in a visitor space to recreate an authentic atmosphere.

Beyond a narrowly focused twentieth-century Western Modernist aversion to decoration, narrating lives through embellishing interior surfaces is a fundamental aspect of inhabiting space. The handprints stencilled with pigment onto the walls of the Cueva de las Manos (Cave of Hands) in Argentina, have been carbon dated to being applied between 7300 BCE and 700 CE. Thousands of cave inhabitants painted people and the animals they hunted and relied upon for their existence. These were overlaid by 829 left and 31 right handprints, including ones with missing fingers, on the walls. Nobody knows why they left their handprints. Archaeologists have speculated that territorial marking, religious or shamanic ceremonies, or maybe even just graffiti to prove they were there, were the reasons. In the Tsodilo Hills in Botswana, more than 4,500 images of animals and humans have been found. The hills of caves contain over five hundred sites representing millennia of inhabitation. The cave paintings at Lascaux in France are believed to be around 17,000 to 20,000 years old. Embellished with over six hundred paintings of flora and fauna, all were painstakingly copied and installed in an adjacent purpose-built museum. Decorating surfaces to reveal stories of an interior's inhabitants, to pass on information in the way of territorial markings or ceremonial memories is an enduring legacy of inhabitation.

42

43

Surfaces don't have to be painted in order to tell stories. *Everyone I Have Ever Slept With 1963–1995* documented the people artist Tracey Emin had slept with, in the literal sense, over thirty-two years. Like a prehistoric cave adorned with paintings, the insides of the tent were embellished with the names of 102 companions embroidered onto the walls. The suggestive title challenges our assumptions, in that Emin also named herself and her grandmother, whom she often napped with as a child. From the outside, the blue tent looked like a normal bit of camping equipment, but inside the thin fabric diffuses the light making the walls appear to glow with the names of each person. Its brilliance lay in the fact that, crawling inside, visitors could not help but think of all the people that they too had ever slept with – including themselves.

Adorning walls with images – and maybe even the names of loved ones – is a way in which we make the interior not just comfortable but also *comforting*. Embellishing our interiors communicates and reflects our lives to others who might just venture inside them – even thousands of years after we are gone.

Essentially, atmospheres derived from built surfaces can be understood in two ways: applied and found. 'Applied surfaces' describes the application of particular materials in order to relay specific identities. 'Found surfaces' refers to the reuse of material left behind in existing spaces as a source of inspiration for the subsequent changes. Every age of the story of interior utilizes surface to create rooms and chambers for life – and also death – that relay distinct atmospheres. Perhaps no other society has invested so much time and labour to ensure survival after death as that of ancient Egypt.

Early Egyptian funerary structures were flat-roofed structures called *mastabas* containing burial chambers cut deep into the ground. The classical Egyptian word for tomb literally meant 'house for eternity' and this is what the *mastaba* represented. Later Egyptian dynasties built pyramids that represented a shift in the idea of death. It was thought that the low-lying *mastaba* was no longer fit for a pharaoh and the associated religious practices devised to accompany their departure from this life. Therefore, pyramids,

42 Tracey Emin used the appliquéd surface of a tent to tell a story in *Everyone I Have Ever Slept With 1963–1995*.
43 Tomb of Meresankh III, Egypt, Old Kingdom, 4th Dynasty (2613–2494 BCE).
44 The Sanctuary of Amun-Re, Hatshepsut Mortuary Temple, Luxor, Egypt, c. fifteenth century BCE.
45 Naos boat of Horus at the Temple of Edfu. Ceremonial boats such as this were common in ancient Egyptian temples, including the 'red chapel' of Hatshepsut at Karnak.

with their associated cosmological dimensions, were built to house the bodies of the rulers who would ascend to their place in eternity – closer to the other gods. The great pyramids, such as those at Giza, were enormous enclosures that from the outside relayed the sheer effort and toil of their construction. Inside, chambers dedicated to the dead would contain the caskets of their carefully prepared bodies, canopic jars containing their entrails, and assorted possessions. Their scale was unsurpassed. Egyptian funerary art and architecture was intended to assist the passage to the next world and hence the tombs of both the great and the less so would contain the stories of their lives inscribed on the walls. The funerary complex of Hatshepsut, one of very few women pharaohs who reigned from around 1473 to 1458 BCE, was one of many monuments built around Thebes (modern-day Luxor) over a period of five hundred years. It includes a mortuary temple known as Djeser Djeseru (holy of holies) that was decorated with scenes of her reign and featured shrines to the gods Anubis, Hathor and Amun. Hathor's shrine had columns that were made to represent a sistrum, an instrument associated with love and music. Anubis was the god of embalming and cemetery and was often depicted with the body of a man and the head of a jackal, as he was in his shrine. Hatshepsut also restored the Karnak Temple Complex, adding a chamber made of red quartzite stone. The 'red chapel' held a boat that would be carried out and used on special occasions depending on calendric requirements. It was carried on the shoulders of priests so that it never got wet. Reliefs all around the room showed how it was transported and used, even when placed on a boat to cross the Nile. Although she ruled and died peacefully, Hatshepsut's successors did everything possible to eradicate her memory, erasing her from inscriptions and removing the boat to a new temple.

The Egyptians were one of the early societies to master the differences between rough-hewn rocks and a polished slab of marble. Roman architecture and interior spaces are also notable for their use of applied surface embellishment in abundance.

Arches, vaults and domes were evolutions in Roman structural technologies that required new ways of thinking about their surfaces. This was expedited through the evolution of *opus caementicium*, otherwise known as concrete. Because it was made thick with a rubble aggregate, cement was often laid out in courses or layers in a timber former and then left to harden. When dry it formed a rough finish that the Romans became very proficient at covering up. We see this in one of Rome's, and maybe the world's, finest interiors: the Pantheon.

Marcus Agrippa built the original structure between 27 and 25 BCE, but it was rebuilt by the emperor Hadrian between 118 and 125/8 CE (contested) in the form it is recognized as today. At 43 metres (140 feet) in diameter, it is still the largest unreinforced concrete dome in the world – a feat that will never be beaten as this type of unreinforced technology would not be attempted today. The interior consists of a cylinder and hemispherical dome of equal measure, ordered around a central axis. The cylinder is divided by two unequal bands: a cornice that links the entrance and the niche opposite; and a cap or cornice that separates the dome from the cylinder wall. The plan is organized by eight recesses, including the entrance and the opposite niche with columns and pilasters of giallo antico marble, pavonazzetto and red-purple porphyry. Projected from the wall, between the niches, are eight temple fronts, or *aediculae*, each containing statues or paintings. The surfaces match the colours and materials of the floor, which is made of squares and circles of coloured granites, marbles and porphyry. These are all arranged along a grid that reinforces the central axis of the main door and opposite niche. The complete effect is masterful, uniting the floor and cylindrical wall through colour, material and organization.

The atmosphere of the interior is manifest through its illumination via just two sources of natural light: the front door and, more dramatically, the dome's central oculus. Come rain or shine the Pantheon is always open via the dome. There is nothing more magical than sitting in that interior for a few hours watching the rain pour through it in

46

46   Light pours into the interior of the Pantheon, Rome, through its permanently open central oculus and animates its decorated surfaces.
47   The dark atmospheres of the interior spaces of the Jingdezhen Imperial Kiln Museum by Studio Zhu-Pei, China, 2020, contrast with sharp accents of direct natural light.
48   The vaulted chambers were designed to be reminiscent of the kilns in the site's former porcelain factory.

a storm or observing that little circle of Roman sunlight move around the sphere, reminding the visitor of how both the building and its occupants are turning around the sun – just like they have done for millennia.

The application of specific materials with which to render geometry and space coherent does not have to be so formal. The Imperial Kiln Museum by Studio Zhu-Pei in the Chinese city of Jingdezhen, renowned for over two thousand years as the centre of porcelain manufacturing, is defined by numerous brick vaults strategically deployed across the site. They were built to represent the traditional brick kilns that once occupied the city and that were uncovered on site during construction. The vaults were constructed by hand-pouring concrete between two brick skins to make the structures as light as possible. Many of the bricks were recycled from demolished kilns. The pattern of the bricks flowing through the interior reinforces the curved geometries of the arcuated construction. The ends of the vaults are glazed and the

unrelenting cave-like qualities of the vaults are ameliorated with a series of punctures that admit shards of natural light into the spaces.

Alongside solid materials such as concrete and marble, paint is another quintessential applied surface. Paint can be used to create dramatic scenes or atmospheres in a room. Fresco painting, often associated with Italian Renaissance interiors, evolved complex and theatrical surface decoration, in which panels, walls and mouldings (such as cornices, doors and their frames) would be used as components in the composition. *Trompe l'oeil* ('deceive the eye') was an effect utilized at first in ceiling designs, where imagery could make interior space appear to break free of the confines of its container. Such illusions were achieved by techniques such as *di sotto in su* (literally 'from below upwards') and its more formal evolution of the perspectively correct *quadratura*. These evolved in late Renaissance painting and used the ceiling plane as the surface to create

49 The walls of the Camera degli Sposi in the Palazzo Ducale, Mantua, Italy, incorporate doors and other details within the fresco to suggest that the room is open to the outside.
50 The ceiling's painted oculus similarly suggests a view to the blue sky beyond the room.
51 To the viewer at ground level, walls and ceiling combine to accentuate the force of the battle between gods and giants in the Sala dei Giganti, Palazzo del Te, Mantua, Italy.

fantastical illusions of a space beyond what was there. The fresco by Andrea Mantegna in the Camera degli Sposi of the Palazzo Ducale in Mantua emphasizes how fresco painting could create the conceit of the view through an oculus to the sky beyond.

Another awe-inspiring example of this choreography is in the Palazzo del Te, also in Mantua, which was designed by Giulio Romano for Duke Federico II Gonzaga. Constructed between 1526 and 1531, the decoration of the rooms of the palazzo was undertaken in two phases. During the first phase, the Sala di Psiche was made between 1526 and 1529 in the north-east apartment. Based on the allegory of Cupid and Psyche, the rooms are dominated by a fresco of a marriage ceremony and feast. In the second phase, 1529–31, the ambition of the patrons is exemplified through representations of Roman triumphs. In the Sala dei Venti, Mount Olympus and the Gonzaga badge appear at the centre of the ceiling and the room is resplendent with scenes of hunting and fighting between gladiators. In the Sala dei Giganti, the walls and ceiling are combined to produce an epic fresco of the fall of the Giants to the Olympian gods. As the battle intensifies, the *trompe l'oeil* painting embodies the demolition of the room with the collapse of the columns and buildings.

Allegorical scenes applied to walls were made long before the Renaissance.

55

THE ROOM | ATMOSPHERES

52

52 Buddhas and Bodhisattvas in the arches of cave 10, Ajanta, India.
53 The restored theatre room of the Palace of Tranquil Longevity, Beijing, China.
54 Eighteenth-century Chinese lacquer panels with red damask wall coverings in Hauteville House, Guernsey.

The rock-carved Ajanta Caves in India are Buddhist monuments made between the first and second century BCE up to around 480 CE. They are believed to be roughly contemporary to the great Stupa at Sanchi (see pp. 68–69) and were rediscovered in the early nineteenth century by a hunting party chasing a tiger, who came across caves 10 and 11 of the thirty or so rock-cut enclosures. Since 1999 an extensive and ongoing renovation of the caves, in particular numbers 10 and 11, has revealed numerous paintings and sculptures that have been accorded world heritage status. The murals are some of the oldest Buddhist paintings still in existence and relive the Jataka stories of the lives of the Buddha including an image of the first sermon at Sarnath. Inscriptions record the names of patrons of the artworks: one mentions Kanhaka of Bahada, a nobleman, others refer to monks named Dharmadeva and Sikhabhadra. Reflecting this sense of community patronage, the murals are teeming with people and alive with drama as opposed to more formal religious imagery.

The colour, structure design and themes of wall paintings can radically alter the sensation of spaces; the messages inherent in a mural are often key. The Palace of Tranquil Longevity in Beijing was built for the fourth emperor of the Qing dynasty in 1771 as part of his retirement complex in the Forbidden City. Comprising twenty-seven pavilions and four courtyards occupying two acres of the complex was the Juanqinzhai, which loosely translates as the 'studio of exhaustion from diligent service'. The western part of the lodge contains the 'theatre room', which had a stage and viewing platform for performances that the emperor was destined to enjoy in his dotage. The silk mural paintings, extremely rare Chinese examples of large illusionist imagery, depict images of the bamboo screens that enclose the opposite side of the room. Beyond the painted screens are painted landscapes filled with pavilions, trees and wildlife such as birds. The paintings also mirror the space's circular moon gate, placing a crane at the entrance to stand watch. The ceiling is painted as a bamboo lattice with vines. It was anticipated that here the emperor could indulge his passion for gardening and the arts. The room had not been touched since the removal of the last emperor in 1924, when many spaces of the Forbidden City were locked up and forgotten. A 2008 renovation revealed its delights anew.

53

54

Along with paint, wallpaper and hangings are other significant forms of applied surface. Wallpaper became particularly popular in Europe and the West in the nineteenth and twentieth centuries as the middle classes began to utilize it in their houses. Its origins are in China and were concomitant with the development of paper making. Early European woodblocks for making religious souvenirs were known as *helgen*. It wasn't until paper-making processes evolved and guilds of paper hangers formed that it became accessible as well as fashionable to paper the walls of your home. Regarded as a frivolous approach to decorating, wallpaper was banned in the seventeenth century by the Puritan government in England. Nevertheless, by the eighteenth century, the fashion for papering walls drove the demand for the export of hand-painted wallpaper from China to Europe. Whether fashionable or forbidden, wallpaper is an enduring applied surface and one whose importance drifts in and out of our interiors. Its use reflects tastes and fashion and can be easily read as a barometer of styles in the way people externalize their desires through atmosphere.

Beyond the use of materials such as marble and stone or the application of paint and paper, there is one surface that can demonstrate all manner of atmospheric conditions. Mirrors are the applied surfaces that are utilized in order to add sparkle and create light as well as to confound and deceive. The Sheesh Mahal (Urdu for Crystal Palace or Palace of Mirrors) is a seventeenth-century pavilion in the Lahore Fort in the Punjab, Pakistan. The Sheesh Mahal is housed in the Shah Burj (King's Pavilion), which was first used for private meetings but was modified by the first maharaja of the Sikh Empire, Ranjit Singh, who built his Harem in the pavilion. The Sheesh Mahal was designed as a semi-octagon formed from a series of arches that are two storeys high. They are encrusted with precious stones and mirrors. Candlelit evenings in the space must have amplified the atmosphere further.

Mirrors can be used to deliberately distort and confound our understanding of the dimensions of interiors by reflecting them endlessly in space. The Portrait Pavilion by HOH architecten and Paulien Bremmer was set in the eighteenth-century ballroom of the Duivenvoorde Castle in Voorschoten, the Netherlands, and employed reflective surfaces not only to dematerialize space but also to reflect the visitors back at themselves. The tiny reflective pavilion mimicked the central motif of the carpet it was positioned on and contained black-and-white portraits including some introduced by visitors. The enclosure was the spatial equivalent of a Facebook page or even a modern selfie as it contained portraits of the visitors set amongst the old masters surrounding it.

The mirror is also a critical component of the retail interior. When customers are trying on clothing the reflective surface is prioritized not only to promote view and depth in space but of course to allow consumers to see themselves as they admire the things that they are trying on. Studio 10 used a huge array of mirrors and other reflective surfaces to create a store for the womenswear brand Geijoeng in Shenzen, China. Situated in a shopping mall, the interior has a mirrored ceiling, reflective walls and a glass block floor. Customers enter from the gaudy mall into a sharp, clinical interior via a glass block-lined corridor. Green terrazzo

55 The lustrous interior of the Sheesh Mahal, Lahore Fort, Pakistan.
56 The mirrored Portrait Pavilion in Duivenvoorde Castle by HOH architecten and Paulien Bremmer, 2010, reflected visitors back at themselves on entering the room.
57 The spectral shimmering surfaces of the 2019 Geijoeng concept store in Shenzen, China, by Studio 10 counterpoint the sharply detailed garments on display.

flooring and green marble plinths, containing frosted acrylic clothes rails, anchor the light-filled space. The mirrors and the reflective surfaces create a blurry ghostly apparition of an interior. This is in sharp contrast to the precise minimalist tailored clothes on display. The mirror is the applied surface that works hardest to appear as though it is not really there.

Interiors are always situated inside buildings. This means that when a building's use changes there will always be the act of stripping back and preparing the existing surroundings to accommodate whatever is to come next. This process can provide motivation for the design of the new additions, and it differs to applied surfacing because it is all about the found conditions on site. The four-storey house known as the Yellow House or Barakat building in Beirut, is a historic landmark located directly on the Green Line, the demarcation that separated the Muslim west and Christian east of the city during the Lebanese Civil War between 1975 and 1990. The early twentieth-century sandstone structure was designed by Youssef Aftimos and latterly Fouad Kozah in a mix of Ottoman revivalist and art deco styles, with latter additions including an open colonnade. The openness of the building and its location made it strategically important for the snipers that occupied the building with a clear sight of the combat zone. Lower stairs in the building were demolished to stop the enemy from intruding. The crossroads in front of it became known as *takaata-al-mawt*, which loosely translates to 'the intersection of death'. The building is both a physical landmark and a symbol of the death and danger that it concealed.

Its ruined shell was saved from demolition in 1997 and, through what became a long journey of protests, activism and political instabilities, in 2017 it was opened as a memory museum and cultural centre with objects tracing the seven thousand-year history of the city. Now known as Beit, or Bayt, Beirut (the house of Beirut), the designer and preservation architect Youssef Haidar decided to retain the scars and histories of the structure, intervening into what he and curator and preservation architect

58   The building's turbulent past is inscribed in the robust restructuring of the walls of the Beit Beirut Museum in Lebanon by Youssef Haidar, 2018.

59   *Internal Theater* installation in the Kunlun Porcelain Factory by One Take Architects in 2021 used mirrors to recall the building's former lives.

Mona El Hallak called the skeleton, flesh and skin of the building. Steel structures were placed brazenly into the openings of the building like an oversized prosthesis. These were designed to respond to new earthquake codes. The skin of bullet holes, craters and scorched plaster work was retained as were bunkers hastily erected by the snipers for protection. Since the conflict is still fresh in the memories of many generations, the museum is still only open sporadically and El Hallak still has many of the objects and possessions found in the ruined building in storage, awaiting installation. Found surfaces, in this case in the Beit Beirut, can tell compelling stories when uncovered and used as motivations for the new use of an interior.

Found and applied surfaces can be used in conjunction with each other in order to create unique atmospheric interiors. Zibo, in Shandong province, is known as the city of ceramics in China. Kunlun Porcelain Factory was one of its most well-known producers, but it was bankrupted and closed down in the 1990s. The abandoned factory had at its centre a workers' club – a social hub for the community. The factory was listed for demolition but before this happened One Take Architects honoured the memories of the lives of the workers by making an installation in the large hall of the club. The exhibit consisted of a series of tall planes clad in mirrored surfaces and focused towards a circular projection at the far end of the hall that showed slides from the days when the club was open. Visitors to the installation stepped between two mirrored walls and were reflected continuously as though in a social gathering with old friends. Three hundred visitors including former factory workers visited the installation for the four hours it was open on 5 March 2021. For a fleeting moment, before the building was taken down, they were reminded of their former working lives and memories.

All atmospheres are reliant on light, whether natural or artificial. When considered as a 'material' that changes space, light can render atmosphere as solid, tangible and *real*. Uniting found and applied materials, and using natural and artificial light, Hiroshi Sambuichi spent a year observing the

60 (Opposite) Hiroshi Sambuichi's installation in Frederiksberg Museums, Denmark, 2017, featured a moss-covered island shrine growing amid the watery environment.

61 James Turrell's works create what appear to be passages, walls and rooms from the manipulation of artificial light.

effects of light on the monumental space of Cisternerne, part of the Frederiksberg Museums in Denmark, in order to make a translation of the Japanese shrine Itsukushima from the island of Miyajima. When in use, the 4,320-square-metre (46,500-square-foot) underground cistern could hold 16 million litres (4.2 million gallons) of water. It was Copenhagen's main supplier of drinking water until it became an exhibition space. It has a unique temperate climate. It is the only dripstone cave in Denmark: as water seeps through the concrete structure from the Søndermarken Park above, it reacts with the air and forms unusual stalagmites and stalactites. Sambuichi allowed water to fill the cistern once again and, by letting natural light enter the space, visitors would be guided to the shrine on an island via a timber walkway made by Japanese craftspeople. The exhibition was illuminated only by the sun, which bounced into the interior via a series of carefully positioned mirrors. The atmospheric conditions of the cistern meant that the small moss-covered island at the centre grew over time. The daylight-only dimensions of the project meant that it was only open as long as the day was light enough.

Artificial light has as much capacity as its natural counterpart to recreate the numinous. In the series Veils, Wedgeworks and Skyspaces, the artist James Turrell has produced what appear to be physical walls and rooms that are all created through the effects of light. So much so that in an exhibition in the Whitney Museum in New York in 1980 one visitor, while leaning back on what they perceived was a wall, fell through the light and broke a wrist. They promptly sued the artist for damages. Lighting can create both good and very *bad* moods.

Making stories through surfaces can also take place via drawing, painting and filming. The historian Robin Evans described a way of representing and then projecting rooms as the 'developed surface interior'.[7] The first example was Thomas Lightoler's 'section' of a stair hall, a drawing published in *The Modern Builder's Assistant* journal in 1742. Evans described a technique that unfolded the drawing of a room with the four fully decorated wall elevations extended from the plan. This process not only prioritized the importance of the room but also accentuated its surfaces.[8] In terms of atmosphere, an interior can be as much a biography of a person as a written account is. Infamously Marcel Proust's bedroom, extensively detailed by Diane Fuss in her book *The Sense of an Interior*,[9] was where he completed *In Search of Lost Time*,

62 The developed surface interior documents the atmosphere of a room by peeling back its walls. Drawing by Thomas Lightoler from *The Modern Builder's Assistant*, 1742.
63 The Kim family search for Wi-Fi signal in their cramped *banjiha* in Bong Joon-ho's *Parasite*, 2019.
64 In contrast, the affluent Park family's house conveys an elegant atmosphere and is slowly commandeered by the Kims.

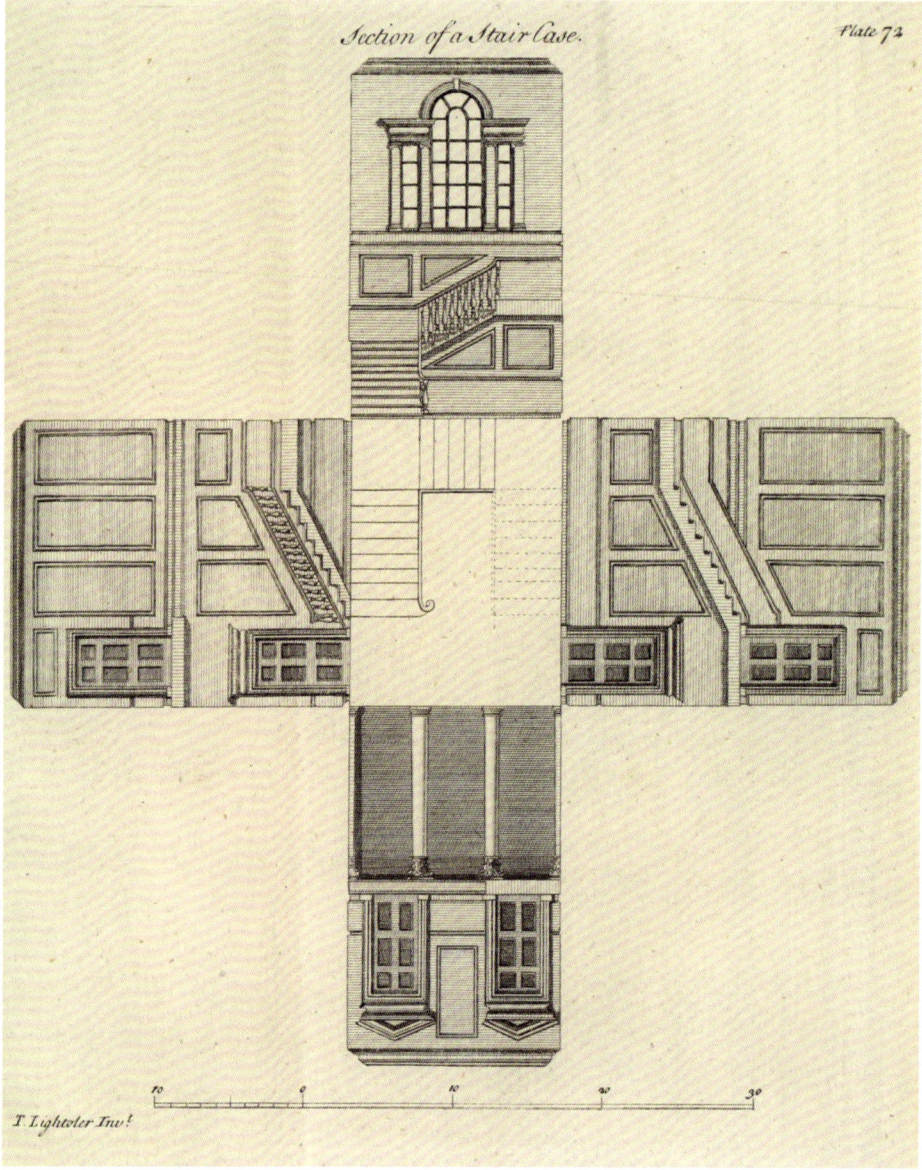

his novel of introspection. Proust lined the walls of his writing room with cork. He worked at night, sleeping in the day, ensuring that the room was always darkened, the curtains drawn – an insular atmosphere heightened by the cork lining. Film has the unique qualities of making very particular atmospheres in space. Two domestic spaces in Bong Joon-ho's 2019 film *Parasite*, by set designer Lee Ha-jun, created two vastly different spaces where the main action took place. The Kim family lived in a semi-subterranean *banjiha*, a working-class apartment in South Korea. Its cluttered and unsettled atmospheres were reinforced by how the two youngest siblings in the family, Ki-Jung and Ki-Woo could only find an unsecured Wi-Fi signal in their bathroom. The confining atmosphere was amplified by the staging of the toilet raised on a platform in such a manner as to severely restrict its use in anything but a cramped sitting position. In comparison, the wealthy Park family was depicted as living in a large opulent house, with wide open spaces, a garden and servants. The atmospheres of the interior were carefully relayed through the set designs while also enhancing the subtle plot lines of the strategic overtaking of the Parks' family life and care by the voracious and mercenary Kims.

Whether applied or found, or constructed through media, atmospheres render enclosure inhabitable to its occupants as reflections of themselves.

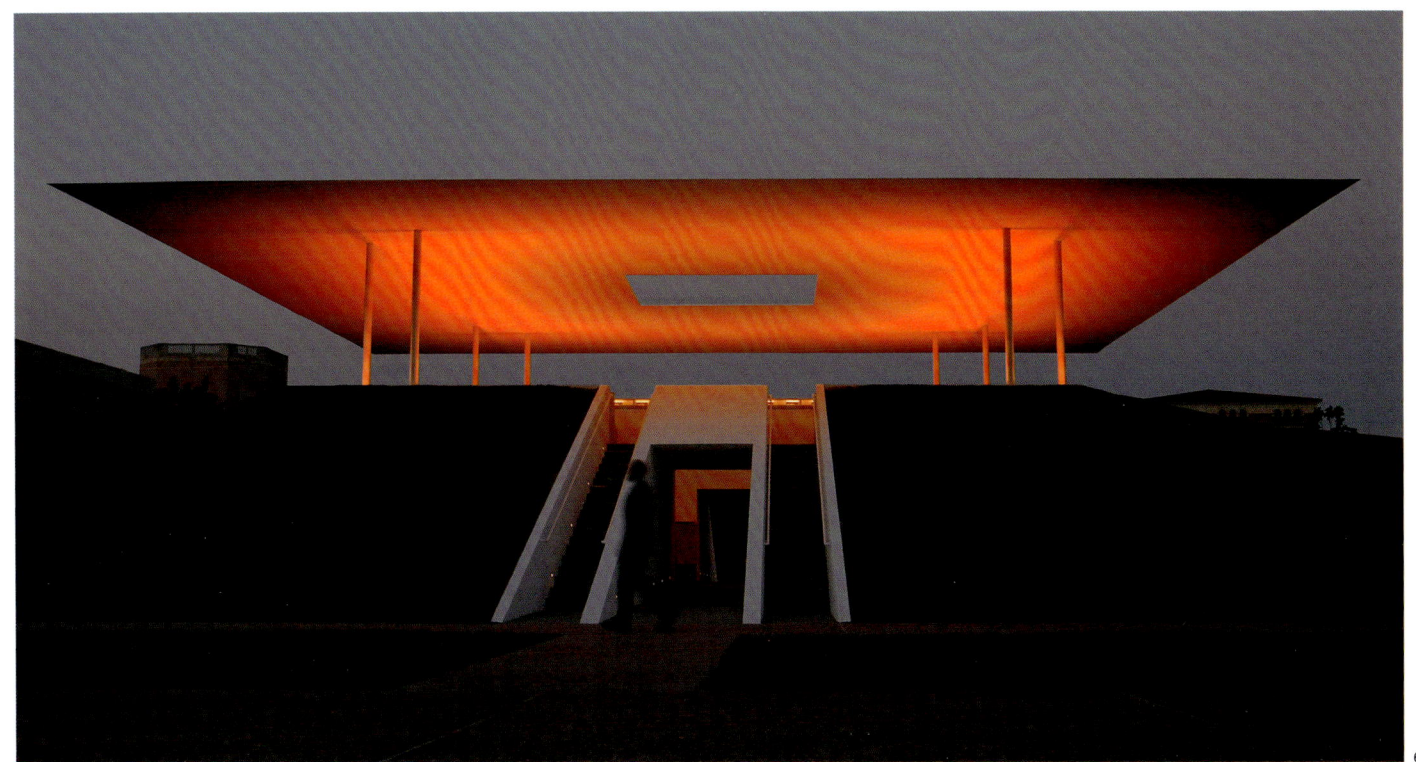

60 (Opposite) Hiroshi Sambuichi's installation in Frederiksberg Museums, Denmark, 2017, featured a moss-covered island shrine growing amid the watery environment.

61 James Turrell's works create what appear to be passages, walls and rooms from the manipulation of artificial light.

effects of light on the monumental space of Cisternerne, part of the Frederiksberg Museums in Denmark, in order to make a translation of the Japanese shrine Itsukushima from the island of Miyajima. When in use, the 4,320-square-metre (46,500-square-foot) underground cistern could hold 16 million litres (4.2 million gallons) of water. It was Copenhagen's main supplier of drinking water until it became an exhibition space. It has a unique temperate climate. It is the only dripstone cave in Denmark: as water seeps through the concrete structure from the Søndermarken Park above, it reacts with the air and forms unusual stalagmites and stalactites. Sambuichi allowed water to fill the cistern once again and, by letting natural light enter the space, visitors would be guided to the shrine on an island via a timber walkway made by Japanese craftspeople. The exhibition was illuminated only by the sun, which bounced into the interior via a series of carefully positioned mirrors. The atmospheric conditions of the cistern meant that the small moss-covered island at the centre grew over time. The daylight-only dimensions of the project meant that it was only open as long as the day was light enough.

Artificial light has as much capacity as its natural counterpart to recreate the numinous. In the series Veils, Wedgeworks and Skyspaces, the artist James Turrell has produced what appear to be physical walls and rooms that are all created through the effects of light. So much so that in an exhibition in the Whitney Museum in New York in 1980 one visitor, while leaning back on what they perceived was a wall, fell through the light and broke a wrist. They promptly sued the artist for damages. Lighting can create both good and very *bad* moods.

Making stories through surfaces can also take place via drawing, painting and filming. The historian Robin Evans described a way of representing and then projecting rooms as the 'developed surface interior'.[7] The first example was Thomas Lightoler's 'section' of a stair hall, a drawing published in *The Modern Builder's Assistant* journal in 1742. Evans described a technique that unfolded the drawing of a room with the four fully decorated wall elevations extended from the plan. This process not only prioritized the importance of the room but also accentuated its surfaces.[8] In terms of atmosphere, an interior can be as much a biography of a person as a written account is. Infamously Marcel Proust's bedroom, extensively detailed by Diane Fuss in her book *The Sense of an Interior*,[9] was where he completed *In Search of Lost Time*,

62 The developed surface interior documents the atmosphere of a room by peeling back its walls. Drawing by Thomas Lightoler from *The Modern Builder's Assistant*, 1742.
63 The Kim family search for Wi-Fi signal in their cramped *banjiha* in Bong Joon-ho's *Parasite*, 2019.
64 In contrast, the affluent Park family's house conveys an elegant atmosphere and is slowly commandeered by the Kims.

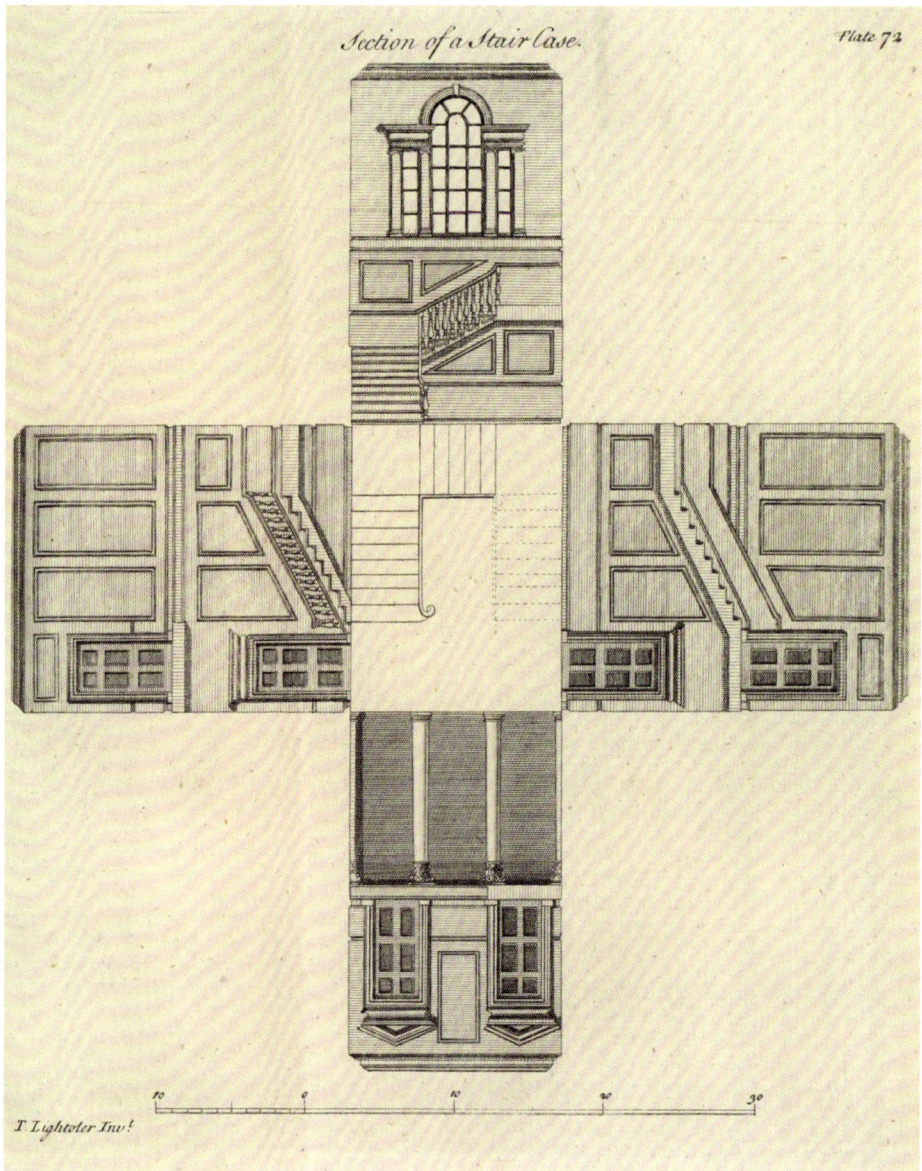

62

his novel of introspection. Proust lined the walls of his writing room with cork. He worked at night, sleeping in the day, ensuring that the room was always darkened, the curtains drawn – an insular atmosphere heightened by the cork lining. Film has the unique qualities of making very particular atmospheres in space. Two domestic spaces in Bong Joon-ho's 2019 film *Parasite*, by set designer Lee Ha-jun, created two vastly different spaces where the main action took place. The Kim family lived in a semi-subterranean *banjiha*, a working-class apartment in South Korea. Its cluttered and unsettled atmospheres were reinforced by how the two youngest siblings in the family, Ki-Jung and Ki-Woo could only find an unsecured Wi-Fi signal in their bathroom. The confining atmosphere was amplified by the staging of the toilet raised on a platform in such a manner as to severely restrict its use in anything but a cramped sitting position. In comparison, the wealthy Park family was depicted as living in a large opulent house, with wide open spaces, a garden and servants. The atmospheres of the interior were carefully relayed through the set designs while also enhancing the subtle plot lines of the strategic overtaking of the Parks' family life and care by the voracious and mercenary Kims.

Whether applied or found, or constructed through media, atmospheres render enclosure inhabitable to its occupants as reflections of themselves.

THE ROOM | ATMOSPHERES

THE ROOM | ATMOSPHERES

Passages

65 The winter solstice illuminates the depths of the internal corridor of Newgrange megalithic passage tomb in Ireland, c. 3000 BCE.

On 21 December 1967, the Irish archaeologist Michael J. O'Kelly was astounded to discover that for just seventeen minutes on the winter solstice the rays of the morning sunrise passed right through the building he was working on. He described how after finding a slit above the entrance to a vaulted inner chamber, one that contained the bones of four children and an adult, light penetrated the room and bounced around the whole interior. It was as though the spirits of the dead bodies had been awoken. Seventeen minutes later, darkness. The building was Newgrange, a passage grave in Ireland, constructed earlier than both Stonehenge and the Egyptian pyramids but not nearly as well known as either. Like Stonehenge, there is little agreement on what exactly it was used for, but the 13-metre (43-foot) high and 85-metre (279-foot) wide mound covers a central space or room that is thought to have had religious as well as calendrical or astronomical significance. The south-facing entry leads to a 19-metre (62-foot) long stone-lined passageway that connects the rooms. O'Kelly and others have excavated human remains and votives around the site, but in the morning sunlight it was this discovery that excited him beyond belief. Newgrange's use as an enclosure built around the importance of a 'passage' became illuminatingly clear.

'Passages' describes the thresholds, doorways, halls, corridors, courtyards, stairs and other openings such as windows that orchestrate the movement of users through an interior. These elements are the instruments for circulation. From the earliest temples, pyramids and castles to the most contemporary houses, museums and hotels, passages are used to link levels and rooms to each other and beyond.

Passages are an integral part of making a room. Thresholds, created at the boundary of inside and out, constitute the beginning of a passage or transition from one place to another – and into the interior. Historically, thresholds are typified by the ancient concepts of sanctuary, or paradise or *hortus conclusus* and *temenos*. Paradise comes from *pairidaeza* in Avestan (an old Iranian language) meaning enclosure. Similarly the *hortus conclusus* ('enclosed garden' in Latin)

66

66 A depiction of the Garden of Eden, a paradise defined by thresholds, by Athanasius Kircher, c. 1675.
67 Inside the *vedika* of the Great Stupa at Sanchi, India, first century BCE.
68 The fluid threshold between canal and interior in the Fondazione Querini Stampalia, Venice, by Carlo Scarpa, 1959–63.

can have spiritual connotations and is often emblematic of the Virgin Mary or the Christian Church itself. *Temenos* describes a piece of ground that is made special through its enclosure. The word derives from the Greek verb *temno* (to cut). *Temenos* also refers to a territory, a field of divinity often demarcated by a fence or a wall, (known as a *peribolos*). All enclosures of this type describe a separation that distinguishes secular and spiritual space, divinity and damnation – thresholds embody the transition between the two.

The stupa, a symbolic Buddhist monument, is essentially a cosmological form, linking the body of Buddha to the universe. It is often expressed via a series of thresholds. A central mass, usually a hemispherical mud mound faced with bricks, is surrounded by a wall or balustrade known as the *vedika* that creates a circular passage for devotion. The *vedika* has openings on four sides, aligned to the cardinal directions, but which are accessed at right angles that are designed to form the *mandala* (from Sanskrit meaning 'circle'). A Buddhist monk or pilgrim will pass through the *vedika* and circulate the stupa in an anticlockwise ritual in order to harmonize their body with the cosmological orders – a process practised in both Buddhism and Hinduism and known as *parikrama*. The great stone stupa at Sanchi, a walled complex of temples in the state of Madhya Pradesh, is one of the oldest stone structures in India and was built over the relics of Buddha in the third century BCE. At 36 metres (118 feet) in diameter, the importance of the stupa is emphasized by elaborate *torana* (ornamental gateways) thresholds at the four openings in the *vedika*. Imitating wooden constructions, two columns support three bent horizontal bars. The beams end in the *sanghas*, the sacred scrolls of Buddhism. Sanchi epitomizes devotional circulation passages.

Thresholds reinforce the flows of other passage elements. The importance of transition and movement through a threshold was an aspect of design that the Italian designer Carlo Scarpa exploited to distinct effect. The Fondazione Querini Stampalia in Venice was designed to render ambiguous the threshold between the tidal waters of the adjacent canal and the interior ground-floor gallery. As the level of the lagoon rose and fell, the waters were channelled into the interior through a gate and contained around the edges of the space. The acceptance of the canal into the gallery rendered the threshold as fluid and as murky as the lagoon waters. Whether devotional or secular, thresholds always symbolize movement and passage between states. The door is an expression of a threshold and thus exemplifies transition from one place to another. It acts as a frame for the journey that has been or is about to be undertaken. The window, while no less important, has a less 'physical' role than a door as we rarely pass through it. Its primary importance is in admitting light and air and facilitating views. The door announces one of the most important passages: the one from inside to out and vice versa. The careful alignment of doors with other openings can entice movement. Doors can signify both openness and entry but also demonstrate obstruction and privacy. This double meaning of invitation and dissuasion is emphasized

by the roots of the word. It is derived from the Sanskrit *dwar*, which is thought to have originally referred to an object consisting of two parts, making one gate or door. It is a duality that is part of the charm of the door: it is always open or closed, makes its user inside or outside and it always separates private and public. The door can be considered a weakness in a wall and therefore all manner of devices have been developed in order to protect it. In castles, drawbridges, portcullises, murder holes, even other doors in the form of gatehouses, were deployed to resist battering rams, fire and the unwanted attentions of intruders. Over time the exterior door became less concerned with the resistance to an intruder and more focused on the welcoming of guests. As one of the first points of a building that the visitor comes into close contact with, the door can be used as a device with which to provide an invitation. Caravanserais emerged in the thirteenth century via the Seljuk Turkish tribes occupying Iran, Syria and Anatolia. Meaning 'a place for caravans', they were designed to provide accommodation along trade routes and to protect the drivers and their animals transporting them and their cargoes. The system of caravanserais was an organized network of rest stops renowned for hospitality towards all travellers. Therefore, the way a caravanserai welcomed travellers through its doors was important. The walls of the enclosure were often devoid of decoration but doorways were another matter. The entrance to the Sultan Han, a 4,500-square-metre (48,000-square-foot) caravanserai in Türkiye, was highly embellished with a marble scalloped tympanum over the door and floral-patterned stone framing. Its decoration indicated to travellers that they could be assured that they were entering a safe haven on their journeys.

Doors can be highly stylized, arched, surmounted by pedestals and often niched. During the Renaissance, pattern books such as Sebastiano Serlio's sixteenth-century *Extraordinary Book of Doors* catalogued numerous ways of making an entrance via the gate, front or exterior door. Serlio depicted doors from the sparingly decorated to the ornately elaborate.

69 The door is a threshold that can both invite visitors and, when fortified, repel invaders. Portcullis at Cahir Castle, Ireland.

70 An expressively decorated invitation to enter at Sultan Han caravansaerai, 1232–36, Türkiye.

71 The door to the Mamluki Lancet Mosque, Kuwait, by Babnimnim Design Studio, 2023, is a powerful and over-scaled articulation of where to enter the building.

Some doors were inlaid with intarsia, a carved wooden decoration with geometric designs. These effects make clear the point of penetration through the external wall into the interior. The doors to the octagonal Baptistry of Saint John in Florence were devised by different artists to exalt and celebrate the transition from outside to inside. The Gates of Paradise, on the east side of the building, took sculptor Lorenzo Ghiberti twenty-seven years to create. Ten decorative panels on the doors utilized perspective to depict the story of Joseph in *rilievo schiacciato* (a kind of very low relief, literally 'squashed'). The narrative devices extolled the entrance to a place of religious significance. The over-scaled and expressive door of the Mamluki Lancet Mosque in Kuwait, designed by Babnimnim Design Studio in 2023, is an example of preparing visitors for the impressive interior behind it. The scale of the door clearly denotes where the entrance to the building begins. The huge opening not only suggests an important interior but concomitantly upon exit it reinforces departure and the passage to a less numinous exterior.

Internal doors can carry on this elaborate game. In Japan, traditional interiors featured opaque sliding paper screens (*fusuma*) to separate spaces. They could be slid back in order to invite movement to the next room, to edit the view to the landscape or to let in more light. The Old Shoin,

THE ROOM | PASSAGES

72　*Extraordinary Book of Doors*, a sixteenth-century pattern book showcasing types of doors by Sebastiano Serlio.
73　The geometric arrangement of mats and screens focuses views into the Middle Shoin and the landscape, seen from room one of the Old Shoin of Katsura Imperial Villa.

the first building to be constructed in 1615 as part of the Katsura Imperial Villa in Kyoto, is arranged as a series of elegantly composed and connected rooms. Each is organized using a system of tatami mats and *fusuma*. The simplicity of the Old Shoin, in contrast to the later shoins, is exemplified by two of its rooms: *Ichi-no-ma* (literally 'room one') made from nine tatami and *Ni-no-ma* (room two) from fifteen. The rooms are separated by *fusuma* that are covered with a paulownia flower decorative motif. Above the screens is a frieze made up of slender cedar uprights topped by a thin white plaster panel that connects to the ceiling. Beyond room two a *shoji* (translucent paper screen) filters light into the space. In the corner is a *tokonoma* alcove, a niche used to hang scrolls, make and display flower arrangements and hold mosquito nets in the summer. It is also decorated with paulownia flower patterns. All doors in the rooms can be slid back to reveal the landscape and the moon-viewing platform. Built out of bamboo, the platform provided views across the garden and also acted as a stage for its occupants. The entire composition is one of beauty, repose and extraordinarily well-considered framing.

The alignment of thresholds, including doors, can create what is called an enfilade. This is an axial arrangement of space comprising a passage lined with columns or, internally, a suite of connected rooms linked by aligned doors. Enfilade encourages movement. The Temple of Horus in Edfu, Egypt, was built between 237 and 57 BCE on the banks of the Nile in Luxor. A tripartite arrangement,

74 The hypostyle hall and the sanctuary of the Temple of Horus, Edfu, Egypt.
75 The enfilade of the Crown Prince's apartments at Schönbrunn Palace, Vienna, with paintings by Johann Wenzel Bergl, mimics an external landscape via an interior passage.
76 The internal corridor within Nagaya House in Kyoto by 2m26, 2020, was inserted in order to facilitate different activities gently separated but alongside each other.
77 A plan drawing of a very early corridor, Beaufort House, London, by John Thorpe, 1597.

the temple, outer hypostyle hall and the entrance are aligned to create a symmetrical passage through the spaces. The 36-metre (118-foot) high entrance gateway frames the passage to the rectangular hall, lined with twelve columns, through the great court. This aligns with the second hall, altar and sanctuary. This is a monumental enfilade of spaces, linked by an axial route that denotes the ceremonial importance of the journey through it. The same impulses drive the creation of an interior enfilade. Rooms can be aligned to invite circulation as well as playing with the views created. The enfilade of rooms at the Schönbrunn Palace in Vienna is lined with painted landscapes that deliberately render the internal framed view as akin to a walk into a garden.

The passage from the outside in is often via a vestibule or hall. This lobby, an antechamber, is essentially a smaller version of the European medieval hall, which originally functioned as a space to unite hosts and all their guests. Once this role became untenable, the hall then became the zone of transition that we recognize in our own homes today. Connected to the entrance hall, the corridor is a passage that encapsulates motion. This is reinforced by its derivation from the Latin *currere* – to run. Rooms in larger historic European houses often had many entrances and

THE ROOM | PASSAGES

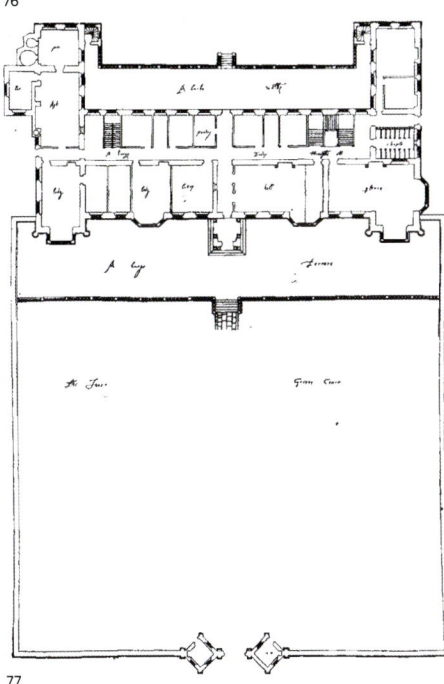

exits. This could give them an unsettled quality, as it was not uncommon to have guests, staff and host in permanent motion, chatting, moving between rooms, servants serving tea, stoking the fire and so on. It was not until the determination of the corridor, reducing the number of doors to a room and facilitating egress from all rooms through a separate channel, that this unsettled quality could be resolved. The historian and writer Robin Evans identified the first appearance of a corridor in Europe in the plan for Beaufort House, in Chelsea, London, designed in 1597 by John Thorpe. In this house the corridor was described on the plan as 'a long entry through all'.

Corridors can also be found beyond the European house. *Nagaya* is Japanese for 'long house' and describes a form of housing typical of the Edo Period (1603–1868). They were organized around a long interior corridor, usually only one or two storeys high and subdivided into apartments that could easily be partitioned again. Each space might have a bedroom and kitchen, but bathrooms were shared. *Nagaya* would accommodate all kinds of inhabitants under one roof: the wealthier having access to rooms facing the street, samurai towards the back and shops at the very end with their owners living in the adjacent spaces. 2m26 architecture studio updated the *nagaya* tradition with its renovation of a house in Kyoto. The studio inserted a sliding timber passage inside the existing building. The same principle of easy subdivision within the long space applied, with activities and furniture freely distributed under one large roof.

In the larger European house, the forerunner of the corridor was the gallery. Galleries originated as covered walkways, essentially a loggia that became enclosed with windows, doors and walls between the columns to keep the weather out and make space to hang paintings and display sculptures. Galleries started to appear as separate passages in houses in the early sixteenth century. One of the earliest in Britain, built during the 1520s, appears in The Vyne in Hampshire. The house's west wing consists of one closed gallery atop another open one.[10] Early galleries

78 Galleries, such as the Long Gallery in The Vyne, Hampshire, UK, were a forerunner of the corridor.

79 (Opposite) Bahia Palace in Marrakesh includes a series of lush courtyard gardens.

were conceived of as links between different parts of the house with the emphasis on the taking of exercise. They were initially sparsely furnished but soon pictures and objects started appearing in order to give the occupants something to look at as they strolled.

Loggias and cloisters are covered corridors that are open to the elements on one or more sides, and they may surround a courtyard. The courtyard is a space set into the building that is open to the air. It served as an internal–external passage, giving access to some of the rooms of the house. Derived from the Latin *cohors* (see p. 33), the 'court' in courtyard is therefore also etymologically related to *hortus*, the enclosed garden discussed on p. 67. This link indicates the enduring characteristic of the courtyard – that is, its connection to the outside and to landscapes. Similarly, a riad (itself derived from the classical Arabic word for garden) refers to a form of courtyard or garden that emerged in the Middle East and thence to the wider Islamic world from the seventh century onwards. Traditionally it was symmetrically arranged into four quadrants with a pool or a fountain at its centre. One of the earliest known examples of a true symmetrical four-quadrant riad in Morocco was uncovered in the Almoravid Palace in Marrakesh, built by Ali ibn Yusuf in the twelfth century. Contemporary Moroccan domestic architecture is still influenced by the riad, with houses orientated around an inner courtyard that not only increases delight but also protection from the hot climate.

Like the riad, the Italian palazzo employs the loggia and the courtyard as internal elements for making passages and circulation through the interior. The Palazzo Venezia in Rome follows a *piano nobile* arrangement, in which the first floor is the principal floor. The stairs enter the upper floor adjacent to a loggia ensuring that guests are reconnected to the outside of the palazzo whence they have just come. Then a sequence of spaces of increasing privacy: the main sala, second sala, inner sala, antechamber, bedchamber, private bedchamber and closet, all serviced by a corridor and two sets of stairs that link the lower

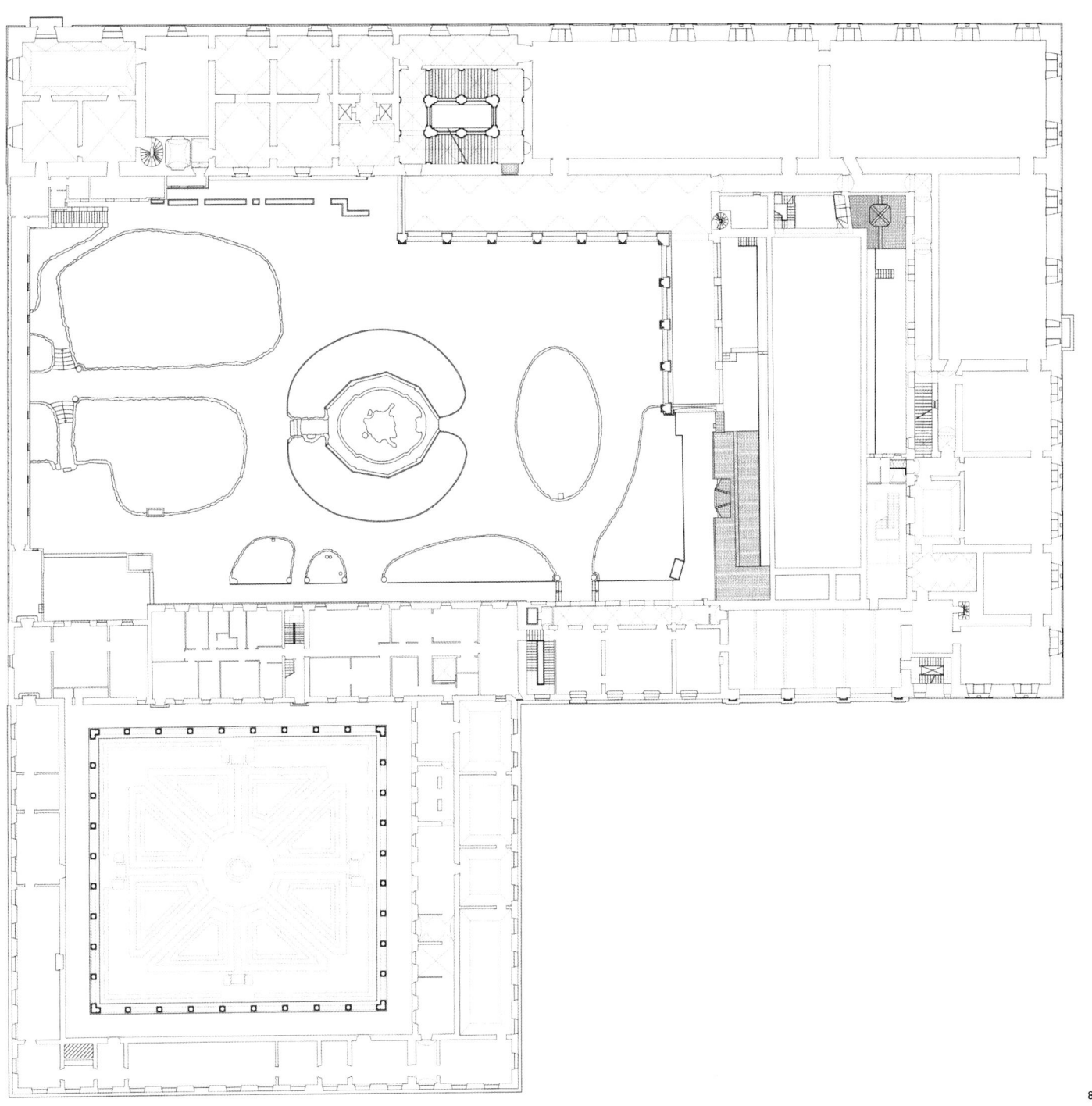

80   (Opposite) The Sala Regia in the Palazzo Venezia, Rome, is on the *piano nobile* and accessed by a passage.

81   Floor plan of the Palazzo Venezia showing the enfilade of rooms and supporting stairs and corridors leading to the Pope's bedchambers (bottom right).

floor kitchens to each of the rooms. The courtyard, stairs and enfilade of rooms were combined to enable the sequencing of movement in the interior to become a journey of delight, as guests moved from the city to the room, from outside to inside and back again.

The traditional Chinese buildings typical of Fujian known as *tulou* utilized the courtyard in a different manner. The *tulou* is formed from a large enclosed fortified wall, usually circular in construction and as much as three to five storeys high, and consists of continuous dwellings containing a small village of approximately eight hundred people. The earliest *tulou* were built in the twelfth century. They resemble small fortified cites, with a single gated doorway in and out. *Tu* means 'earth' and *lou* is a tall building. Jiqing Lou is the largest *tulou*, built in 1419. At four storeys high it has fifty-three rooms on each level and is served by seventy-two staircases. As with riads, its central courtyards act as temperate spaces, cooling the structure. They would also serve as a communal space, with many becoming the centre for ceremonial and ritual gatherings as well

82

82 A 'plugged-in' reading room and amphitheatre emerging from the window of a *tulou* in the Lantian Village Project by Rural Urban Framework, 2019.
83 The theatrical transitions in the double-helix stairway between the floors of the Château de Chambord, Loir-et-Cher, France.
84 Once purely defensive structures, later stairs expressed style as demonstrated by the combination of medieval, Gothic, Renaissance and classical at the Château de Blois, France.

as social activities. A set of projects in Lantianvillage in 2019 by Rural Urban Framework set out to adapt the *tulou* for present day requirements. This primarily involved exploring the circulation aspects of the buildings. One *tulou* had already been adapted to become a school and was further revitalized with a 'plug-in' element: a small amphitheatre connected to an opening in the outside wall, behind which was the library. Another *tulou* received a new stair tower in the courtyard.

The Latin *passus*, from which passages is derived, means step. Steps embody movement and when many steps form a stairway, they became one of the most common forms of passage to appear in an interior. They are always carefully arranged transition points between floors, sometimes placed discreetly but often for show. Whether private or public, stairs distribute visitors between rooms and form integral links to other passages such as corridors, courtyards and galleries.

Early stairs were instruments of defence for an interior and its occupants across many cultures. The stairs of a European castle exemplified this role as they were built not just for security but also for the quick evacuation of the upper levels of the keep. Important possessions would be stored in the keep, and it was common to locate the stair to it inside a narrow circular void or chamber. Stairs were constructed to run from the ground to the uppermost level often without linking any intervening floors in order to protect the most valuable household effects from unwanted intruders. This would also ensure its position was known only to those who had visited before and therefore delay any invaders as they tried to find it. Sometimes the stair was formed from timber, so that it could be easily removed or pulled up like a drawbridge in times of extreme danger. More often, however, the castle keep stairs were stone and spiral, mostly narrow and attached to the walls of the stairway chamber. This made them easier to defend. The attacker's sword hand, usually the right, would be constrained in this narrow chamber, making it difficult to achieve a clean swing of their weapon during an attack. Early stair designers carefully considered the height of the step, the

83

84

riser: low for the armour-clad knight's quick ascent or high to increase their defence from above. Fighting in these dark, narrow cylindrical chambers, unsure of your footing on the uneven steps as your opponent tried to counter your movements from above must have been precarious in such a perilous situation. Early stairs were not about social ceremony but instead were the spaces of defence and conflict.

Post-feudalist stair designs underwent a transformation. Relieved of their defensive duties, they became elements of wonderment and opportunities for dramatic expression in the vertical movement between spaces. The Château de Chambord in the Loire Valley perfectly illustrates this shift from defence to delight. Designed and built in the early sixteenth century as an enormous hunting lodge for Francis I, the building has all of the typical elements of a castle such as a wall with a moat, a central keep (*donjon* in French) and four bastion towers at each corner of the building. But these are purely decorative. At the centre of the building is a partly open double-helix spiral staircase. Any visitors undertaking

85 The helicoidal Borromini staircase, Palazzo Barberini, Rome, made access to the different levels of the building easier than with a circular equivalent.
86 The ascent to the Vatican Palace was exaggerated by the narrowing, false-perspective stair of the Scala Regia.
87 The plan and elevation of the stair reveals its carefully considered illusions of distance, from *Templum Vaticanum et Ipsius Origo*, Carlo Fontana, 1694.

the 274-step journey view each other sporadically through the central light well that both stairs are wrapped around as they traverse the chateau. The layers of stairs and their semi-open character exemplifies how the passage had now become a space that spoke less about defence and more about the theatrical transition of its users between the floors of the building.

The Italian palazzo typifies the evolution of what we may now recognize as the sophisticated social stair. The important rooms of the house, the main entertaining spaces and the family rooms, were elevated to the upper floor and given the title *piano nobile:* the *noble* level or floor. Invited to ascend the stairs to these rooms, the chosen guests were bathed in light from lanterns positioned above the flights of steps. For a fleeting moment they became actors in a performance as they arrived and were swept upwards towards the fun in the rooms of the home. Palladio's famous four books set out a series of standard forms of stairs for palazzos and their structure. These fairly rudimentary suggestions were surpassed by Borromini's exuberant helicoidal stone stair in the Palazzo Barberini in Rome and by Bernini's linear equivalent, the Scala Regia, in the Vatican. False perspective in the form of an exaggerated narrowing barrel-vaulted colonnade is used to maximum effect in the ascent towards the Vatican Palace. These stairs were designed to be the dramatic passages of transition between the various levels of the inside spaces of the buildings. The private stairs of the palazzo were often spiral and set unobtrusively into the deeper aspects of the house. Used for servicing the upper-level apartments and their chambers they not only allowed servants to support the host in their private rooms, but would also enable a discreet escape to the lower levels of the house if a very disagreeable guest had arrived. Often located close to the *camera* (chamber) or the *studiolo*, where the family held the valuables of the house, the service stair was an echo of the speedy exit required from the castle keep.

Akin to its Italian counterpart, the British stately home grappled with the ways in which its guests could be elevated in the interior. As the influence

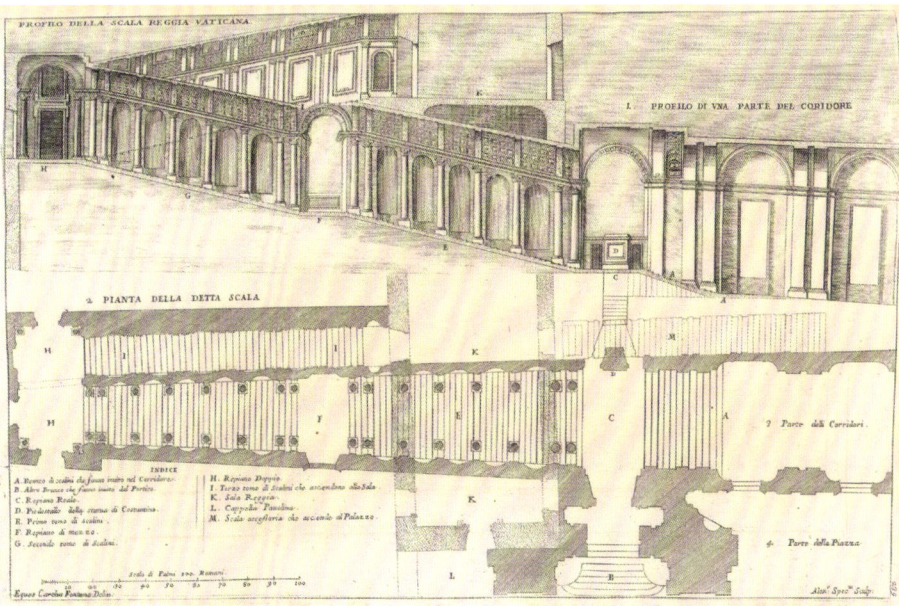

88 Looking up towards the processional staircase from the half-landing at Hardwick Hall, Derbyshire, UK.

89 Bricked-up openings were common in England due to a tax on windows between the seventeenth and nineteenth centuries.

of the medieval hall waned, a room – the chamber or the parlour – was elevated to facilitate separate entertainment for the chosen few and make clear the hierarchies of the household. Entertaining guests in it meant that the journey there needed to convey this new position or status. The most important chamber at Hardwick Hall in Derbyshire, UK, is on the second floor. The journey to it is facilitated by a great stairway lined with hangings and tapestries. These give those ascending it a running commentary on the family wealth and status as they journey up to the parlour. This large, grand room is also hung with tapestries and contains a frieze depicting hunting scenes from the surrounding countryside. The entire journey constitutes a narrative of the family's life relayed by the very rooms they inhabited.

Thresholds, doors, corridors, courtyards and stairs are elements of circulation that will often be complemented with views – windowless rooms are possible but not favourable. The sizes and shapes of windows as well as their adornment in the form of coverings, screens, shutters and layers of glazing, is always directly influenced by regional variations in weather. For instance, windows in hot climates are often smaller or screened to filter out direct sunlight and heat. Cooler northern climates might aim to accommodate more light but resist chillier air. In England the value of windows was such that until 1579 they were considered to be furniture and could be designated in wills and estates. They were sometimes left to heirs as individual pieces of property, independent of the house. In the seventeenth century, the number of windows a house had was subject to a tax when William III designated them as an indicator of wealth and status in England and Wales. In response, landlords bricked up openings to escape the tax. The law wasn't repealed until 1851, the year that the biggest window of them all was built: the Crystal Palace (see p. 243).

In its early incarnations, the window was often just an opening in whatever

THE ROOM | PASSAGES

90 (Opposite) The delicate latticework of a *mashrabiya* in the House of Suhaymi, Cairo, 1648, lets light and air in but ensures discretion.
91 The large bay window of Deanery Garden, a late nineteenth-century Arts and Crafts house in Berkshire, UK, designed by Edwin Lutyens.

material from which the building had been constructed. As the window grew in sophistication, it became fitted with a frame, which in turn required modifying and elaborating with mouldings, pilasters and entablatures. Covering and finally glazing were to follow. The relative simplicity of the concept of a window (i.e. a hole in a wall), belies how effectively it can be deployed in the interior to initiate movement. The bay or bow window became popular in the eighteenth century, built onto the façade of the building, to express a room externally and expand the view to the exterior. It could be a place for looking out of as well as a room to be seen within. The origins of the bay lie in the narrow, shaded alleyways of Middle Eastern cities into which *mashrabiyas* projected. The *mashrabiya* was designed not always to facilitate view, but instead was a device to keep the room cool. The protruding bay is enclosed with delicate latticework that allows air into the room. The *mashrabiya* affords views of the street without its occupant being observed: an important consideration for privacy.

The bay window in British domestic architecture is usually a large addition to the main room. Its proportions ensure that its impact is as much on the building's façade as on the room that it extends. The bay was a motif used particularly in Victorian architecture. Arts and Crafts houses utilized the bay as a room within a room. William Lethaby remodelled the façade of Avon Tyrrell house in Hampshire, ordering it with a series of two-storey bays. Edwin Lutyens's Deanery Garden in Berkshire was organized around a large rectangular bay window that connected the interior to the garden, which was planted by horticulturalist Gertrude Jekyll.

Both doors and windows have the capacity to express mass, by opening the enclosure through which they penetrate. All passages are instruments of circulation and movement.

Objects

92 Objects, particularly houses, relay the stories of life. Do Ho Suh, *Rubbing/Loving Project: Seoul Home*, 2013–22.

Sitting in a white-walled gallery in the Museum of Contemporary Art in Sydney was a replica of the artist Do Ho Suh's childhood home in Seoul. *Rubbing/ Loving Project: Seoul Home* (2013–22) was a copy of the *hanok*, a traditional Korean house, he and his family had lived in in the 1970s. The artist covered the building in sheets of mulberry paper, a soft off-white material that has funerary associations in Korea. He then gently rubbed graphite across the contours and lines of the building onto the paper to make a facsimile of the surfaces of the structure. The sheets were left on the building in all weathers for months, ageing and distorting them. Suh peeled the sheets off and fixed them to a wire-frame structure to make the copy of the house. He explained how 'rubbing' and 'loving' were words that he initially struggled to pronounce in English but that when written in Korean they were the same word. The object, a map of the house, relayed Suh's care and attention for his family and in particular admiration for his father, who spent much of his time in the building. The project emphasized how objects can transcend their mere tangibility and materiality and mean so much more. Whether large or small, objects narrate the lives of inside spaces. They might be imported into the space and be freestanding – a chair, a statue – or they can be built in and fixed into the fabric of the space, like a banquette or a sculpture in a niche. The reuse of objects from elsewhere brings new meanings to a space. Whichever way objects are deployed, as we can see in Suh's work, they will often relay not just stories about their previous use but they will also hold and recall meanings and emotions.

Furniture describes objects that reveal the habits and the social proclivities of civilizations. Throughout time, the seating arrangements in a room, though a seemingly simple consideration, have been used to indicate status: for example, being seated at the head of a table or on a throne. Seating has not always required a chair, and to elevate your repose from the floor has far reaching consequences not just for the organization of interior spaces but also for etiquette. Squatting and sitting

93

93 Floor surfaces may influence habits such as the removal of outdoor footwear in a tatami mat room in a Japanese traditional house.
94 Empire style chair by Nicolai Abraham Abildgaard inspired by the ancient Greek *klismos*.
95 A pair of elaborately carved walnut-backed *sgabelli*, Florence, c. 1575–1600.
96 A tall, elegant French high-backed chair, fifteenth to sixteenth century.
97 A quartzite seated figure of Pharaoh Nynetjer dating to 2810–2767 BCE, Egypt, early evidence of the relationship between status and seated repose.

cross-legged is favoured in some Asian, African and Central and South American societies – working, relaxing and dining often take place in these positions. Postures can be influenced by climate, dress and lifestyle. Cold floors and tight clothing discourages kneeling and squatting. Some nomadic tribes, such as the Bedouin, traditionally utilized mats and rugs for sitting while others, such as the Mongols, favoured foldable and portable furniture. If the custom is to sit on the floor on mats, then footwear will need to be considered. Tatami mats organize the dimensions of Japanese rooms, but they also require the formal etiquette of removing outdoor footwear and acquiring slippers before entering the space.

An elevated seating position on a piece of furniture of some kind reflects status and subsequently hierarchy. Archaeologists have found early forms of seating in the dry environments of the sealed tombs of the pyramids. These were mostly stools, but one of the earliest pieces of evidence of a throne was represented in a statuette of Pharaoh Nynetjer (c. 2785–2742 BCE). Tables have rarely been found. It's been speculated that this is because they were left outside the tombs with offerings for the gods upon them, hastening their disintegration or theft. Stools were common in Egypt and used by all levels of society, while chairs were status symbols and used by high nobility and officials until around the eighteenth dynasty (c. 1580– c. 1314 BCE). Early Grecian and Roman forms of seating included the throne, *klismos*, couch and stool. The Greek *klismos* was similar to the chair that we recognize today, with legs, a seat and a backrest. The *diphros* (stool) was often foldable and used by all, including important dignitaries and the general population. A stool typical of the Italian Renaissance was the *sgabello*. This would often have an octagonal seat, sometimes with a cushion placed upon it, and trestle legs. It was often carved, sometimes painted or inlaid with intarsia, and had a fan-shaped backrest. The *panchetto* was its three-legged counterpart and could be equally elaborate. Along with the bench, these types of seating and their deployment are recognizable to us today and form most of the sitting furniture that we still use in both domestic and public spaces. Furniture for sitting started to represent

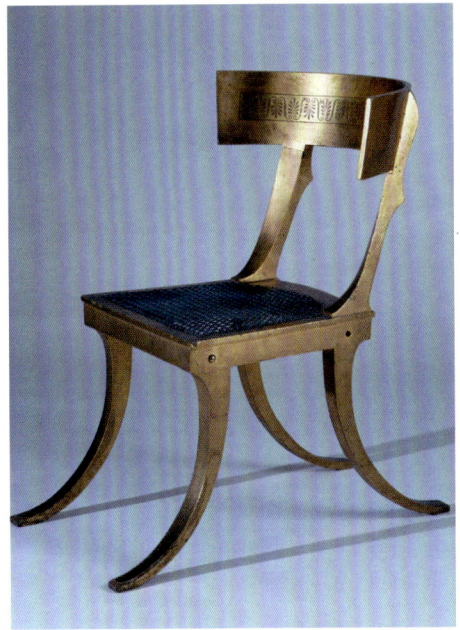

94

95

96

97

the increasingly stratified and hierarchal nature of society in medieval Europe. The highest-ranking person in the room would be afforded a chair, usually ornately carved, sometimes upholstered or cushioned and with arms. For the next level down were chairs without arms. Below that, people sat on stools with back supports, and below them backless stools. Last in the seating hierarchy were folding stools – those ranking even lower were made to stand.[11] In general, any ancient house interior could be understood as a carefully orchestrated, highly nuanced arrangement of status and power told through furniture. In domestic spaces, movable chairs, tables, benches and other items of furniture were often lined up against the wall until pressed into service. When the need arose, it would be pulled into place in the room and then returned back against the wall when done with. Furniture placed against walls, between doors or below windows sometimes complemented the structure, proportion and appearance of the room. Thus, to some degree, furniture was considered an object of display and not always of utility. This initiated the unification of the treatment of the space with that of the furniture within it, effectively implementing the idea of built-in or fixed, as opposed to free-standing, furniture.

Like the chair, the bed is an object that has always reflected the ebb and flow of human nature and status. Throughout time, it has been both public and private, singular and communal and the site for the journeys from life to death. It is no coincidence that the *chambre* or chamber, essentially a public and political set of spaces, was also used as the word to describe where the bed was located. Ancient Egyptian, Greek and Roman beds were couches, some with headboards, all used for the act of reclining and, often, entertaining. Beds evolved to become seats of power and the place from which order was established in courts and empires. Throughout the fifteenth century, different parts of Asia were ruled by dynasties including the Ottomans, Safavids and Mughals who constructed palaces of elaborate splendour in Istanbul, Isfahan, Agra, Delhi and Lahore. The Topkapi Saray (palace) in Istanbul was the centre of the Ottoman government until 1856. Bedrooms in such palaces were private affairs that were clearly demarcated along gender lines. The bedroom of Sultan Murad III was a lavishly decorated space covered with Iznik tiles and calligraphic Qur'anic inscriptions infused with botanical imagery. In contrast to European bedrooms of the time, the chambers of the Topkapi Saray were strictly private and off-limits to functionaries and diplomats. Traditionally, the Harem was the part of the palace reserved for the women of the court, including female members of the royal family. Murad broke with this tradition and had his bedroom installed in the Harem, indicative of a more open approach towards ruling and effectively redistributing power to his mother and eventually his widow.

The private and public narrative of a bedchamber was played out in the bedroom of Louis XIV at Versailles. Unlike the privacy of the Saray, here the bed was an instrument or object of power from where the king could watch and order his courtiers, the cloying nobility and seduce his numerous mistresses. The balustrade surrounding the bed was the demarcation between who was allowed into his inner chamber and who was outside of it.[12]

Radical and experimental items of furniture are imbued with many of the formal values of their historic counterpart, but they may also contest how we position our bodies within or on them, contain political or social messages or employ new technologies in their material and construction. The Faraday chair by the design studio Dunne & Raby is an enclosure that hypothetically protects its user from electromagnetic rays. Described as a chair but really a daybed, it draws attention to the constant unseen radiation that surrounds us. Formafantasma's Ore

98　The privy chamber of Sultan Murad III in the Harem of the Topkapi Palace.

99　Named after physicist Michael Faraday, the Faraday chair by Dunne & Raby, 1995, was designed to resist 'unseen energies'.

100　Advocating for the responsible distribution of e-waste, Formafantasma's Ore Streams, 2017, recycled electrical components to make furniture.

Streams project examines how waste from electronics, often neglectfully disposed of and sent to developing countries for reprocessing, could be redesigned to make new furniture, such as chairs. The Spanish designer Martí Guixé painted an off-the-peg cheap plastic chair to send a message that its lack of value made it useful and good quality. His argument was that this kind of chair is democratic, inexpensive, robust and its lack of perceived value makes it very valuable. Ironically his intervention made the chair become increasingly costly to buy. Innovations in which furniture and rooms intersect stretch the bounds of the relationships between sitting, sleeping, rooms and the body and space. Dutch architect and designer Rolf Bruggink inherited a family chest of drawers that nobody else wanted, with the understanding that he could reorder the heirloom in any way he wanted. He cut away large sections and updated it with a new element in order to create contemporary furniture. It is an approach that he followed for his family home in Utrecht, the Netherlands. Bruggink used salvaged elements from the demolition of a building next door to make a new house. The interior was constructed using no drawings, instead the house was pragmatically fabricated according to the size and availability of the various materials that were extracted from the site.

The story of the interior as told through the formation of the room is as much about reusing old objects as it is about the creation of new ones. Interior architecture, design and decoration

100

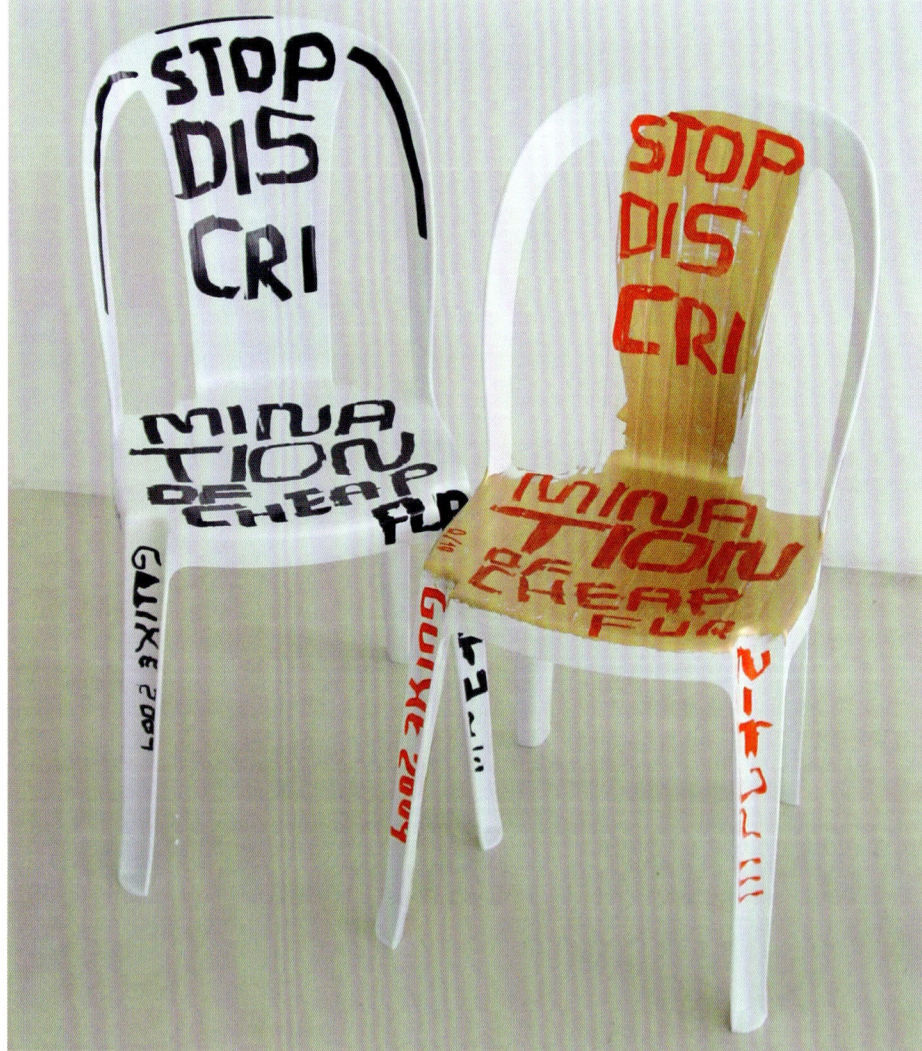

101 Rolf Bruggink's Cut Furniture project alleviated the guilt of rejecting unwanted heirlooms by transforming them into multiple contemporary pieces.

102 Martí Guixé elevated low-cost objects like this Monobloc chair to the status of bespoke artworks. *Stop Discrimination of Cheap Furniture*, 2004.

103 In collaboration with Niek Wagemans, Bruggink formed his home from salvaged materials such as radiators (seen here) cladding the main intervention within a late nineteenth-century coach house.

all utilize found objects. Salvaged, spoliated and ready-made elements have already been used elsewhere and so their reuse in a new context imbues that interior with unique atmospheres. These are meanings that are impossible to recreate in new-build spaces.

Salvaging is shorthand for the rescue and the subsequent redeployment of demolished building materials in another place. Salvaging elements of rooms and placing them in a new space creates a composite of new and old, one that necessitates a mix-and-match aesthetic. On the roof of a central London apartment block is the home of Adam Hills and Maria Speake and their family. They are the founders of the London-based Retrouvius, the architectural salvage specialists. The flat was initially designed by Hill's father but when they took over and updated it, they reworked it, using many of the found and salvaged objects that had passed through their practice. The hallway was furnished with terrazzo columns extracted from a Liverpool department store. Kitchen cabinets came from stripped-out museum display cases and internal screen doors were rescued from a Lutyens bank interior. The rooms were composed of found objects, reused and integrated into an existing building in order to make it anew.

Making use of salvaged items requires the designer of the new interiors to consider how to work with the meanings carried forwards from the existing objects. S+PS Architects embraced these challenges when they designed Collage House, a large family residence in Mumbai. They were well aware that many of the salvaged elements they wanted to redeploy in the construction of the house – reclaimed features such as doors, windows and columns – were materials from demolished buildings around the city. To reuse them in a manner akin to the informal settlements of Mumbai might send the wrong signals. Without fetishizing the materials, they embraced the ad hoc nature of the ensemble of new and old. They incorporated the demonstrable energy savings of working with the 'not new' while also emphasizing the more abstract aspects of the narratives, memories and unique stories of the salvaged elements.

104 Retrouvius used display cabinets from museums to impart rich new narratives to a kitchen in Rooftop Home, London.
105 Reclaimed doors and windows enriched the living room of Collage House, Mumbai, 2015, by S+PS Architects.

106 Old and new windows collected by Flores & Prats Architects for their transformation of a derelict building into Sala Beckett, Barcelona, 2017.

107 Forgotten elements of various Prada fashion shows became *Ex Limbo*, an installation by Rotor at Fondazione Prada, Milan, 2011, showing how material can flow back into use.

'Window corner' celebrates elements extracted from the city to make the new façade. The resultant building and interior is a recombination of both the new, old and the strangely familiar. The salvaging of materials always highlights the merging of the pragmatic qualities of what can be found and used, with the carried-over meanings of the materials' previous lives.

Salvaging extracts materials from buildings that are often about to be demolished. They are inventorized, brought up to any necessary codes or regulations, before being 'passported', so that they can be redeployed in other projects. The work of design practice Rotor prioritizes a curiosity for salvaging and passporting materials. *Ex Limbo* was an installation formed from the forgotten scenographic elements of Prada fashion stage sets designed by OMA. Gathered from their numerous storage spaces from all over Italy and laid out in their warehouse in Milan, the exhibition brought back to life the material that was considered out of use or 'in limbo'. Re-energizing material and returning it from perceived waste back into use always begins with the processes of inventorizing. In designing the Sala Beckett theatre in Barcelona, architecture studio Flores & Prats documented the hundreds of doors and windows in the existing derelict Peace and Justice Cooperative building in Poblenou district. The designers started inventorizing all of the paving, windows, doors, wooden staircases, mouldings and ceiling roses not just in order to incorporate them back into the new design for the theatre, but to also carry the ghosts of the building elements forwards, creating continuities between the past and future lives of the building.

Salvaging creates continuity. It is an approach that can include the reclaiming of a room or even a whole building. Ricardo Bofill reworked a cement factory on the outskirts of Barcelona to make his new house and offices. La Fábrica consisted of over thirty silos, machine rooms and subterranean galleries. The remnants of the industrial building became interior elements that created a unique backdrop and ultimately an unusual atmosphere in the space. The cement factory was a relic of the 1920s and had been abandoned for many years. Its reclamation and reuse as a home and studio is ongoing and for over fifty

108 The inventory of found doors and windows that were reinstalled into the Sala Beckett, Barcelona, by Flores & Prats.

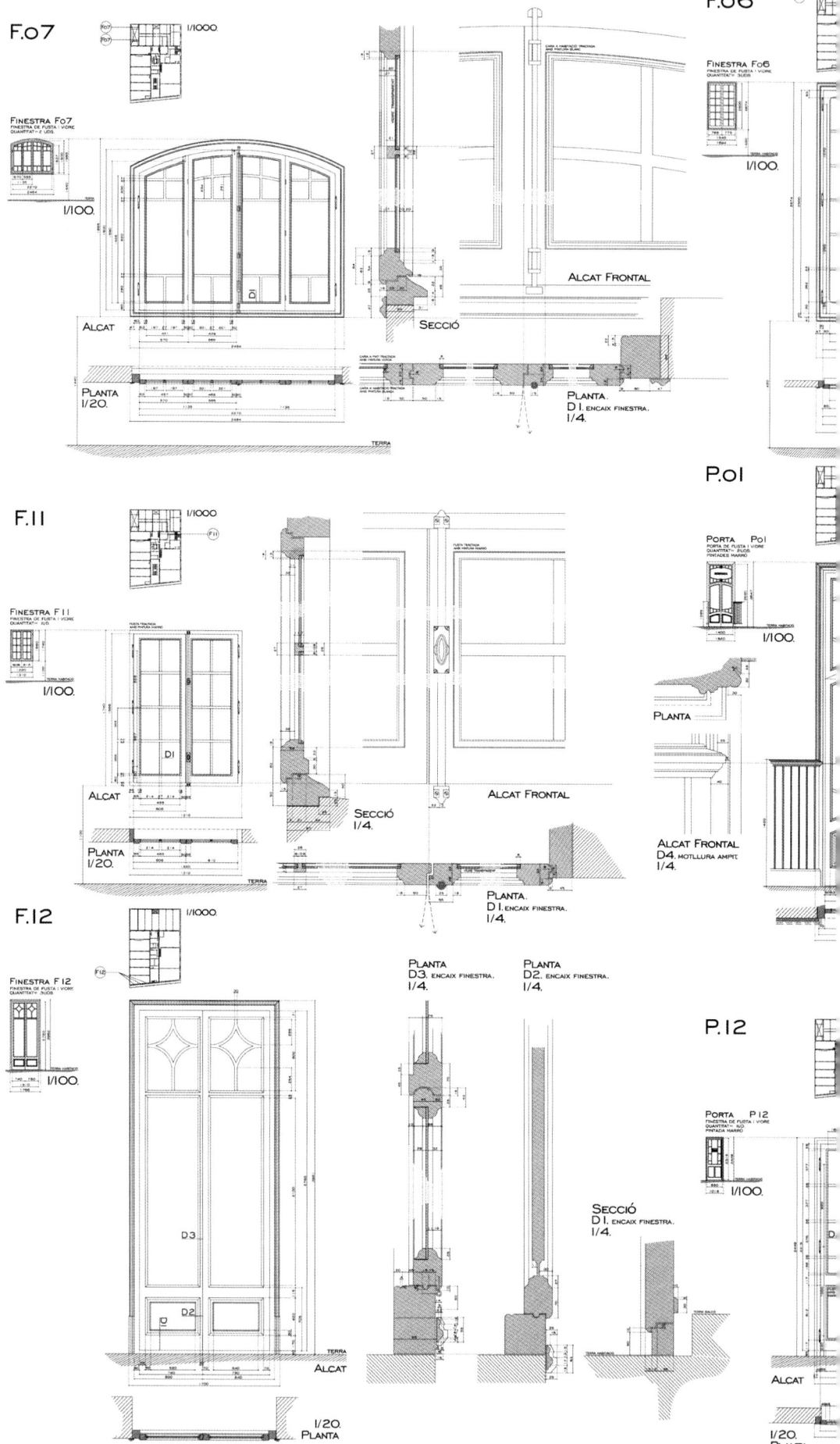

THE ROOM | OBJECTS

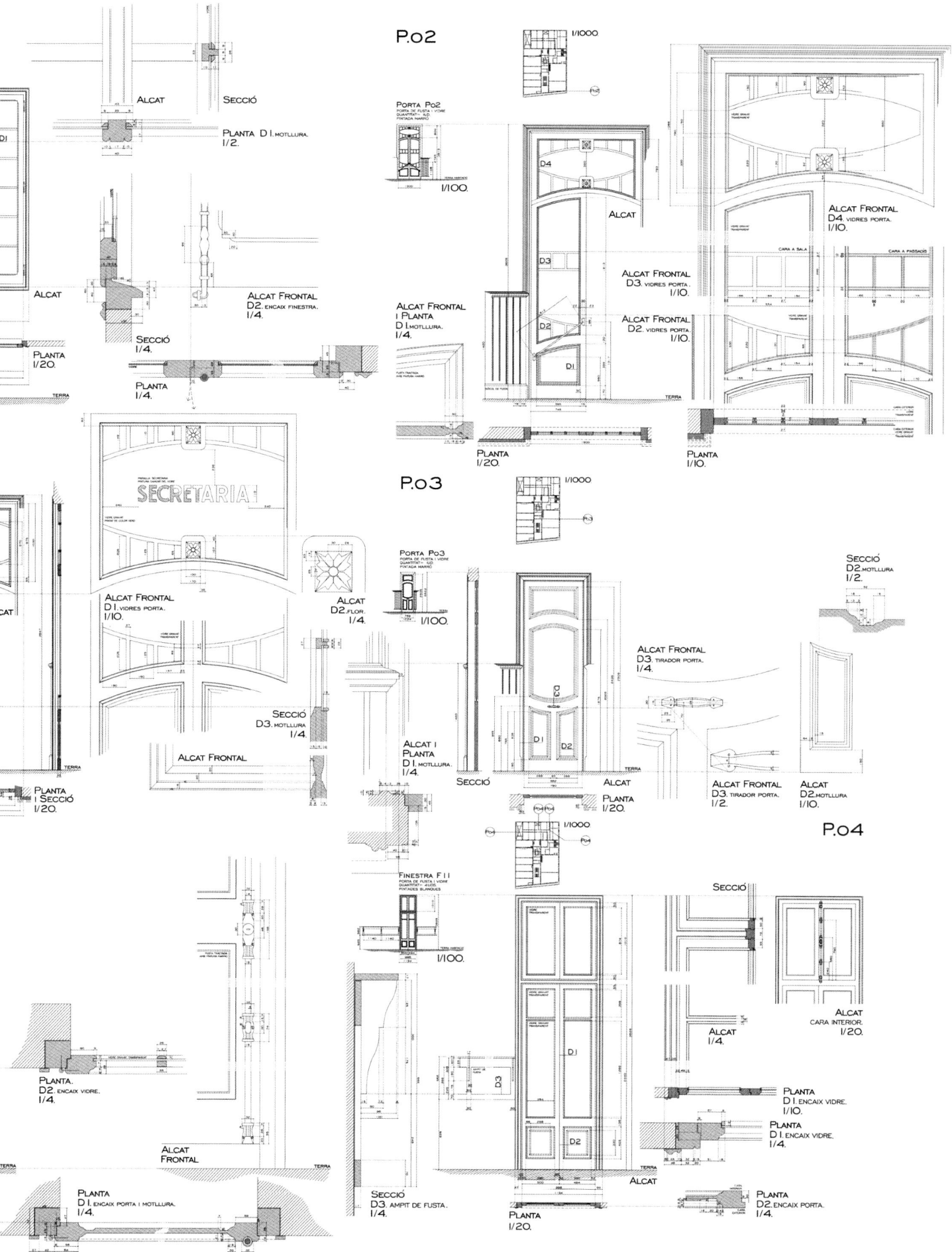

109   The ongoing metamorphosis of an abandoned cement factory into the home and studio of Ricardo Bofill, La Fábrica, Barcelona, 1975–present, emphasizes the decaying infrastructure.
110   The Arch of Constantine made use of *spolia*, engraving from *Speculum Romanae Magnificentiae*, 1583.
111   The pulpit fabricated from reappropriated material in the ninth-century CE Cathedral of Santa Maria Assunta on Torcello, near Venice.
112   The Serpentine Pavilion by Sumayya Vally, London, 2021, was composed of numerous meaningful fragments of the city's buildings.

years the designer has been reworking the spaces to house a sprawling set of domestic and work interiors distributed amongst the industrial landscapes.

Object reuse can be traced back through time and can be described through the study of what archaeologists refer to as *spolia*. An archaic term, rarely used outside the study of Roman and medieval antiquities, it describes the recycling of existing architectural elements by incorporating them into new buildings. *Spolia* is the Latin word for 'spoils', a phrase used to describe the act of taking trophies, usually armour and weaponry, from the enemy after a battle. The spoils of war would either be worn as trophies or used to decorate the victors' houses and temples. It is an approach that foregrounds legacy, pragmatism and epitomizes the desire to make new things from the existing, sometimes with violent intentions. Using *spolia* results in interiors that can be understood as a collage, or an assemblage of fragments, one made up from other times and places. *Spolia* usage falls into two approaches: pragmatic or ideological. Pragmatic when a fragment that was to hand fit the job required. Ideological when the choice and form of reuse was deliberately provocative and intended to evoke specific messages and responses.

The triumphal Arch of Constantine was erected to celebrate the victory of Constantine I at the Battle of Milvian Bridge in Rome in 312 CE. The arch drew extensively on *spolia* reclaimed from other monuments. Elements from the second century, sourced from Trajanic, Hadrianic and Aurelianic monuments, were recast with Constantinian sculptures added. It also included elements from the era of Maxentius, the Roman emperor whom Constantine had defeated at the bridge. Maxentius had drowned during the battle and Constantine subsequently had his body recovered from the river into which he had fallen and then beheaded – just to make sure. The arch is an amalgam of pragmatically and ideologically reused *spolia*. It is composed from elements taken from many different monuments in order to express Constantine's power over them all.

In the ninth-century CE Cathedral of Santa Maria Assunta on the small

110

111

Venetian island of Torcello, is a pulpit constructed from spoliated objects. Its steps are made from reliefs that were sawn and cut to provide an edge and balustrade to the stair. The steps were formulated using a series of leftover fragments. The carvings were treated quite forcefully and were cut to fit the steps and then edged with a reclaimed frieze detail. The carvings on the friezes are datable to the eleventh and the twelfth centuries and research has uncovered the fact that they were dedicated to Chronos and Kairos, in antiquity the personifications of time. The spoliated objects were deliberately retained and reused for their explicit connections to time.

The arch was clearly arranged in order to aggrandize Constantine; the components of the pulpit were chosen to compact time into one formal element. Pragmatism and ideology are embedded in their spoliated structures.

The use of *spolia* is as contemporary as it is ancient. The twentieth iteration of the Serpentine Pavilion in London 2021 was designed by Sumayya Vally of Counterspace. The pavilion was constructed from fragments of spaces related to diasporic and cross-cultural communities of the city. The pavilion referenced the city's first mosques such as Fazl Mosque and East London Mosque. It also used elements from Centerprise Bookstore in Hackney and entertainment and festival sites such as the Four Aces Club and the Notting Hill Carnival. The space was made from a series of abstracted formal vignettes taken from the community spaces to make a symbolic pavilion of furniture. Upon closing, numerous fragments of the pavilion were redistributed back to significant locations in London. New Beacon Books in Finsbury Park received a section for display and seating. The Tabernacle in Notting Hill and the Albany in Deptford fragment made seating and performance spaces and so on. The return of the fragments to the city formed an important part of its legacy.

The term 'readymade' characterizes an approach to making interiors that utilizes 'off-the-peg' objects. Marcel Duchamp defined the idea of the ready-made in the early twentieth century, foregrounding *choice* as the primary strategy for creating art. Readymades established choosing something already imbued with meaning, associations and connotations and, like *spolia*, could be entirely pragmatic but also ideological in their choice and subsequent reuses. Ben Kelly personifies ready-made approaches to designing interiors. He uses off-

112

113 The exemplar readymade: Marcel Duchamp's *Fountain*, 1917, replica 1964.
114 Dry Bar, Manchester, UK, by designer Ben Kelly, utilized found objects such as telegraph poles and engineering bricks to create hard-wearing spaces.
115 The rough exterior of a shipping container opens to reveal the domestic interior in Push Button House, 2009, by Adam Kalkin.
116 A meeting room for the design agency Reactor in Santa Monica, 2012, by Brooks + Scarpa housed in a reappropriated shipping container.
117 Air-conditioning units bought online were bolted together on-site to make Tubular Baitasi, Beijing, 2015, by PAO.

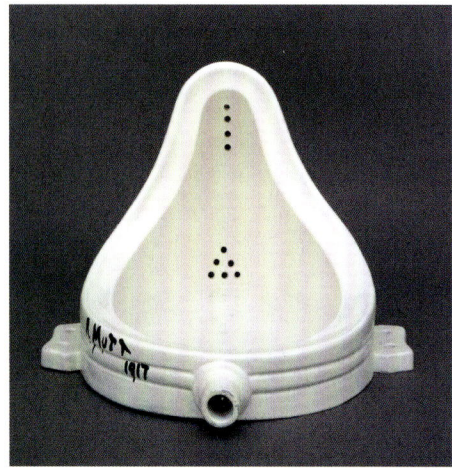

the-peg and found elements such as traffic bollards, factory-standard plastic screen doors, telegraph poles, industrial glazed bricks and hazard signs appropriated from motorway hard shoulders to make spaces. Kelly used these readymades in order to create distinct interior spaces such as The Haçienda nightclub and Dry Bar in Manchester and the Science Museum basement galleries in London. The use of ready-made found and spoliated elements created a distinct collage-like identity for the spaces.

Readymades can be adapted to conform to exact sizes or measurements, ensuring that they are fit for very particular uses. The emergence of the shipping container as a ready-made element, able to be refitted and repurposed for a variety of new uses, has become omnipresent. Container reuse is now a byword for cheap, sustainable, easily attainable built interiors. The Bohen Foundation in New York is a gallery inhabited by three moveable shipping crates that become an office, a meeting room and a bookshop. The designers cut the containers open to facilitate flexible working spaces and put them on rails so they could be easily moved to create different configurations of gallery and workspace. Two petrol tanks from the back of a lorry were used in order to create the rooms within an apartment in a former parking garage in New York. One was braced horizontally across the space, which was used for two bedrooms; the other, placed vertically, contained the bathrooms on two levels. Both were adapted with hydraulics to create doors that could be opened and closed to ensure privacy in the home. The Push Button House, designed in 2009 by Adam Kalkin, was situated inside a standard 6-metre (20-foot) container. It was named after the fact that at the push of a button all four walls of the object could be opened

115

116

117

or closed, revealing a domestic space inside. The interior was a refined space with wooden floors, sumptuous upholstery and coffee-table lamps; all in stark contrast to the corrugated rusted steel shell within which it was contained. The standard sizes and ease of transport of shipping containers mean that they can be used for workspaces, leisure and retail as well as domestic spaces. They can be cut and shaped to make space like a meeting room – as in Reactor, a workspace designed by Brooks + Scarpa in Santa Monica – or stacked, as found, to make new space for coffee bars – like Kengo Kuma's Starbucks in Taiwan. The container is a readymade with arguably no substance, qualities or design intentions. Its off-the-peg status denotes a perfunctory storage box, one that is conceived to be easily reproducible and simple to transport. It was never intended to house an interior, yet its refitting and repurposing, with a new and sometimes unusual reuse, can irrevocably alter its condition and fill it with a new life.

Sophisticated networks of digital ordering and delivery systems increase access to ready-made objects. People's Architecture Office (PAO) used Taobao, a Chinese online shopping platform, to order elements that they then used to make interior spaces. Tubular Baitasi is an event space in Beijing that was built using HVAC components delivered to the site and constructed by workmen. Their Courtyard House Plugin system can be used to upgrade traditional houses quickly and efficiently by adding bathrooms and kitchens and thereby avoid their demolition due to their lack of modern amenities – a prefabricated solution to making anew.

If architecture is viewed stereotypically as 'new build', then the story of the interior as told through objects is a narrative that prioritizes the existing, the already made and the not new, as the primary way in which to shape the world around us.

Technologies

118 The split screen between Doris Day and Rock Hudson in *Pillow Talk*, 1959, emphasized the uniting and also separating capacities of the telephone.

In the film *Pillow Talk* (1959), Jan Morrow, an interior designer played by Doris Day, and Brad Allen, a composer and womanizing bachelor played by Rock Hudson, share a party phone line in their apartment block. This is problematic. Morrow uses the line for work and Allen is always on the phone, chatting to dates he is trying to seduce. Morrow overhears a love song Allen has composed his dates, its mostly the same tune but with the name changed for each call. In an iconic scene they are each in their separate bathrooms and they share the line as they recline in their bathtubs. The director uses a filmic device whereby the wall between them is split. They are in different apartments, but at the same time they are joined together in conversation. The intimacy of the call is played out via their feet touching on each side of their respective bathroom walls, separate but together. The fun and flirtatious connections created both in the dialogue and spatially in the mirroring of their movements is facilitated through the phone call. The call unites them and intimates that they might be more compatible than they fully realize.

All technologies have significant spatial impacts and have the capacities to unite and bring people together but also to separate. In *Pillow Talk* the telephone brings together two people in a building, emphasized by the split screen, but anything from air movement, plumbing, wiring, heat and light, television, radios, Wi-Fi, escalators, lifts, even revolving doors are technologies that have all impacted significantly on interior spaces and how people use them.

Technologies can be utilized to enhance or mitigate environmental conditions through the orientation, organization and construction of interiors. Temperature can be controlled via cross-ventilation and passive cooling in buildings. Both techniques focus on improving natural air movement in interior spaces with low or no energy consumption, often just by positioning openings opposite each other. Older technologies can help to understand these issues. Windcatchers or 'scoops' are thought to be of Iranian or Persian origination and are used to passively draw cool air into and through interior spaces. At night they can assist with cooling the space as cool air is drawn in and warm air driven out of them via a process known as 'night flushing'. *Ab anbar* is a term used to describe a water reservoir in Iran, where the hot climate makes the retention of cool drinking water of primary importance. In order to resist earthquakes they were usually subterranean, sometimes built under mosques or caravanserais. They usually had numerous windcatchers positioned carefully around them, effectively circulating air to cool the water and keep the atmosphere aerated. MAS Architecture made a contemporary version of a windcatcher for Dubai Design Week in 2019 to showcase how this passive technology was as contemporary as it was ancient. Constructed from 480 sheets of

119 *Ab anbar* (water reservoir) with windcatchers in Yazd, Iran.
120 Barjeel, a cooling wind tower in Dubai, 2019, by MAS Architecture was constructed with a combination of recycled cardboard and aluminium.
121 Circular wind-resistant Tekin yurts in Turkmenistan, constructed to ameliorate the harsh conditions of the landscape.
122 The Kyrgyz devised *kibitka* to resist air pressure from strong winds.
123 The decentralized entrance-hall fireplace in Conisbrough Castle, a twelfth-century stronghold in South Yorkshire, UK.

recycled cardboard the 6-metre (20-foot) high structure afforded its visitors a moment to cool off. Instead of chilling water, the tower cooled the visitors as they checked their phones as cool air was drawn down through the structure.

The *kibitka* operates on an air-pressure modulation model to pacify winds and aid ventilation. It is a dwelling devised centuries ago and employed by numerous nomadic tribes of Central Asia such as the Kyrgyz, Uzbek and Turkmen. Its circular form and structure were devised to prioritize its demounting and transportation as well as to ensure a resistance to wind, an important consideration for the harsh open landscapes they were situated in. The cylindrical structure supported a roof ring that allowed light and air into the interior and released smoke from the centrally placed fire. This opening helped to mitigate extreme differences between external and internal wind pressures, reducing wind loading on the tent. The doorway area was reserved for household and work activities, such as cooking, while the ceremonial and symbolic functions such as worship took place at the rear. A formal hierarchy of the guest of honour, hosts, children, kinsfolk and male and female

visitors would be arranged around the central fire. The circular enclosure and its wind resistance and smoke expulsion were akin to windcatcher technologies.

As well as air movement and cooling, an enduring theme of the story of the interior is the provision of heat. A hearth is often the focal point of a room – and indeed *focus* is the Latin word for hearth. The importance of the hearth in ancient Greek society is indicated by the fact that it was ascribed its own deity: Hestia (or Vesta to the Romans) was the goddess of hearth and fireplace. In Roman houses the *atrium* was the central space in the house that contained the hearth. The hearth has been so fundamental to a domestic space that in Europe from the ninth right up to the nineteenth century, like windows, it was not uncommon for them to be taxed. In parts of Italy, a basic rental space was called a *camino*, a hearth or fireplace.

The positioning of the hearth and a fireplace, and the venting of the resultant smoke, is a recurring concern in the organization of the room. Its primary role was to afford warmth and the ability to cook. Its manifestation began, like in the *kibitka*, in the centre of the room away from the walls, and primarily with a brick or stone base. In the Middle Ages and in a European domestic setting, it was decentralized and integrated into the wall. Conisbrough Castle, dating to 1163, in Yorkshire, UK, demonstrates this radical shift that altered the focus of the room. The removal of smoke is always an issue with fire. With a centralized hearth, ventilation was achieved through shuttered holes in the roof that drew the smoke up and out. The smoke would be utilized to facilitate the drying and curing of food hanging from the rafters. If the roof was thatched, the smoke would fumigate insects. All elements of the fire were used efficiently.

Decentralizing the hearth meant that a flue could be made in the cavity of the wall – a chimney. The hearth and its chimney could be developed as a focal point for the decoration of the room. The Italian architect Sebastiano Serlio drew ten designs for fireplaces in his fourth book on architecture. These employed classical elements, columns supported by pilasters or brackets and even caryatids (pillars in the form of

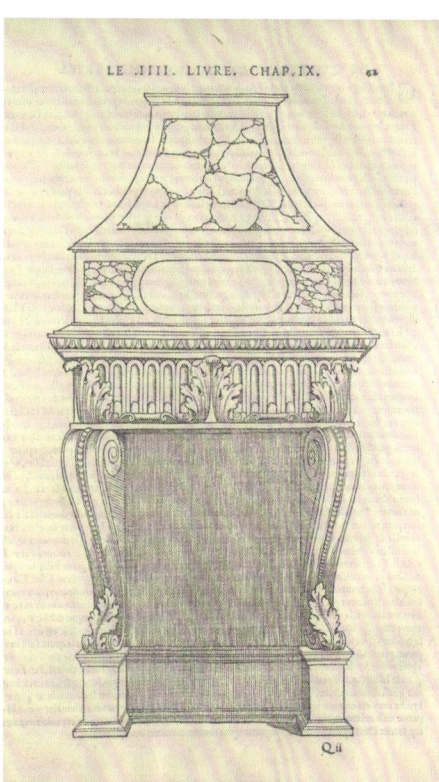

female figures). The Palazzo Davanzati in Florence deployed its fireplaces on the narrowest wall or corner. The Serlio-inspired conical hood of the hearth was made a feature of the room. As the centralized fireplace moved to the side of the space, complex internal-wall flues and chimneys enabled upper-level floors to be heated with fires. In the Middle Ages in Europe, the number of rooms in the homes of the wealthy grew exponentially from an average of three to six or seven per house. Fireplaces were moved to adjoining walls between rooms so that they could warm both at the same time. The hearth became an expedient device linking spaces, yet, it was also arranged pragmatically so that one or more could be vented by a singular flue or chimney. More fireplaces meant more rooms in a domestic interior, which in turn externally meant that the number of chimneys represented the wealth and status of a family to their neighbours.

In Britain, like Italy, the fireplace became integral to the decoration of the room. In the drawing room of Loseley House in Surrey, the fireplace in the drawing room is an elaborate confection of pilasters, corbels and figures that connects to the cornice of the room and enhances the ceiling mouldings. In an idiosyncratically British

124 Sebastiano Serlio's fourth book of architectural details displayed numerous fireplace examples, *Five Books on Architecture*, 1545.

125 Serlio inspired the fireplace in the bridal chamber of Palazzo Davanzati, Florence.

THE ROOM | TECHNOLOGIES

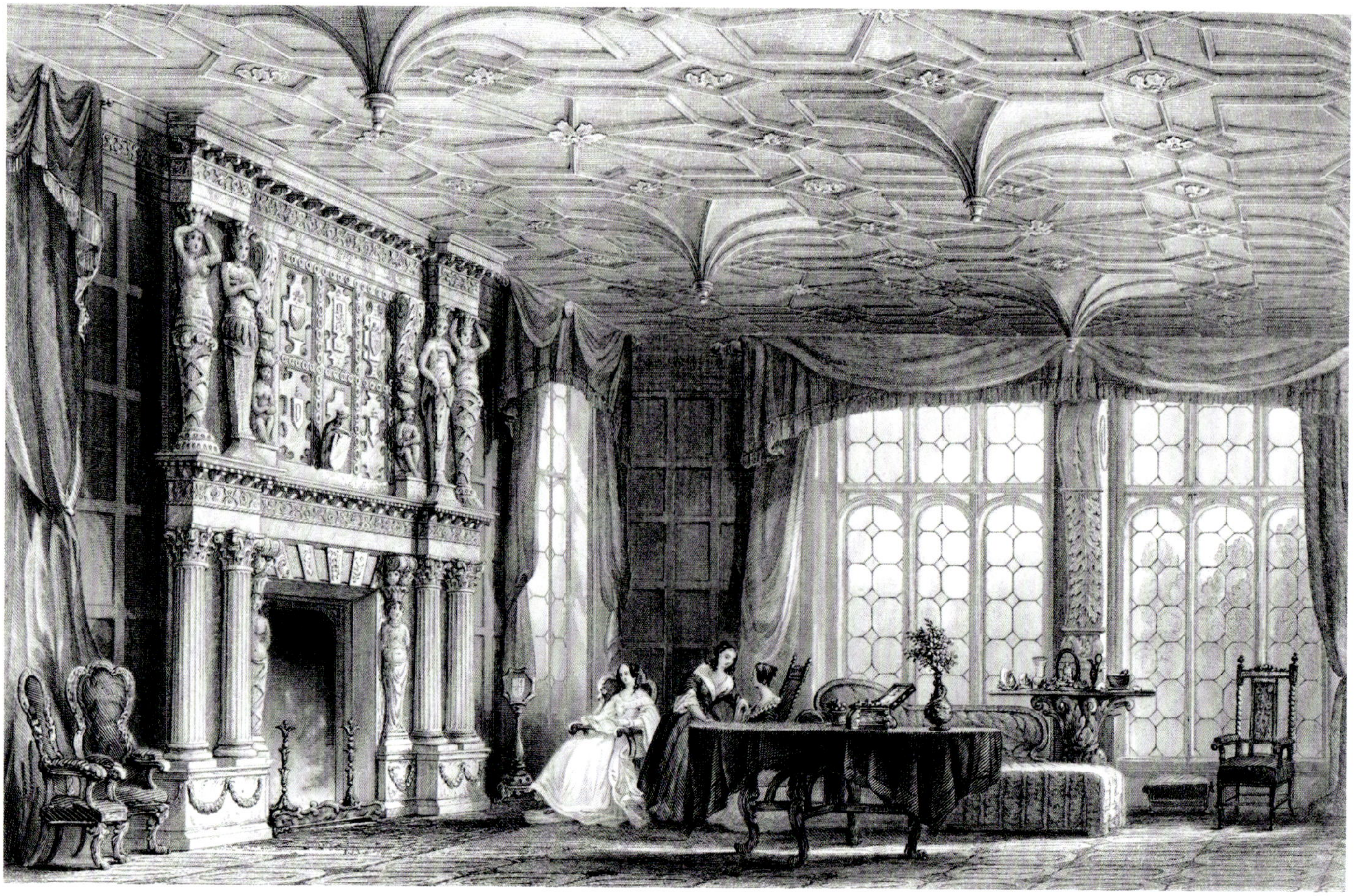

126

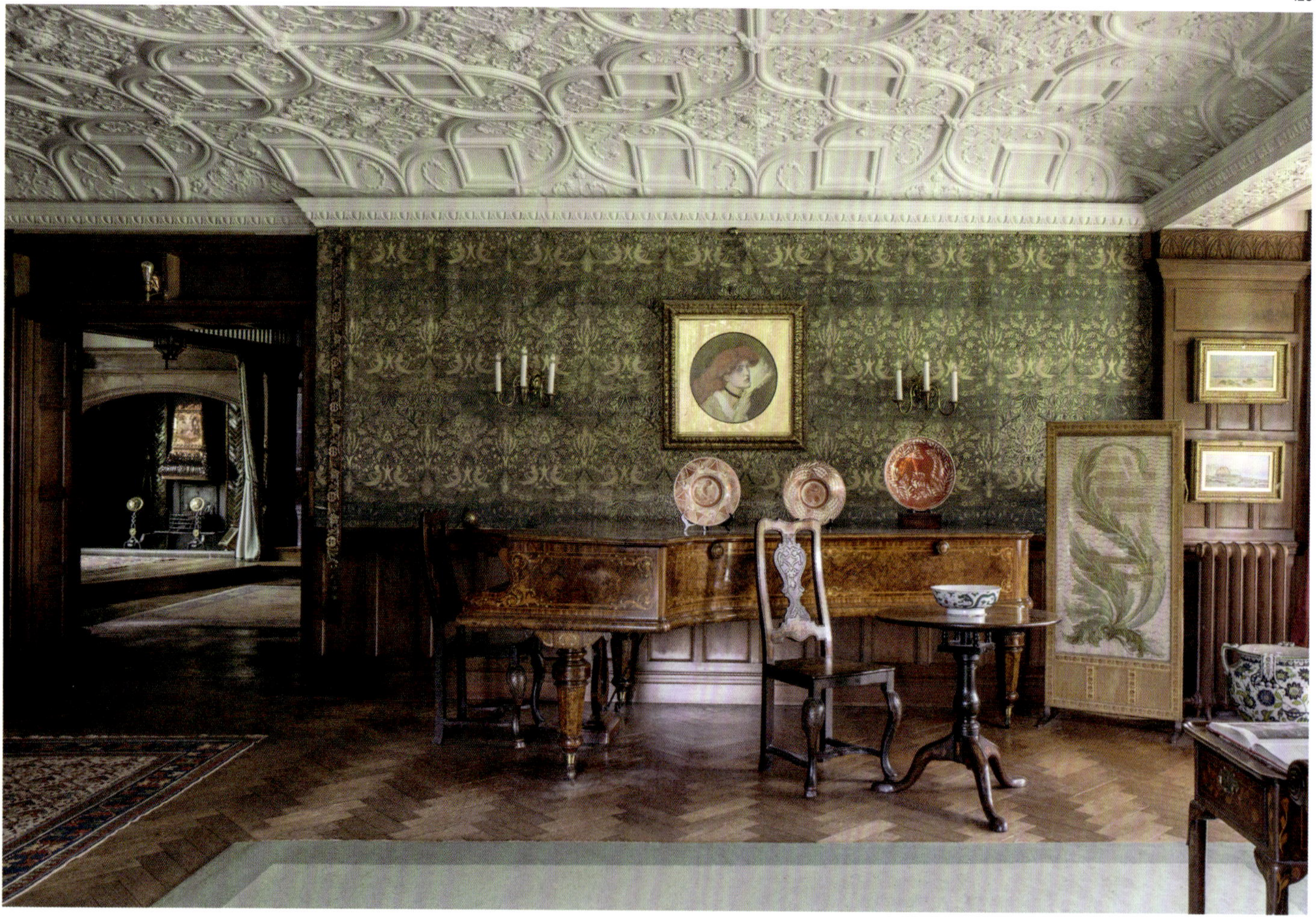

127

126 Loseley House drawing room, Surrey, UK, where the fireplace, cornice and ceiling mouldings were unified to create a coherent interior.
127 The fireplace in Wightwick Manor, West Midlands, UK, by William Morris was positioned to be invitingly on view through different rooms.
128 A traditional Korean heating system, the *ondol* heats floors in the interior via an outside hearth.

manner, the inglenook originated as a recess around the hearth, which made the fireplace become almost a room itself. The inglenook prioritized the gathering of families around the fire. Romantically inspired late nineteenth-century Arts and Crafts designers favoured them as they relayed a moral dimension to an interior, bringing the family together around the interior's main source of heat. William Morris designed one at Wightwick Manor in Wolverhampton for Theodore Mander in 1887. Its scale invited the family to gather and socialize in the warmth together.

Warming a room can be entirely decentralized by the use of underfloor heating systems. The *ondol* is a traditional Korean method of warming solid masonry floors via a 'firebox' or stove in an adjoining room. The smoke would be drawn horizontally, rather than vertically, underneath the floor to heat a room. Japanese interiors can be warmed with a *kotatsu*, derived from the *irori* – essentially a panel or square dug from the floor into the ground and used as a fireplace. As tatami became more popular the *kotatsu* was elevated from the ground and took on a table-like role. It was subsequently used for heating, cooking and gathering around to keep warm. In China, the *kang* is a heated platform that traditionally occupies one third of a room. In Iran and Afghanistan the *korsi* is a low table for gathering, heating and cooking. All floor-level systems inform how the room is heated but more so how inhabitants can gather

128

129 An elevated table-like heated *kotatsu* within a traditional inn, Oita, Japan.
130 A family in their traditional house with a *kang*, a heated platform, in Kashgar, China.
131 An elevated *korsi*, used for heating and gathering in Iran and Afghanistan.

129

together around them. They do not need to be central or situated by a wall. Their venting can take place via doors and windows.

The remote boiler combined with a distributed radiator system known as central heating is a technology that significantly impacted upon the interior. In England, the late eighteenth-century engineer William Strutt designed a central hot-air furnace system that heated outside air through a series of ducts, ventilating and warming a new mill building in Derby. Realizing the effectiveness of the system, Strutt collaborated with the engineer Charles Sylvester in 1819 to construct a novel heating system for a hospital, also in Derby. Once mechanical systems of air movement became considered in the design of a building, their integration impacted not just on the interior but also the form and structure of the spaces.

As important as heating a room, cooling interior spaces relies on efficiently moving chilled air. Willis Carrier, an engineer tasked with solving a humidity issue in a printing press company in Brooklyn, USA, is usually credited with the invention of the first modern air-conditioning system; but it was Stuart Cramer who coined the term 'air conditioning'. Carrier patented an 'apparatus for treating air' which could regulate humidity. Most air-regulating instruments were for industrial purposes. The first major

130

131

THE ROOM | TECHNOLOGIES

132 The Milam Building in San Antonio, Texas, 1928, is a very early example of unified architecture and air movement.
133 The long corridor of the 1922 Royal Victoria Hospital, Belfast, was built directly atop an air-moving vault.

public building built with mechanical air treatment to facilitate human comfort was the 1922 Royal Victoria Hospital in Belfast. The hospital was partly reliant on natural ventilation systems, opening windows for cross-ventilation. But it also incorporated a very new and modern system of ventilation to meet the hygienic needs of the patients. The building was organized around a 150-metre (500-foot) long and 3-metre (9-foot) wide brick tunnel through which air was pumped via a pair of enormous fans, driven by waste steam from the laundry. Air was pulled into the engine rooms via windows and filtered through hanging curtains of coconut fibres, kept moist with sprinklers. Cleaned of the Belfast environment, the air was then passed through the vault and distributed into each of the 'pavilions' of medical spaces and wards arranged off the first-floor corridor above the straight line of the vault. The mix of passive and mechanical venting enabled the interiors to be freshly aired and free from germs.

The first fully air-conditioned high-rise structure was the Milam Building, built in 1928 in San Antonio, Texas. As in numerous other early experiments in air movement, the basement was filled with plant machinery, in this case a huge chiller room that was filled with ice. Compressors then pumped the chilled air up into the twenty-one-storey building. The architect George Willis and engineer M. L. Diver distributed generators on every other floor behind the elevators, forming a service core of machinery, which then fed the cooled air through three main corridors and into each separate office. The corridors acted as return ducts for the warmed air.

The generation and movement of wind, heat, water, light and power between the city and the home is the story of innovations in networking and distribution. These are inventions that have enormous impacts upon the interior and its organization. The technologies for distributing both fresh and waste water is known as plumbing, derived from the Latin *plumbum*, the term for lead. The Romans used lead piping to convey both fresh and waste waters. Other ancient civilizations used clay. In Mesopotamia, archaeologists have uncovered a network of clay sewer pipes at the Temple of Bel dating to c. 4000 BCE as well as clay tubing used to capture rainwater, while the city of Uruk has been found to contain the remains of the earliest brick latrines from c. 3200 BCE. Copper waste pipes have been found in ancient Egypt at the pyramid of Sahure. Lead, clay and copper are still used for plumbing

today, although lead, while favoured for its malleability, has been phased out in most newly built homes of today due to its associations with poisoning.

Electricity has proved more difficult to distribute. In the middle of the nineteenth century, interiors were illuminated by candles or oil or other fuel-burning lamps. Soot from the oil, or gas, or candle created an unenticing air quality. Early experiments in electricity were undertaken in the 1860s by Thomas Edison and Joseph Swan, who resolved and subsequently commercialized Humphry Davy's first experiments with incandescent light, or light bulbs, in the early nineteenth century. Thomas Edison had learned from his experiences as an operative in the US telegraph system, which enabled what might be arguably a more important invention than the light bulb, the routing of small electrical currents through cabling networks and systems. So, while the bulb was the visible outcome of the power surging through buildings, streets and cities, the miracle was the development of the electrical distribution network to facilitate it. The development of grids and networks, for instance the National Grid in the UK (1925) and USA (1950), facilitated controlled networks of power in cities and homes.

In January 1882, Holborn Viaduct in London became the site of Edison's first coal-fired power station, which drove electric street lighting on the viaduct for a short while. Six months later Shanghai became the first electrified city in China and remained the only such for what was to be the next six years. Pearl Street in Manhattan followed in the summer, and before long swathes of large populous cities were being lit at night with electric street lighting. The first house in England to be built to fully embrace and integrate electric light to its interior was as recent as 1889. Stokesay Court in Shropshire,

134 Shanghai in the 1930s with neon lights outlining the buildings.
135 Cranbourn Street and the Hippodrome, London, c. 1903.
136 Stokesay Court was one of the first British interiors to consider and integrate electric lighting, heating and plumbing into its design.

136

designed by architect Thomas Harris, had lights in its great hall integrated into the arches. Crank handles for opening windows, water pipes tucked into wood panelling and speaking tubes for the staff to communicate with each other meant that the house was a machine, albeit one for being comfortable in. By 1900, manufacturers were listing electric fans, toasters, roasters, heaters, cigar lighters, even hair curlers. The fact that the supply was piped direct to the home created a burgeoning market for all these goods.

The impact of many of these service innovations, such as the electrification of interiors and the movement of air and water, was furthered in the US, where the first tall multi-level buildings were emerging. In cities such as Chicago and New York the evolution of skyscrapers sped up technological

137 The foyer of the Rookery Building, Chicago, 1885, a pioneer of integrated service technologies and space.
138 Monadnock Building, 1882, in a photo taken before its 1938 remodelling shows the original elevator cages and interior fenestration.
139 Revolving doors allow people to flow in and out of a building without disrupting the interior climate.
140 Revolving Door Structure, drawings and patent plan by Theophilus Van Kannel, 1888.
141 House of the Future by Alison and Peter Smithson, Daily Mail Ideal Home Exhibition, London, UK, 1956.

advances. Histories of tall buildings tend to focus on structural innovations, but there were also important interior technological advances. For instance, in how water supplies could be delivered at high level at the right pressure, and how airflow could be facilitated and regulated at such heights. An open window at ten storeys high could easily see the contents of a desktop disappear in a harsh breeze. Workers needed to be kept warm and also see what they were doing when dusk fell. Most important was the question of how these innovations could be integrated into the building without taking up too much of the enormously expensive yet highly profitable floor space?

The ten-storey Montauk building (now demolished) in Chicago was the first in the US to be designed – in 1882 – to integrate electricity. This was swiftly followed by the Rookery (1885), Monadnock (1892) and Marquette (1895), each one using more sophisticated technologies for air, heat and water movement. Fully integrated electric lighting alleviated any reliance on gas appliances but also overcame the need for large, expensive and space-consuming steam-driven engines in the basements.

Among these many innovations in air movement, heating and lighting in the nineteenth century is the little-known US Patent 387,571. In 1888, Theophilus Van Kannel responded to a problem inherent with tall buildings by inventing the revolving door. Tall buildings were particularly susceptible to a thermal stack (hot air rising) effect which, when doors were opened on the ground floor, created vertical draughts that could be quite significant and disrupt the interior climate. 'Always Closed', as per the slogan of his company, Van Kannel's door would literally *never* be open. It would revolve and allow regular volumes of people into the lobby while never fully opening to whatever the weather was doing outside. There was a mechanical solution in the form of an expensive internal air movement system, but Van Kannel's 'airlock', was a more expedient way of maintaining a constant temperature between inside and out – while also keeping the dirt and smells of the city outside. As each door panel turned, it created an airlock, meaning that the external weather was contained within each compartment until it opened to the inside, pacifying the outside as it mixed with the interior. Revolving doors still do the same job today. A public space such as a retail environment in a mall, a place where the inviting open door to the passing customer is a very important selling device, will often feature a blast of hot

139

141

140

air as shoppers walk in. That is doing the exact same job as Van Kannel's door in ameliorating temperature and airflow between inside and out.

Domestic spaces have long been the evidence for changes in patterns of social activities and behaviours. They have always been a vehicle for speculation and experiment. Rooms in the home, such as the kitchen or bathroom, in their capacity as spaces that are primed to incorporate new features such as electricity, central heating or smart technologies, have always ensured that the home is the space for innovation. In the early twentieth century, components of the home were scrutinized for ways in which they could be made more efficient, resulting in groundbreaking designs such as the Frankfurt Kitchen (see p. 166) and Alison and Peter Smithson's House of the Future. In 1972, the exhibition 'Italy: The New Domestic Landscape' at the Museum of Modern Art (MoMA) in New York commissioned twelve 'environments' that advanced the thinking around the concerns of domestic spaces of the day. These included Ettore Sottsass's Microenvironment (see p. 171) and Joe Colombo's Total Furnishing Unit (see p. 193). Colombo decided that the house should be utilized as an integrated environment where objects and spaces were considered together, echoing the twentieth century's preoccupation with appliances and house machines. The speculative nature

142 (Opposite) For Jungle House in Darlington, Australia, 2019, CPlusC Architects carefully considered its sustainable credentials, employing a glass interior skin with planters outside of it to passively cool the rooms via transpiration.

143 The home was formed from a reused two-storey derelict shop-top house.

of the environments examined many issues that are arguably still a part of today's domestic landscape.

Inhabitation is intrinsically linked to the notion of privacy. Writer and curator Justin McGuirk has noted that increasing prevalence of technologies that collect data for your home – smart devices such as speakers, thermostats, doorbells and locks, and the companies behind them, such as Amazon, Google and iRobot – means that the idea of home as a sanctuary is fast eroding. This is compounded by phenomena such as Airbnb and social media platforms, where the interior has become open to the public. The upshot of this is that never before have our private domestic spaces now undertake performative roles in our lives.[13]

Enclosures, atmospheres, passages objects and technologies all embody the primary components of the story of the interior. Each is present in historic and contemporary interior spaces. We will see how they have been manifest and distributed from the nineteenth century onwards in the next part of the story of the interior.

The Private Interior

Rooms and the Home

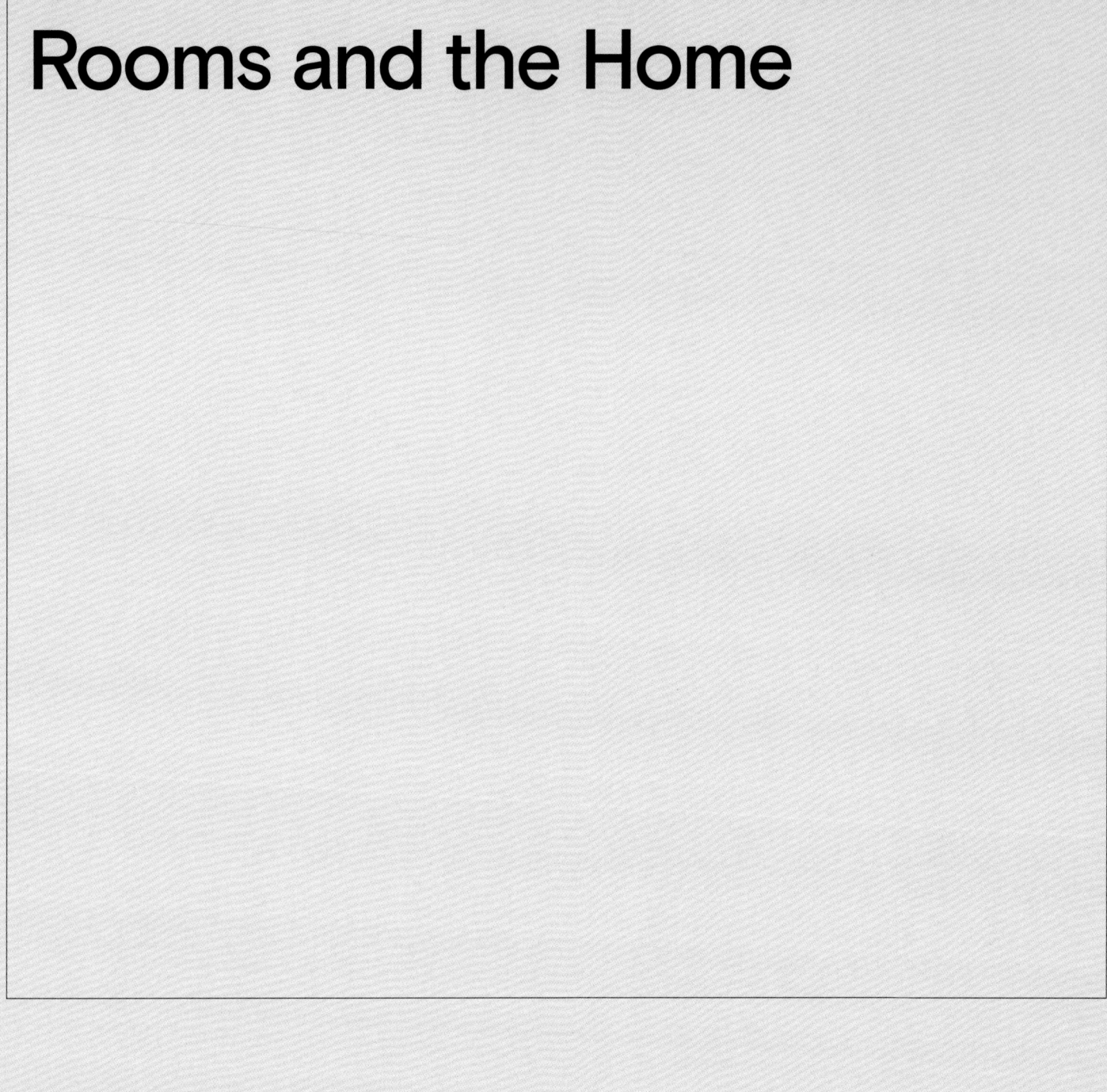

The private interior develops the proposition that the room is the primary inside space. It demonstrates how evolutions of the thematics of enclosures, atmospheres, passages, objects and technologies create living, sleeping and dining rooms, as well as the kitchen and the bathroom. These are the universal domestic spaces that form the main rooms of any home. The private interior accommodates numerous forms of social display and expression made through aesthetic choices in possessions such as furniture and decoration, to name just two. These are decisions and practices that have evolved numerous forms of taste and, by association, status for their owners. On this basis the private domestic interior always reflects its inhabitants, the relations between them and their patterns of acquisition and consumption. The rooms of the private interior are:

01   The enclosed timber box of the bedroom of The Day After House, Madrid, TAKK, 2021.

02 The multi-level and multi-use living spaces of the House NA, Tokyo, Sou Fujimoto, 2012.
03 The extended fireplace by Michael Graves in Charles Jencks's Cosmic House is crowned with female busts representing the months of spring by Penelope Jencks.

Living Room

Living rooms are the spaces for receiving guests, for gathering and entertaining. Living rooms epitomize the ambiguous relationship between the private and the public within the home. They are *majlis*, parlours, divans, salons, drawing rooms, studies and studios. Distinctions between living, dining, sleeping and even bathing have changed significantly over time in domestic spaces. Living rooms and the connections between them and other spaces are the enduring backdrops to the ways in which we live our interior lives.

Kitchen

Living, dining and sleeping are all activities that need to be *serviced*. The kitchen is a service space from which the rest of the home is supplied with refreshments. Often, the kitchen also houses the utilities that support the cleaning of the home. The role of a kitchen in a house is akin to a theatre. It may have a front and backstage: spaces which are public and for entertaining an audience, such as seating at a bar or a table; and then there are spaces such as larders or utility rooms for activities that are kept in the background. This distinction has not remained static, and over time what was once below stairs and hidden away is, in a modern home, often considered the epicentre of the house. The kitchen is the room where performance, technologies and the roles of families and their guests are played out.

Dining Room

In all the many rooms of the house the dining room is the space with the relatively shortest of histories. It contains a very specific act and therefore reflects its close associations with the actions of eating, drinking and entertaining. Dining accommodates social rituals connected to networking and status represented through enjoying food and drink. These are often embodied in the furniture and utensils used in the processes of entertaining, along with the technologies of food production and the atmospherics of the gathering. Dining rooms have shifted between being integrated into the kitchen and then, through rituals such as the takeaway or TV dinner, have become a part of living rooms. Such shifts are intrinsically linked to changes in patterns of how and where food and drink are consumed and whether it is done alone or with families and guests in the house.

Bathroom

The bathroom and its associated activities of cleaning and waste play a significant role in the modern domestic interior. Its function in the removal of waste has remained relatively private in nature; its role in ablution, caring for the body and even socializing less so. Its status as the site where we are at

04 The precursor to its private counterpart, a communal bath at the Sagamiya Hotel, Izusan, Japan.
05 At Croft Lodge Studio, UK, by Kate Darby and David Connor, 2017, work takes place against the backdrop of a 300-year-old dovecote.

our most vulnerable in the house has lent it well to expressions of anxiety about the body and danger in film. Horror movies often use this room to expose and heighten our fears of the unknown. Bathrooms and who can use them can be contested spaces, or they can simply be accepted as the interiors that everyone has to visit, usually numerous times a day.

Bedroom

We spend a significant proportion of our lives in bed. So, it is no surprise that its position, design and the evolution of the room to accommodate it has occupied much thought throughout the history of domestic spaces. Along with the bathroom, it is the space in the home that is explicitly named after the main element of furniture that it contains. This is not to say that the bedroom is a mono-functional room. The histories of the bedroom, the bed, and the boudoir describe the lives and the deaths of the occupants of a home – all linked in a fluid spatial story. In some histories, the bedroom was a public room in which only the powerful came close to the person lying within it. Other bedrooms were hidden away, becoming cells or spaces where its occupants were singly in repose. Whichever way the bed and its room is organized, it was and still is a space that has always corresponded to the way in which we represent the reclining body and its needs.

Living Room

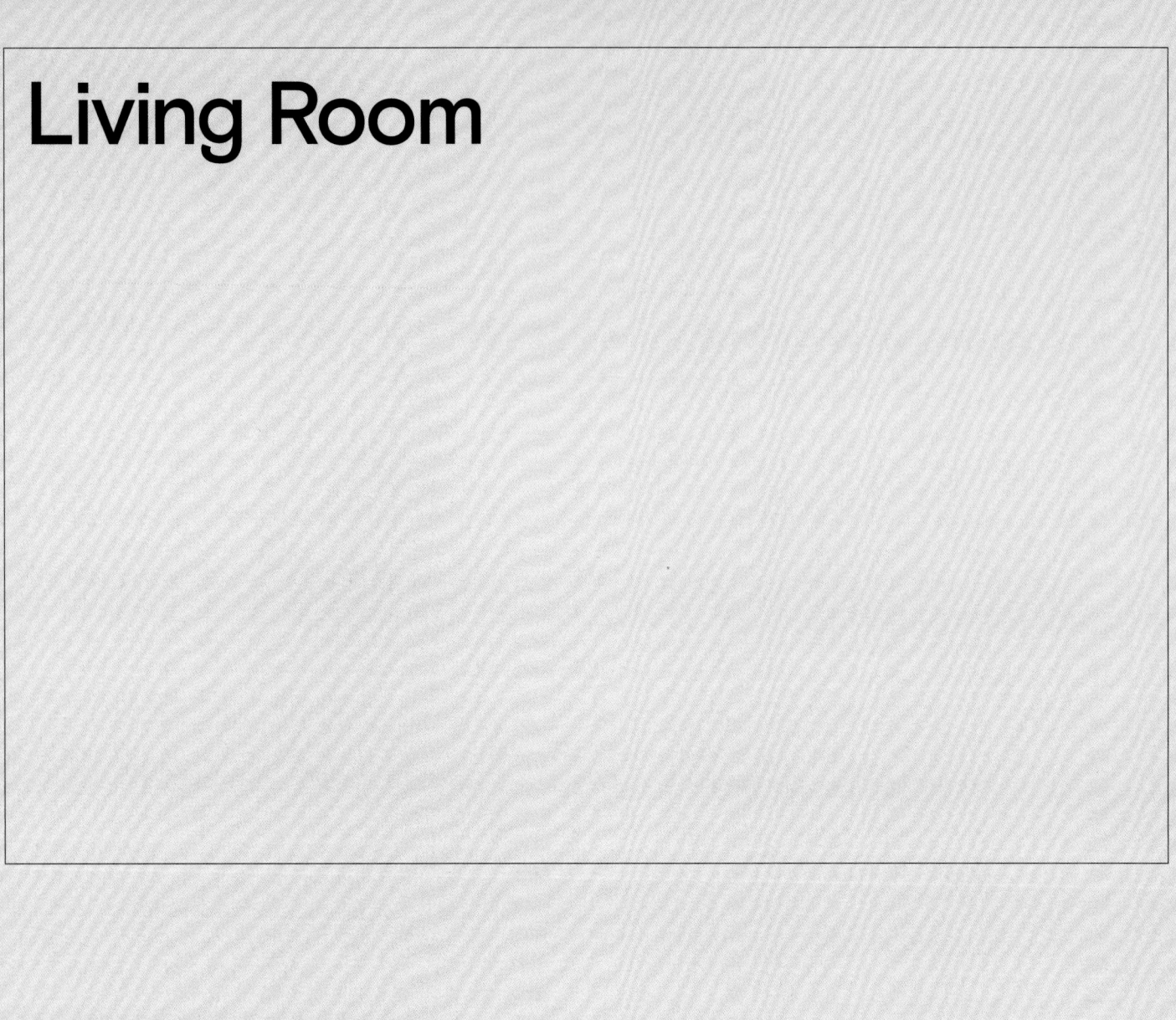

06 The robust intervention of a steel frame in the living room of Katsuhiro Miyamoto's collapsed Zenkai House, Takarazuka, Japan, 1997.

In the city of Takarazuka, near Osaka, Japan, the studio of the architect Katsuhiro Miyamoto was rebuilt within what was once his family home. The project, known as Zenkai House – mixing *zen* meaning 'totally' with *kai*, 'collapse' – was reconstructed after the Great Hanshin earthquake, a disaster that struck the Hyogo Prefecture of Japan in the mid-1990s. Like so many houses in Takarazuka the building collapsed when its heavy masonry monsoon-resistant roof, sitting on top of a structurally inadequate timber frame, gave way during the seismic activities. Miyamoto did not want to forget the disaster that had devastated the town and the lives of so many people. He wanted to rebuild his home to memorialize this tumultuous period of history. To do this, he restructured the house using a steel frame that, while bringing the building up to current legislative code for future earthquake resistance, intervened unsentimentally upon the surviving timber structure. New life and living was manifest robustly in the transformation of the home.

Miyamoto's office was placed in the bedroom where he grew up. He positioned his desk alongside a surviving timber column, a support that was still marked by notches his parents made when documenting his growth as a child. What was once the ground-floor living room of the house became the main reception of the studio, a room in which we sat when I interviewed him about this project. What became apparent during our talk was how this interior epitomized the disaster and the life and work of Miyamoto. Crashing through the room was a diagonal steel beam that braced the new structure while binding together the remnants of the timber frame. Like a fallen tree unceremoniously collapsing into the space, this dramatic element juxtaposed structural gymnastics with the traditional tatami-mat interior. The resulting space was a composite of past and present where new and old structures were intertwined, symbolizing their unstable history but presenting hope for the future of the building and the lives of its occupants.

07

07 A *majlis*, the UNESCO-recognized universal living room, constructed at the Venice Biennale by Simón Vélez and Stefana Simic, 2021.
08 Residents sitting on the *engawa* of a traditional 1880s Japanese house enjoying the ambiguities of being neither completely inside nor outside the home.
09 A shaded *jagli* in Tharangambadi, India.

Zenkai House embodies *living* in rooms and how the stories of interior space can reflect both the good and the bad memories that can inhabit them. Private domestic living rooms range from *majlis*, sitting rooms and parlours, to *engawa*, drawing rooms, *thinnai*, libraries and lounges – for entertainment and entertaining within. Their layout, furniture, decoration and resultant ambience and mood all reflect how they typify relations between people, families and their guests. As the Zenkai House demonstrated, atmospheres and memories can be manifest in the way in which the solid matter of materials and structure are deployed, to create unique stories of the lives of interior spaces.

Living rooms are as public as they are private. This is primarily because they are the spaces into which we bring guests to be hosted and entertained. Living rooms always contain elements of display, exhibiting status and relaying standing through furniture, decoration and possessions to those who are invited into them. This unique combination has meant that the particular form of living room known as the *majlis* has been recognized by UNESCO on its List of Intangible Cultural Heritage of Humanity.[1] An Arabic *majlis* originated as the space where councils sat to preside over the choice of a new caliph; legislative bodies in many Arabic-speaking countries, including the parliament of Iran, are still referred to by the term. In domestic spaces, a *majlis* is a parlour, lined with cushions where entertainment and the comfort of guests is prioritized as communities, families and their hosts come together. Their designation as world cultural heritage was because they play an important role in the transmission of stories. These are the histories and the intangible heritages of the communities and families who live in them.

To celebrate their universal qualities and heritage status the designers Simón Vélez and Stefana Simic installed a *majlis* in the gardens of the Abbazia di San Giorgio Maggiore for the 2021 Architecture Biennale in Venice. The bamboo structure was designed and built in Colombia and the textiles that

covered it were handwoven in Morocco by the Ain Leuh Women's Cooperative. This *majlis* was created to celebrate the story of the universal living room, where life was embodied in its very walls. A *majlis* is a room where histories, genealogies, songs, folk stories and poetry, as well as clarifications on rights and adjudications on disputes are all shared between generations.

Early living rooms emerged as distinct spaces within the cave, hut, tent and hall and were created only for invited guests. Once hierarchies within the interior were established all manner of rituals and activities for the selected participants could take place. These distinctions between space and certain people meant that the journey to the living room needed supervising. Thus, all living rooms need a 'reception'. These are spaces that emphasize a place to arrive at, often while also demarcating the threshold of a home. A reception space doesn't always have to be a room and it may not always even be *inside*. In traditional southern Indian and Tamil dwellings, a *thinnai* is a shaded veranda located outside the entrance to the home. The *jagli* or *jagli katte* also describes a shaded raised platform often surrounded by low walls located at the entrance of a modest Indian home. Both *thinnai* and *jagli katte* invite guests to take some rest, to sit, take water and be formally hosted. When not hosting guests, families use the external room to eat, drink and hang out, gossip and cool off on a hot day. Like all receptions they are a filter or buffer between the outside and inside of the home. Like the *thinnai* or *jagli katte* the *engawa* is a veranda or porch-like reception in a Japanese house located at the edges of the floor where the interior tatami end. *Engawa* are often screened from the living room and enclosed by overhanging eaves, offering shade and protection from the weather but open to the outside. They are often raised off the ground with a stone step defining an invitation to the elevated platform level of the house. *Engawa* accommodate the *genkan*, a porch or mat where guests remove their shoes before entering the main living rooms of the home.

A portico is a sheltered reception space usually attached to the entrance of an important home. Its grandiosity

10 The cooling environment of a *thinnai*, with comfortable outdoor seating, in Goa, India.
11 The symbol-laden carved columned portico of the entrance of a *Chefferie*, home of the village chief, Bandjoun, Cameroon.
12 A typical Yemeni living room, or *diwan*, prioritizing hospitality and socializing, Sanaa.
13 Parlour stairhall with built-in bench at the Metcalfe House by McKim, Mead & White, Buffalo, New York, 1884.
14 The reception-hall inglenook fireplace in Frank Lloyd Wright's home and studio, Chicago, 1889–98.

is often designed to impress status upon its visitors. The *Chefferie* (headquarters) of the chief of the Bandjoun region in Cameroon features elaborately carved semi-open colonnades, supporting a traditional heavily thatched conical roof. The carved timbers of the columns and walls are of spiritual symbols, often concerned with warding off evil spirits and bad weather that may ruin ceremonies or harvests. The aspirations and symbols of the portico or *porte-cochère* (covered entrance) are reduced to the porch in most modern domestic settings, prioritizing shelter over its grandiose antecedent. The *engawa*, *thinnai*, the *jagli katte*, the portico and the porch are all the reception spaces of transition, a spot to pause, rest and then be welcomed deeper into the living rooms.

The reception inside a home is usually conceived as a distinct chamber positioned before the living room that is a filter or buffer of both people and climate. In Islamic architecture the *diwan* or *divan* is a reception hall. Its formal manifestation is as a council chamber. Its domestic version is an entrance hall that tempers the weather as well as people. The name of the hall evolved from the furniture it contains. *Divan* is the name for a long piece of seating, the type usually found lining the walls of chambers such as *majlis*. An American equivalent could be found in the Metcalfe House, built in 1884 and designed by McKim, Mead & White. It buffered the external climate and filtered people by incorporating a resting bench alongside the staircase. It formed the entrance to the home of Erzelia Stetson Metcalfe, in Buffalo, New York. It was reached via another chamber, the porch, and once guests entered they could rest and await their hosts in an inglenook, a fireplace flanked by built-in benches creating a warming wait on a winters day. Similar to Metcalfe's home is Frank Lloyd Wright's reception space in his own home and studio on the edge of Oak Park in Chicago. Upon entry guests were escorted to a reception-hall inglenook with built-in furniture around a fire. Guests would feel as though invited right into the heart of the home. Yet, Wright played a spatial trick. A mirrored panel above the arched opening of the

reception created the illusion of an endless space in what was assumed to be a contained room. Wright wanted his guests to experience the contrast between enclosure and expansiveness, and to signal that this was a pause before their consideration for entry deeper into the home. The *divan* and the entranceways of Metcalfe and Lloyd Wright all epitomize welcoming yet cautious receptions. They all filter guests into a waiting space before their acceptance into the living rooms of the home.

Receptions are passages made to distribute guests between rooms once they have been received into the home. Charles Rennie Mackintosh designed the Hill House for the publisher Walter Blackie between 1902 and 1904. The house's entrance is on its side, signalled by a chimney with a small adjacent upper window, intimating an entrance to a castle – a playful nod to the client's baronial aspirations. Blackie's work and family life were inseparable, therefore the more public living rooms of the house, such as the library, drawing and billiards room (latterly a cloakroom), are adjacent to the entrance. Once inside, guests are distributed along a single passage with slight attenuations in particular steps and decoration demarcating the changing levels of

15 The choreographed entrance sequence of the Hill House, by Charles Rennie Mackintosh, Helensburgh, Scotland, UK, 1902–04.
16 The meditative and eternal journey of the curved central passage of the White U by Toyo Ito, Tokyo, 1975–76.
17 Exterior views from the White U are limited and the role of the courtyard in reinforcing internal contemplation is evident in the building's plan and sections.

privacy of the rooms leading off it. For instance, entrance hall and library are accessed via the same level as outside. This first part of the living hall is simply decorated and painted white. Halfway down the passage four steps elevate guests to the same level of the more private dining and drawing rooms. The break between levels is signalled by a fireplace set into the wall, alongside the four steps. Its location at this junction alludes to a warmer welcome waiting deeper in the home. The ornamentation in this part of the space reflects this in its elaboration. A timber screen separating stairs and fireplace initiates a sequence of similarly proportioned wall panels. These are divided with thin strips of timber making panels that orchestrate the rhythm of the movement of the hall. In each panel, a painted upper frieze completes the high wainscot and deep cornice approach to the junction of the wall and the ceiling. Ceiling joists are exposed, adding to the sharply defined rhythmical organization of the passage. A series of gaslights with an open top, converted to electricity in the 1920s, are small elaborations on Mackintosh's style of mixing organic and orthogonal design languages using intricately composed motifs and materials. The reception hall engages the visitor in a distinct poetic pattern of sequences that not only articulates movement, but also creates a unique public-to-private reception experience.

Moving guests through a reception is not always about public and private relations. White U, a home designed by Toyo Ito for his older sister in Nakano, Japan, was essentially an elongated passage within which the occupants

were invited to make a journey of reflection. The home was organized around a long, curved corridor, enclosing a central garden courtyard, through which movement was conceived as a contemplative journey. The house was designed to bring together a family grieving the loss of their father. The living room was thus combined with the hall to make living, movement and time for grieving inseparable. The kitchen and bathroom were at one end of the U and two bedrooms placed at the other end of the journey. Natural light in the hall was carefully controlled. A strip of glazing in the roof and two windows facing into the central courtyard, along with a sparse furniture arrangement, reinforced the introspective nature of the interior. In contrast to the Mackintosh-designed sequence, the White U interior was blank and abstract, with no ornamentation for the visitors to reflect upon or admire. Of paramount importance was the solace and quiet of the calming interior, designed to reinforce reflection as hosts and their guests moved silently through it.

Once guests have been accepted and welcomed, the living room can be entered. There are many terms used to describe rooms for 'living' in. Parlour is an old-fashioned term that is rarely used in contemporary interior design. Its name is derived from the French *parler* (to speak), reinforcing its meaning as a separate space where the invited are free to chat and gossip. The parlour originated in monasteries. The outer parlour was where the nuns or monks could conduct business with visitors. The inner parlour was where those who were constrained by vow could undertake conversations between themselves. Outer parlours were usually situated by the main entrance to expedite visitor relations at a discreet distance from the inner workings of the monastery. The inner parlour was usually connected to the cloister, the space for informal discussion between the devotees.

This history characterizes the atmosphere of the parlour. Its dual-purpose public/private qualities and its associations with conversation endured among the European and American bourgeoisie in the eighteenth and nineteenth centuries. Like its monastic

18 Wayside Inn, South Sudbury, USA. The formal associations of a parlour mean that it is now more commonly a public interior.
19 The Salon de la Princesse at the Hôtel de Soubise by Germain Boffrand, Paris, 1735–39, exemplifies the unification of leisure, cordiality and status.
20 The public-yet-private salon and living room of the Maison de Verre by Pierre Chareau and Bernard Bijvoet, Paris, 1932.

antecedent, the parlour would often be positioned near to the entrance of the home. In working-class Western homes a parlour was the word often used to describe the best room, one kept for guests and special occasions. This might include entertainment, but it would also involve moments of significance in the lives of the family such as death. In some households, the parlour would be the space for the wake, when the passing of a family member was grieved. Families would gather to pay their respects to the body, usually placed at rest in an open casket. Parlour curtains would remain tightly closed to the outside world when the deceased lay in the room. This is why the parlour has funereal associations. Its close affinities with formality and death meant that it has not endured, and it is rare for a contemporary comfortable living room to be called a parlour. Instead, its public qualities are emphasized, as demonstrated by the beauty, massage, tattoo or pizza parlours of the city.

Akin to the parlour is the salon. Its similarity to the word 'saloon' means it is often understood as a public room, like one found in a bar or public house selling alcohol. Like the parlour, its meanings associate the room with a private but also a very public role. This ambiguity characterizes the domestic salon; a place of entertainment, networking and connections.

The oval Salon de la Princesse at the Hôtel de Soubise in Paris, designed between 1735 and 1739 by the French designer Germain Boffrand, includes all these attributes. Hercule Mériadec de Rohan, Prince of Soubise, commissioned Boffrand on the occasion of his marriage to Marie Sophie de Courcillon. The organization of the mansion and the distribution of the rooms was arranged around two salons, one placed above the other, with the ground floor for the prince and the first floor for the princess. The Salon de la Princesse was designed in a flamboyantly Rococo style and was envisioned to be for the 'assembling of company'. This invitation placed the princess at the centre of the social and cultural activities of the house. While the Prince's salon expressed stability and reason, hers was of pleasure and sociability. The ornament of her salon is organized around eight arched bays, incorporating windows, doors and mirrors in their decoration. The arches are surmounted by gilded cartouches that connect to a sky-blue ceiling. Eight paintings by Charles-Joseph Natoire in between the arches depict the story of Cupid and Psyche, the myth of the beautiful princess who earns trust through industry and diligence. The Prince's salon below is the same shape but is less flamboyant and depicts allegories of politics and prudence, geometry and poetry – effectively *his* role in public life.[2] Both salons express not only their public roles but also the gender politics of the day.

The role of the Parisian salon had changed very little almost two hundred years later. The bourgeoise salon endured as the public-yet-private space of entertainment and status, characteristics that were evident in the first-floor salon of the Maison de Verre. The glass house was the home of a Dr Dalsace and his family. The doctor's gynaecology practice was situated on the ground floor of the three-storey building. The first-floor double-height salon was the place for entertainment and literary gatherings. Dalsace was a prominent member of the French Communist party and throughout the late 1920s and early 1930s he held regular gatherings of the intellectuals of the time. Walter Benjamin, Pablo Picasso, Max Ernst and Jean Cocteau were visitors. Just like its oval counterparts in the Hôtel de Soubise, the salon in the Maison de Verre was to provide a public and private statement to the peers of the Dalsace family as the centre for Parisian socialites to gather, confer and gossip.

In warmer climates, the filtering of heat impacts upon the sequences of entering and being received in a living room. Dar Jamai Museum in Meknes, Morocco, constructed as a palace in the nineteenth century, is organized around a riad, a planted courtyard with water and fountains greeting and cooling guests before they ascend the stairs to the first-floor salon. There, the grand vizier, effectively the head of government, would greet guests in a *divan*-lined room. Also known in Arabic architecture as a *bahw*, the salon is situated in a domed and alcoved room where guests were entertained under an ornately carved wooden ceiling surrounded by fractal patterns of mosaic tiles, known as *zellij*, covering the walls. The journey to the salon was designed to cool the visitor down before being welcomed into the room.

THE PRIVATE INTERIOR | LIVING ROOM

21 Painted wall designs in a traditional mud house in Oualata, Mauritania; the thickness of the walls resists extreme temperatures.
22 The drawing room of Elsie de Wolfe's home, Irving Place, New York, 1845.
23 Recessed *zidaka* niches filled with possessions set into the walls of a home in Lamu, Kenya, give the room identity through atmosphere.

All types of salons serve the same purpose. To invite guests into the home to socialize, relax and be entertained but also to ensure that the status and position of the hosts are extended to the visitors through their material forms. Cooling guests within living spaces is of paramount importance in hot climates. Oualata (or Walata) means 'shady place' and was once an important trading post on the trans-Saharan route in Mauritania, a stop off for caravans transporting gold and salt between Bambuk and Idjil. The town is made up of some of the oldest stone settlements on the African continent. The houses are organized around shaded courtyards, sheltering travellers and townspeople from the harsh sun. Each is made of thick rammed-earth walls covered in *banco*, a red clay mixture, and decorated with white geometric patterns. Oualata offered free bed and board to its visitors as they passed through, and living rooms were kept cool with minimal openings to the outside set deep into the thick walls. Furniture was sparse and kept close to the cooling walls. The old town was made a UNESCO world heritage site in 1996 and today focuses on tourism rather than hosting traders arriving from across the desert.

Other formal domestic rooms include the drawing room, a space derived from the sixteenth-century notion of withdrawing – a legacy of the action of exiting the large open ancient hall, tent or hut space. 'Withdrawing' described a room or a chamber to which the host and selected guests could repair for more privacy. The drawing room was multi-functional and could accommodate both daytime and night-time activities. Guests in a bourgeois home may be received in the drawing room in the morning, or they may gather there prior to lunch or an evening meal. Like the salon and the parlour, entertainment may take place in the room, with music or games such as cards. It would also provide a quiet haven, when not being used for entertaining, for reading and private conversation. The furniture of the room was as much about comfort as it was about presenting the family to guests. Irving House, the home of interior designer Elsie de Wolfe in New York in the late nineteenth century, contained

THE PRIVATE INTERIOR | LIVING ROOM

a drawing room that displayed many of these qualities. It was on the first floor of the house, adjacent to the dining room. It was a long and narrow space, punctuated by a columned arch. Emanating from the arch was a series of wall panels that gave the room order and framed the artwork and antiques. Because of its narrow qualities, furniture was positioned at the edges of the room. A small bay window was treated as a greenhouse and contained cut flowers and a window box. To complete the effect of a small garden, De Wolfe had a fountain installed in the space. As polite conversation flowed so did the sound of trickling water. Drawing rooms can also be focused upon calm and stillness. In the 1970s Swiss artist Hermann Stucki invested money from his sales in an exhibition into a derelict house in Lamu, an island in Kenya. Made from coral stone and mangrove timber he spent two decades restoring the eighteenth-century building, organizing it around a series of shaded courtyards. The quiet introspective rooms were filled with found Indo-Swahili antique furniture, a hybrid of Gujarati, Omani and East African aesthetics – a product of the location of the house close to passing trade. The thick walls of the cool, pale living rooms were recessed with *zidaka*, decorative niches for containing possessions, pottery and paintings, giving splashes of colour to the serene interiors. Irving House and the house on Lamu Island both provided living rooms for rumination when withdrawing into them.

The study or studio is like the drawing room in that it is a space where work is undertaken away from the hustle and bustle of the home. It is a room to withdraw to. *Studiolo*, a diminutive of studio, was historically a small room within a Renaissance palazzo and a space set apart for private study. *Studiolo* could also describe a piece of furniture, usually a cabinet made to contain precious books and objects with an attached writing desk. *Studioli* would often be positioned in the corners of the palazzo or odd-shaped leftover spaces in the plan of the building with few windows. This was to ensure warmth but also to focus the user's mind on their work without

24 Federico da Montefeltro's *studiolo*, designed to inspire its occupant, in the Palazzo Ducale, Urbino, Italy, 1476.

25 The pivotal role of the studio in Casa Luis Barragán, Mexico City, meant it had its own entrance to the street and connections to the living, dining rooms and garden.

any external distractions. Much like its historic counterpart, the contemporary studio represents concentration. In Mexico City, architect Luis Barragán's house contains a studio that is the epitome of focused thinking and rational thought. The home is made up of two houses carefully joined together and reworked to provide space for Barragán's family and his studio. The close proximity between work and living resulted in the home becoming a laboratory – a place to test spatial ideas. Barragán was a particularly tall person and the rooms in the house were designed to fit his proportions. A result of these experiments are the small anterooms that compress entrances to his exact height before the full height of the rooms unfolds as you enter them. The studio and house has a bespoke interior built around the dimensions of the designer.

Like Barragán, the Italian designer Achille Castiglioni used his living space and studio as a laboratory for experiments. Castiglioni's design was not as formal as Barragán's and instead relied on the seemingly happenstance positioning of his collection of objects. Located in Milan in a series of four rooms on the ground floor of an eighteenth-century palazzo, the studio – now a museum – portrays Castiglioni's thinking and processes. Alongside his objects are his archive of drawings, prototypes, models and books. His studio is an autobiographical account of his life and work, a rendition of his character. It was and still is a witty, playful space, full of oddments stacked up in glass cabinets, accessible and ready to be extracted and used for a design. The juxtaposition of various objects he collected in the cabinets meant unusual associations could be made between them, an effect always expressed in his work. Studios are the rooms of focus, but they can also accommodate chance encounters between possessions and people to inspire their occupants.

24

THE PRIVATE INTERIOR | LIVING ROOM

25

Study, studio and library are closely related rooms. 'Library' is etymologically rooted in the Latin term *librarium*, a chest for books. The public library has stood for the collective expression of reading for centuries. The domestic library was also devised to symbolize learning, but in a more private fashion. Early home libraries were created to display collections of manuscripts, books and important precious objects. Prior to the seventeenth century in Europe, books were comparatively rare and unaffordable, so they were kept locked in a *librarium* with other valuables – often in the *studiolo*. As books became more readily available the ways of displaying and rooming them, became more important, especially in larger houses.

The display of books in the home was often undertaken in such a manner as to impress guests of the intellectual cachet of their host. It is still an impulse in interior spaces today. Library House, by Shinichi Ogawa & Associates, in Tochigi, Japan, is dominated by a tall library/living room located centrally in the single-storey pure white box of a house. The huge room is back-lit by a courtyard and top-lit by a large glazed opening in the roof. As well as creating overwhelming displays, the shelving of books can have a more functional role. In the main room of the Carrer Avinyó apartment, by David Kohn Architects, in Barcelona, an upper-level balcony mezzanine studio/library is balustraded with a bookshelf, keeping the reader safe. Larger libraries require vertical access, often via ladders or stairs. Bookshelves can even double up as stairs as well as display cases. In the studio of Ezio Gribaudo in Turin, the levels of the interior are linked by a sinusoidal wooden staircase. Gribaudo was an artist and publisher and the books he produced were ingeniously

26 The library is a room of focus and study in a house such as the Château de Groussay, Montfort-l'Amaury, France.
27 Achille Castiglioni's studio in Milan was an extension of his thinking and processes where work, objects and ideas intermingled.

28 The book wall of Library House by Shinichi Ogawa & Associates, Tochigi, Japan, 2012, dominates the main living space.

29 The high-level library and its book-shelving balustrade forms a balcony that connects bedrooms and kitchen in the Carrer Avinyó apartment by David Kohn Architects, Barcelona, 2012.

stored in the open risers of the stair. Whichever approach to a library is taken, one of its primary concerns is to provide a retreat, a space for a moment of reflection, even if the room becomes a part of the journey such as a stair or balustrade and overlaps with the other rooms of the interior.

Contemporary planning in domestic interiors has questioned the limitations of the cellular room. Modern domesticity has prioritized better connectivity through designing in 'open plan'. This development didn't mean that the complexities embedded in cellular rooms dissolved, it just made rooms more fluid in the living relationships between them. These complexities were examined in two projects of the twentieth century, one exploring the efficiencies of these connections and the other enhancing their complexities. Ken and Jo Isaacs' Living Structure, designed in 1954, was an experiment in the economics and functionality of living rooms made through modular systems of construction. It was part of a system they conceptualized known as the Matrix Research Project. This was a network of grids that could be city-scale or be reduced to the sizes of modular living units and furniture. They were made from off-the-peg materials such as plywood and pieces of readily available 2 × 4 timber. They could be erected in just two hours with a pair of pliers and a screwdriver. The newly wed Isaacs built and lived in their own structure in their apartment for several years, developing and refining the two-level system of seating, bed and storage. Their experiment questioned how rooms could overlap and be seamlessly connected within one frame, dissolving the walls of traditional room layouts.

Open-plan living and the erasure of internal walls in the domestic interior has been a recurring motif in modern design. Contrary to spatial

30 Ken and Jo Isaacs' Living Structure, 1954, was designed to test modularity and expedient construction methods.

31 Taking 'open-plan' to its logical extreme, The Withdrawing Room, by Diller + Scofidio, 1987, drew attention to barriers between rooms while the furniture dissolved them by moving through the walls.

simplicity, this seamlessness can increase complexities in the interior. These issues have been explored in The Withdrawing Room an installation by Elizabeth Diller and Ricardo Scofidio. Based in an old timber-frame house and designed to question open planning and domestic conventions, the designers divided and sliced up the furniture and the walls of the rooms. The inhabitant was imagined moving between newly opened rooms questioning the domestic rituals they would normally undertake in the home. The dinner table was suspended between floors, the bed could move between rooms. It was designed to provoke reflections on the complexities of gender and property rights and challenge etiquette in an open-plan set of rooms. It poked fun at the formalities of what might be described as a 'regular house'. Both Living Structure and The Withdrawing Room were characterized by responses to open planning. Both prioritized the dissolution of cellular spaces in favour of a seamless flow between living rooms, while The Withdrawing Room exposed how openness did not necessarily mean straightforwardness.

Seamlessness between open-plan rooms can be extended to the approach of bringing external landscapes inside. Relationships between homes and their gardens has been an enduring design idea. It is an approach that can

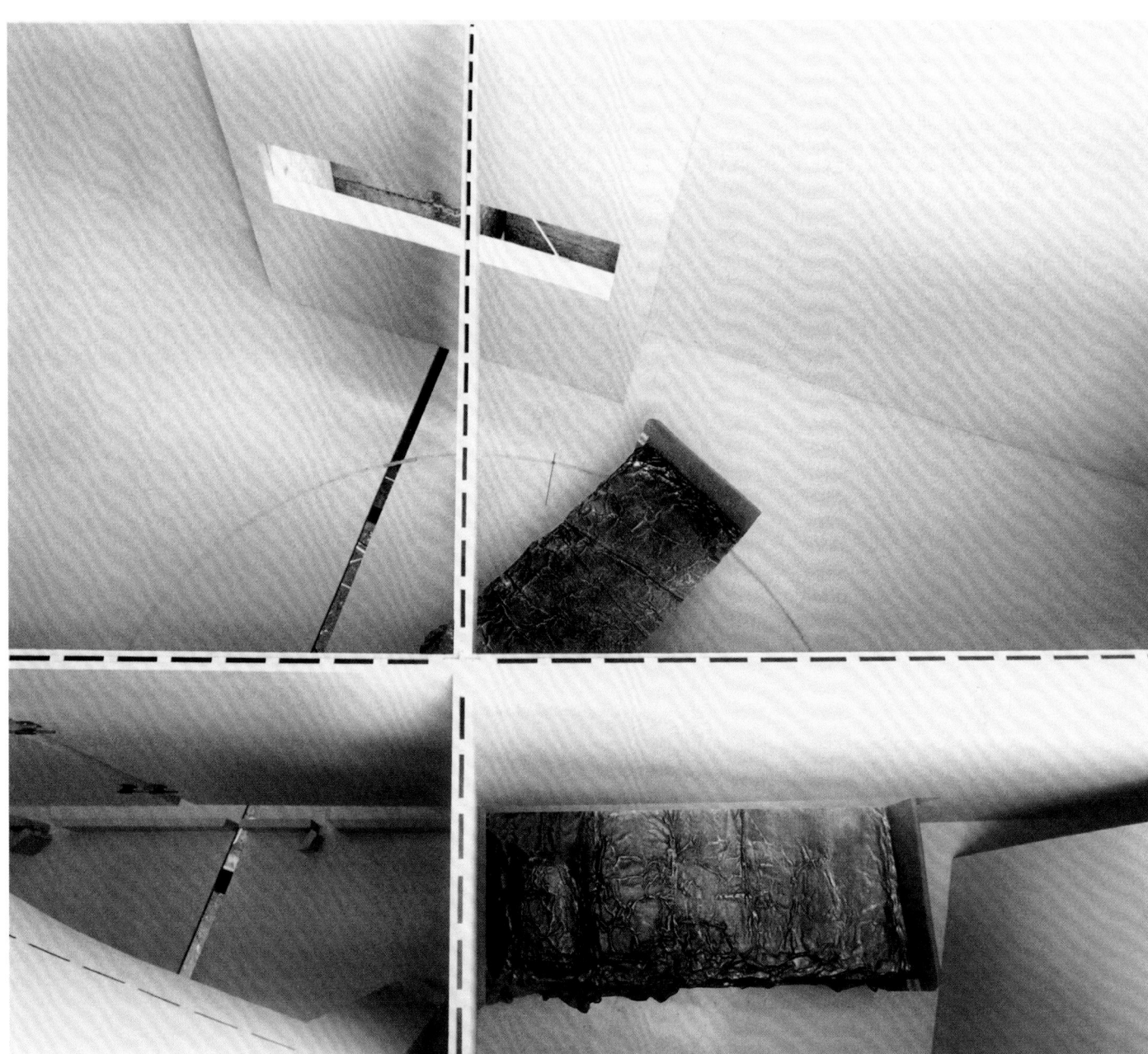

lead to some unusual interior space relationships. Casa das Canoas, by Oscar Niemeyer, in Rio de Janeiro, incorporated rocks brought crashing through the glazed walls of the home right into the living room. Frank Lloyd Wright re-enacted the river running below his Fallingwater house in Pennsylvania by rippling the concrete floor of the living room and even embedding rocks from the riverbed within the surface. Seamless connections in open plan between an interior and the surrounding landscape features can cause problems. Loewy House in Palm Springs, California, was designed between 1946 and 1947 by Albert Frey for Raymond Loewy. The external courtyard swimming pool was designed to enter the living room alongside the lounge furniture. After several guests had accidentally fallen into the pool, a metal barrier was erected around the edge of the water. Extending the flow of an open-plan interior to the landscape, bringing in rocks and water into living spaces, created seamless links between inside and out but also numerous trip hazards and, for some, a quick unplanned dip in the pool.

The combination of open-plan design and advanced networking technologies such as Wi-Fi means that the separation of something like work, previously contained within a study or

library, can now take place in any room or environment. This impacts upon private living rooms in that different types and scales of furniture become the critical elements in defining spaces within a fluid open system. The Casa Lazzari, situated in an apartment block in Milan and designed by Romano Juvara in 1974, predicted these issues by creating one large room that was conceived as though a landscape of furniture. Each coloured modular piece of furniture defined the room, separating the space into two main uses: living and dining. The living space was defined through a full-height wall cabinet and leather settee. Dining was realized by shelving and a red table. All of the elements were linked through their glossy primary-coloured finishes, reinforcing the fluid and yet geometric qualities of the open-plan interior space. In 1965, the collector Giobatta Meneguzzo commissioned Nanda Vigo to devise the interior of a Gio Ponti designed house. The house was named The Beetle Under the Leaf after Ponti's design made the building look like an insect beneath some vegetation. Vigo covered the entire surface of the interior with 20 × 20 centimetre (8 × 8 inch) white ceramic tiles. The flow of the interior was increased as no doors were used inside. Grey fur lined the centrally placed fixed furniture and the spiral stair, linking the ground with the basement. The warmth of the fur offsets the clinical tiling, which links the lines of the interior to the windows. These in turn frame the Vicenza forest where the building was situated. Open plan is reinforced by the reflections of the lines of the tiles in the glass windows and doors extending endlessly into the landscape surrounding the home.

Furniture that defines open-plan interiors may sometimes make a strong statement with regards to utility. Like the Isaacs' Living Structure project, inhabiting furniture can

32 Casa das Canoas by Oscar Niemeyer, Rio de Janeiro, 1951–53, incorporated external features such as rocks into its interior.

33 At Loewy House, by Albert Frey, Palm Springs, 1946–47, bathers could splash their way right into living room.

propose novel and efficient ways of utilizing space, especially if within a compact environment. George Ranalli's apartment in New York, designed and built in 1975, combined the dining table, a bed and a library into one single element, leaving the rest of the studio apartment in use as living space. In Omaha, Nebraska, Randy Brown designed his own home and workspace using a series of off-the-peg materials sourced from the local hardware store. Brown even managed to satisfy local building codes by convincing the planners that this interior building was just a piece of large-scale built-in furniture. Utility is of primary importance, but that doesn't mean fun has to be overlooked. Italian design group Memphis created fun-filled statement furniture that characterized late twentieth-century postmodernism. The fashion designer and collector Karl Lagerfeld filled his Monte Carlo apartment with Memphis furniture in 1983. A visit to the home might incorporate taking dinner within the colourful boxing-ring dining space or a drink in bright red and yellow armchairs. The perception of the serious fashion designer must have been dramatically offset by the comedic effect of the furniture in the apartment.

Living rooms memorialize and reflect life. They encapsulate the stories of the occupants and in the right hands these narratives can be relayed to maximum effect. In A House for Essex, designed by the collective Fashion Architecture Taste, or FAT, and the artist

THE PRIVATE INTERIOR | LIVING ROOM

34 Frank Lloyd Wright's Fallingwater, 1939, united the living room with the landscape by embedding rocks extracted from the river bed below into the floor.
35 In contrast with the relentless white tiling the grey fur-covered furniture invited its occupants to touch. The Beetle Under the Leaf, Nanda Vigo and Gio Ponti, 1965.
36 The various areas – living, dining, kitchen – of Casa Lazzari, by Romano Juvara, Milan, 1972, were defined by furniture.
37 The primary colours unified each autonomous space within the open plan.

THE PRIVATE INTERIOR | LIVING ROOM

38 George Ranalli combined dining, shelving and bed into one harmonious unit, devoting the rest of his 1974 Manhattan apartment to living space.
39 A House for Essex memorialized the Essex everywoman Julie in its double-height fireplace and inglenook, Grayson Perry and FAT, 2014.
40 Karl Lagerfeld assembled numerous pieces by Memphis design group to populate his Monte Carlo home and express his inimitable style.

40

Grayson Perry, all the symbolism and focus of the interior revolves around the desire to build a living room that narrates the story of Julie Cope: the everywoman of the county of Essex where the house was built. Her story is manifest as a huge fireplace set into a large red wall in a double-height living room. The inglenook, with doors to the kitchen and dining room on either side, has upper-level balconies, accessed via the wardrobes from both guest bedrooms. This huge piece of furniture incorporates a yellow ceramic life-like scale figurine of Julie. At varying times of the day, guests emerge from the doors onto the balconies aligning themselves with the statue and thus reinforcing connections and affinities between the symbolic host and the guests. The home is site specific, representing past, present and possibly futures of its guests and the county of Essex through Julie. The interior spaces of this building, like so many living rooms, provide the enduring backdrops to the ways in which we live our lives.

Kitchen

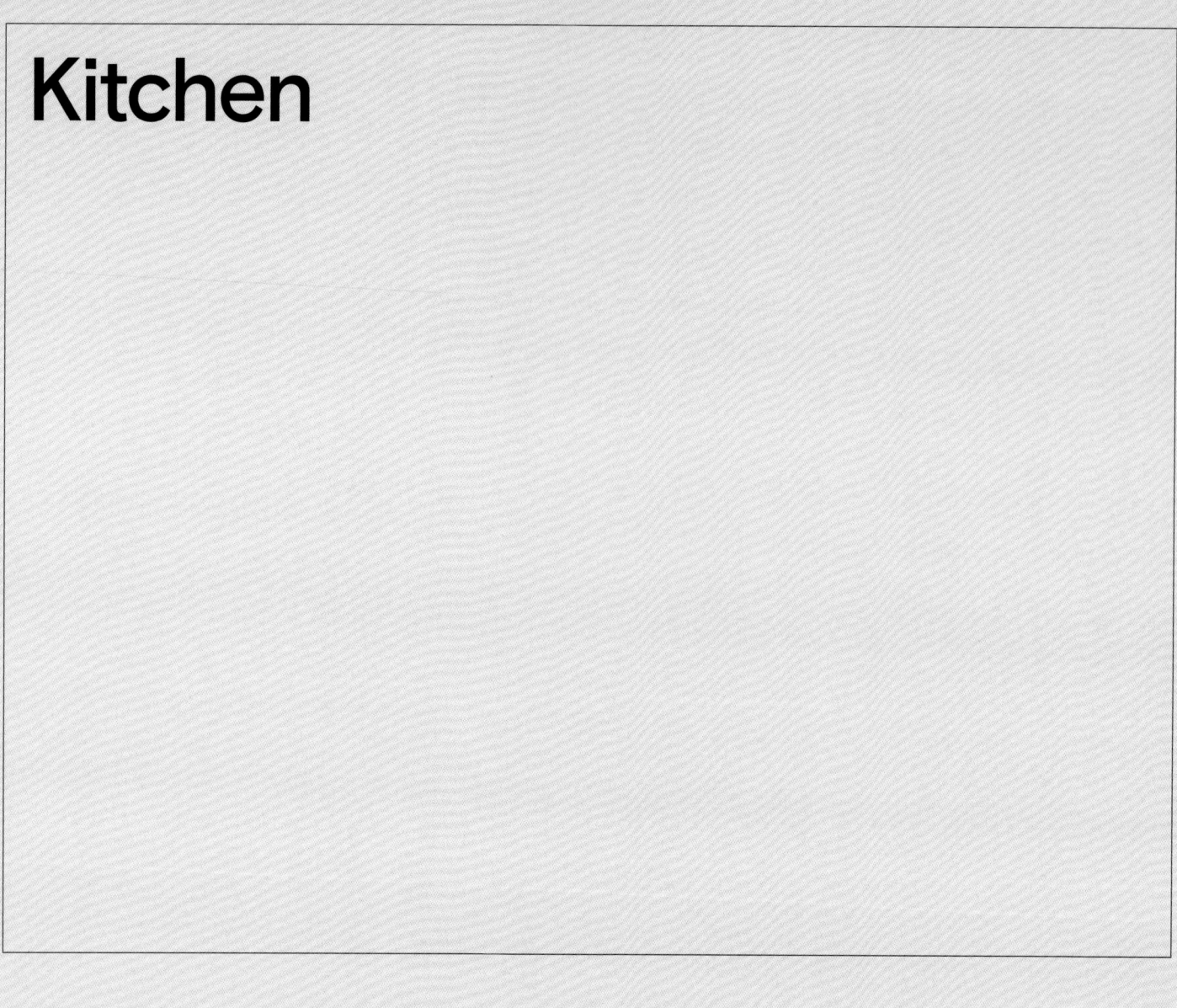

41 The efficient and economic Chulah Cookstove designed by Yasmeen Lari for rural communities in Pakistan to reduce harm associated with open-flame cooking.

Unlike any other domestic room, the kitchen is the space that substantiates the intersections of technology, politics and the distribution of labour and gender relations in the home. Its histories tend to document the preparation and creation of food and drink to support the inhabitants of a house. This simplistic perspective overlooks how it represents technical and human revolutions as it manifests the care and nurturing of the householders through their sustenance. All these complex issues are laid bare in Yasmeen Lari's Chulah Cookstove project. The Pakistani architect and humanitarian designed the stove to be cheap, accessible, easy to fuel and efficient. Whether internally or externally positioned, it epitomizes all the issues and roles of the kitchen. It was created for rural communities in Pakistan, to enable families to reduce cooking with open fires, a process that increases carbon pollution as well as the risk of domestic fires and exposure to smoke and burns. The stove is fuelled from abundant waste such as cow dung and sawdust bricks, reducing the daily need to search for firewood and, by extension, reducing deforestation by up to 70 per cent. The stove is built from mud and lime and constructed as a raised platform in or outside the home. It contains a fire chamber, a place to wash and prepare food as well as store utensils, and a chimney to channel away sparks and smoke. It costs just US$8: 6 to make and 2 to train workers to build them. Their popularity has meant that people have personalized their stoves, painting them bright colours and using them as shared spaces to meet and prepare food together. They can also be used to heat homes in the cooler months of the year. The stove symbolizes relations between technology, the distribution of labour and community. Like all rooms and technologies for preparing nutrition, it incorporates both labour and leisure – centred on bringing people together through food.

Appliances such as a stove or an oven and devices that cool and keep food germ-free, such as a fridge or a freezer, are always central to the organization of a kitchen. Until the mid-nineteenth century, the Japanese kitchen was called *kamado*, meaning stove. It was a symbol of the family home, much like a hearth or fireplace was central to domesticity in European cultures. The stove was housed in the *doma*, a feature of traditional Japanese homes known as *minka* (folk houses). It was usually positioned between the *engawa* and the *genkan* (see p. 135).

42 A kitchen as a part of the *doma* (dirt floor) of the Suzuki House, a traditional Japanese home built in the early nineteenth century in Fukushima.
43 The Harumi Aparments, by Kunio Maekawa, 1958–59, exemplified the shift in Japanese interiors from traditional to modern.
44 The *doma* is still relevant as a spatial device; in House in Takaya by Suppose Design Office, 2011, it became a passage between rooms.
45 Allan Wexler's Crate House, 1990, demonstrated the fluctuating importance of rooms with mobile units that could be shifted in and out of the central home when needed.

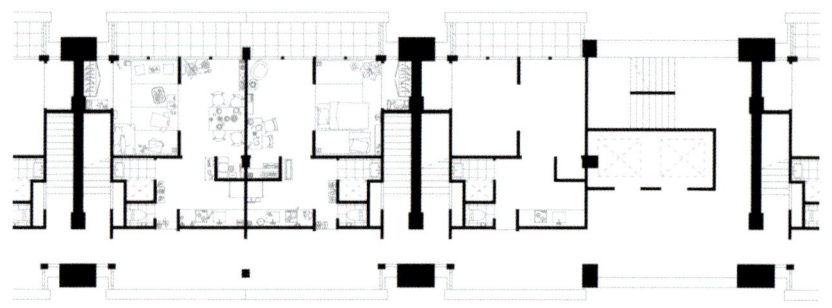
43

42

44

Doma means 'dirt place' and was a covered area of compacted earth that sat between the outdoors and interior. *Doma* were where the kitchen was located. Keeping this indoor/outdoor space covered but upon the earth meant that the potential for fire in what were predominantly timber buildings was reduced. *Doma* could also be used as workshops as it was better to keep the dirt in these spaces and keep waste smells away from the living rooms of the interior. Gathering and eating together was separated from the *doma* on a raised platform above the earth. Over time, the proximity of the *doma* and the raised sitting and eating area meant that they became combined, and in more modern dwellings became the *daidokoro*, the word used for kitchen today. The evolution of technologies such as running water, gas, light and waste removal meant that the *doma* was superseded by the modern *daidokoro*, bringing the kitchen fully inside the modern Japanese home and combining it with dining and living. Early and mid-twentieth-century Japanese public housing, known as *danchi*, merged kitchen and living into modern *daidokoro*. The 1958–59 Harumi Apartments designed by Kunio Maekawa in Tokyo were Modernist Brutalism on the outside but the interior kitchen and living arrangements were a mix of modern and traditional designs. This contrast accentuated how traditional interior space relations in the kitchen were being incorporated into contemporary buildings. The

45

doma has not entirely disappeared. A modern interpretation of its inside/outside ambiguities featured in a house by Suppose Design Office in Takaya, near Hiroshima. Instead of locating the kitchen in the *doma* they used it as a corridor between rooms, a passage that could be utilized, much like its traditional forebear, for numerous activities. The dirt path linked a series of rooms that could open or be closed off to the *doma*. Its traditional role as a space for mess was retained, and it acted as an overflow to the rooms of the house, a space for children to play or for neighbours to hang out and catch up in. Each room was separated from the *doma* by an elevated wooden platform and could be closed off with sliding glass doors.

The kitchen is often described as the functional command centre of the home.[3] Its connection to dining, living, storage (for example the larder) and the garden (for picking ingredients such as herbs) is paramount. This means that its location in the home has always shifted in relation to the importance of the rooms near or around it. This flexibility has been explored in several experimental projects. Described as a 'non-functional look at function' Crate House by Allan Wexler distilled the house down to its basic idea as an entity requiring different elements of connectivity and servicing.[4] It distinguished the components of the home by making them into a series of moveable elements. In Crate House, kitchen as well as bedroom, bathroom and living room were all contained in mobile units, boxes that could be pulled into the central room when needed or rolled out when not. Crate House demonstrated how the kitchen, usually more fixed than other rooms due to connections to water and gas supplies, was flexible: it could be drawn closer to the living space when required and then slid out and away from the other rooms when not. Its flexibility was its principal feature.

Like a theatre, houses have both front and backstage spaces; some are public and for an audience, while others are for the discreet workings of the house. As demonstrated in Crate House this distinction does not remain static, and over time the focus of the home can move. The Rotating Kitchen

46 Rotating Kitchen by Zeger Reyers, 2009, turned the space into a large appliance, mixing all of its ingredients and conveying the performative aspects of the kitchen.

47 The thick mud walls of a kitchen in a home near Matetsi, Zimbabwe, integrate the storage of utensils and ingredients.

48 Storage cabinets and utensils incorporated into bespoke units in a traditional home in Rajasthan, India.

by Zeger Reyers was a project installed in the Kunsthalle Düsseldorf, Germany in 2009. In the installation, a cook prepared food in the kitchen for the visitors to the gallery. After feeding them, the cook tidied the kitchen, put the pots and pans in the dishwasher and then exited the room for a break. This initiated the next part of the installation. In a fifteen-minute sequence, the kitchen rotated a full 180 degrees and emptied out all the cupboards, upturned the pans, threw the waste onto the floor and emptied the contents of the dishwasher across the floor. This carried on until the kitchen was completely trashed. It was apparent that the turning room had become a blender, churning the utensils and food with the waste to become one large mixture of trash. It was as though the kitchen has rebelled against its user. Both projects offer an amusing take on the role of the kitchen in the home. They both describe the flexibility of the room but also the importance of the user at the centre of it and how critical its efficient functioning must be when they are using it.

Storage and display in a kitchen do not always have to be such movable feasts as demonstrated by homes in Matetsi, Zimbabwe. The thick mud walls are recessed to make niches that hold the utensils for the kitchen. As well as ensuring that they are easy to access, the possessions are displayed in such a fashion as to make the walls come alive with the colour of the plates and tins and bags of food. 'Fitted kitchen' is a term usually applied to the exacting measured relationships between appliances and units in a room, here the kitchen's features are literally integral to the mud walls. In a traditional dwelling in the Thar Desert in Rajasthan, India, the units and appliances are formed from the walls of the hut and placed atop a solid earth plinth. Each of the storage units and the oven are painted the same colour to suggest their connection to the space, but all are expressed as standing on legs above the supporting shelf. This creates storage for pots and utensils between the legs of the units. Whether movable as in Crate House or the Rotating Kitchen or fixed and embedded as part of the construction of the walls, expedience, utility, care, and status are all expressed in how kitchens are constructed and their contents displayed and utilized by their occupants.

The Tuareg people are a Berber nomadic group who founded the town of Agadez in the Sahara desert in Niger. The construction of rammed-earth dwellings provided shelter from the harsh climate, and motifs depicting ancestral beliefs decorating the walls inside and out were designed to ward off evil spirits. The embellished reveals around windows and doors were deep and designed to keep out direct sunlight. These sculptural motifs extended to the structures of the insides of the dwellings, with walls constructed of earth and roofs of timber joists covered with branches. Giving a new dimension to the notion of fitted kitchens, house builders would incorporate furniture into these structures. Kitchens were designed to be integral and would incorporate appliances such as ovens and preparation spaces. Columns would be niched to hold utensils. The kitchen, its appliances and the religious motifs of their decoration were all considered as integrated elements in the life and structure of the home.

47

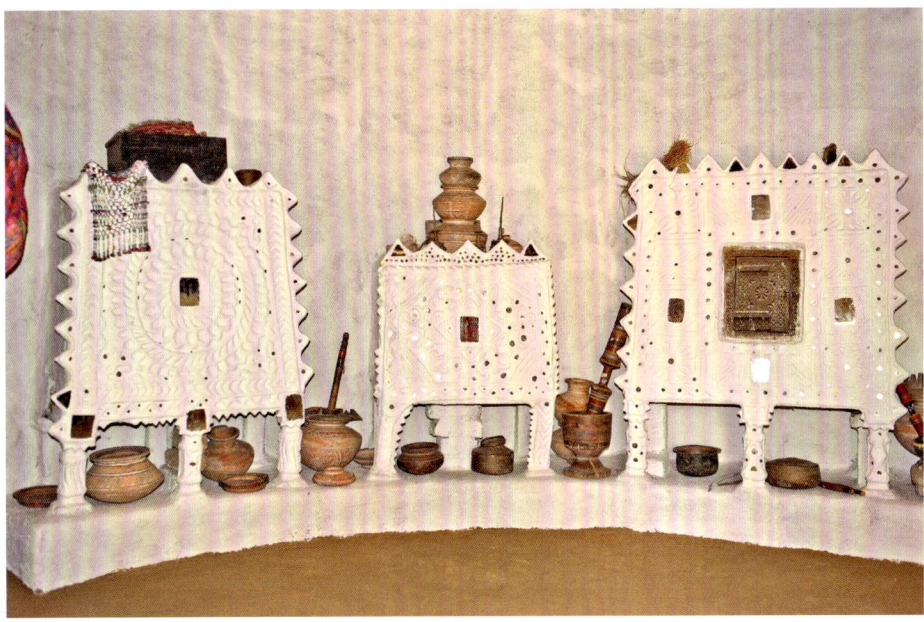

48

The kitchen exemplifies the advancement of technologies and appliances, the evolution and testing of labour-saving devices and the latest gadgets – all of which have played a role in the evolution of both the pre-modern and the contemporary room.

All are critical in understanding the kitchen as a part of the home and its role in family life. The contemporary domestic kitchen is where dinner parties and the various 'performances of consumption' take place alongside everyday practices such as cooking. Its gendering has been subject to much debate, and for centuries it has represented equalities and inequalities within a family's domestic structure.

In the twelfth-century European home, the kitchen was separate from the great hall, a space for the cooking (usually over a great fire), presentation and the storage of food. There it stayed until the seventeenth century when it emerged from 'backstage' and took a more prominent role in the accessible ensemble of rooms in a house. Since then, the kitchen has represented two definitive attitudes: the changing approaches to social life, and the status of gender roles in the family both within and outside of the house. In large and prosperous seventeenth- and eighteenth-century English houses,

49

the kitchen was discreetly tucked away and staffed by servants. Depending on the wealth of the household, servant numbers could be impressive, with cooks and maids, butlers, footmen, gamekeepers – an entire army of service staff. In numerous period dramas, as in real life, the kitchen, usually located in the basement, was the centre of this industry and the space where the daily routines of each great house took place. In his standard account of the planning and building of these eighteenth-century British houses, *The Gentleman's House, or How to Plan English Residences*, architect Robert Kerr described the kitchen as the room that should have 'the character of a complicated laboratory, surrounded by numerous accessories specially contrived … for the administration of the culinary art in all its professional details'.[5]

Kerr's kitchen placed it at the heart of a group of sculleries, larders, pantries, pastry, salting and smoking rooms, bakehouses, beer and wine cellars. He described its requirements in terms of light, temperature, dryness and aspect in detail. It couldn't be damp, and in some parts of the world an even northern light was preferred. Preferably stone on the floor and glazed bricks or other wipe-clean material such as tiles on the walls. These qualities set a template and have endured in contemporary kitchens. The modern kitchen's importance to the house, when now it can be a social living and sitting room, means that its contents must also communicate the aspirations of the owners. Gadgets, appliances and utensils – the tools of the room – indicate status and therefore contribute to the performance of wealth. Furthermore, the materials of the space – stone, marble, steel and tiles – are not just hygienic surfaces that speak of cleanliness, but they are also indicators and aesthetics of style and wealth. They are the characteristics of advertised

49　The expressively carved and decorated walls of Sidi Kâ house, Agadez, Niger, where the kitchen was formed as a structural element in the interior.

50　Staff in the kitchen, the centre of food preparation, production and storage, at Minley Manor, Hampshire, UK, 1903.

aspirational kitchens in magazines and on television.

A significant aspect of the kitchen's history is bound up with its role as a social instrument. It can be an indicator of ideological focus and the ambitions and desires not just of its inhabitants but also of governments and the state. The kitchen's gendered associations mean that it has been subject to all manner of political and moral ideologies focused on the home and the family unit. In other words, kitchens and their occupants have always been the subject of principled instruction. In 1841 Catherine Beecher's *A Treatise on Domestic Economy* appeared, explicitly dealing with the kitchen, its user and the furniture within it. It came at a time of unparalleled advances in industrialization, and it championed the increasing functionalism and rationalization of the kitchen. Inspired by Beecher, Christine Frederick published her home economics text *Household Engineering* in 1915, in which she adopted Frederick Winslow Taylor's principles of industrial efficiencies in engineering and mass production (see p. 306) and applied them to the kitchen. Frederick sought to rationalize domesticity with Taylorism and make the kitchen more efficient in how it was organized and used. Setting up an experimental kitchen in her own home in upstate New York, she used time-motion studies to document patterns of movement within the household. She plotted daily practices like cooking, washing-up and attempted to simplify the work spent on numerous menial tasks. She published her findings widely, beginning in *Ladies' Home Journal* in 1912 with a regular article on 'New Housekeeping' extolling these labour-saving efficiencies.[6]

To rationalize and professionalize homemaking, Frederick recommended that the female of the house, and it was gender-specific, needed to be liberated to enable *her* to attain a mastery of *her* work. Thus, independence would arrive through *her* efficiencies in the kitchen and ultimately the rest of the home. Frederick brought about efficiencies in the standardization of worktop heights and recommended layouts for kitchens. While she sought to advance familial roles and the health of the home and kitchen, the promise of independence

THE PRIVATE INTERIOR | KITCHEN

51 Christine Frederick experimented with rationalist time-saving planning in the kitchen in *Household Engineering*, 1915.
52 As a place of work, the kitchen has been subject to numerous experiments in efficiency. Kitchen featured in Woodward & Lothrop department store, c. 1905.
53 Margarete Schütte-Lihotzky's iconic Frankfurt Kitchen, 1926, was designed to minimize movement but ultimately became restricting rather than emancipating.
54 Lilian Moller Gilbreth's 'work triangle' still informs kitchen designs today.
55 The Kitchen Practical, 1929, was a model interior by Lillian Moller Gilbreth designed to save the homemaker time and wasted motion.

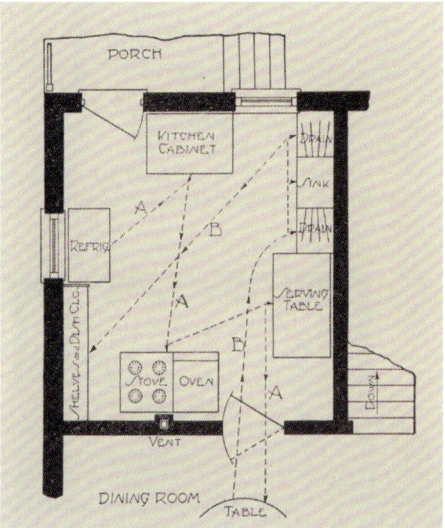
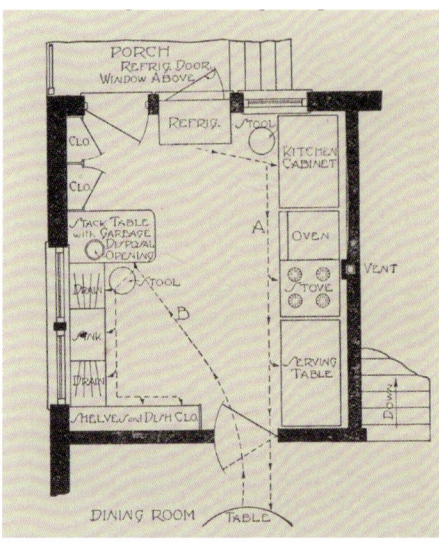

for the *housewife* remained elusive and instead reinforced gender stereotyping of whom the kitchen was primarily aimed at and for.

Frederick and Taylorism were adopted in the modern age and played into the notion that the home could be a rational efficient machine, sweeping away the clutter of the Victorian home. The kitchen could function like a laboratory, an approach that fitted perfectly with the purifying aspirations of functionalism. In Europe, this approach manifested itself in the famous kitchen designed in 1926 by Austrian architect Margarete Schütte-Lihotzky. The Frankfurt Kitchen, as it became known, was designed for social housing, of which there was a shortage after the First World War in Germany. The kitchen was unique in many ways, not least in that it separated itself into a room, a break from the kitchens of previous workers' houses that overlapped with other elements of the home, such as bathing, sleeping and living. The kitchen was designed to be narrow and primarily for one person (normally female) to work in. Its slender proportions were a conscious decision to minimize movement and thus increase efficiencies, primarily through reducing the steps taken in the space. Dedicated storage, fitted cupboards, fold-down ironing boards and integrated appliances meant that it was the first 'fitted' kitchen. This meant that it required new appliances to be designed for it. It allegedly freed up time to be 'productive', either through work outside of the home or via more leisure time with the family.

This rationalized kitchen was fitted in over ten thousand apartments in Frankfurt. Householders were initially flummoxed by its newness and how to operate it. In the 1970s and 1980s the Frankfurt Kitchen was criticized for precisely the inefficiencies that it aimed to resolve. Rather than emancipating the user it was aimed at, its dimensions restricted them to the room. The isolation of the kitchen also meant that it wasn't open to the other spaces, keeping the user apart from the workings of the home and, ultimately, their families.

Another instructor of kitchen design, Lillian Moller Gilbreth was an engineer in the US and a key figure

53

in modernizing the kitchen – but with a more thoughtful and inclusive approach to the user. Rather than rationalizing functional impulses, her work focused on designing kitchen spaces for the disabled. Her rehabilitative studies were directed at how efficiencies could support the elderly and disabled to help them be independent. Gilbreth's studies explored 'circular routing', bringing equipment and surfaces closer together to minimize motions and any steps to get to them. Her 'work triangle', arranged around the three key pieces of equipment: fridge, sink and stove, was groundbreaking and is still often utilized in modern kitchen planning. She suggested that the ideal measurement of the triangle was no more than 8 metres (26 feet). Because she prioritized the standardizing of equipment rather than bodies at the centre of planning, she pioneered bespoke kitchens that were made explicitly for all types, non-gender specific and for a full range of abilities of users. She went on to design the Heart Kitchen in 1948 and wrote *Homemaking for the Handicapped* in 1966, which demonstrated the use of bespoke appliances and kitchen environments for the less abled. Gilbreth was a pioneer of designing spaces that could be adapted to all kinds of users' needs and requirements.

The eternal wrangle between the functionality of a kitchen and its status (due to its positioning away from the social rooms of earlier houses and its associations with service) meant that in a post-war US it became engaged in the battle for hearts and minds in the consumption of new technologies, gadgets and devices with which to impress friends and family. Post-war America effectively redirected its military might towards ideas of labour-saving by designing new and improved domestic machines. This approach fed post-war recovery through increased consumption and, ultimately, renewal through built-in obsolescence. The kitchen was the new battleground for capitalism and consumption. In the late 1950s, to promote understanding and cultural exchange at the height of the Cold War between the US and the USSR, both countries decided to host exhibitions of American and Russian progress. In June 1959, the Soviet exhibition took place in New York, the US equivalent in July in Moscow. In New York, the Russians displayed huge statues of heroic workers, satellites and a model of a nuclear-powered icebreaker. In Moscow, the Americans focused on lifestyle. Hundreds of manufacturers filled the hall, featuring products such as shoes, basketballs, cars and food. Pepsi-Cola gave out free samples to passers-by, an act which

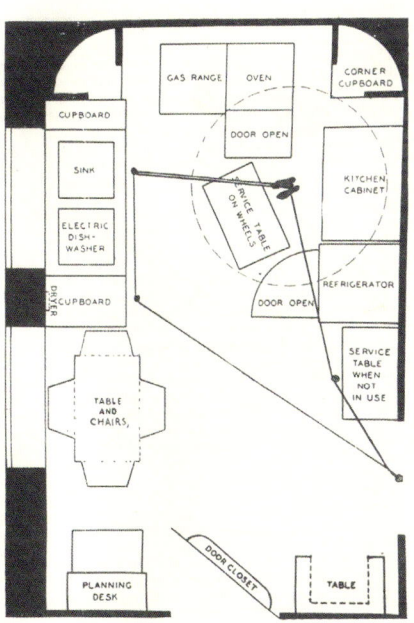

54

55

56 Nikita Khrushchev and Richard Nixon during the heated ideological 'Kitchen Debate' at the American National Exhibition in Moscow, 1959.

57 'Type F' unit apartment showing a built-in kitchen, Solomon Lisagor, Moscow, 1929–33. Such apartments were built to accommodate a rapidly growing urban population.

later led to them becoming one of the first American companies to strike a deal with Russia.

It was at the Moscow exhibition that the so-called 'Kitchen Debate', an exchange of their differing ideologies, took place between the leaders of the US and Russia, primarily in the kitchen of a full-scale suburban house – cut in half – representing the affordable and typical American dream home. The kitchen was filled with gadgets including a dishwasher, fridge-freezer, a range and a hob. During the debate, First Secretary of the Communist Party Nikita Khrushchev allegedly informed Vice President Richard Nixon that his grandchildren would live under Communism. Nixon told Khrushchev that *his* grandchildren would live under freedom. The location of the exchange was deliberate. The kitchen in the exhibition was used to summarize the differences between East and West. It symbolized the tensions of the Cold War and the domestic differences between two opposing ideologies. The kitchen was chosen deliberately to emphasize the politics of space.

Russia's aversion to 'democracy' in a kitchen was not new. In the early twentieth century, a post-revolutionary Russia intensified its industrialization. This meant that its significant rural population migrated to the cities for work. To accommodate this rapid change, communal apartments were hastily constructed. Inside the new apartments, Lenin decreed a new revolutionary 'interior topography' – a landscape of rooms in which families from different social groups would share the kitchen and the bathroom. These new arrangements afforded opportunities for residents to be monitored, as their daily routines, contacts and thus their beliefs would be witnessed, shared and relayed to other interested parties. In essence, the kitchen became an instrument of the state. A war zone where watchful eyes overheard and reported every move.[7] One of the early experimental communal apartment blocks was the Narkomfin Building. Designed by Moisei Ginzburg, a couple of years later than the Frankfurt Kitchen, the communal kitchens of the block were the exact dimensions of the German prototype. There were individual kitchenettes in each apartment, but these were small, and each resident was invited to share the main kitchens in the block. The block was a radical attempt at collectivist living and as a 'social condenser' brought different families together to share the kitchen, laundry, crèche, library and gymnasium. It was a collectivism that also facilitated surveillance. The communal kitchen was a revolutionary act designed to free all users from the isolated drudgery of housework. Narkomfin had fifty-four apartments, each differentiated in how far they were to be collectivized. As soon as it was finished Stalin rejected the collectivized position as Trotskyist. The building has only recently been saved from demolition and has been redesigned by Ginzburg's grandson. It now has forty-four apartments, each with its own separate, and private, kitchens and bathrooms.

A significant kitchen moment in the later twentieth century was the *Womanhouse* project. *Womanhouse* was initiated in early 1972 in California. It was set up by Judy Chicago and Miriam Schapiro, from an initial idea by Paula Harper, as part of the Feminist Art Programme started at the California Institute of the Arts. It took the form of an installation in a domestic home: a disused seventeen-room Hollywood mansion that was selected for demolition. The rooms in the house were each used to stage various installations. Inevitably, due to its gendered associations, the kitchen became a focus for the exhibition. The *Nurturant Kitchen* was painted in a lurid shade of pink, a colour, as one of the artists Robin Weltsch described it, that represented the body of the woman and thus the home. The body theme then took over. Walls, ceiling and some of the furniture were covered in foam fried eggs that morphed into breasts as the pattern continued.[8]

Plates of food were laid out as though a factory plant assembly line, highlighting the repeated requirement to keep feeding a hungry family and aligning labour with a low-paid factory worker. Aprons that represented the female body were hung in the adjacent pantry. Performances took place in the living room, including a woman in a housecoat and slippers repeatedly ironing sheets. The installation raised

58 Nakagin Capsule Tower, Kisho Kurokawa, Tokyo, 1970–72. The modular capsules were constructed off site and bolted onto the structure.
59 The capsules were highly rationalized rooms in which every item needed for living was incorporated within the structure including televisions, phones and a tape player.
60 *Preliminary Project for Microenvironment* by Ettore Sottsass, c. 1971, included a kitchen as a communal asset.
61 The combined utilities of Joe Colombo's Minikitchen, 1963, make a unified and efficient piece of furniture.
62 *Nurturant Kitchen* by Vickie Hodgetts, Robin Weltsch and Susan Frazier, a part of *Womanhouse* by Judy Chicago and Miriam Schapiro, 30 January–28 February, 1972.

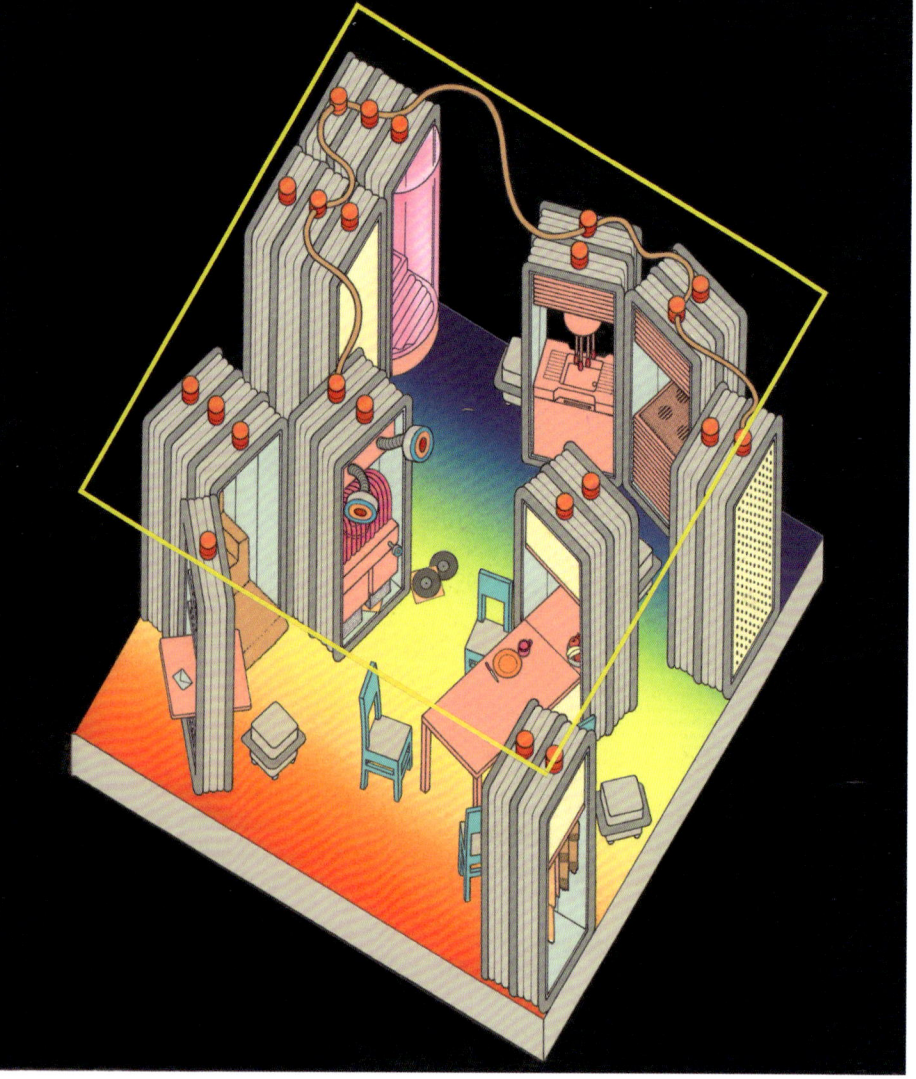

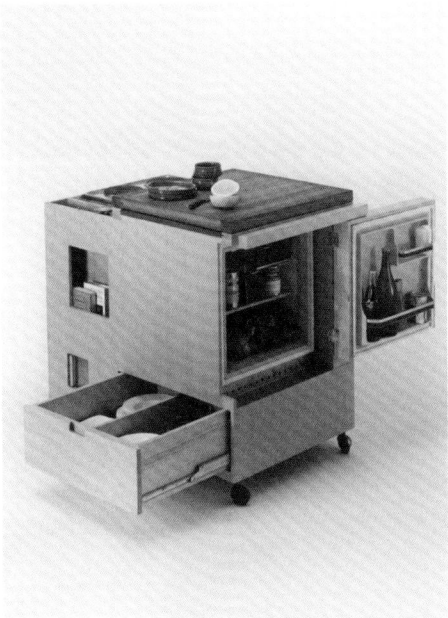

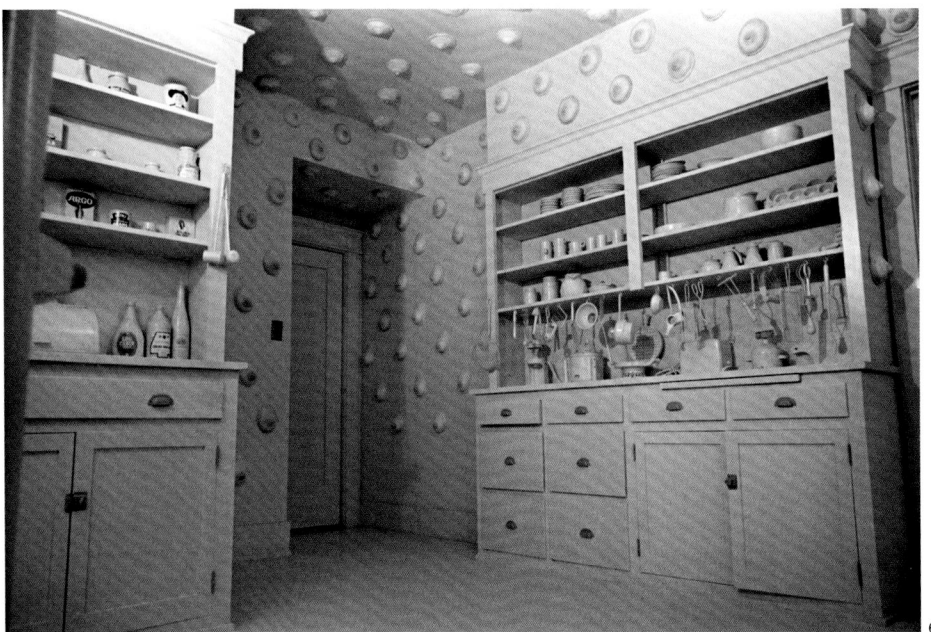

feminist consciousness among young Californian women students who wanted to shape a very different life to that of their mothers' and grandmothers' generations.

Forms of experimentation and therefore economizing, particularly through the design of appliances, are recurring features of the kitchen. Italian designer Joe Colombo made the Minikitchen in 1963, a movable device that contained all electric appliances and the equipment needed to cook food for six people. It included a stove, refrigerator, drawers and working surfaces and was carefully considered right down to the can opener and the space for cookbooks. For the 1972 exhibition 'Italy: The New Domestic Landscape', Ettore Sottsass developed his *Preliminary Project for Microenvironment* that included a mini-kitchen. He anticipated a future in which ownership was not a critical concern. Instead, domestic arrangements were considered as a series of shared containers into which equipment could be placed and choices made about what could be utilized each day. At an urban scale the careful reduction of the kitchen to make an economic home reached a particular conclusion in the Nakagin Capsule Tower. Designed in 1970 by Kisho Kurokawa, the building had 140 capsules bolted onto the structure. It was designed for bachelor Japanese 'salarymen', whose long working hours meant an efficient capsule for living, sleeping and eating was needed. Each capsule, designed like an aircraft toilet, contained a wall of cabinets, a kitchen with storage and a reel-to-reel tape deck, all fitted into the 4 × 2.5-metre (13 × 8-foot) space. The capsules were built off-site and, when delivered, hung on the main structure with just four bolts. Though designed to be easily removed and upgraded, this flexibility never happened, ensuring its limited longevity. Its demolition began in 2022.

The size of the kitchen and the adaptability of its components for upgrading have always been important. In a quiet suburb of Kyoto, a traditional timber townhouse (*machiya*) from the 1950s required updating for its new owners. Traditional *machiya*, often one or two storeys, would consist of *doma* and tatami-matted rooms with a narrow street frontage screening a long building and occasionally enclosing a courtyard. Junko Nakatsuka and Luke Hayward of Atelier Luke redesigned the interior for clients who had bought the house from the daughter of its original owner, retaining a *doma* entrance and creating a service area consisting of a bathroom and a new kitchen at the entrance to the interior. The roof of the new service core created a tatami-mat mezzanine bedroom, accessed by a ladder from the kitchen. The compact kitchen, inserted into the wall of the core, exhibits a mixture of traditional and contemporary craftmanship. Its black-tiled worktop is counterpointed by a traditional *washi* (paper) lacquered splashback. The cabinet was restored

63 A flexible and adaptable kitchen set-up that can be used to colonize disused buildings, by Aixopluc, 2020.
64 The compact and carefully considered kitchen of Terrace House by Atelier Luke, Kyoto, 2021.

by traditional craftspeople. The kitchen is discreet, with a subtle blend of traditional and contemporary features.

Modularity and building reuse are both enduring technological responses in kitchen design. Aixopluc (the Catalan word for 'shelter') is a design practice that has created a series of modular elements that can be put together to make a home. The Homeful system of furniture can be installed in disused spaces, thereby rehabilitating them. Its prototype was built in an empty warehouse space above Aixopluc's studio. The project was called Alfondac, after the Arabic word *al-fondaq* that describes a place for an overnight stay and a storage place for grain. The practice uses the space to house guests, who can make the interior their own during their stay. The system comprises a series of enclosures that can be used to form walls and thus rooms. They are serviced via a quick fix of cables and pipes running through the space.

The kitchen is the room of the house that encapsulates politics, technologies, the familial and gender roles and dogmas of the day.

Dining Room

65 *Art and Money; or, The Story of the Room* in the Peacock Room by James McNeill Whistler and Thomas Jeckyll, 1876–77.

The Peacock Room was the name of the dining space in the London home of shipping magnate Frederick Richards Leyland. The design of the room was started in 1877 by Thomas Jeckyll, a Gothic Revival architect. He initiated the work with a view to making a porcelain room or *Porzellanzimmer*, creating a walnut timber framework to hold Leyland's extensive china collection and frame his tapestries and furniture. The shelving was to surround the room, accentuating its geometry, and incorporate eight 'drop-ceiling' pendant lights. It was a carefully considered work of unified interior artistry.

Jeckyll fell ill during the project and his friend James McNeill Whistler, who was working on the designs for the hallway, didn't just take over the project but transformed it, creating tensions between Jeckyll and Whistler.[9] Jeckyll was being erased from the project, a situation that progressed his illness and hastened his demise. The scheme was organized around his painting *The Princess from the Land of Porcelain* (1864–65), which Jeckyll had installed above the mantelpiece. Whistler didn't like Jeckyll's colouring of the room and instead – in order to make the painting the focal point of the room – decorated the walls in the blues, greens and golds of a peacock's plumage. In the final act of cancelling Jeckyll, Whistler covered his timber frame with gilding, ensuring that each piece of pottery was framed by gold. Whistler and Leyland subsequently fell out, and Leyland refused to pay the artist. This acrimonious state of affairs resulted in Whistler breaking into the house and painting two peacocks on the wall which he entitled *Art and Money; or, The Story of the Room*. The room was later dismantled and sold along with the painting to an American industrialist, who had it shipped to the US. It was reconfigured in the Smithsonian Institute in Washington, where it still resides today.

But this is not the end of this dining room story. Whistler was made bankrupt towards the end of his life, and, in a twist of fate, Leyland was his main creditor. One day as the creditors arrived at his studio to liquidate Whistler's assets, they were confronted by a painting

66 Darren Waterston's *Filthy Lucre*, a reworking of the dining room that emphasized the complex relationships between art, patronage and capital.

67 *Conversation Pieces* explored how furniture could promote dialogue through inviting guests to dine and debate, Milan Design Week, 2014.

68 Nendo's perspectively skewed dining table and chairs displayed a dinner service at the 2015 'Feeding the Planet'-themed Milan Expo.

of a large peacock-man playing the piano. Whistler titled the work *The Gold Scab: Eruption in Frilthy Lucre (The Creditor)*, the sentiment of which needs little explanation.

This dramatic story inspired the artist Darren Waterston to remake the Peacock Room in 2014. Waterston portrayed it as a ruin with decaying shelves and replaced the porcelain with pots picked up from a flea market. The Peacock Room was considered a moment of aesthetic perfection, yet it tainted everyone who came into contact with it. Jeckyll lost his mind, Leyland lost his wife, who in turn lost their children, and Whistler lost his patron, friends and ultimately his practice. Waterston drew on this narrative to create an allegory of the art world, making a statement on art, patronage, money and its relationship to life and work. It is a dining room story that goes beyond creating a room in which to eat, drink and entertain.

In all the many rooms that constitute the private interior, the dining room could be classed as the one that is both indispensable and also superfluous. Essential because the dining room is a space for eating, a place that brings a family together to meet and discuss the day's events over food. It is necessary for entertaining, dinner parties and in turn its furnishings and decoration will project the status of its host. But it is unnecessary because together or alone, eating is an activity that can really be undertaken anywhere – so do we really need a room in which to do it? To dedicate a space

67

68

solely to the consumption of food could be considered as bordering on extravagance; this affords the dining room an importance and a prominence. When there is one in a house, it is a statement that food and gathering are considered to be a fundamental feature of the home and the functioning of the daily rituals and lives of its inhabitants. Because of its non-essential qualities, it is often a space that is *performative*, that is, a room that is about *show*, a room for all manner of acts of display. Because of this characteristic, as demonstrated by the Peacock Room, it is a useful device for display and a vehicle for exhibitions.

At Milan Design Week in 2014, a project entitled *Conversation Pieces*, designed by students at the Geneva University of Art and Design (HEAD), revolved around dining and the centrepiece of an over-scaled coloured dining table in a large show apartment. For the duration of the exhibition, guests from the worlds of design were invited to a themed dinner party, gathering around the table in the dining room. The show was designed to create a room in which debate and exchange could take place. Dining and dialogue were captured around the table in the brightly coloured room. A year later, dining rooms and tables featured at the Milan Expo. This time the Japanese design studio Nendo used a perspectively skewed dining table and chairs to create an exhibition space for a set of specially commissioned black tableware. The twenty-four-seat dining table was positioned in a 11 × 3-metre (36 × 10-foot) long white room in the Kengo Kuma-designed expo pavilion. The black installation was angled from front to back to allow viewers to see the whole dinner service, yet in order to make this exaggerated view work the chairs at the far end of the room were over 3 metres (10 feet) high. Visitors could use the chairs as ladders and climb up to see the items on the table. Both exhibitions used the features of dining to evoke conversation and display.

Because of the social capacity of a dining room it is often used as a narrative instrument in films. Dining rooms, tables and food feature in numerous movies throughout the history of the medium. In *Eat Drink*

69

70

THE PRIVATE INTERIOR | DINING ROOM

69 Dining plays a central role in Ang Lee's *Eat Drink Man Woman*, 1994, acting as a metaphor for open dialogue between parents and children.
70 The dining table as an expression of community (however treacherous) in Leonardo da Vinci's *Last Supper*, Santa Maria delle Grazie, Milan, 1495–98.
71 The table in *Citizen Kane* by Orson Welles, 1941, was used to illustrate Charles and Emily's increasing emotional distance.

Man Woman (1994) by Ang Lee, the preparation and consumption of an elaborate Sunday dinner for all the family becomes a tradition where the father, a retired master chef, makes food for his three unmarried daughters as a way of gaining insight into their latest romantic challenges. Food and room can be a metaphor for open dialogue. In *Citizen Kane* (1941) by Orson Welles, the dining table and in particular breakfast becomes a metaphor for the relationship between Charles and Emily Kane and their gradual distancing and emotional separation as Charles spends much of his time at work at the newspaper of which he is the proprietor. Dining scenes are repeated throughout the film, placing the characters further and further away from each other at the table. The window behind them darkens and the way they address each other, even their clothing, becomes more formal as they grow apart because of his devotion to work over their marriage.

In both exhibitions and films the dining table, utensils and food are utilized as devices for exchange, conversation and dialogue. This is deliberate and chimes with all manner of symbolism, particularly religious imagery. One of the most famous dinner scenes in history is the Last Supper. The table is an altar, one of ritual upon which sacrificial blood is spilt to cleanse worshippers of their sins – a fundamental part of the Holy Communion in Christianity. The table is a symbol of family and community and where blessing is provided via the provision of sustenance.

The performative dimensions of dining are evident in one of the most dramatic and theatrical historic dining rooms in Britain in the pavilion that the Prince Regent (later George IV) built for himself in Brighton on the south coast of England. This embodied dining as both event and theatre. The architect John Nash redesigned the pavilion, beginning in 1815 adding to redevelopment plans

72 A cross-section drawing of the Brighton Pavilion revealing the scenography of the rooms aligned enfilade, 1821–25.
73 The drop-chandelier illuminating the dining table of the banqueting room in the Royal Pavilion, Brighton, redesigned by John Nash, 1815–22.

by Humphry Repton, with Frederick Crace and the painter Robert Jones designing the interiors. The extravagant Indo-Islamic exterior hosted an exoticizing Chinese-Mughal-Islamic inspired interior. The main dining or banqueting hall was aligned enfilade with the music rooms and the saloon, emphasizing their entertaining capacities. Placed adjacent to the kitchens, the room and its dining table were arranged underneath one of the pavilion's large domes and lit by a huge chandelier in the form of lotus flowers held by dragons and mounted to the ceiling with another larger dragon. A further four chandeliers accentuate the vaulted corners of the room, which are decorated with chinoiserie and columns that terminate in palm leaves. Framed painted panels depicting various Indian and Chinese figures line the walls. The room is an extravagant stage set for the enjoyment of frivolities and food. Historically, the dining room has revolved around the furniture of the space and the disposition of the guests invited in to participate in food. Small tables called *trapezai* were used by the ancient Greeks and brought into a room laden with food. The diners reclined on couches (*klinai*) under which the low tables could be stored when not in use. Roman houses contained *triclinia*, formal dining rooms named after the arrangement of three couches formed around a table. Food and drink were served to the guests and entertainment provided as they reclined. Dining was central to Roman domestic life and the houses of the wealthy had at least two or more *triclinia*. Their size and exclusivity was determined by the status and number of guests invited into them.

Even today the dining room is a space that requires very specific objects to ensure that it functions. The table is one of them. In 2001, Sarah Wigglesworth undertook the design

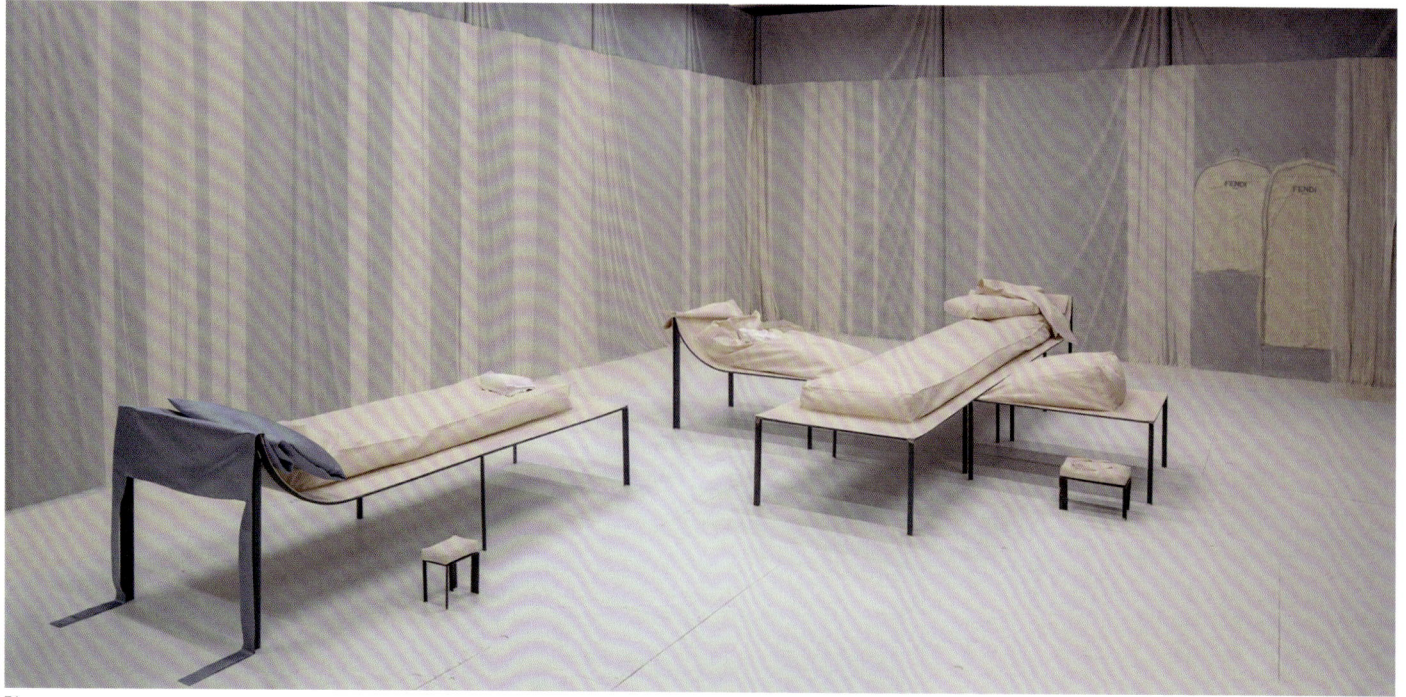

of her and her partner's house/studio in London, using the idea of 'the life of the table' to inspire the new building. She mapped out the stages of its life in three drawings: the first depicted the table before the guests arrive; the second the messiness of the event itself; and the third shows the leftovers of the party. The drawings show how the prescribed setting out of a building and its interior can only ever provide an outline or guide for the ways in which they will be really utilized. It is an enduring idea because Wigglesworth's table represents the fact that dining is an act facilitated by its furniture. When made a separate space, the dining room becomes the place that contains very specific social rituals and connections and, in the case of the Peacock Room in particular, the challenges that these traditions embody.

The table is such an integral part of the dining experience that its presence can define a dining 'room' even when food is taken outside. In Uzbekistan *tapchan* are dining tables and chairs – essentially a room – all combined into one movable piece of furniture. The *tapchan* can roll into any location, usually under the shade of a tree in hot weather. It is then covered with a rug, then several quilted blankets known as *kurpachas*. They are made from silk or cotton and are considered an important part of a household's collection of linens, sometimes part

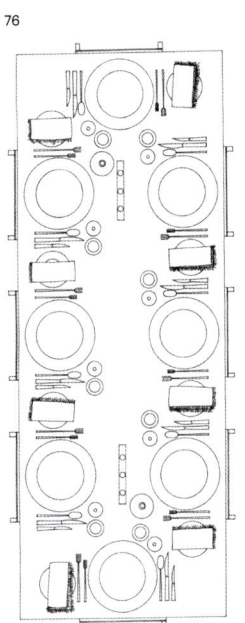
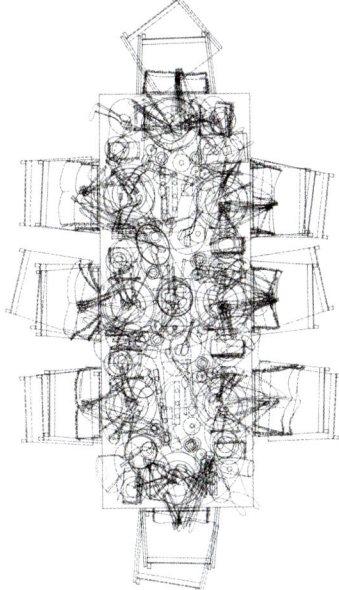
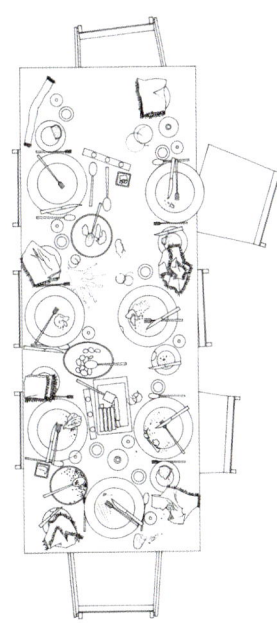

74 Lukas Gschwandtner's interest in how bodies reclined on furniture led him to create the *Modern Triclinium* installation for Fendi at Design Miami, 2022.

75 In a Roman *triclinium* (dining room) three couches surrounded the banquet table, facilitating both conversation and the serving of food and drink.

76 An Uzbek *tapchan* combines chairs and table to form a movable open 'room' so that dining can take place in any convenient location.

77 Sarah Wigglesworth's documenting of the beginning, middle and end of a dinner party informed the design of her home. *The Disorder of the Dining Table*, 1997.

of a young woman's dowry when she marries into a new family. At the centre of the *tapchan* a white cloth is laid out for the food. After food, coffee, gossip and chat, sleep is possible – or the *tapchan* is cleared and moved away to shelter, ready to receive guests for its next meal.

Not all dining rooms have such a tight control of the relationship between room and furniture. Open planning in dining rooms has not only dissolved the walls of the room to create a more flexible space but has also relaxed the formalities of dining together. In the twentieth century, the expression of flexibilities in space meant that designers sometimes used free-standing or movable screens instead of walls to denote different rooms. This placed further emphasis on the design and appearance of the furniture in the room. The Peter Behrens House in Darmstadt, built in 1901, moved the dining table off-centre and located the furniture towards the room's bay window. The elaborate ceiling design, with organic motifs, contained hanging lights which illuminated the interior and the table. The table was positioned on top of a rug that further distinguished the positioning of the dining moment.

In Robie House, Chicago, by Frank Lloyd Wright, the table and chairs became almost room-like in themselves. Tall-backed and compositionally integrated with the corners of the table, they were designed to establish a room within a room in the long main space on the upper floor of the house. Total fluidity in dining space arrived with the Mies van der Rohe-designed Villa Tugendhat in Brno, what is now the Czech Republic (also known as Czechia). Dining is but a 'zone' as opposed to an enclosed room. The dining area consists of a circular polished stone table surrounded by Mies-designed tubular steel chairs. This space is enclosed by a curved Makassar ebony screen. Dining was made distinct but not separate and open to the flow of the interior. Late twentieth-century postmodernism furthered the erosion of formalities around dining and thus loosened distinctions between furniture, atmosphere and room. Dining experiences could become even more adventurous. For fifteen years, between

78

79

1972 and 1987, Verner Panton and his family used their home in Binningen, Switzerland, to experiment with his design work. Among many remarkable spaces, the dining room became an experience, where, through light, the ceiling of the room dominated the dining table. When designing the London flat of Adam and the Ants guitarist Marco Pirroni in 1985, David Connor drew on a punk aesthetic for the dining space in the large entrance hall. Surrounded by chairs clad in 'dog fur', the location of the dining table in the reception area expressed the client's wishes for the act of dining to be distinctly informal. Both Panton's and Connor's interiors were designs that challenged the relationship between food, atmosphere and the rituals of dining.

The loosening of the dining room as a distinct entity has dissolved the distance between it and the kitchen. The kitchen-diner is a contemporary version of the room in which both spaces are brought together, often in the form of the combination of elements of furniture. The integration of both rooms has been typified by the amalgamation of kitchen island and table. In Nieby Crofters Cottage in Germany by Jan Henrik Jansen and Marshall Blecher, the central kitchen island continued to form a long solid polished-concrete dining table. The continuous piece of furniture emulated a production line of making and then eating food. The island-table does not have to be long and linear and can instead be joined in a T-plan as it is in Almost Cube House by LAND Arquitectos on the Pacific coast of Chile. The view to the sea from the interior is enhanced by floor-to-ceiling windows in the dining room/kitchen. The house is wrapped on three sides by a second skin of slatted timber screens to protect it from the sun and strong winds in the exposed landscape. Light passes through the screens making strong shadows throughout the interior of the home. The screen is folded back for the glazed areas, allowing unfettered views from the combined dining and kitchen furniture element to the sea beyond.

Dining requires specific considerations not just in relation to etiquette and furniture but also in

78 The combination of furniture and decoration forming the *Gesamtkunstwerk* (total work of art) of the Peter Behrens House, Darmstadt. 1901.

79 Dining room furniture can be used to reinforce the geometrical dimensions of the room. Robie House, Frank Lloyd Wright, Chicago, 1910.

80 The spectacular shell ceiling and elaborately furnished dining room of Verner Panton's home in Binningen, Switzerland, 1972–87.

81 A semi-circular wall and specially designed chairs demarcated the dining 'room' of the fluid Villa Tugendhat, Mies van der Rohe, Brno, Czechia, 1928–30.

THE PRIVATE INTERIOR | DINING ROOM

82 The theatrical intentions of Marco Pirroni's dining room in his Marylebone flat, London, as drawn by David Connor, 1985.
83 The resulting entrance hall and dining table captured the anarchic spirit of the client's wishes and conveyed the subversive attitude that punk embodied.
84 A long concrete plinth doubles as a kitchen island and dining table in Nieby Crofters Cottage, Jan Henrik Jansen and Marshall Blecher, Germany, 2022.
85 The view from the kitchen-diner in Almost Cube House optimizes landscape and light, LAND Arquitectos, Pichilemu, Chile, 2017.

187

THE PRIVATE INTERIOR | DINING ROOM

86 The mirrored dining room in Mimi Calpe, a nineteenth-century villa turned hotel in Tangier, Morocco.

87 (Opposite) Light pours through the lantern above the dining table in the breakfast parlour of John Soane's home in London, c. 1813.

relation to atmosphere and lighting. In the early nineteenth century, different mealtimes, such as supper or breakfast, would sometimes have been accommodated in separate spaces. Breakfast rooms didn't mean you *had* to eat within them – and they were considered usually as a 'morning room' – but their existence would provide an opportunity to take the first meal of the day in natural light. One of the finest examples is John Soane's magnificent breakfast room in his own London house. The design of the room is orientated towards a central lantern, set into the middle of a canopied domed ceiling. Underneath the lantern, a small round table provided a place for one or two people to take their morning meal and gather their thoughts for the day ahead. In good weather, breakfast would be bathed in the light of the morning sun as it passed over the home through the roof lantern and onto the table.

Soane used numerous mirrors across his interiors to reflect light and create endless vistas of space, but they can also be deployed to enhance how people see themselves within the rooms of the home. Mimi Calpe, a decadent nineteenth-century villa on a hillside in Tangiers, Morocco, was the centre of social life in the city in the mid-twentieth century. Tangiers' history as an international zone meant it became a melting pot of different cultures and influences. Arab, Jewish, Berber and Christian cultures have all left their mark on the city. The villa's decoration and eclectic mix of furniture reflects this diversity. Its dining room's central table, adorned with candles and lit with large globe lights, is reflected endlessly into the mirrored walls and ceiling that surround it. Now an exclusive hotel, the nights are probably quieter than when the city's social elite congregated in the villa to eat and drink while admiring themselves in the reflections of the room's shiny mirrored surfaces.

Atmosphere and lighting are dependent on climate, particularly when dining is performed al fresco. In climates that are reasonably warm year-round, as in Mexico or India, the boundaries between outdoor and indoor living can be made porous and flexible. The Casa Los Tigres in Nuevo Vallarta in western Mexico, a collaboration by César Béjar and Fernando Sánchez Zepeda, is a

88 In tropical climates, ventilation and protection from the sun are central considerations for dining. Karai by RAIN, Chennai, India, 2023.
89 Casa Los Tigres by César Béjar Studio and Fernando Sánchez Zepeda, Mexico, 2023, allows dining to drift into the central courtyard.
90 The white-enamelled engineering bricks in the dining room of Victor Horta's home and studio, Brussels, 1898–1901, project a cool finish.

large villa in two volumes with a central courtyard in between. One block is solid, with few openings, while the other, private block is counterintuitively much more open and transparent. The closed block contains the combined living, dining and kitchen, which spills out through a set of foldable glazed doors into the central courtyard. The courtyard therefore becomes an open dining room for the family. A courtyard and a dining room can be a very compatible combination in a warmer climate. In the coastal region of Kuvathur near Chennai, a family home was designed by RAIN studio of design to resemble a simple and humble *nalukettu* house, a traditional building in a rectangular shape with four rooms or halls joined to a central courtyard (known as the *nadumuttam*). This type of building was usually for a large family, encouraging them to live together. As families grew, the number of halls could be increased accordingly. The record is a thirty-two-hall, three-courtyard *muppathirandukettu*. The courtyards increased ventilation and light and encouraged socializing and the taking of food together. In RAIN's interpretation, four halls with adjoining bathrooms and sea views were distributed around the central courtyard with the kitchen-dining space on the same axis as the entrance at the flat end of the rectangular plan. In this combined space, the family and friends could gather and cook, eat and socialize together.

Modernism's desire to unify through the *Gesamtkunstwerk*, the total work of art, meant that formal dining rooms were often a harmonious concoction of decoration, lighting, table and homewares such as cutlery and ceramics. Victor Horta built his own house and studio on two plots of land in Brussels in 1901. The building provided a home for him and his daughter. Horta was an exponent of art nouveau, and the house clearly demonstrates the sculptural organic qualities of this style. Placed on the first floor, the dining room is arranged with the table facing the door to the garden. The entire room is organized by a series of arched bays, each rendered in white-enamelled engineering bricks. These were originally purchased with a view to cladding the exterior façade with them.

Instead, they were brought inside and used to lend a clean and clinical feel to the interior. Each of the vault edges is outlined with elaborate gilt-ironwork. Ironwork also links the main lighting for the central table. Each arch is elaborated with alternating bands of white and cream marble at its base, connecting to a skirting that articulates the junction between the mosaic floor and the wall. Built-in furniture stored the tableware and contained the heating element for the room. Elaborate scrolls of carved timber embellish the doors and thresholds of the room. This total work of art resulted in an engineered, clinical yet also organic atmospheric dining experience.

Just a few years later and close to the location of the Horta house, the Palais Stoclet interior was being designed by Josef Hoffmann. Its dining room is organized around a very different set of surface treatments: a series of large friezes by the artist Gustav Klimt that surround diners at the central table. Two friezes on the longitudinal walls of the rectangular room are dominated by the motif of the tree of life, with blossoms, butterflies and birds. On the left wall, *Expectation* depicts a single figure that corresponds to an embracing couple on the right wall titled *Fulfilment*. Allegedly both images were inspirations for Klimt's most famous later work *The Kiss*. Built-in sideboards, lacquered to a deep shine anchor the friezes in the room, ensuring a solid black baseline skirting. This

91

92

connects to a monochromatic tiled floor topped with a rug upon which the table and chairs are positioned. The highly polished dining table is surrounded by sumptuously upholstered leather chairs. In quite different fashions both Horta's and Hoffmann's dining spaces made socializing through eating a sensuous affair.

Mealtimes are influenced by factors that include culture, tradition and working hours. In the 1700s in Europe, dinner was eaten at 3 p.m. moving to 7 p.m. in the 1800s, creating space for a new development: 'luncheon'. The deregulation of mealtimes, and the room that contained them, began with experiments in how the standard family unit experienced its meals. The dining room and its usually adjoined counterpart the kitchen were transformed by the development of technologies such as the microwave and even the television – when sharing a takeaway dinner watching the TV together can be a regular activity for many. The shift in patterns of eating and the timing of when food is taken, along with the fact that a dining room might only be used a few times each day,

91   Gustav Klimt produced nine drawings that were realized as mosaics for the dining room of the Palais Stoclet by Josef Hoffmann, Brussels, 1905–11.
92   The loosening of conventions and innovations in technology have impacted upon the formalities of the dining room. Ronald and Nancy Reagan in the White House, 1981.
93   Total Furnishing Unit, a portable home for a family of four by Joe Colombo in collaboration with Ignazia Favata, 1972.
94   Telematic House by Ugo La Pietra, 1983, foregrounded the use of screens in every room of the house.

means that the formality of this room has been challenged. Food can be taken anywhere in a domestic interior; it does not require a specific room or even a table.

Some of these changes in processes can be traced back to a period of change in furniture in the nineteenth century. Cheaper, mass-produced furniture that allowed an easy reconfiguring of the home, meant that heavy, formal dining tables and chairs were not necessary. Post-war technological advances in kitchen equipment such as ovens and microwaves informalized food preparation. Even the way in which the traditional family set-up changed, with more parents working and often in shift patterns or differing hours, irrevocably altered how a family would take its food. Experiments in eating in the home have led to innovations in the rooms that accommodate it. Joe Colombo's Total Furnishing Unit hypothetically explored these changes in the celebrated exhibition 'Italy: The New Domestic Landscape' at MoMA, New York, in 1972. A portable unit contained the living space for a family of four, with a kitchen and dining table and chairs that doubled as a lounge and relaxation room. Meals could be taken together or whenever you wanted, informalizing the experience. In Ugo La Pietra's 1983 Telematic House the television and its importance impacted significantly upon the home. Dining was arranged around the television schedules and food was always taken in front of a screen, a real takeaway experience.

Like many spaces in the domestic interior, dining is subject to the vagaries of social conventions, technologies and politics. Dining rooms have become less formal and their designation as a separate room has disappeared from many domestic interiors, especially in smaller homes. This is the case in large and dense cities where it is just not possible, economically and spatially to have a separate space for eating. This is realized in an extreme form in a place such as Hong Kong, regarded as one of the most unaffordable cities in the world, where land prices and rents are high and thus affordable homes are very much out of reach of the many workers of the city. This has led to the development of a phenomenon

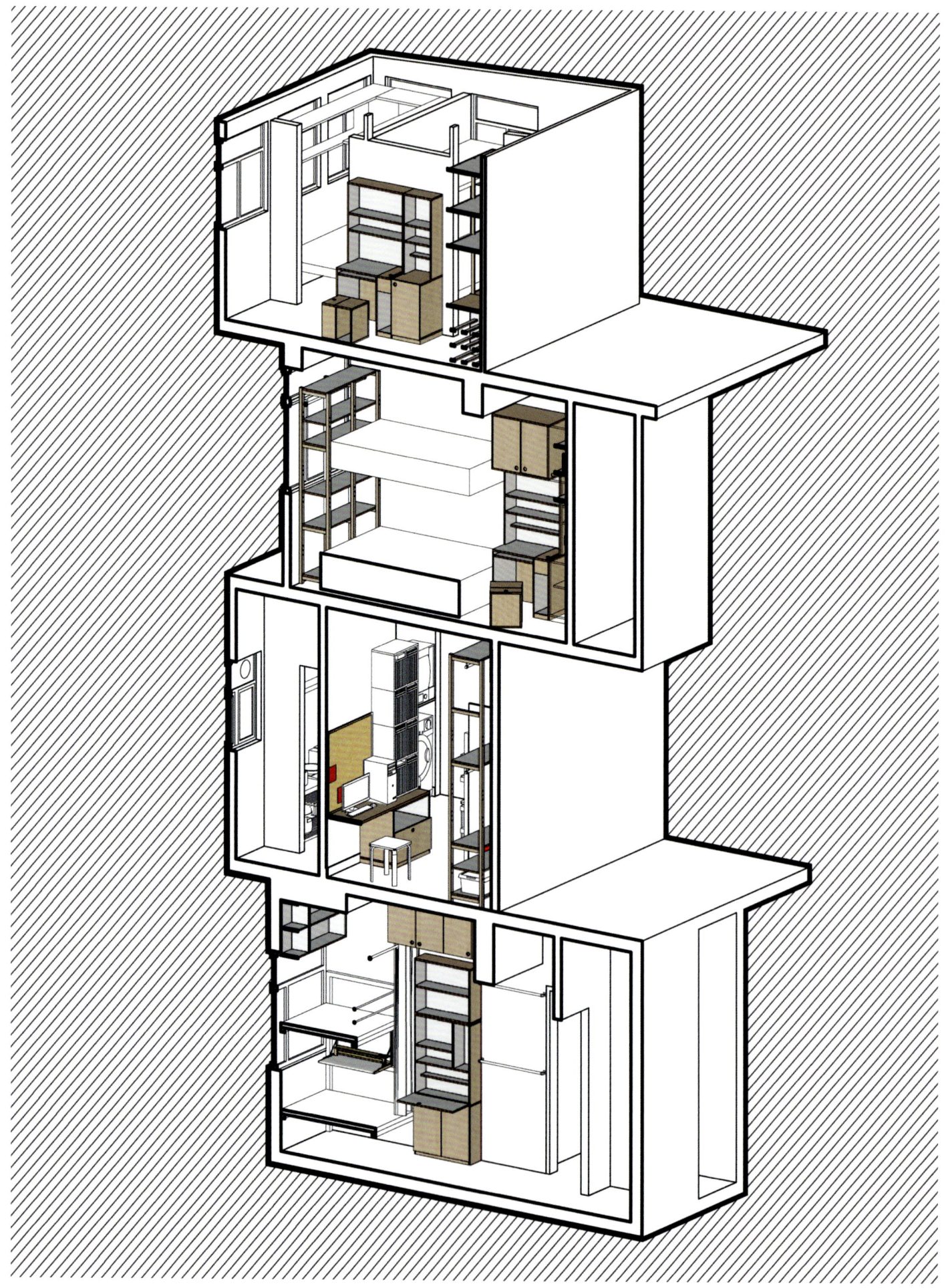

THE PRIVATE INTERIOR | DINING ROOM

95 DOMAT's Home Modification scheme, 2013–present, allows for the organization of cramped conditions in Subdivided Units in Hong Kong.

96 The modular, standardized designs can be reassembled when families move and are durable enough to survive several years.

known as the SDU. Subdivided Units are small apartments in residential blocks that unscrupulous landlords divide up and rent at what appear to be cheaper prices but are in fact more lucrative (for the landlord) as many more rentals can be squeezed into the space of one regular apartment. Averaging 9 square metres (97 square feet), there are allegedly 220,000 Hongkongers living in SDUs in often illegally cramped conditions, with limited access to good ventilation and utilities such as water and power, and no privacy between family members. DOMAT, a design practice run by Maggie Ma and Mark Kingsley, raises awareness of people and communities that don't have access to architects. The Home Modification scheme developed a series of modular furniture units that can be temporarily installed into an SDU to allow children to do their homework, the storage of clothing, food preparation and also dining. DOMAT realized that the furniture needed to be removable to ensure that landlords did not think that the apartment was renovated and therefore could raise the rent. Residents own the elements and can take them with them when they move home in what is a precarious existence. DOMAT designs numerous cabinets and units to facilitate many uses for the families who own them; they can be adjusted to suit the family's needs. They are adaptable and users add plug sockets, decorations and textiles to make them their own. In the extremely tight situation of living in a small room, all activities including dining can be undertaken within a few adaptable modular units.

The dining room is a space that is always intrinsically linked to the changing patterns of inhabitation through the accommodation of how and where sustenance is consumed, with whom and at what time.

Bathroom

97 Bricolage and salvaged elements form the bathroom in Willie Bester's home, South Africa.

Growing up under apartheid in South Africa, the artist Willie Bester knew from an early age that space and its contents were politically charged. As South Africa transitioned to democracy in the 1990s, Bester and his wife Evelyn bought a plot of land in Kuilsrivier, a formerly 'whites-only' enclave east of Cape Town. Enlisting Carin Smuts from CS Studio Architects, they designed and built a home/studio, a building that challenged local regulations. These were controls reminiscent of the rules Bester had always been subject to in his life, the imported aspirations of a Global North suburban respectability. Instead of conforming, the house became a landmark and an extension of his art, forming a unique new family home and studio and a rebuke to the inherent racism of the state.

Bester's work originated in his impoverished upbringing, which compelled him to be imaginative and inventive in utilizing discarded items. Assembling found objects through welding or joinery, his sculptures became powerful statements not just of his life but also of those of a generation lived under apartheid. The new house was treated as though a found object. It was built with discarded matter and covered inside and out with sculptures formed from abandoned materials. The front gate, entitled *The Myth of Civilization* was constructed from bike wheels and car parts and painted a vivid blue. On his studio roof he built a 9.5-metre (31-foot) high, bright red scrap-metal tree with branches draped in wire-mesh fencing gathered from Robben Island Prison, where Nelson Mandela was incarcerated. The interior follows this logic. Spaces and the furniture in them were assembled from all manner of discarded material: car parts, pipes, salvaged railway sleepers, scrap metal and all painted in bright vivid colours. The bathroom of the house is a sight to behold. The toilet is placed in a bright yellow cubicle, with building site hard hat and safety glove signs outside it. The sink is mounted on a green gloss-painted steel column to which several waterpipes and taps are attached. Reclaimed industrial switchgear, meters and gauges adorn the column, all painted in vivid shades of red, yellow and blue. It is reminiscent of a Heath Robinson contraption and

98 Bathing is a communal activity in many cultures. Kodakara-yu public bathhouse (*sento*), Tokyo.

99 Constructed in 1741, the Cağaloğlu Hammam, Istanbul, is a public bath for both men and women.

looks as though it was extracted from the engine room of a large steamship.

Like the house, the bathroom is an extension of the ideas and life of its designer. The transformed discarded materials represent the politics of space by referencing waste and the discarding of the mass-produced goods of the affluent and wealthy. Bester's work reassembled these scraps and forged them into new identities. It is a form of resistance, not just to Global North throwaways but also to over-production and conformity. Ultimately the house expressed the aspiration to represent new values and identities. Bester's work spoke of his experiences as a black artist in South Africa; his home is a vibrant and colourful reproach to the controls of oppressive regimes. All bathrooms are the representation of related social and political issues. They signify our bodies in space through the values we hold regarding its care and cleaning. Bathrooms and our bodies may have changed little over time, but politics and care in society and how they are formed in space is always a moving target.

The core components of both the public and private bathroom have changed little over time. There is usually a tub of some kind for water and a receptacle for waste. From the combination of these basic elements a myriad of vessels and ways of arranging them in space have been conceived. The bathroom is also the site of all manner of concerns. Intimacy, technical innovations, bodily functions, gender issues, social collectivity, sexualities, politics, infrastructure and waste: all are enacted through the fine art of porcelain and plumbing.

Bathrooms, powder rooms, cloakrooms, washrooms, wet rooms and lavatories have either been taken as an individual pursuit or, quite often, as a collective activity. Cultures have been built upon how ablutions are taken. *Sento* is a public bath in Japan, less prestigious than an *onsen*, where spring water is prized. This is a space where segregated utilitarian bathing facilities are often used to offset smaller domestic bathrooms. The *hammam*, or Turkish bath is another space for the collective cleansing of the body, often undertaken in extravagant surroundings with numerous other bathers. Bathing and culture are inseparable.

The first recorded bathing rooms

THE PRIVATE INTERIOR | BATHROOM

100 One of the oldest known bathing structures, the Great Bath found at the ancient city of Mohenjo-daro, Pakistan, is believed to be around five thousand years old.
101 The Forum Baths at Pompeii, Italy, were a complex of communal *tepidarium* (warm), *frigidarium* (cold) and *caldarium* (hot) rooms.
102 Bathing in Edwardian Britain was considered medicinal and often involved entering the water from a mobile beach hut to protect modesty, c. 1910.

102

date as far back as 3000 BCE. The Great Bath excavated at Mohenjo-daro in Pakistan was a 12 × 7 metre (39 × 23 foot), 2.4-metre (8-foot) deep water-tank structure entered by a staircase at either end. Its adjacency to a well ensured water was abundant. It was allegedly used for special religious functions, purifying the bathers and renewing them – an enduring aspect of all kinds of bathing. In ancient Greece bathing was part of the routine of exercise, often undertaken communally, briefly and usually in cold water. In ancient Rome and in many Islamic countries, bathing was a time for relaxing and was a communal ceremonious activity. Cleansing was also a ritual required before prayer. Some baths were part refreshment part medicinal.

In the medieval monastery the bath was strictly a spiritual cleanse, not to be enjoyed at all, and instead to be taken as penance. In Victorian and Edwardian Britain, bathing was often considered medicinal and involved 'taking the waters' in the sea or in a spa as a treatment. All of these characteristics of water imbibing, refreshment, cleansing and ablution are still an important ritual of bathing today and have influenced the modern bathroom experience.

Bathing was a prominent part of ancient Greek and Roman cultures, though only the very wealthy had bathing facilities at home. Equipped with running water, steam rooms and sunken baths in mosaic-tiled rooms, bathing was often a collective activity. The sixteenth century domesticated bathing in Europe,

103

104

103 A garderobe was a small medieval toilet chamber, often set into the walls of castles, which directed waste into a cesspit or moat.

104 Before a definitive bathroom emerged, tin or copper tubs were dragged into the living room or kitchen for all the family to take turns in. Sutton-in-Ashfield, UK, c. 1950s.

105 The bathroom in Stanley Kubrick's *The Shining*, 1980, was significant as a site of terror in the film.

106 Marilyn Monroe's bathroom scene in *The Seven Year Itch*, Billy Wilder, 1955, represented her dilemma in attempting to escape her predatory neighbour.

107 Jeroen Offerman's working replica of the shower set from *Psycho*, 1960, was unfinished at the back to represent how the scene was a constructed narrative. *The Portable Psycho Shower Scene Stage Set Party, Part I–V*, 2010–12.

202

with portable tubs, barrels, tin or copper baths, bowls, washstands and ewers (a pitcher, but also the name used for the servant who bore it) that would usually be brought to rooms and be filled with either hot or cold water. The rich would have servants to assist with the process while the poor would have filled the tub themselves, albeit much less frequently than their more affluent counterparts. A curtain might be draped around the receptacle, to offer some privacy and hold in the steam. With a very small number of exceptions (for instance the Palace of Versailles, which had over one hundred separate bathrooms), the domestic bathroom was essentially abandoned in Europe after the Romans, and ablutions were not assigned a definitive room. The toilet was the same and facilitated by a bedpan or bowl, to be filled and evacuated by either yourself or some other unlucky soul. Bathing was often connected with religion, which had less to do with physical cleanliness and more to do with the removal of the spiritual stains contracted by encountering death and disease.[10]

A separate room called the bathroom emerged in the late nineteenth century in the European domestic interior. It was still without a toilet, yet it privatized the act of cleansing. The toilet was a separate entity and, for the most part, remained external to the main home until it was brought indoors in the early to mid-twentieth century. The development of the toilet is closely related to the evolution of drainage and the removal of waste from the domestic environment. The bathroom's connection to the infrastructure of the city, in order to channel harmful waste as far away from the home as possible, has always been critical for reasons of hygiene and disease prevention. Throughout time there have been chutes linking to cesspits and basement areas used to collect waste for the disposal of 'night soil'. Chamber pots were used by the more important members of the household and often kept in the pantry when not in use. The forerunner of the toilet, with its own room, began as a close-stool: a box with a lid, usually primitively decorated. In France these were known euphemistically as *garderobes* (literally meaning 'wardrobes') and the term is still used to describe the toilets of medieval castles today. Developments in

plumbing meant that in the second half of the eighteenth century, increasingly sophisticated inventions, such as the water-filled S-bend, were designed to keep smells out of the interior. The invention of flushes, supplied by water held in tanks in the room, in attics or on roofs, gave rise to the recognizable version of the toilet as it is known today.

Along with the bedroom, the bathroom is one of the few spaces in a private interior where we disrobe. Intimacy and vulnerability are therefore mixed with the rituals of cleansing, creating a potent combination. Realizing this, numerous movie directors have used the bathroom as the site in which to exacerbate our feelings about ourselves. Alfred Hitchcock's *Psycho*, Stanley Kubrick's *The Shining* and even Billy Wilder's *The Seven Year Itch* – with Marilyn Monroe's toe stuck in the tap – all used bathroom scenes to demonstrate anxieties ranging from apparent helplessness to downright terror. Janet Leigh's shower scene in *Psycho* is one of the most iconic images of modern cinema. It inspired a film by the artist Jeroen Offerman entitled *To Become, Shift, Transfer, Copy and Erase Janet Leigh*. The artist explored how recognizable the actress and the set were by making a full-scale replica of the scene and slowly removing elements to reveal how much could be taken away before the bathroom became just an ordinary washroom.

The bathroom elevates our exposure, making it fertile ground for installations that heighten these feelings. *Don't Miss a Sec.* was an artwork by Monica Bonvicini inspired by watching gallery goers at art show openings. Desperate not to miss a second of the partying, free drinks and gossip, she decided to make a bathroom from which all of the networking and showing off could still be observed. She designed and built a two-way mirrored glass box with a toilet inside. From the outside, passers-by see themselves reflected in the box, while the user, sitting inside, could see out and still watch proceedings. The toilet has been installed at numerous art openings around the world, sometimes in the streets outside of them. The project is not for the faint hearted; when sitting on the toilet, users feel as though they are in full view of those

108 The iconic silhouette of the inclined body rendered as a tiled surface in the Villa Savoye, Le Corbusier, Poissy, France, 1928.

109 *Don't Miss a Sec.* by Monica Bonvicini, 2004, revelled in how its user could see without being seen via a two-way mirrored bathroom placed in a public location.

110 The bathroom of Le Corbusier's Cabanon in Roquebrune-Cap-Martin, France, 1952, was separated from the interior by only curtain.

outside. But, when using the bathroom, they never miss a moment of the all-important party. The installation typifies so many aspects of the bathroom. It is a space we all need and use, several times a day, and it embodies both exposure and concealment – the basis of all bathroom experiences.

The twentieth century evolved the moral tone surrounding the bathroom's 'civilizing' capacities. Le Corbusier's bathroom in the Villa Savoye in Poissy, France, with its curved tiled recliner, invited the body to lay down naked before slipping into the adjacent bath, rendering the clinical bathroom and the body as inseparable elements. Cleanliness in the building began at the front door with a washbasin, inviting visitors to cleanse before entering the space. Le Corbusier was obsessed with the bathroom and its fittings, thinking of them as beautiful industrial mass-produced objects. In many of his houses, a sink or bidet would be strategically located, often with unusual prominence. He situated a bidet prominently in the bedroom/living room that was his design for the 1927 Weissenhof Estate in Stuttgart, Germany. In his own house, much to the consternation of his wife Yvonne, he put the bidet in the middle of a room. Historians describe how Yvonne would cover it with a tea towel when they had guests.[11] In the Cabanon, the holiday cabin that he designed for himself in Roquebrune-Cap-Martin in the south of France in 1951, the one-room space meant that the toilet and basin had no door – meaning that there was no separation between all functions in the space. It was clear that one of the most infamous modern architects of the twentieth century was obsessed with the bathroom.

From the mid-twentieth century, the bathroom became the site for experimentation. Buckminster Fuller rationalized the bathroom as well as the

108

THE PRIVATE INTERIOR | BATHROOM

109

110

THE PRIVATE INTERIOR | BATHROOM

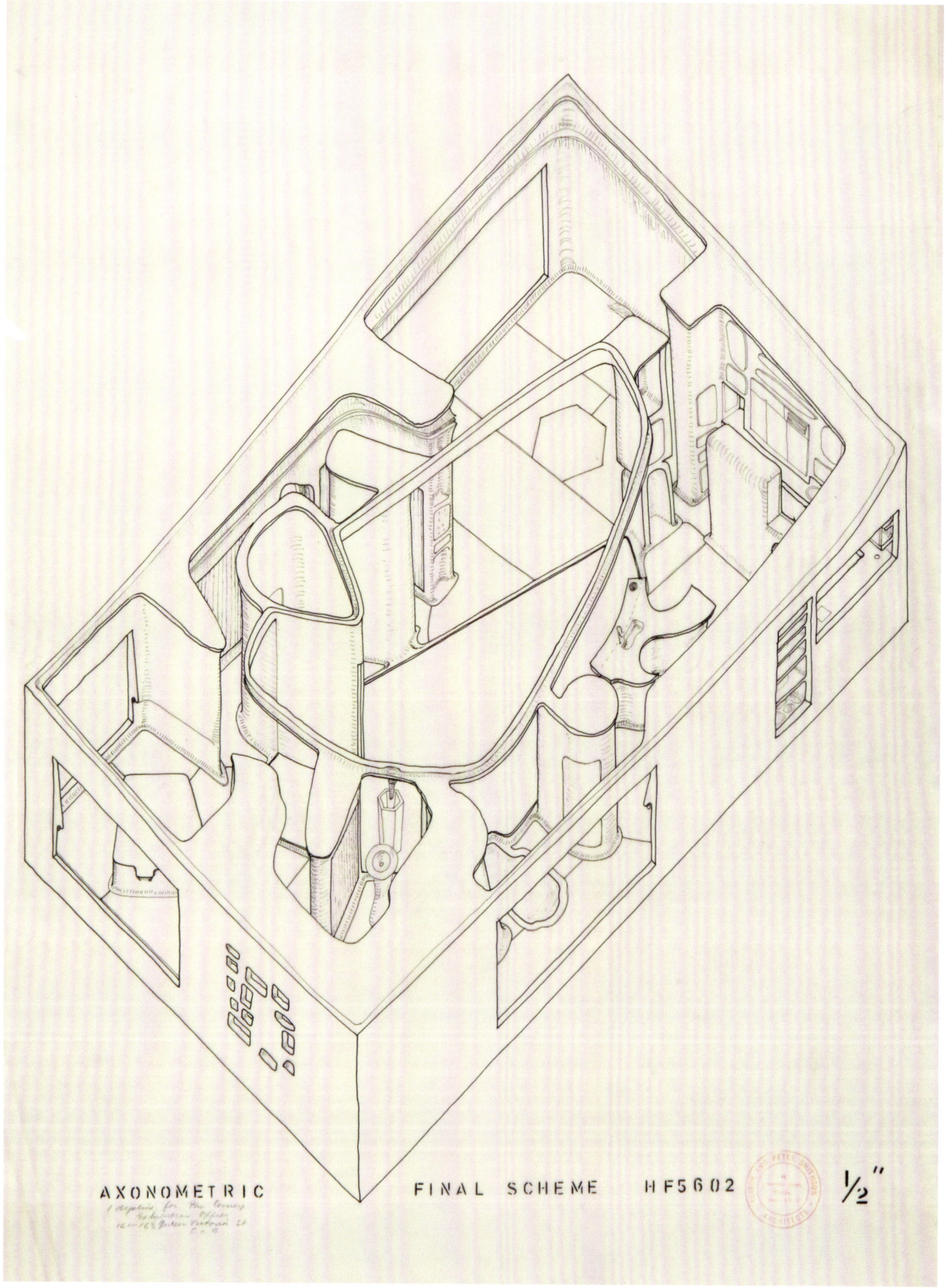

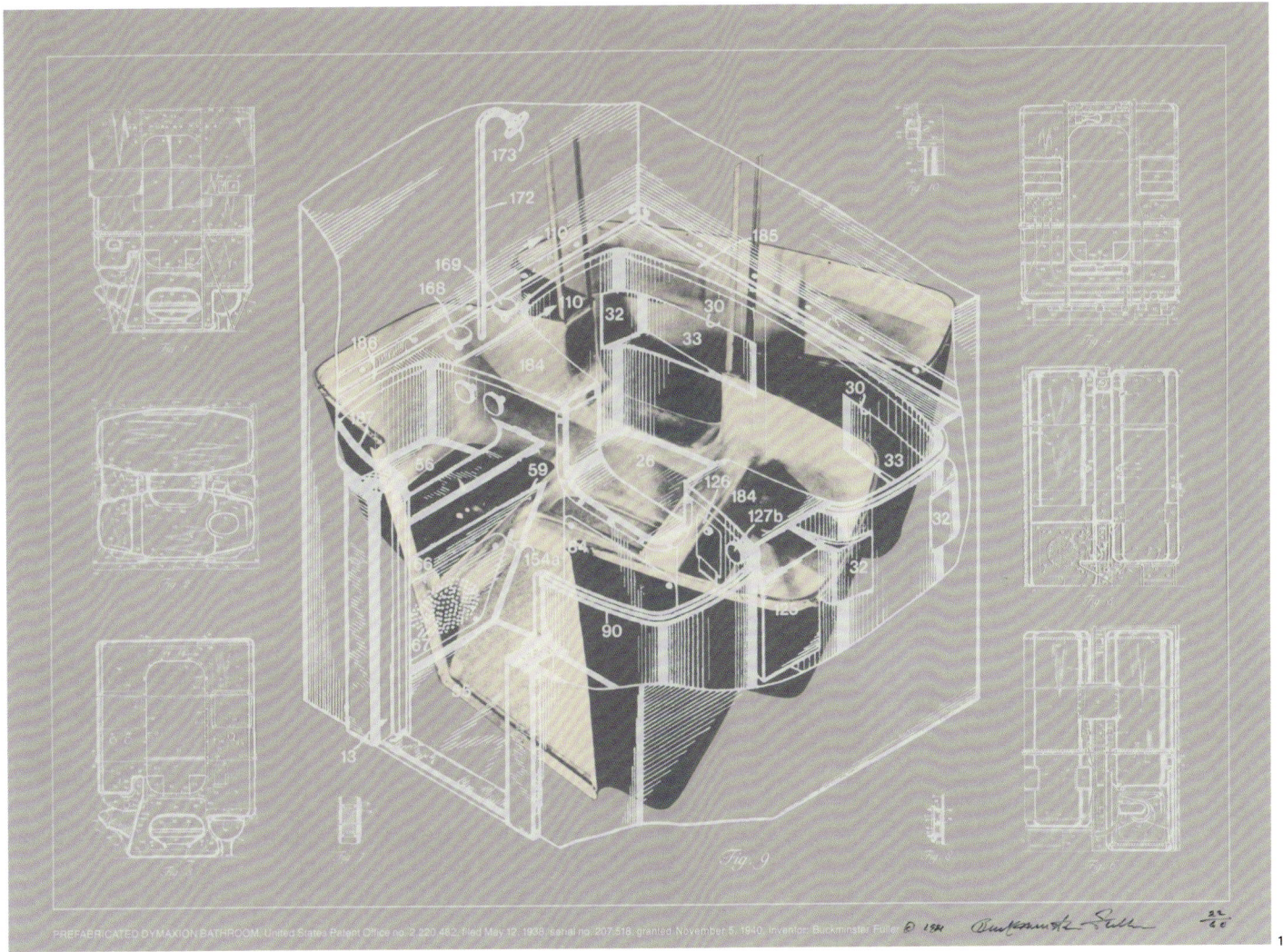

111 The final scheme of Alison and Peter Smithson's House of the Future, 1956, shows how all elements including the bathroom were built-in.

112 Buckminster Fuller's Prefabricated Dymaxion Bathroom, 1936, comprised just four stamped sheets of metal or moulded plastic.

use of the waste left in it. In 1931, he was a researcher for the American Standard Sanitary Manufacturing Company. Designing a toilet, he extruded the bath and sink into a complete and seamless room. His Dymaxion House incorporated this specially developed bathroom. The Dymaxion bathroom, as it became known, was marketed as an independent unit by the Phelps Dodge Corporation. He even developed a solid waste system that shrink-wrapped the expelled contents for later use. Fuller was a toilet obsessive. Alison and Peter Smithson's 1956 House of the Future designed the bathing area as a large room, adjacent to the dressing room, with a self-cleaning temperature-controlled red tub. It had a shower that also dried its users and a sun lamp for warmth and tanning. The sinuous, integrated features of the room hinted at a futuristic aesthetic. But really, the most revolutionary aspect was that it was a separate and private space – a revelation in a post-war Britain just getting to grips with bringing its outside privy indoors.

As well as technological concerns, the bathroom has the capacity to be a site for the construction of artifice – often via the ingenious use of surfaces. This characteristic can lead to a variety of unusual forms of self-expression. Austrian architect Otto Wagner installed a glass bath in his Viennese apartment in 1898. Paul Rudolph went a step further and installed a glass-bottomed bath that was viewed on entrance to his apartment in New York. This must have created a surprise for anyone entering the interior when one of the most intimate and private rooms of the house was clearly on display.

The aesthetics of the wall and floor surfaces of the bathroom have always been an important concern, yet the 'wipe-clean' requirement common today has not always been prioritized. In the eighteenth century the Ndzundza Ndebele people of South Africa transitioned from grass huts to

113 A glass bathtub was installed in the bathroom of Otto Wagner's apartment in Vienna and was exhibited at the 1900 Paris Expo.

114 The prominence of the bathtub in Paul Rudolph's penthouse in New York meant anyone taking a soak could be glimpsed as one passed from the kitchen into the main living space.

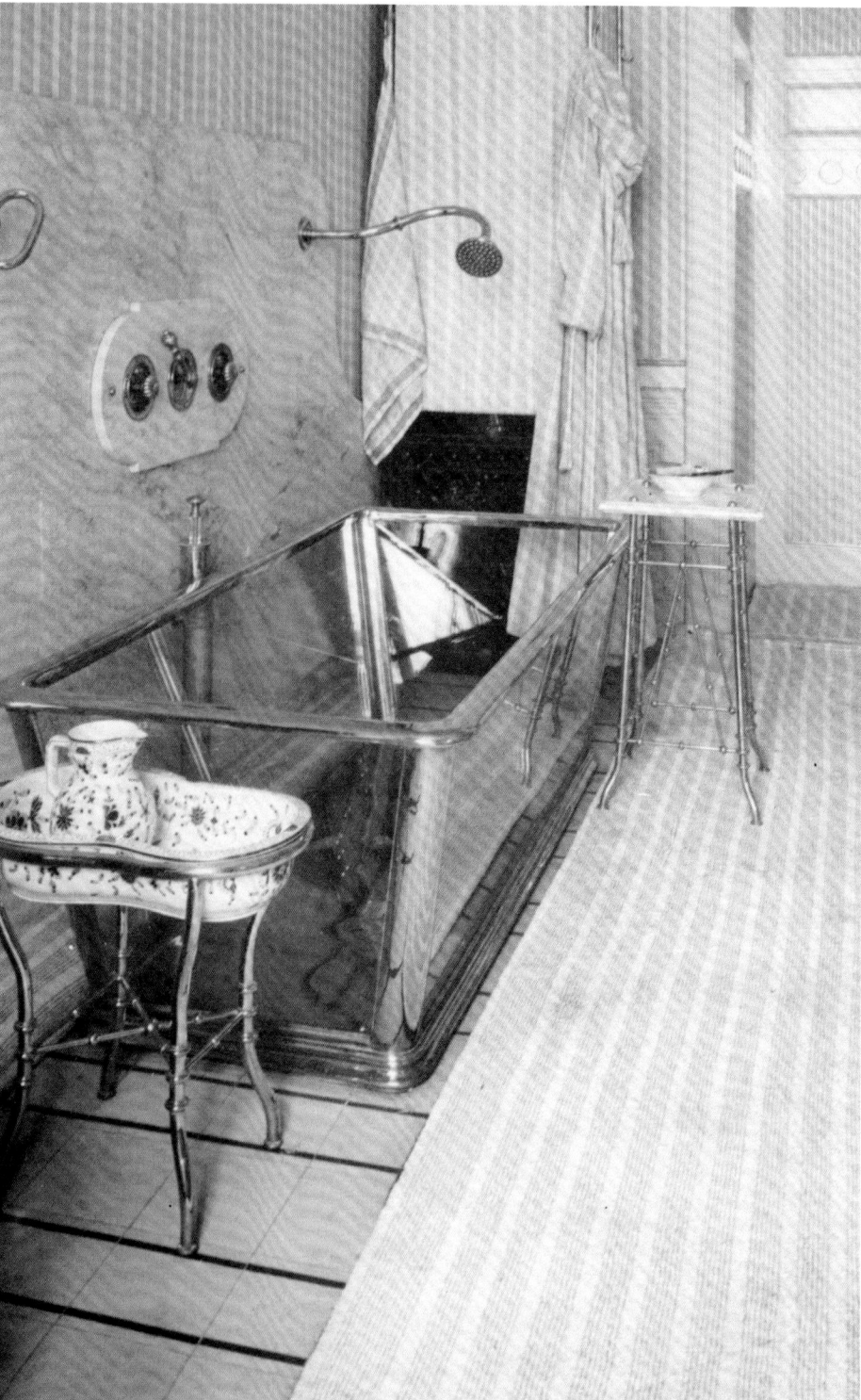

113

mud-walled constructions and, after suffering defeat in war with the Boers, expressed their grief through wall painting. Vibrant, colourful geometric symbols, often painted by women, represented a good household, both inside and outside of the dwellings. The graphics relayed grief but also signified the resistance to the oppression of their foes, the Boers. The bathroom of artist Esther Mahlangu's home in Mpumalanga province carries on this tradition and the standard fittings are contained in a room of vibrant colours and forms. Red, yellow, sky-blue, green and pink, often outlined by sharp black and white lines, are codes. They can symbolize the status of the homeowner, offer prayer or make announcements such as marriage. Like all interior decoration, the paintings imply status and convey taste, extended to all spaces including the bathroom, a function of embellishment that is as ancient as it is contemporary.

The same coding signals and status effects can be applied to very different sorts of bathrooms. In the 1960s, the actor Jayne Mansfield's bathroom was lined with pink fur and replete with a heart-shaped bath, embodying her celebrity and the glamour of this period. Her husband Mickey Hargitay had been a plumber before becoming Mr Universe and thus with great expertise made the space an elaborate gift for his wife. Gender relations in the home can be exemplified when bathrooms are custom made for partners. Paul Nash's bathroom for the dancer Tilly Losch, designed in 1932 in the London home of Losch and her husband Edward James, was a never-ending shimmer of reflective mirrors and dimpled glass surfaces. Losch must have seen herself a hundred times when she was inside the space. Different but the same, both Mansfield's and Losch's rooms were created to place the occupant at its centre. The pink fur-lined room cocooned Mansfield in wall-to-wall softness: an acoustically silent retreat where no one could hear you scream. Losch's bathroom, with its shiny surfaces of plate glass, neon tube lighting and even an exercise barre, would endlessly mirror the dancer for whom it was made. In both spaces, the female body was fetishized and trapped in the eternal gaze of their admirers. Like Esther Mahlangu's bathroom, they contained implicit codes and messages in their surfaces, pertaining to values attributed to the users.

Despite being considered the most private of rooms, the bathroom can be placed centre stage. The Italian designer Carlo Scarpa placed a bathroom 'pod' at the threshold of the main bedroom in Villa Ottolenghi on the shore of Lake Garda in Italy. Fitted with two-way glass (transparent on the inside and reflective on the outside) the room is prominent yet totally discreet at the same time. Similarly, in the Kaufman apartment, a rooftop penthouse in London designed by Simon Conder Associates, the toilet and bathroom were located in opaque glass circular units right in the middle of the floor. Testing the relationships between private and public through the location of the bathroom can be extended to the placing of the elements within it; there can be nothing more exciting than a bath with a view. The Nest is a lodging house in Namibia on the Namib Tsaris

115 The expressive geometric decoration of the bathroom in artist Esther Mahlangu's home contrasts strikingly with the orthodox suite installed in it.
116 The shimmering and reflective surfaces of Tilly Losch's bathroom, designed by Paul Nash, London, 1932.
117 Jayne Mansfield in the pink carpeted bathroom of her lavishly decorated home, 'The Pink Palace', Los Angeles, 1960.

THE PRIVATE INTERIOR | BATHROOM

Conservancy near to Sesriem by artist and architect Porky Hefer. The building was designed to appear as though part of the landscape and took inspiration from the nests of the sociable weaver bird that dot the landscape. The off-grid bespoke house was made by local craftspeople, while the hand-bent steel frame was clad in granite from the site and Namibian reed thatch. Bricks were made on-site, and the timber was locally sourced kiaat and Rhodesian teak. In a climatic response to the harsh, hot surrounds inspired by the weavers, the building skin is separated from the interior making it cool in summer and warmer in winter. It is raised off the ground to let cool winds pass underneath it. The bathroom interior echoes the external thatch, and the bath is placed as a free-standing object with a view to the landscape beyond. The nearest city is 400 kilometres (250 miles) away, so the promise of nothing but the animals in the landscape seeing you in the bath is alluring. Even in a more populous location, a bath with a view can still heighten the delights of a long soak. Neri & Hu's Waterhouse at South Bund hotel in Shanghai was remodelled from a derelict ex-Japanese army building. In many of the rooms the bathroom is placed centrally in the space and enclosed by glass walls. In one particular room, the bath is located in a window with a view over the city and with only the neighbours to look back and view the bather.

No bathroom is complete without a mirror. It is an object that one can use to reflect on themselves as well as the space around them. British designer Oliver Hill's design for the London townhouse of Robert Hudson in the 1930s placed a scalloped-edged bath in the middle of the room and reflected the central tub in a full-height mirrored wall. Stepping out of the bath and being reflected in the facetted screen must have made the occupant feel as though they were shimmering in the space. The design collective FAT used the bathroom to make a playful installation based on an 'en-suite' sharing of the most intimate room in the house. *Bathroom Sweet* was intended

118 The prominently located yet impenetrably finished circular glass bathroom units of the Kaufman apartment, Simon Conder Associates, London, 2000.
119 The bathroom of the Villa Ottolenghi, Carlo Scarpa, Verona, Italy, 1978, was a free-standing room at the threshold of the main bedroom.
120 The view across the rooftops of Shanghai from the tub of a room in the Waterhouse at South Bund hotel by Neri & Hu, 2010.
121 The Nest by Porky Hefer Design, Namibia, 2018, was inspired by the sociable weaver, whose nests optimize temperature regulation in the hot climate.

THE PRIVATE INTERIOR | BATHROOM

122 The strips of bevelled mirror, fluted oval bath and seaweed-patterned wallpaper complete the bathroom at North House designed by Oliver Hill for Mr and Mrs Robert Hudson in the 1930s.

123 *Bathroom Sweet* by FAT, for the British Council's 'Hometime' touring exhibition in China, 2003, was a bathroom retreat for an imagined celebrity couple.

for a celebrity couple with two sets of bathroom equipment. Two baths, toilets, showers and sinks – all in baby pink – were glued together, uniting the couple in a make-believe room surrounded by a shower curtain.

Our most exposed moment in the home lends the bathroom the potential to explore our identities through experimentation. Alex Schweder's works *Plumbing Us* and *Bi-Bardon* explored the meanings of the porcelain systems of our toilets and bathrooms. Placing a conjoined urinal either side of a stud wall in *Plumbing Us*, meant that both users, who were usually separated, were connected to each other through the toilet drain. Judy Chicago's *Menstruation Bathroom* (1972), a part of the *Womanhouse* project (see p. 169) was a room in which the messy realities of this space were made evident. Terence Koh's *Untitled (Medusa)* is a white box that looks plain and simple on the outside, while inside is a jet black room with a urinal and a shelf of religious icons, all presented as phallic imagery. All these projects force the viewer to question the sexual dimensions of this space. The bathroom's propensity to enable us to reflect on our bodies and their functions can extend to reflection on our sexuality and gender.

Shifting attitudes towards the body and bathing, and the sexual revolution of the 1960s and 1970s, precipitated changes in intimacies and bathroom spaces. Large baths for more than one, hot tubs, 'his and hers' basins all signalled a room that was no longer for one. In the so-called 'living bathroom', mirrors, tables, even chaise longues and chairs became part of the fixtures and fittings of the room. The living bathroom was a space of leisure for a good long soak and socializing. As bathroom expert Barbara Penner states, 'With the move towards more casual, sexually liberated lifestyles, bathrooms began to be more widely treated as places of leisure, sociality and sensuality – places for regeneration as well as "ablutions".'[12]

As well as its emergence as a living space for leisure, the contemporary bathroom reifies the experimental qualities of its ancient forebears. Its hygienic requirements can be extended to render it as a diagnostic tool, with smart technologies leading the way as to how your bathroom may be able to understand your body and its needs. Moreover, it is arguably because of the room's close associations with our bodies that it has emerged, especially in the 2020s, as a battle ground for inclusivity. These fundamentals are evident in its capacity as a space

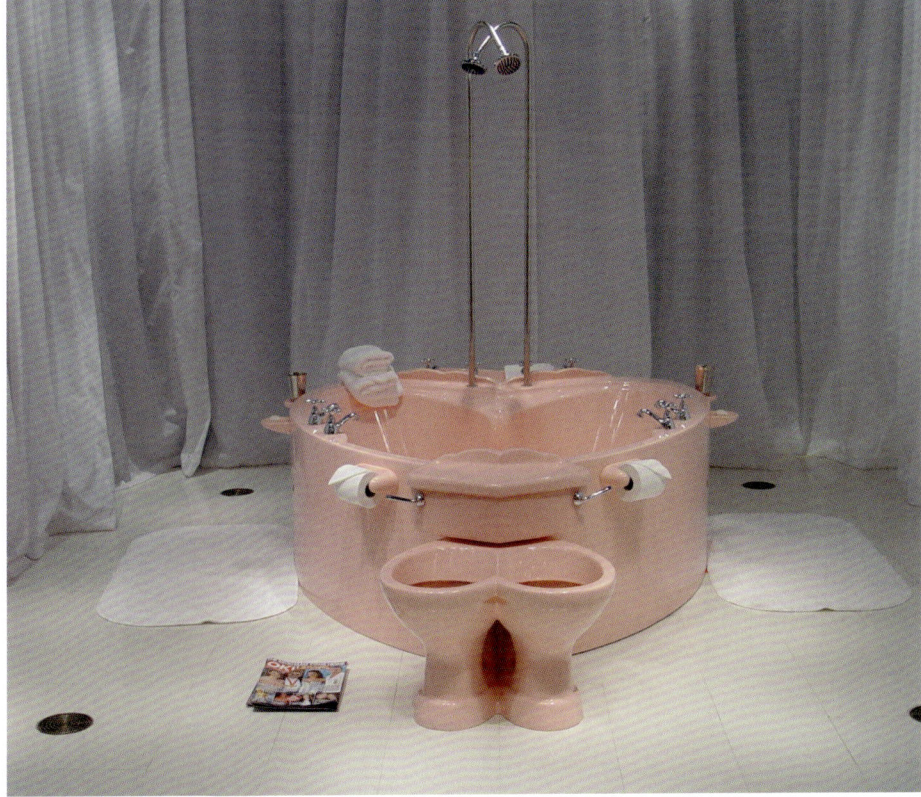

124 Driven by technological and social necessities, the bathroom has always been the site of experimentation. *Plumbing Us*, Alex Schweder, 2009.

125 *Menstruation Bathroom* by Judy Chicago, originally created in 1972 as part of *Womanhouse* (see p. 169). Shown here is the 1995 reinstallation at Los Angeles Museum of Contemporary Art.

126 *Untitled (Medusa)* by Terence Koh, 2006; the outwardly clinical appearance belies its subversive interior.

THE PRIVATE INTERIOR | BATHROOM

126

for measurement and regulating of bodies in space. Ernst Neufert first published his *Architects' Data* in 1936 and it is still in print today. Designed to rationalize the sizes of rooms, objects and utilities it became a template for space planning. Its peer is the *New Metric Handbook*, first published in 1979 and in its seventh edition. In both books, diagrams of bathroom sizes, tubs with bodies in them, shower trays and sinks all standardize the measurements of the body and bathroom furniture. In 1966, Alexander Kira produced *The Bathroom*, an extensive study of fittings and use of all aspects of the design of this room. But, more importantly, for the first time it brought the user into consideration and acknowledged how varied the group of people under that label just might be. Access issues, equality in facilities, even issues

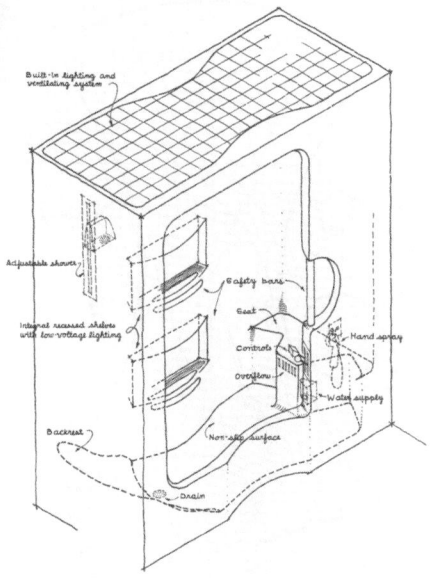

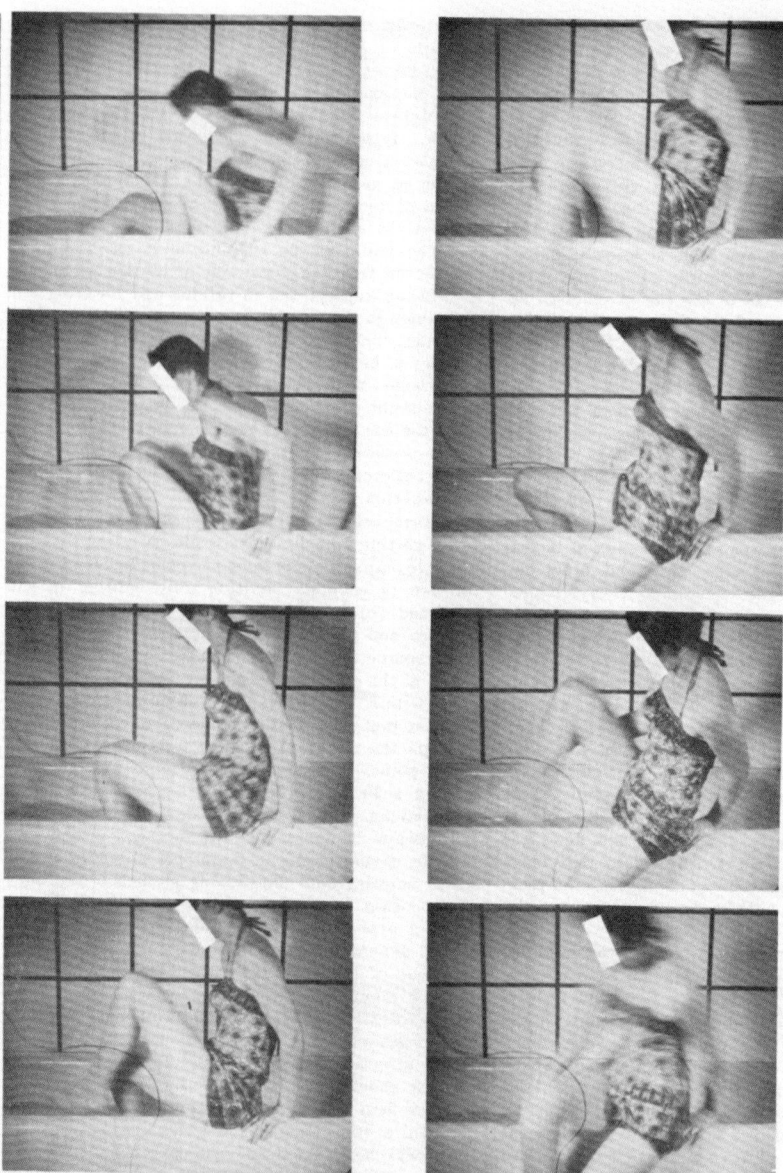

127 Alexander Kira's bathroom studies were the first to recognize the variations in users and how these should be accommodated.
128 Smart home mock-up construction by the Institute for Smart Cities at the University of Kansas.

around racial segregation (Kira was working in the US) were incorporated into the study. So too was the world's first principle of accessible buildings and facilities for all, known as A117.1 and issued by the American National Standards Institute (ANSI) in 1961.[13] Kira's ambition was to establish a fresh set of criteria for the room that would focus on the variances in the anatomy and behaviour of its users rather than a one-size-fits-all approach. For instance, Kira's study noted that the bathroom sink was used for washing hands, face and hair. The existing standard bowl and tap arrangement did not accommodate anything other than washing hands in a pool of water at the bottom of the sink.

Thus, a new sink had to be designed to accommodate these different uses. It was deeper and bigger and the tap more flexible. He did the same analysis on and made changes to bathtubs (too low), showers (too small) and toilets (too high).

Building on Kira's work, the advent of various smart technologies has meant that the bathroom's relationship to bodily functions makes it an excellent place for testing all kinds of metrics and data about health. Researchers at the Institute for Smart Cities at the University of Kansas are utilizing all kinds of technologies to measure our well-being through the elements of the home, including the bathroom.

Floorboard joists can be wired to provide data on movement and can detect falls as well as irregularities in walking to diagnose limps, tremors, Parkinson's disease, even diabetes (which can cause issues with nerves and change patterns of walking). Smart mirrors monitor dental plaque, eye reflexes and even asymmetries associated with strokes. Toilet sensors will be able to detect dehydration, kidney and liver issues, and even be programmed to prescribe the appropriate medication all through the analysis of our waste.[14] Other researchers have been developing a bathtub that monitors its user's heart, detecting arrhythmias and other conditions. It is, as the director of the Smart Cities Institute Joe Colistra says, as though the home becomes a medical device that can predict how to take care of you before you even have noticed you need looking after.[15]

The public bathroom has much to learn from its private counterpart. In the home, the bathroom has always been the site of shared usage by all genders. Public bathrooms have been the sites of discrimination and danger for many, especially the LGBTQ+ community. For transgender people in particular, choosing which bathroom to use can be challenging at best and, at worst, lead to unsafe situations. Designers and architects of public spaces are realizing this and have been

129 The public bathroom as the site for private emancipation was exemplified in the film *The Ladies Room* by Mahnaz Afzali, 2003.

130 Public bathrooms can learn from private ones as in the gender-neutral bathroom of the RISD Student Success Center by WORKac, 2019.

addressing inequalities in these spaces. The modern gender-neutral bathroom can alleviate concerns and maintains the privacy of the user. Architects at WORKac collaborated with a queer student organization to design gender-inclusive toilets for the Rhode Island School of Design (RISD) Student Success Center in the US. Six enclosed toilets with a shelf, mirror and vanity light were arranged around a central communal wash basin. Their research showed that all-gender washrooms with an open plan create busier and thus safer environments.

The history of the bathroom's significant role as a space that typifies rationalism, measurement and standardization means that when it manages to wriggle free of these constraints it becomes a place of delight and liberation. This was exemplified in two films centred around a public convenience. *Zananeh* (2003), also known as *The Ladies Room* by Iranian film director Mahnaz Afzali, centres around a ladies' washroom in a public park in Tehran. The bathroom is populated by all kinds of women who come to enjoy the camaraderie and atmosphere of the space. It is one of the few places in the city free from the prying eyes and surveillance of men and where women would share cigarettes and talk to each other about all kinds of subjects while being free to remove their veils. *Perfect Days* (2023) by Wim Wenders follows the life of Hirayama, a public toilet cleaner in Tokyo. Every day he travels across the city to clean the conveniences in the Shibuya district, starting at dawn and finishing after a long day. He listens to music, reads and takes great pride in the precision and thoroughness of his work. At the centre of the bathroom are the rituals and ceremonies of daily lives, spatialized by our ablutions – often much more communally than we care to recognize. The bathroom is the space that equalizes its users.

Bedroom

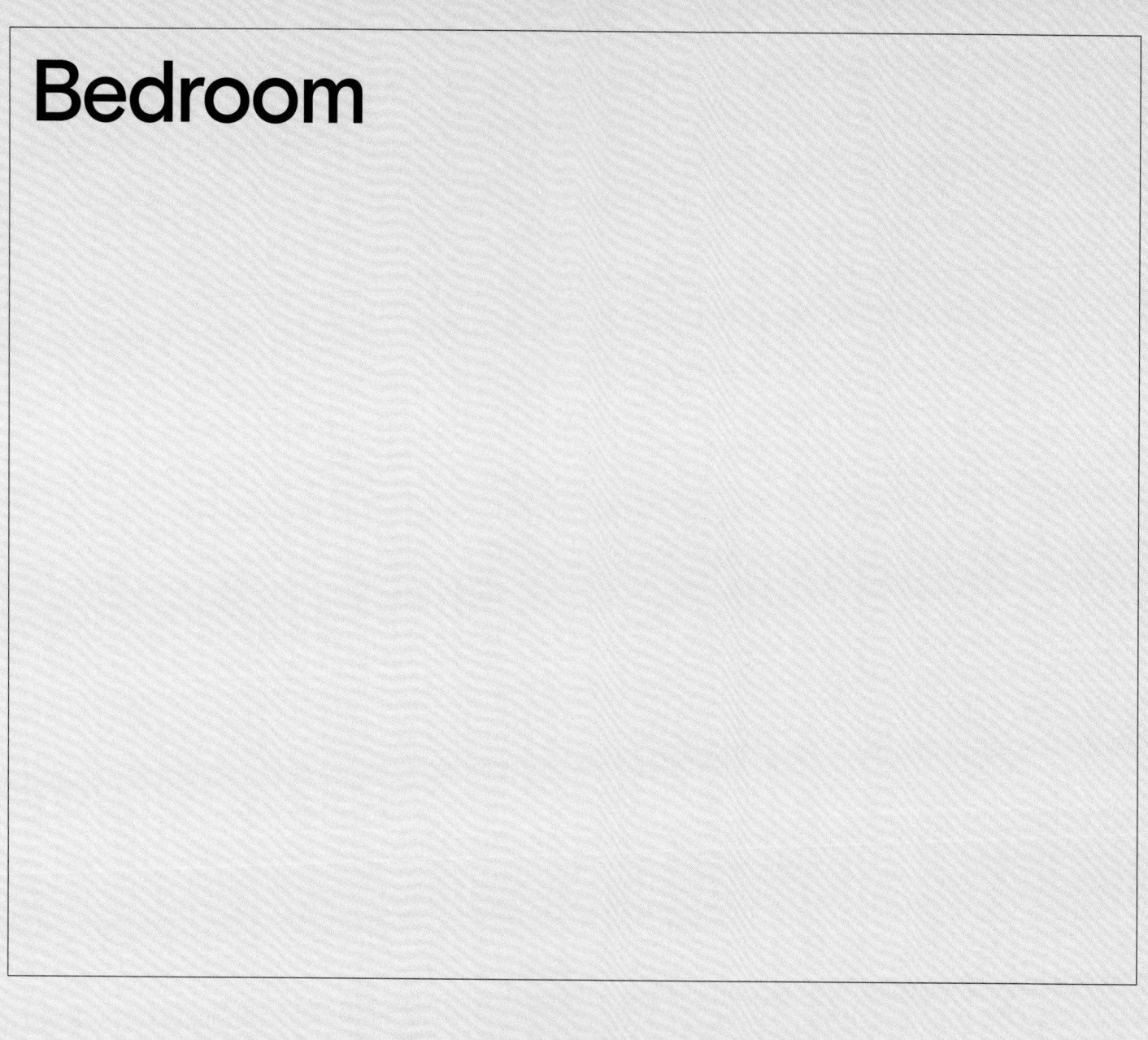

131   A room in which to sleep does not always have to be enclosed by walls. Youth to Youth Bedroom, Batlab Architects, Budapest, 2014.

The story of the bedroom and the bed describes the space in which the lives and the deaths of the occupants of a home are all linked in a fluid spatial story. As the historian Michelle Perrot states, 'The bedroom has been the cradle of civilisation, at once productive of social norms, a place of creation, and a site for experience … it corresponds to the ways in which we represent the body and its needs'.[16]

Raised above a doorway in an apartment in Budapest, Batlab Architects designed a bed 'room' for their young clients. It was not a traditional 'room'; it didn't have any walls. Instead, it was a platform with a mattress and a glazed balustrade, to stop sleepers dropping out of bed onto the floor below. Two staircases on either side of the platform were made distinct from each other. A steeper one was enclosed in orange painted fibreboard and finished with steel-plate stair treads. The other was open and its angle was shallower. It was a bedroom that unlocked all manner of issues relating to the room in which we sleep. The relationship between private and public was very ambiguous. Visitors would be able to see their hosts in their bed. The designers described how the two stairs were used by either client on the journey they take to their bed and each side was tailored to represent the partners. While looking very contemporary, the bed exemplified numerous historic and traditional associations of public and private, masculine and feminine, that have always surrounded the room, and the piece of furniture it contains, in which we sleep.

Over time, the kitchen has merged with the rest of the house and, along with the dining room, has become a public place. The bedroom has undergone the opposite journey. Sleep and its preparation were once very public activities. With its rituals of dressing and undressing, processes of ablutions in an en suite (if lucky enough), sleep and the bedroom are now effectively very private entities. This is a relatively recent pheno-menon. In many historic or collective spaces, such as tents, huts or large halls, sleeping would be undertaken communally with little thought towards separation. You often slept where you could and next to

132

133

whomever would accept you alongside them; only the royal or very wealthy would have their own bedroom. It wasn't until the mid-sixteenth century that a separate room for sleeping and procreation became discernible in domestic architecture.

A very famous bed bears witness to the sleeping proclivities of the past. The Great Bed of Ware was made in the sixteenth century and originally placed in an inn in Hertfordshire, near London. It is imaginatively carved with foliage and motifs of flowers but also with lions and satyrs – virility symbols hinting at the bed's increasing attraction as a tourist destination for travellers from London. It is over 3 metres (10 feet) deep and wide and could accommodate up to eight guests at any one time. All would have been strangers; it was common at an inn to never know who you might sleep with that night. Many of the guests left their mark on the bed by carving their names into its woodwork or even leaving wax seals. It was so famous that it was mentioned in Shakespeare's *Twelfth Night* (1601) and Ben Jonson described it in his comedy *Epicoene* (1609). In the 1930s the bed was acquired by the Victoria and Albert Museum in London and is still on display today complete with the seals and carved graffiti of its numerous guests and their various sleeping partners.

The ancient Greeks used the word *kamara*, which would apply to any vaulted or arched covered place of rest and which over time came to represent a room for sleeping. Wealthier Romans had a *cubiculum*, a small private chamber to which to retreat to sleep. *Cubo* is to lie down and is closely related to cubicle, a niche in a Christian catacomb, a link that highlights the relationship between sleeping and death. In the latter part of the sixteenth century in Europe, rest would be taken in an alcove or on a bed in a corner of a larger room, such as a hall. In its simplest form the bed would consist of a level platform, supplemented by cushions, and sometimes enclosed with curtains and a canopy to denote separation. Seclusion in bed enclosures became more prevalent in the later Middle Ages with more sophisticated beds having carved, canopied, sometimes even mirrored and highly

132 The Great Bed of Ware is an iconic bed that could be considered a tourist destination, England, 1590–1600.
133 Wealthy Romans slept in a *cubiculum* like this one from a villa at Boscoreale, near Pompeii, whose walls are decorated with frescoes dating from *c.* 50 BCE.
134 The state bed at Osterley Park, London, was a sleeping enclosure reserved for the privileged.
135 As a symbol of royalty the king's bed was always separated by a balustrade. The bedroom of Louis XIV at the Palace of Versailles.

135

134

decorative drapes and frames, with higher backs within which to secrete its occupants.

Emerging in the mid-seventeenth century, the French bedchamber embodied the nuances of the boundaries between private and public territories. The increasingly sophisticated approaches to the arrangement of rooms in the larger houses began with the importance of the *chambre,* within which the bed was placed often in an alcove. To reach this room was to participate in an elaborate social game of status. Leading to the *chambre* would be a *cabinet*, an anteroom, for waiting in and often full of personal possessions. This would be linked to the main *salle* or *salon*, from which guests would be drawn and admitted to the inner rooms for a formal meeting. In important houses in France, the bedroom was a public room where social rituals such as the *coucher* or the *lever* (evening and morning receptions) were performed. Access was bestowed upon high-ranking individuals in the king's favour. State beds, such as that at Osterley Park by Robert Adam or Louis XIV's at the Palace of Versailles, were placed at the heart of operations. At Versailles, the bed was placed in a room covered in velvet tapestries and encrusted in 60 kilograms (132 pounds) of gold, unceremoniously removed during the Revolution. The king's bed was surrounded with a balustrade upon which to lean. To transgress this barrier without an invite was to risk rebuke, possibly much more if the king was in a bad mood. The king's bed was the space of complete power, and proximity to it reflected standing. It was well known that where the king slept, power resided.

Reflecting the increasing privacy of the bedroom, the ceremonial role of state beds became less important from the eighteenth century onwards. In contrast, poorer houses contained beds that were communal. Families would sleep together, even including guests, although protocols concerning distancing the females of the household from others would be observed.[17] The location of a bed and its room can further privacy and deepen seclusion and separation from the other more public rooms of a house. This might be achieved by burying bedrooms underground. Matmata in Tunisia is a Berber town where some residents constructed troglodyte dwellings, carved from the featureless sandstone landscape. Each dwelling was begun by digging out a large rectangular courtyard with a well, dug down to the water table; from the sides of the sunken courtyard several caves were then excavated. These rooms are painted white inside and out to reflect the harsh sun and keep

136 Furniture is carved out of the same rock as the room itself in a Berber underground homestead, Matmata, Tunisia.
137 The sanctuary of a room in which to retire and relax. Elsie de Wolfe in her boudoir, 1896.
138 Traditional domestic room planning linked the boudoir with the 'mistress of the house' leading to gendered associations that persist to this day. Photograph for *Country Life*, 1907.

the subterranean rooms cool. Bedroom furniture is carved out of the rock. The application of textiles, rugs and blankets softens the rooms and the inhabitants' possessions further offset the spartan feel of the space.

Some resting spaces have unique meanings. The term boudoir allegedly derives from the French *bouder* (to sulk), suggesting a room in which to brood. A more reasonable explanation suggests a derivation from the space known as the bower, the second chamber in a medieval castle. The former etymology has led to some rather biased associations and preconceived overtones that are found in histories of planning. Robert Kerr in his influential book on domestic layouts was stridently clear that the boudoir was the private parlour for the mistress of the house.[18] He stated that the boudoir was a morning room and therefore should be positioned accordingly in the house for the householder to catch the morning light. Designers such as Elsie de Wolfe understood a boudoir as a room where she could plan and organize her work and routines. It was like an office in the home. It was also a room to which to retire to at the end of the day. Her own boudoir was a space that 'in the rare evenings when I may give myself up to solid comfort and a new book ... becomes a haven of refuge after the business of the day ... It is a sort of room of all trades, and good for each of them.'[19]

In the twentieth century, the boudoir still had some currency in the larger modern home. In the hands of modern designers, the boudoir, or 'lady's room' was deployed to particular effect. Adolf Loos used a boudoir as an important room in many of his houses. The Zimmer der Dame in the Villa Müller is at the centre of the home and is an intimate enclosure, overlooked by the stairs

THE PRIVATE INTERIOR | BEDROOM

139

140

surrounding it. The room is viewed through various openings and windows and hence its occupants were watched as both hosts and guests circulated the house. Aspects of voyeurism are unavoidable. The boudoir in the Villa Cavrois by Robert Mallet-Stevens is a much more relaxed and less strictly ordered affair, with the furniture dispersed casually around the room. A daybed is built into the side wall, while the dressing table is free-standing, allowing it to receive maximum daylight for reading or working and creating a much freer room and atmosphere. Franca Sozzani was the editor-in-chief of *Vogue Italia* for almost three decades. When seeking a retreat from her busy life she would return to a house in Derb Zaouia in Marrakesh, which for decades she had been renovating with the artist Kris Ruhs. Arranged around two courtyards, one with a garden the other with a pool, the rooms were filled with textiles, furniture and art that Sozzani found on her travels. The bedroom evoked a boudoir with its soft textile coverings across the bed, carpets and large cushions on the tiled floors. The original walls of the room were preserved, and the carved timber ceiling was restored, creating a moody atmosphere. When designed by a woman, the boudoir became a more relaxed, informal and less voyeuristic space.

Increasingly, in the latter part of the twentieth century, the boudoir became

139 The informality of the boudoir in the Villa Cavrois, Croix, France, by Robert Mallet-Stevens, stands in stark contrast to some of its more restrictive Modernist counterparts.

140 The Zimmer der Dame (lady's room) in the Villa Müller, Prague, by Adolf Loos was structured with built-in furniture and was overlooked by the adjacent stairs.

141 Antique silk throws, pillowcases, rugs and cushions adorn *Vogue* editor Franca Sozzani's bedroom in Derb Zaouia, Marrakesh.

141

an anachronism. It lost its lustre and was considered a luxury. It is no longer a regular feature of contemporary domestic design, dissolving into the bedroom as the specific space in the home to be on one's own.

The bed and the room surrounding it have always represented the social norms and relations of a household. Lina Loos's bedroom, designed by her husband Adolf, created an integrated room where the bed and flooring were formed into one continuous surface. The bedroom was draped all around with white *batiste,* a fine cotton or linen often used to make lingerie. This was hung up to door-height and covered the cabinets in the room. The floor was a blue carpet, upon which a luxurious white Angora rabbit-skin rug extended all the way over the bed. The intimate and atmospheric conditions of the bedroom were deliberately contrasted with the adjacent timber-panelled living room. The soft and sensual disposition of textiles and colours created a very particular atmosphere in the home, distinctly separate from the other rooms of the house. The covering of the bed in the Loos apartment fetishized the horizontal surface upon which the invitation to lay down was clearly signalled to the newlyweds. In a completely contrasting bedroom fantasy, Carlo Bugatti, the Italian furniture, silverware and interior designer, created the bedroom of English politician Cyril Flower. Designed at the same time as Lina Loos's bedroom in 1903, it was an Egyptian fantasy, with the bed connected to a highly elaborate headboard. Beds and their rooms are clearly stage sets for some to act out their dreams.

142 A recreation of Lina Loos's bedroom, originally designed by her husband Adolf, by Hubmann Vass Architekten, Vienna, 2014.
143 The Egyptian revival fantasy bedroom in Surrey House, London, designed by Carlo Bugatti for Cyril Flower, c. 1903.
144 The carefully composed Hill House bedroom in Helensburgh, Scotland, UK, by Charles Rennie Mackintosh, 1902–04, with the bed located in its own vaulted space.
145 The placement of the study in the bedroom in Jože Plečnik's house, Ljubljana, symbolized the close connections between work and his life.

In contrast to Loos's sensual surfaces, again dating to between 1902 and 1904, Charles Rennie Mackintosh's bedroom in the Hill House expresses a much more glacial, northern European sensibility towards bedroom design. The bed is positioned in its own vaulted alcove, integrated with yet separated from the composition of the room. Its positioning suggests that it is less the main act and more of a side issue in the space. Even more frugal, the same reserved quality can be seen in the bedroom of Jože Plečnik's house in Ljubljana, his home from 1921–57. The simplicity of the room, sparse yet carefully arranged with books and a worktable close to the bed, relayed a precise focus of dedication and piety, quite different to the intimacies of the Loos, Bugatti and even Mackintosh rooms.

Twentieth-century Freudian analysis extended the bedroom's significance to become the centre of the sexual atmosphere of the home. The Italian interior and furniture designer Carlo Mollino demonstrated this theme for his clients and in his own domestic arrangements. In the late 1930s he designed two iterations of a small apartment for his friend Giorgio Devalle in a housing block in Turin (the first version was dismantled and redesigned in a larger setting). Both foregrounded the bedroom as the site of theatrical, atmospheric experiences. The bedroom in the second version, Via Alpi 5 (the first was at Via Alpi 3), consisted of walls and ceiling lined with upholstery and a cabin door reminiscent of an ocean liner for the adjacent bathroom. At the centre of the composition was a bed with a green velvet couch in the shape of an exaggerated pair of lips, an invitation that no one could resist. The design for Mollino's own apartment,

also in Turin, was a relatively strait-laced affair. This apartment was kept secret and used as his photography studio, where he took many erotic polaroids and photographs – often of clients' wives. The bedroom was a simple affair, a bed on a podium surrounded by drapes and a leopard-skin wall. Hundreds of butterflies were arranged, by Mollino himself, on the wall. Possibly to remind himself of the beauty of nature as he slept.

The bed in its room can be conceived of as a part of a larger ensemble of artefacts. Eileen Gray's iconic Modernist villa E-1027, built 1926–29, placed a daybed in the living room alongside an adjustable side table designed especially for the home. Jean Dunand's bedroom for Templeton Crocker, made at the same time as E-1027, relied on the effect of incredible lacquerwork. Dunand learned lacquering from the

146 The overt symbolism of the lip-shaped sofa in the bedroom of Casa Devalle, by Carlo Mollino, in Turin, reflected the erotic overtones of the room.

147 Mollino's own bedroom in his private Turin residence was the place he kept all his most treasured objects.

148 A daybed in the living room of E-1027 by Eileen Gray in Roquebrune-Cap-Martin, France, 1926–29, ensured its occupants could relax outside the formalities of the bedroom.

149 Bedroom by Jean Dunand in the Templeton Crocker residence, San Francisco, as set up in a Paris photography studio, c. 1927.

Japanese artist Seizo Sugawara, who, incidentally also taught Eileen Gray. Dunand designed the bedroom, dining and breakfast room in Crocker's San Francisco penthouse. Newly divorced, in 1927 Crocker needed an apartment to express his new status. Dunand turned the walls of the bedroom into a woodland scene. The lacquered panels shone with muted silvers, greens and warm red-browns. Furniture was upholstered in goatskin and grey chamois leathers, with matching grey curtains hung at the windows. Crocker was a naturalist, author and explorer, and the scene that surrounded him in the evenings must have given him great comfort as he closed his eyes to sleep, imagining he was out in the wilds.

As well as giving comfort, one feature of the bed is to symbolize the dreams that take place within it. Beds can be intensely private, providing space to focus the mind. Marcel Proust famously wrote from his bed, declaring, 'It would seem one can only write well in bed…. For the bed is like no other. While at one time it was the place of birth, of suffering, and of death, today it is still the site of our dreams and our pleasures.'[20]

The four-poster bed is an enclosure to which to retreat; it removes the occupant from their surrounds. It became increasingly popular in the eighteenth century and remains so as a symbol of luxury and status. The exemplary type of the four-poster is the state bed. It was a symbol of power and prestige and often the most expensive item in a house. The state bed was the 'best bed' and was reserved for special occasions and, therefore, it was rarely slept in. Such beds would be canopied, under a great swathe of luxurious textiles, drapes, swags, fringes, testers, valances,

headcloths, curtains and cords, all supported on a timber frame. The grand or state bed heyday was in the eighteenth and nineteenth centuries. After this their usefulness and popularity waned, especially when the idea of the formal room parade was no longer an essential element of interior life.

Twentieth-century designers like David Hicks continued to use the four-poster bed to signify grandiosity and to make a statement in the bedroom and the home. Meanwhile a thoroughly modern version of the four-poster enclosure exists in the series of timber bed-boxes made by Harry Thaler Studio in a temporary home commissioned by the contemporary art museum Museion for guest curators and artists. To increase the fluidity of the space the units are on wheels and can be moved around the room.

Reusing unusual elements can create the same effect as the enclosed

150 David Hicks used a four-poster bed to make a statement in Easton Grey House, Wiltshire, for Peter and Didi Saunders, 1966.

151 A contemporary version demonstrating the enclosing properties of the four-poster bed in Atelier House by Harry Thaler Studio for Museion, Bolzano, Italy, 2012.

152 Repurposed petrol tankers create sleeping pods in an apartment on the site of a former parking lot. Morton Loft, LOT-EK, New York, 2000.

153 An elevated view from the bedroom of Lodge in the Pigüe by Mestizo Estudio Arquitectura, Ecuador, 2024.

four-poster. In the Morton Loft, LOT-EK reused the tank of a petrol lorry that had bulkheads that corresponded to the exact size of a double bed. One section of the tank was craned into the apartment and raised up in the double-height space. Then two bedrooms were created in the tank by utilizing the bulkhead as a divider. Hydraulic arms lift the heavy doors for fresh air and close them for privacy when occupants want to go to sleep. Another section of the tank was stood upright on its end and the bulkhead in the middle enabled it to be used as a two-storey bathroom. Both bed and bathroom containers were connected with a steel staircase. The rest of the space was left open. Being ensconced in a box may be conducive to sleep for some, but a unique location may also provide the right context for relaxation. Mestizo Estudio Arquitectura created a one-bed lodge high up in the Amazonian rainforest in Ecuador using recycled steel tubes from the oil industry and natural materials such as rocks, wood and bamboo from the site. The lodge is raised off the edge of a ravine with a scaffold and elevated among the tree canopy, even incorporating a large pigüe tree into the shower room. A gabion wall filled with rocks from the site anchors the back of the building and contrasts with the full-height glazed wall in the bedroom that faces out to the terrace and view beyond. Sleep must be peaceful high among the treetops.

The bed is the only piece of furniture that has dictated areas of the city. In the UK 'Bed-sit land' was the name, in the mid- to late twentieth century, given to parts of a city characterized by unscrupulous housing practices. A bedsit being the name given to houses in multiple occupancy (HMO). Historically they arose from the subdivision of large houses into smaller sublets in big British cities such as London and Manchester to accommodate younger people leaving home, students and those wanting short-term lets. Often they were made using cheap materials and filled with poorly maintained furniture, with shared facilities such as a bathroom and kitchen. They were usually viewed as unsatisfactory, and many governments have attempted to phase them out through planning laws and regulation.

One-room or studio living, doesn't have to be so unprincipled. Innovative solutions for space saving can be seen in designs by Studiomama in London where beds and their rooms can be foldable or portable with no fixed abode. Bao House by Dot Architects takes the idea of a movable bed to the extreme by attaching it to the back of a bicycle and allowing it to roam through the streets of Beijing. Beds within boxes, within the room, make enclosures in an open space in order to minimize sound and create a quieter environment for sleep. Small-space living does not have to take place in poorly designed interiors.

Sleeping requires certain conditions. Light, sound and the regulation of temperature are very important considerations to maintain a comfortable and uninterrupted rest. In large, noisy, hot cities this can be challenging – increasingly so in globally warmed times. TAKK design studio overcame these challenges in The Day After House. This involved the stripping back of an existing 110-square-metre (1,184-square-foot) building in central Madrid, removing its external windows to turn part of the interior into an open terrace. They subdivided the flat into summer and winter houses. The 60-square-metre (646-square-foot)

winter house was separated from the open terrace by retractable glazed doors. Kitchen and dining were placed along one wall. Anticipating forthcoming warmer winters, the living room and kitchen were made open plan, while the bedroom was formed as a pine-clad insulated box on stilts – free of the interior yet deriving its properties from the scale of the room. The apartment and bedroom were made from material sourced and reused from the Rioja region's wine-making industry. Pine was sourced from packaging and crates, charred cork lined the walls and shutters, and openable screens enable the apartment to be cross-ventilated, eliminating the need for air conditioning. The blackened cork stores carbon and holds the heat in the winter. The acoustics and temperature of the bedroom can be carefully controlled. Second-hand duvets were used to insulate the bedroom and large weights, stones from a nearby quarry, along with artificial flowers were suspended outside the box. The stones are counterweights to prevent the wood bending, the flowers for decoration. Reminiscent of a medieval hall, all the family sleep in the bedroom in order to reinforce energy saving but also links between them. In contrast, the summer house was finished with cement. A prominently positioned bathroom in the open terrace, enclosed by a thick, pink curtain, hosts bath times for the young family.

Because we spend so much of our life at rest, sleeping in a bed, it has become the site for research into how our body functions. Doctors and scientists study how we sleep and recommend what is the norm. Hygiene specialists and psychologists describe the ideal conditions of a bedroom in terms of layout, air quality, what light is suitable and appropriate acoustics. Even moralists aim to prescribe how and with whom we should sleep within it. The bedroom has an incredible capacity to be experimented with and can be used as a predictor of futures. In high-density cities with growing populations and the associated challenges in finding the right spaces to house them – whether multi-occupancy homes, flat-shares or bedsits – living rooms might be considered a luxury. Bedrooms become the spaces for

156

154 A foldable bed maximizes the living space in the one-room 13m² House, Studiomama, London, 2016.
155 Sleeping can take place in beds that are movable. Bao House, Dot Architects, China, 2012.
156 Bedrooms can be cooled and heated naturally through ventilation and insulation as in The Day After House, TAKK, Madrid, 2021.

living, working, dining and leisure. The bed has become multi-functional, and its flexibility has become critical. Transformable solutions such as Ori, an automated living unit designed by Yves Béhar in collaboration with MIT Media Lab, conceals the bed within a wall that contains numerous other elements needed for a small-space living unit. Smart technologies can even monitor our health in our beds. Researchers at the University of Missouri developed a smart mattress for elderly people in a residential home that, along with room sensors and monitors, can predict if a resident is becoming unwell or may even fall in the home. Hydraulic bed sensors monitor night-time restlessness, heart rate, respiration and temperature activities, even dehydration. Early onset dementia can be diagnosed if the patient is often restless and disorientated in the night.[21] Today the bed and its room can be an instrument of diagnosis, at the heart of our well-being.

The bed is often a final resting place, the place where many end their days. The role that the room and the bed have to play in this destiny is open to challenge. The Reversible Destiny Foundation was founded by Shusaku Arakawa and Madeline Gins. With the view that death was reversible and not preordained, they developed art and buildings that attempted to challenge the logic of theirs and anybody else's ultimate demise. Numerous projects

157

158

such as parks, buildings and cities were designed to shake the inhabitants out of their usual routines, challenge their perceptions and provoke physical and mental responses to the spaces. They believed that this would stimulate immune systems and ultimately make inhabitants live longer. In East Hampton, New York, they designed the Bioscleave House, a single-family home added to an existing building. 'Bioscleave' was their development of the term 'biosphere', and they described the lifespan-extending villa as an interactive laboratory of everyday life. Steep and uneven rammed-earth floors surround a sunken central kitchen, with adjacent dining table. The challenging topography of the interior landscape is accentuated by random coloured poles and a painted interior in forty different colours. Randomly uneven windows complete the disorientation. The two bedrooms and one bathroom were kept open to the main room and covered in cork, ply, pink and green paint, fake stone and copper, and part linoleum and carpet floors. The heightened, possibly overwhelming, cacophony of colours and materials were designed to, in the designers' words, keep

157 Experiments in flexibilty in bedrooms can be seen in Ori Living – Robotic Furniture by Fuseproject and Yves Béhar with MIT Media Lab, 2016.

158 Increasing urban populations means that separate rooms become a luxury. Bedrooms can become spaces for living and working as well as sleeping.

159 The challenging terrain of the Bioscleave House by Madeline Gins and Shusaku Arakawa, East Hampton, New York, 2008, was intended to prolong life by perpetually stimulating the senses.

159

the users 'tentative'. The environment means that they have to actively negotiate any activity. You couldn't simply walk across the floor to go to your bedroom, instead you had to navigate what was a very unstable and challenging terrain. Gins and Arakawa passed away in 2010 and 2014 respectively. It appeared that the conditioning of the occupants' senses didn't work as thought.

In their simplest form beds are plinths, separated from the floor and accommodating the body in a full and comfortable repose. In their most sophisticated forms, beds represent power, desire, sex and death and can be the seat of power in domestic interior spaces – all channelled through the promise of a very good night's sleep.

THE PRIVATE INTERIOR | BEDROOM

The Public Interior

The City and the Room

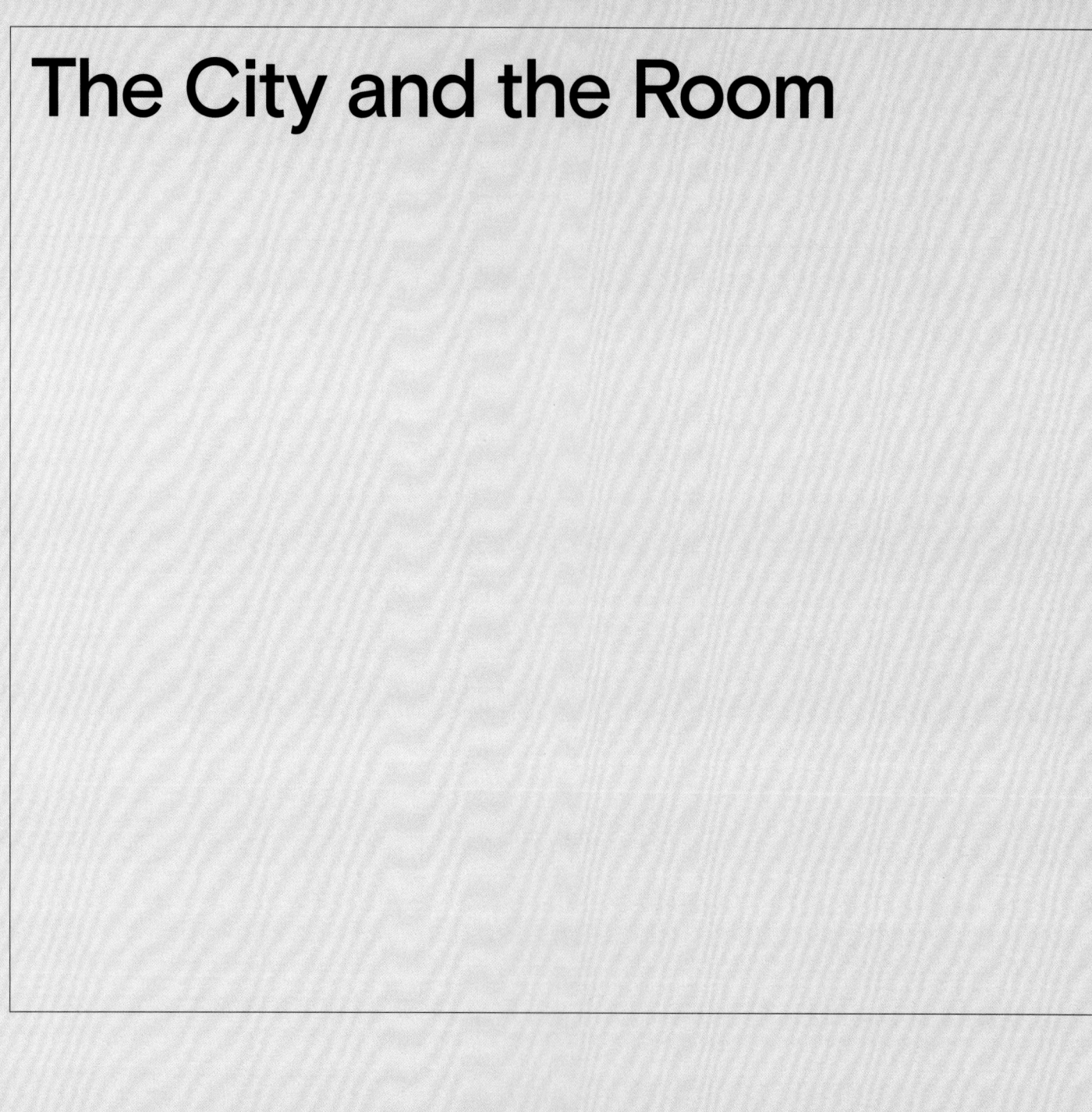

01 Sculptures, fountains and trees in the indoor garden of the Crystal Palace in Hyde Park, London, 1851.

The Great Exhibition of the Works of Industry of All Nations took place in London's Hyde Park in 1851 inside a specially built temporary structure. Histories of the Great Exhibition tend to focus on the building's dazzling design, its complex engineering and the logistics and speed of its construction. Some histories focus on how the goods of a rapidly industrialized world were gathered under one roof, demonstrating the might of a global manufacturing revolution. More recent histories focus on its extractive legacies and imperialist ambitions. Very little is written on how the building represents the emergence of the modern public interior.

The Crystal Palace, as it became known, was a public interior that showed how a structure could be erected to enclose activities that did not have any direct correlation with the contents within it. While not the first building to do so, the Crystal Palace was an enclosure so dramatic in scale and content that it demonstrated a radical shift in relations between the interior and the city. It was a structure that clearly delineated the differences between inside and out. The noisy brash interior full of people and machines and the genteel parkland that surrounded it were abruptly separated and differentiated. Situated between these two conditions was

a skin of glass and iron, forming the backdrop to the gigantic exhibition. The Crystal Palace's wide, column-free structural spans, atriums of glass and steel and well-ordered circulation for large crowds are characteristics that reappear again and again across different types of the public interior – a testament to its influential impact. These elements can be traced in the great public interiors of railway stations, airports, department stores, offices and restaurants, museums, theatres – the public palaces of the world. The public interior has five types:

Social
Social interiors are the spaces where we gather to enjoy leisure time, often in the company of others and usually through eating and drinking. Social interiors are cafés, bars and restaurants. Sociability can also involve staying in hotels, clubbing, travel and may enhance our well-being when we receive treatment in a hospital or a clinic. We may also socialize to be part of a community with a specific aim such as worship. However we socialize, the scenography for these activities is specifically designed to reflect its users.

02 The UK pavilion at Expo 2010 in Shanghai was conceived by Thomas Heatherwick as a 'cathedral to seeds', housing 250,000 kernels in acrylic rods.
03 The atmospheric Nike SuperRep showroom, a temporary space built in 2019 and designed by Robert Storey Studio, London.

03

Shop
Shops, department stores, arcades and malls are the spaces of commerce and consumption. Their focus is the production of an interior environment that stimulates desires for the possession of *things*. This section explores the role of the interior in these numerous forms of display and acquisition.

Work
The term 'work' describes environments that fuse economics, politics and communities of workers together in often bespoke spaces. Offices, studios, workshops and factories are traditionally places where we spend much of our work time. Emerging technologies have loosened the boundaries between places for living, working and also entertaining. Work shows how an office is becoming an increasingly ambiguous entity.

THE PUBLIC INTERIOR | THE CITY AND THE ROOM

04 Daylight filters through holes in the mosaic ceiling of the covered bazaar in Isfahan, Iran.

05 The huge expanse of the organic, flowing ceiling in Beijing Daxing International Airport, Zaha Hadid Architects, 2014–19.

Infrastructure

Transport networks such as railways, underground systems, roads and airports, as well as digital networks, are all instruments for the circulation of people and goods around the world. All are realized as accumulations of systems, logistics, financing and ultimately buildings. Infrastructure describes the spatial manifestations of transport, communication and the financial systems of the world. They can be manifest in newly built spaces as well as by the reclamation of structures whose original purpose has been made redundant by change.

04

THE PUBLIC INTERIOR | THE CITY AND THE ROOM

05

Culture

Public cultural interiors are museums, exhibition halls, libraries and schools. They are performative spaces such as theatres, cinemas and include scenography such as stage sets. They can be world's fairs, Expos and large spectacular events. They are all public interiors where knowledge is held and then disseminated through information and experiences, usually through the digestion of exhibits, books, shows and performances. Cultural public interiors can be site-specific or non-site-specific environments.

Social

06 The social fog of fun that was Alcoholic Architecture by Bompas & Parr in Borough Market, London, 2015–16.

07 The Grand Lobby, Raffles Hotel, Singapore, opened in 1887 and is famous for the Singapore Sling cocktail, invented in 1915.

In London's Borough Market, Bompas & Parr created Alcoholic Architecture, an inhabitable cloud of gin and tonic that guests were invited to enter (wearing a waterproof outfit) and then inhale the vapour – having been warned to 'breathe responsibly'. The designers described the installation as 'meteorology combined with mixology'.[1] It was an interior born out of its atmospherics and designed to unite its visitors within one cloud of booze. The sheer delight of the taste of the atmosphere created an intoxicating sensorial interior experience – a social fog of fun.

Social public interiors are spaces where people enjoy leisure time. They may eat, drink, dance and be alone or in a group. These activities take place in cafés, bars and restaurants as well as hotels and clubs. They are all places of sociability and hospitality created with very specific identities in order to draw in particular clientele. Because of these characteristics, social interiors often reflect how fashions change. They may not be fashionable for long before their users move onto somewhere more 'of the moment'. Others become timeless classics. Institutions such as Raffles in Singapore, Harry's Bar in Venice and El Floridita in Havana are all synonymous with the cities in which they are located.

The café and the bar are often orientated around the type of beverages they serve. Tea, coffee, alcoholic and soft drinks all demarcate types of interiors in which to imbibe. Tea drinking has been a significant part of both ancient and contemporary cuisine and medicine, as well as a spiritual undertaking for over 4,000 years in China and Japan. Tea rooms are carefully choreographed interior spaces, designed for tea preparation, consumption and the formalities that surround these processes. The Japanese *chashitsu* (tea room) was historically a place for geisha to entertain guests. Modern tea rooms are now called *kissaten* and are distinct to nosier cafés and bars in that they are quieter spaces to drink. Japanese tea ceremonies derive from Zen Buddhist and Shinto influences. They include the informal *chakai*, a light meal, or the formal *chaji*, a full dinner service lasting up to four hours. The ideal formal tea room is systematized as

4.5 tatami in plan with a low ceiling and a hearth for the preparation of the drink. It is considered important to enable seated guests to observe the preparation and making of the tea. These prevailing requirements and traditions can be updated for a more contemporary experience. The Beijing Tea House by Kengo Kuma, overlooking the Forbidden City, utilized plastic beams and polycarbonate panels to update the traditional aesthetic of the tea room. Translating the city's masonry vernacular, the lightweight structural elements were designed to be reminiscent of the paper screens of a traditional tea room interior. Light passing through the plastic was intended to project a zen-like atmosphere. Contemporary teahouses and their ceremonies do not even need to be situated in a building. Teahouse Ø, designed by Pan- Projects, re-enacted the soothing processes of a tea ceremony but within a floating pavilion on a canal in Copenhagen. The experience was designed to align its users with nature and the calming influence of the water upon which the room floated. Ø means 'island' in Danish. This particularly small island had a motor attached to it, and if the occupant got bored with the view they could manoeuvre off to another part of the canal and relax with a totally different outlook.

Imbibing tea was historically considered a novel contrast to the taking of alcohol. The appearance of teahouses in Britain was an early twentieth-century phenomenon that developed in relation to the Temperance movement, promoting abstinence and teetotalism. Margaret and Charles Rennie Mackintosh's Willow Tea Rooms were designed for Catherine Cranston and her brother Stuart, tea importers in Glasgow. The rooms catered for a cross-section of society as a place in which to do business as well as play games such as billiards and cards. One of the most elegant spaces was the ladies' room: the Salon de Luxe. Margaret Mackintosh's close collaboration with her husband ensured that the room spatially demonstrated its occupants' requirements for comfort as they slipped away from their consorts to enjoy a different kind of atmosphere. The theme of the room was based upon

08

09

08 Hollow blocks of plastic form the Beijing Tea House, a remodelled *siheyuan*-style building by Kengo Kuma and Associates, located in front of the Forbidden Palace, 2014.
09 Tea-drinking is a ceremonial process that can be undertaken both privately and publicly. Tatami room in a traditional country house in Japan.
10 A translucent wall of acrylic surrounds visitors to the floating Teahouse Ø by Pan-Projects, Copenhagen, 2019.
11 High-backed chairs arranged in the Salon de Luxe or 'ladies' room' in the Willow Tea Rooms, designed by Margaret and Charles Rennie Macintosh, Glasgow, 1905–04.

Dante Gabriel Rossetti's poem 'O Ye, All Ye That Walk in Willow Wood', a quote from which was placed in a frame on one side of the silver and purple silk-lined room.

The Temperance movement originated in the US where it emphasized the moral and medicinal implications of overindulgence – and eventually led to the nationwide prohibition of alcohol in 1920. Its impact on cafés and bars throughout the early twentieth century was in the advocating of fun and indulgence *without* alcohol. When Prohibition was lifted in 1933, the Canadian distillers Seagram commissioned Morris Lapidus to create a celebratory bar for its workers' use in the Chrysler Building in New York. Its 4.6 × 8.75-metre (15 × 29-foot) plan,

12 The long and thin executive bar of the Seagram office by Morris Lapidus, Chrysler Building, New York, 1936.
13 Social activities, such as backgammon, fuelled by caffeine imbued Ottoman coffee houses with life, c. 1870–75.
14 The formal organization of the interior of the Viennese *Kaffeehaus* informed the decorous arrangements of its patrons, Vienna, 1895.
15 The elevation and plans of the British Coffee House, Robert and James Adam, 1777.

with a height of just 2.5 metres (8 feet) was a distillation of the streamlined elegance of the host building. There was a bar on one side of the room, for standing only, and seating opposite for eighteen guests on a gently scalloped leather-upholstered banquette. This was complemented by loose seating and small tables with recessed ashtrays. The bar exuded Seagram's business wishes to create a prestigious space in the city, a feat that the company would achieve at a larger scale twenty-five years later with its own Mies van der Rohe-designed headquarters on Park Avenue. The back bar was mirrored with glass shelves displaying the company's products. At the far end of the room, evident on arrival, was a trademark Lapidus design: a timber wall punctured by a series of portholes. Each one contained a bottle of Seagram alcohol. The space celebrated the end of Prohibition with a thirst-quenching flourish.

Coffee houses have a long history. Emerging in the fifteenth century in the Middle East and spreading via the Ottoman Empire, Damascus and Persia, they were places to meet, play games and drink. Caffeine meant conversation and coffee houses were places of discourse, some of which was politically motivated. This meant that authorities would often view them with suspicion and subject them to raids or occasional bans. The history of caffeinated dialogue imbued the coffee house social interior with its enduring capacity for getting things done expediently. The coffee houses of the eighteenth century were environments not only in which to socialize, but also to undertake the day's business. In London, the coffee house was an early social condenser, mixing the different classes of the city all in the pursuit of trade. The eighteenth-century British Coffee House on Cockspur Street, near Charing Cross station, designed by Robert and James Adam, was famous as both a centre of business and a stop-off for travellers. At its height of popularity in the 1840s, at least four coaches would arrive per day. This café, like many in London at the time, was situated in an ordinary town house and was reassuringly domestic in the organization and apportioning of its

14

15

rooms, a feature that undoubtedly ensured its guests' comfort and facilitated their deal-making.

The role of coffee in business and speculation was emphasized in the design of the typical Viennese *Kaffeehaus* (coffee house), an interior that played a central role in the social and working life of the city. Its layout provided space to meet and work, and also to play. Like its London counterpart, it developed in order to attract a certain clientele. But, in contrast to London's all-welcoming approach, Vienna's coffee houses were orientated directly towards the proclivities of the middle classes. The cafés provided spaces and facilities that allowed their customers to stay for longer. Games and ladies' rooms became the norm. Once invented, telephones were installed to enable business to be undertaken in the private rooms adjacent to the central main hall. The *Kaffeehaus* became a place that provided from morning through until evening, ensuring its importance in the business and social lives of the city.

THE PUBLIC INTERIOR | SOCIAL

16

17

18

Co-working, when socializing and business are combined, is a logical extension of the historic coffee house. A worker on a laptop nursing a drink and monopolizing a power socket is a familiar coffee-shop sight across the world. Recognizing this overlap between social and working spaces, Lukstudio designed a co-working environment for Atelier Peter Fong in Guangzhou, China, combining work with good coffee. Three white boxes were neatly slotted into the ground floor of an existing block, evenly distributing the spaces between drinking and working and bringing life back to the street amid the concrete structure. Co-working does not always mean workers huddled over a laptop. In Seoul, designers Workment created Eert, named after the clients, a social workspace in a three-storey 1970s building in Mangwon-dong, a rapidly commercializing residential area. A coffee and tea bar on the ground floor was organized around a long table that slid through the interior and linked up the bar and social spaces. To discourage solitary laptop-orientated working, a sewing repair shop was placed in the entrance to greet customers. Encouraging working together in a different way, the repair space fostered a more communal co-working ethos in the coffee bar.

The worldwide popularity of coffee has meant that its sustainable credentials have become scrutinized. Its ubiquity also means that consumers seek unique experiences when imbibing it. 14sd/Fourteen stones design created Koffee Mameya Kakeru by reworking an old warehouse in Tokyo for the barista Eiichi Kunitomo. The building was left as found and a rectangular white-oak frame was inserted into it on its central axis. One end signals the entrance and inside is a U-shaped bar from which the baristas prepare and serve the coffee. The interior is like a temple created to elevate taking coffee to the realm of a high-level gastronomical experience. Kunitomo described the barista's status as akin to that of a sommelier, and the interior was made in order to celebrate this focus. In stark contrast to the central role of a barista, 2050 Coffee in Kyoto is a self-service space. It draws its customers into the shop in order to raise issues around the sustainability of the drink. Created by Teki Design,

16 Lukstudio's space for Atelier Peter Fong in Guangzhou, China, 2016, was organized into three different enclosures, containing café, work and office room.
17 Workment artfully distressed the existing building for Eert Mangwon café, Seoul, 2020, to ensure that visitors felt the layers of history as they ate and drank.
18 The self-service and information hub that is 2050 Coffee by Teki Design, Kyoto, 2024, is designed to raise awareness of coffee's sustainability.
19 The elevated experience of imbibing at Koffee Mameya Kakeru by 14sd/Fourteen stones design, Tokyo, 2022.
20 Despite coffee's ubiquity, the space provides a unique experience where the barista collaborates with chefs to develop pairing menus.

its position is that, as climate change challenges coffee production, in the future the drink will become an expensive luxury. Inside the space, taps dispense five types of drip-coffee. Each comes with information explaining that an increasingly difficult problem for a world hooked on caffeine is how we will be able to feed our addiction when it becomes prohibitively expensive and scarcer in the future.

Historically, inns and taverns across the world were places where travellers could stop and be offered hospitality. They were usually located on significant roads and close to civic or religious buildings. Their popularity grew as the influence of monasteries declined. Less pious than an overnight stay in a monastic cell, inns and taverns offered more comfort for the travel-weary guests. All manner of social practices such as eating, drinking, news-gathering, business transactions and fun could be found in them. A stay might also entail fraternizing with other travellers and workers, some of whom offered illicit services, making them often unpredictable places.

Taverns and inns evolved to become 'public houses' of which the British pub is a renowned example. Pubs were often realized as a series of rooms or saloons linked by a continuous circular or horseshoe-shaped bar. This subdivision of the pub ensured that it could cater for a variety of clientele served from one place. This would sometimes include a public bar for workers, the saloon for clerks and a private bar for the middle classes. Learning from the example of the Viennese coffee house, pubs often had billiards, skittles or other games

THE PUBLIC INTERIOR | SOCIAL

21 Neighbouring rooms of the Prince Alfred, Maida Vale, London, are separated from each other by carved and glazed screens.
22 The seemingly expansive interior of the compact American Bar by Adolf Loos, Vienna, 1908, was achieved through the deployment of mirrors to endlessly reflect the ceiling.
23 La Maison du Café was designed by Charles Siclis, Paris, 1933, to expedite seamlessly its patrons' transition from the street to the bar and back out again.

rooms. With the curved bar at the centre, serving all rooms, the space could be viewed as an efficient machine, but one that discreetly differentiated its clientele. Each room facilitated the various ways in which its customers took their drink: standing at the bar, sitting, individually or as a group. The extensive use of glass in the screens separating each room, especially in the Victorian pub, meant that a sense of 'the others' in the adjacent rooms was palpable. The Prince Alfred, in Maida Vale in north London, which is still in operation today, was organized in this circular manner. It was planned around five rooms serviced by a central bar. The screens separating each room could be swivelled and opened, suggesting some flexibility between the drinkers in their allotted rooms but also facilitating quick and convenient access for bar workers collecting glasses (or stopping altercations) between them.

As Bompas & Parr demonstrated, alcohol is a social lubricant that expedites many intoxicating social events. Alcoholic drink types can influence bar design. The American Bar in Vienna by Adolf Loos prioritized cocktails, or 'American drinks', which had become fashionable. Still open today, it was announced to the street by a gaudy backlit mosaic sign. Its small footprint of 4.5 × 6 metres (15 × 20 feet) was offset with a mirrored panel running above wainscot-height around the room. This reflected the higher part of the compact bar, endlessly mirroring its orthogonal coffered marble ceiling, making what appeared to be an endless series of adjacent rooms. This spatial trick didn't just relieve the claustrophobic effects of the small interior space; like its Victorian pub counterpart, it suggested other adjoining rooms full of guests making the small bar seemed crammed with atmosphere and life.

The social importance of the café, bar, the brasserie and the pub have endured throughout the twentieth and twenty-first centuries. Their role in the city was the same then as it is today: to provide refreshment while people socialize or do business. In 1930s Paris, new types of bars emerged that either adhered to the traditional form, where guests took time to sit, drink, eat and socialize, or differed, in that drinks

would be taken standing up and often at pace. La Maison du Café, by Charles Siclis, epitomized the latter. Situated on a busy street corner, utilizing its prominent location, it opened the four bays of the existing building to the street with floor-to-ceiling doors to allow coffee drinkers to drift freely in and out. The outside corner façade was decorated with a bronze relief by Léon-Ernest Drivier, a collaborator of the sculptor Rodin. The copper and bronze bar was placed deep into the space and dominated by a series of large, shiny coffee percolators. Behind the curved bar was a fresco of people consuming coffee by the Mexican artist Ángel Zárraga. Customers would dash in to order their pastries and coffee, consume them standing, while admiring the gleaming surfaces of the café, and exit as quickly as they had entered back into the busy street. When full, the café was a blur of activity and a seamless extension of the surrounding city.

The story of the café and bar in the latter part of the twentieth century can be characterized by the desire to use any means possible to stand out and attract new clientele. The 'spectacularizing' of the interior through theming gathered pace in Japan in the mid-1980s. Designers from outside Japan working in Tokyo at the time brought an entirely different outlook when it came to capturing the unique qualities of the city. In 1986, Nigel Coates designed Caffè Bongo, a bar situated on the ground floor of the Parco department store in the Shibuya district of Tokyo. The café perfectly summed up the moment. It was a riot of styles with a series of disparate elements collaged together. The café experience began with the entrance signalled by a wing of a Boeing aircraft rammed unceremoniously into the façade. The wing continued inside the space and was propped up by a series of cast-iron columns, salvaged and imported from the UK. Pedestalled classical statues were positioned on top of it. Spanners, bolts and hinges were embedded into the poured concrete floor alongside televisions playing Federico Fellini's *La Dolce Vita* on loop. The ceiling was frescoed like the interior of a Renaissance church. The overall effect was of a theme park for the young and fashionable of Tokyo to play in.

24

25

Prioritizing speed and the impact of the experience and trend, the pop-up or guerrilla social space provides a quick-fire temporary solution to capturing the interest of the moment. The Movement Café by Morag Myerscough in London occupied a space adjacent to Greenwich railway station, and there were just sixteen days to build and open it in advance of the 2012 Summer Olympics. For speed, off-the-peg materials such as shipping containers and scaffolding were used. Tweets by the poet Lemn Sissay were painted onto panels above the café to attract customers disembarking from the nearby train. Pop-ups are designed to make an impact in the short time they are in existence. They are designed to impress upon the visitor a very specific identity, sometimes aligned with a product. The Courvoisier Bar was a pop-up that celebrated the brand and its famous white brandy-making grapes of the Cognac region in southern France. Designer Yinka Ilori channelled the waters of the Charente river into a fountain-shaped bar in the department store Selfridges in London. The colour and patterns of the circular counter were designed to suggest that the guests were in the middle of the river as they consumed samples of the drink. The pop-up was open for just three weeks before disappearing, leaving just a colourful image burnt into the retinas of anyone who saw or drank in it.

Restaurants are closely aligned to the same social impulses and collectivization as cafés, pubs and bars. Their visual impact is critical, and their ambience often reflects the type of food and the service that they provide. They can also be used to make commentaries on the issues of the day. SUPERFLEX is a collective of Danish artists who have used food and their forms of distribution to articulate particular ideas about the world. Their 2009 project *Flooded McDonald's*, painstakingly recreated an interior of the fast-food restaurant in a film studio in Vietnam and made a twenty-one-minute film of it slowly filling with water. As the water engulfed the space, packaging, along with a statue of Ronald McDonald, floated by. At the end of the film, the electrics short-circuited and the whole place disappeared into darkness. This comical yet apocalyptic

24 A collage of inspiration, from Renaissance to aircraft wing to Fellini movie, at Caffè Bongo, Nigel Coates, Tokyo, 1986.
25 Tweets by poet Lemn Sissay were painted onto the façade of the Movement Café by Morag Myerscough, London, 2012.
26 The Courvoisier Bar by Yinka Ilori at Selfridges, London, 2023, made the drinker feel immersed in the flowing waters of the Charente river.
27 *Flooded McDonald's* by SUPERFLEX, 2009, intimated complicity of large multinational companies in the escalation of climate change.
28 Times Square McDonald's by Landini Associates, 2019, was part of a plan to reinvent the identity of the world's largest restaurant chain.

movie provoked its viewers to reflect upon the food that they consume from this restaurant chain and the role that it plays in the climate emergency.

'Restaurant' derives from the French *restaurer* meaning 'to restore', or 'refresh', and it is the role of the food and the ambience of the space to do just that. Food can be fast or it can be taken at a more leisurely pace. McDonald's is the world's most famous fast-food restaurant and, since its inception in 1940, has expanded to over 41,000 restaurants in 100 countries. Its role is to serve quick and cheap uniform food to numerous customers anywhere in the world. In contrast, the interior design of its branches is often much more varied than this uniformity suggests. Brand iconography of colour and materials is often deployed in differing ways. The McDonald's in Times Square, New York, provides a serene antidote to the chaotic context outside of its walls. The three-storey restaurant is fronted by a glass façade overlooking the square. This flagship store designed by Landini Associates has twenty-one self-service kiosks aiming to serve thousands of customers per hour. Topped with a huge 862-square-metre (9,279-square-foot) billboard, the building projects gigantic images of hamburgers across the street, attracting hungry customers from all sides of Times Square.

Fast and cheap food does not necessarily mean the environment in which it is produced and consumed has to have the equivalent aethetics. The Four Seasons restaurant, designed by Philip Johnson in the Seagram Building in New York in 1959, embodied not just the food but also the importance of time in the city. It consisted of two 18 × 18-metre (60 × 60-foot) rooms with 6-metre (20-foot) high ceilings, linked by a corridor. Located on the ground floor of Mies van der Rohe's Seagram Building, in Midtown New York, the restaurant became an institution and the place for which the term 'power

26

27

28

29

29 Brasserie by Diller + Scofidio in the Seagram Buiding, New York, 2000, frames its clientele to afford particular views of their food and each other.
30 The sinuous columns of rattan in the Spice & Barley by Enter Projects Asia, Bangkok, 2020, create an identity for the interior and also discreetly hide the services.
31 A cluster of interlocking timber-lined rooms aligned with key views of London's skyline formed Studio East Dining, Carmody Groarke, 2010.
32 The temporary Zero Waste Bistro at WantedDesign in New York, 2018, was built on themes of circular economy, material innovations and sustainable design.

lunch' was coined. Johnson conceived the space as a filter of the public plaza that Mies created in front of the Seagram. In a carefully considered sequence, guests entered from the busy street, through the semi-public lobby and into the quieter seclusion of the restaurant. Diners entered and either went left to the formal dining room, which was focused around a central pool, or right to the bar and grill – and their power lunches (see p. 11). In 2000, in the basement of the same building, Diller + Scofidio redesigned the Brasserie to create a new restaurant that, in a building famed for its transparency and views, responded by interpreting looking in a new way. Diners arriving at the space were filmed as they entered. This entrance was replayed sequentially on screens above the bar. A large timber wrap enclosed the main dining space in the middle of the room, framing not just the diners but also a spectacular entrance sequence, via stairs into the centre of the restaurant. As it had been for decades, the Four Seasons and the Brasserie ensured that the Seagram was the place to 'do lunch'.

A focus on materials, their provenance and the sourcing of food in order to encourage sustainable practices and avoid waste has become critical in the contemporary restaurant. This approach may take many forms. Rattan is the name for numerous species of tree that can be used to create strips of material for weaving textiles, mats, objects such as baskets and even furniture. If farmed and managed correctly its use can be sustainable, but populations are becoming extinct due to deforestation. Rattan is native to South East Asia and architecture firm Enter Projects Asia utilized it extensively for a bar and restaurant selling beers from around the world in a glass-façade hi-rise tower in Bangkok. The interior was conceived as a series of rattan towers flowing from floor to ceiling in the glazed box. Their striking aesthetic also serves a practical purpose in masking the beer pipes, lighting and air conditioning. Modelled using software such as Maya and Rhino the sculptural liquid forms were built by local craftspeople. The project ensured the survival of two rattan factories on the edge of the city when many

have closed down due to cheaper plastic imports. The golden forms are not dissimilar to the flowing beers enjoyed by the customers.

Reusing material is a strategy that ensures localized connections between space, place, food and its consumption. In London, Studio East Dining was constructed in just ten weeks from scaffolding and other materials left over from the adjacent Olympic Stadium building site. The pavilion sat on top of an existing warehouse building, forming a series of rooms framing views of the surrounding landscape. The interior, which existed for just three-weeks, could seat 140 covers. When it closed, all the materials were recycled. All that was left were the memories of the interior and the food. In New York in 2018, Zero Waste Bistro served five-course meals to thirty diners at a time over three days at WantedDesign. The food was conceived and prepared by chef Luka Balac and used locally sourced ingredients as well as overlooked byproducts of the food industry. The most striking element of the project was the environment in which the food was consumed, an enclosure fabricated from panels made of recycled Tetra Pak cartons. The panels were sourced from a recycling plant and came in whatever colour and pattern was being processed at the time. This meant that on closer inspection the barcodes and labels of the former lives of the packaging could still be discerned in the walls. Like Studio East Dining, the restaurant was taken down and its materials dropped back into the circular economy of reusing matter.

Provenance can be made evident in numerous ways. Restaurant Moes, designed by Superuse, was a seasonal restaurant in Amsterdam relying on produce grown nearby; the same approach was applied to the design of its interior. Using a 'Harvest Map' approach, whereby material is sourced from within a specific demarcated range of the site, designers extracted over 60 per cent of its material from the surroundings. This included a series of wayfinding lightboxes salvaged and extracted from nearby Schiphol airport, giving the interior a unique aesthetic along with its local food. Provenance, expressed through reusing existing

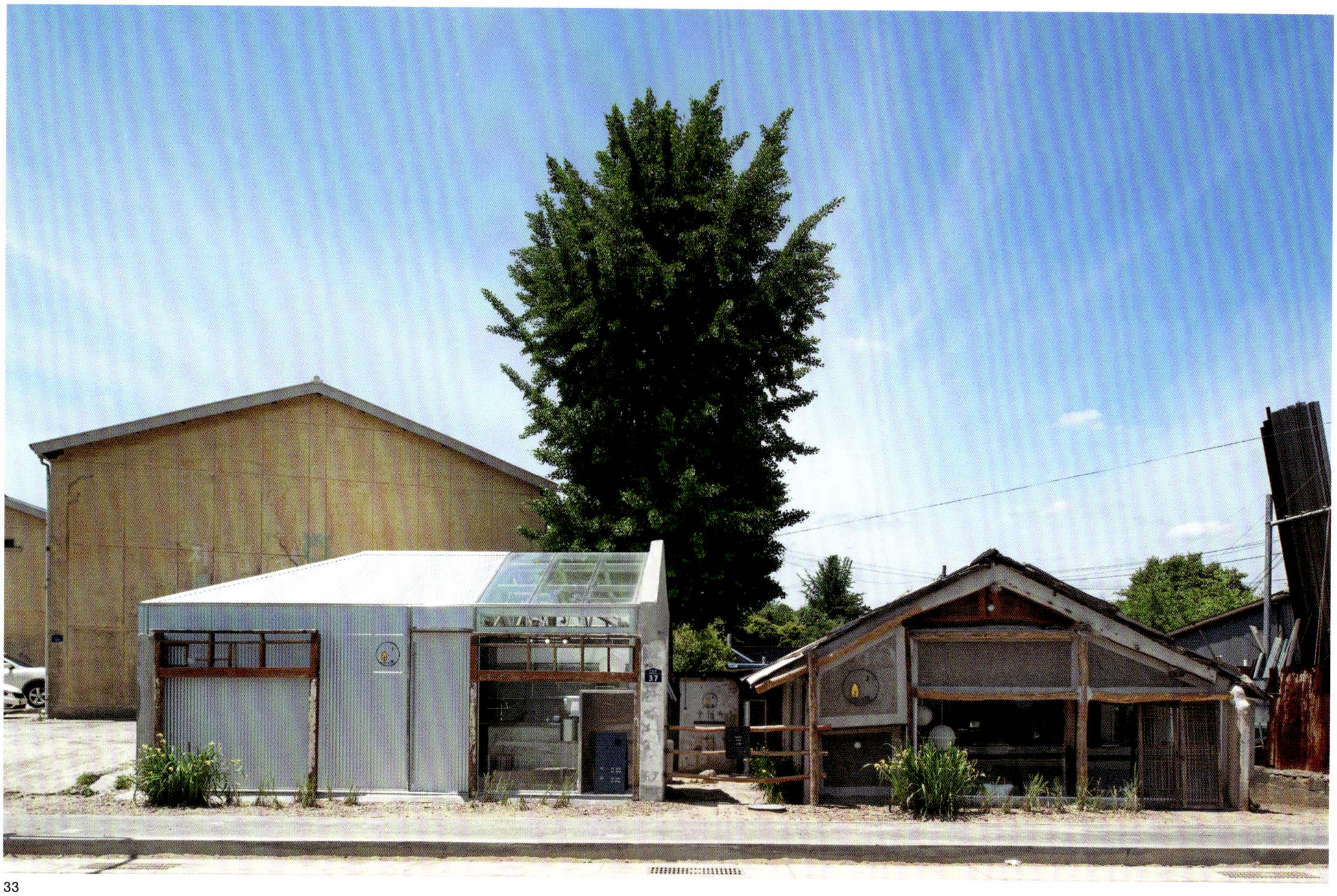

33

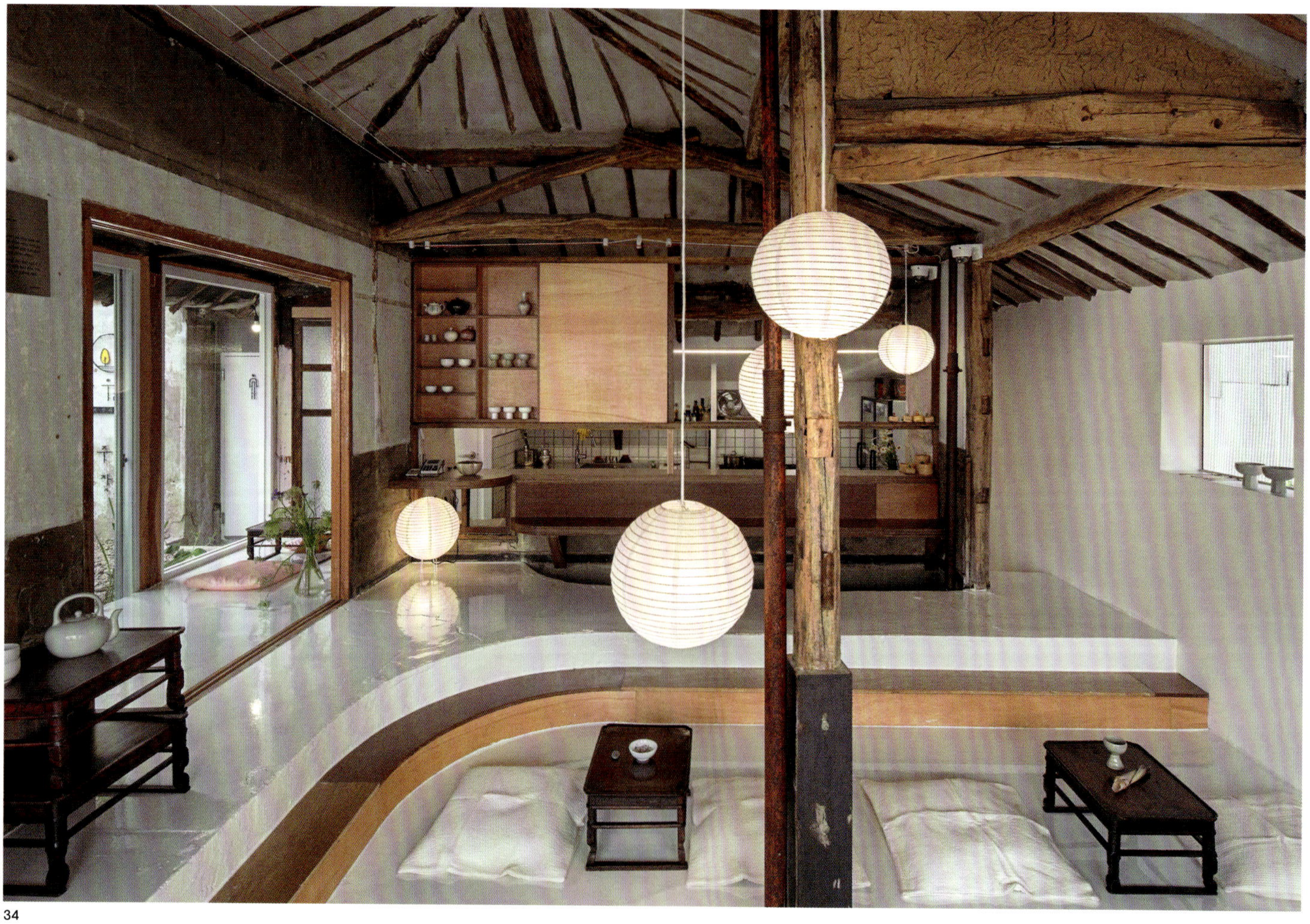

34

33 Two houses, built in 1955 and 1962, were joined together by Starsis to make the restaurant Suwŏlok in Buyeo, South Korea, 2018.
34 Instead of stripping out the years of additions and repairs, the designers celebrated the buildings' idiosyncrasies.
35 An ethos of local, seasonal food was aligned with a design approach for Restaurant Moes by Superuse, Amsterdam, 2012, that extracted building materials from the surroundings.

buildings, means that adjacencies and proximities are always critical. Suwŏlok, in Buyeo, South Korea, is a project by Starsis consisting of two roadside houses, each over sixty years old, one a timber-framed shack, the other a tin shed. Both should have been demolished, but instead the designers unpicked the buildings, exploring the layers of their respective histories and taking great care and enjoyment in the various odd and half-baked repairs made to them over time. Like a series of courses of a meal, with contrasting flavours, instead of correcting the buildings, the designers enjoyed each layer as a part of the overall story. Inside these two spaces, linked by a central courtyard, they deployed furniture, a kitchen and services such as toilets and storage, in order to make an idiosyncratic restaurant interior. Like so many social projects, the uniqueness of the space, the originality of the food and its maker were all designed to create memorable social experiences.

Alongside food and drink, social public interiors can include places to stay. The 'route' or 'destination' hotel was as much a feature of ancient times as it is today. Ancient Greek *leschai* were meeting places or simple hostels, usually on a trading route with the *pandokeion*, its city counterpart. *Tabernae* and *popinae* were common features of roads and towns in the Roman world. *Khans* were Middle Eastern and North African hostels offering travellers food and drink; monasteries and caravanserais were business stop-offs along trading routes. Contemporary hotels maintain these primary themes of hospitality and home when travelling. Conrad Hilton suggested that each hotel is a stage set with a focus on escapism. In his view the best hotels were places of discretion, where guests could go to act out their anonymity to whichever degree they desired, stating, 'In a hotel guests should find what they dream of at home'.[2] Along with Hilton, one of the most famous hoteliers was César Ritz. Learning his trade through years of being a waiter and gaining a reputation for pioneering new levels of service, he worked with the famous chef Auguste Escoffier, who at the same time was radicalizing French cooking and its methods. Together they set up the Ritz

36 Zein-o-Din caravanserai is one of 999 such inns built during the reign of Shah Abbas (1588–1629) to provide facilities to travellers.
37 The Imperial Suite at the Ritz in Paris, redesigned in 2016, includes a living room, two en suite bedrooms and private dining room and kitchen.
38 Digital displays afford a dynamic, everchanging welcome to guests in the lobby of the Cosmopolitan hotel in Las Vegas, by LAB Design Studio.
39 The New York Bar, Park Hyatt Tokyo, made famous in the film *Lost in Translation* as the meeting place for the jet-lagged Scarlett Johansson and Bill Murray.

Hotel in Paris. Artists, writers and all the famous of the day made their way to the hotel and it became the centre of late nineteenth and early twentieth-century Parisian cultural life. Marcel Proust was a patron and Ritz took great pleasure in the notion that Proust, 'did his writing in his cork-protected bedroom, but to experience life, he went to the Ritz'.³ All of the rooms in a Ritz hotel had their own en suite bathroom, unheard of in those days. Ritz originated levels of service where the customer was always right, ensuring a very loyal clientele.

The lobby is a room that in the more functional hotels will just be a desk. But in the best places it sets the tone and atmosphere of service and space. Lobbies are the stylish living rooms of their respective cities. Media such as film can make lobbies more famous than the hotel itself. The lobby and bar of the Park Hyatt in Tokyo was immortalized as the place for the jet-lagged Scarlett Johansson and Bill Murray to meet and watch over a sleeping city in the 2003 Sofia Coppola film *Lost in Translation*. Contemporary lobbies can be enhanced by media. The lobby of the Cosmopolitan hotel in Las Vegas, by LAB Design Studio is a multimedia experience that immerses guests in a space dominated by a series of filmic columns. Each pillar houses full-height screens featuring dancers activated by the guests. A dramatic reception in which to collect the key to your room.

Lobbies can be slower paced – large rooms or environments in which to relax, hang out and socialize. The elegance of the SAS Royal Hotel lobby in Copenhagen, designed by Arne Jacobsen, was formulated as a timeless flowing landscape of furniture dominated by the spiral stair that invites guests up to their rooms. In the 1980s 'boutique' hotels were originated by the hotelier Ian Schrager, who caught the mood of a trendy clientele searching for new interior locations and experiences in which to socialize. The rooms were important but took second place to the lobby, which announced how cool and attractive the hotel was to the in-crowds of the city. The Royalton Hotel, designed by Philippe Starck,

THE PUBLIC INTERIOR | SOCIAL

40 The open and flowing interior landscape of the SAS Royal Hotel by Arne Jacobsen, Copenhagen, 1960.
41 The long elevated 'catwalk' of the lobby of the Royalton Hotel, Philippe Starck, New York, 1988.
42 The ziggurat-like lobby of the Hyatt Regency by John Portman, San Francisco, 1973, dominated by Charles Perry's *Eclipse* sculpture.

remodelled an old Midtown gentlemen's hostel and the new design was based around an entrance lobby catwalk. Guests had to sashay almost the whole length of the building to get to the reception desk, ensuring a parade past drinkers and diners. Lobby inhabitants could watch each other and the arriving guests from a series of large chairs distributed across differing levels of the space. If this fashion show became tiresome, then a discreet whisky bar tucked away to the side of the entrance was available for quieter liaisons.

Lobbies can be awe-inspiring spaces. The hotels designed by John Portman, namely for the Hyatt and Westin brands, in Atlanta, San Francisco and Los Angeles were all organized around huge, monumental atriums. The seventeen-storey Hyatt Regency in San Francisco is a stepped wedge of a building. Its interior is dominated by a full height 'ziggurat' lobby illuminated by a glazed roof at the top. Guests are overwhelmed within the giant space of the public interior lobby as they circulate between reception, bar and shops, or take one of the egg-shaped lifts to the upper floors. Reusing buildings for hotels can focus on the unusual qualities of the host spaces to provide uniqueness.

The Jaffa Hotel in Tel Aviv by John Pawson was placed inside an old monastery. The lobby and the lounge were located in the chapel, a striking setting in which to meet or to just relax. Shangri-La Shougang Park in Beijing, designed by Lissoni & Partners, is located inside the remains of a derelict factory that had once been China's largest steel mill. The designers combined the remnants of the plant's industrial elements with sleek, luxurious surfaces to create a new five-star hotel. The reception and hotel lobby were designed in the 20-metre (215-foot) high cavernous main hall and are dominated by a red spiral stair leading to lounges and places to eat and drink. The fragments of the factory provide a jarring contrast to the lustrous surfaces of the hotel lobby. In contrast to the bombastic nature of the Shangri-La, the Capsule Hotel and Bookstore

43   A maximum of twenty guests can find peace and tranquillity in the Capsule Hotel and Bookstore by Atelier Tao+C, in Zhejiang, China, 2019.
44   The bar and lounge of the Jaffa Hotel by John Pawson, Tel Aviv, finished with colours picked out from the existing paintwork of the former chapel.
45   (Opposite) A former steelworks, housing 60,000 workers, now the Shangri-La Shougang Park hotel, Beijing. Lissoni & Partners, 2019–21.

in Zhejiang, China, by Atelier Tao+C was designed to emphasize reflection and quietness in the communal spaces of the building. Also designed in an existing factory building, the project is like a residential library, with books as the focus of the experience. The interior was treated as though an extension of the surrounding landscape. Guests are invited to meander through the lobby space and find a place to perch and become absorbed within the shelves.

The hotel room has the potential to create a unique space for the weary traveller to unwind in. After all, the room is the central focus of the hotel. It must deliver a domestic 'dream', according to Conrad Hilton. This might mean isolation and being completely away from other guests. The Krane is a disused piece of dockside lifting machinery in Copenhagen, which once shifted coal from barges. Now, it has been repurposed to host a small one-room hotel, a singular experience high up above the docks. Isolation can sometimes be everything in a hotel stay. Connected to the room and if designed thoughtfully, the bathroom can provide the opportunity to relax and dream. A former town hall in East London, with its municipal interior atmosphere, provided a unique backdrop for a crisp and modern new insertion. Rare Architects placed the bathroom as though an independent object within this unusual

THE PUBLIC INTERIOR | SOCIAL

46 The Krane by Arcgency, Copenhagen, 2017 affords its guests unrivalled solitary views of the Nordhavn waterfront.
47 The free-standing enclosed bathroom in the large rooms of the Town Hall Hotel by Rare Architects, Bethnal Green, London, 2010.
48 The reception and entrance lobby of the Waterhouse at South Bund, Neri & Hu, Shanghai, 2010, is located in what was once a Japanese Army headquarters.

context. Hotels, lobbies and rooms have for centuries provided unique places for the traveller to rest, often reusing buildings with complex histories as in Neri & Hu's conversion of an army headquarters into the Waterhouse at South Bund hotel in Shanghai.

Social public interiors are also nightclubs, health clubs, members-only spaces or interiors that bring communities together such as spaces of worship. These environments are all created to imbue the collective with a particular direction or purpose. They are the spaces of intoxication and places to escape the everyday whether through dance, health or devotion.[4]

Precursors to nightclubs were dance halls, jazz clubs and coffee bars; these later became discotheques and even 'super clubs'. Because of their nocturnal timescale they often accommodated unorthodox communities, people seeking like-minded souls – the counterculture. All of which required spaces in which to foment new ways of thinking. Ultimately all clubs were and still are heady places where everyday modes of being can be tested and reworked.

48

They are stages where various identities, genders and sexualities can be explored. This separateness to everyday life has ensured that their designs exemplify creative freedoms. Space Electronic opened in Florence in 1969, based in an old car engine repair shop. It was furnished with salvaged washing machines and had a parachute suspended from its ceiling. It hosted performances and events as well as an architecture school and a garden on its dance floor. Ugo La Pietra designed Bang Bang in Milan in 1968, a club underneath a boutique. Visitors accessed the club via a two-person cylindrical lift that mimicked the clothing display upstairs. Nightclubs can include 'guerrilla' activities: Smart Mobile Disco by Konstantin Grcic and Miu Miu Club by AMO were mobile and temporary event spaces, either formed into pieces of furniture or inhabiting existing structures for events. If you could not get to the club, then these mobile units would come to you.

Studio 54, Area and then Palladium in New York became *the* places to be seen and representative of the city they were in. The Haçienda in Manchester

49   Gruppo 9999's Space Electronic in Florence, 1971, was furnished with salvaged materials including an old parachute.
50   Smart Mobile Disco by Konstantin Grcic, 2018.
51   Bang Bang nightclub was accessed via a cylindrical lift hidden in Altre Cose boutique. Aldo Jacober, Ugo La Pietra, Paolo Rizzatto, Milan, 1969.

was one of the first spaces specifically designed for nightclubbing in the UK. Designer Ben Kelly was commissioned to convert a former yacht showroom to house bars, performance spaces and the all-important dancefloor. The interior was rendered as though an exterior industrial environment, using the language of the street, the motorway and the factory to delineate its various spaces. Traffic bollards and reflective motorway cats-eyes ringed the dancefloor; hazard stripes were placed upon the columns. Akin to a factory door for forklift trucks, a plastic-sheet screen ruffled the hair of clubbers as they passed through into the main dance hall. The design of the club was pivotal for many – myself included. Manchester's heritage as the first industrial city was celebrated in a post-industrial space for dancing and socializing.

Arguably, gathering people for worship is not dissimilar to assembling them to dance or socialize through eating and drinking. They all bring participants together with the aim of communing with each other to form an enlightening experience. The world of social public interiors has proposed numerous elaborate and sometimes luxuriously appointed designs that encourage and support interaction.

THE PUBLIC INTERIOR | SOCIAL

THE PUBLIC INTERIOR | SOCIAL

52 Backdrop by Keith Haring at Palladium, 1985, a former music venue in New York converted by the owners of Studio 54 into a nightclub.
53 Studio 54, New York, 1978. Iconic venues often become representative of the city they inhabit.
54 Urban landscape elements like traffic bollards and hazard stripes relocated into the night club interior. The Haçienda by Ben Kelly, Manchester, UK.
55 A place of worship constructed from off-the-peg crates. KotaKrat by PSA Studio, Tangerang, Indonesia, 2019.

But socializing can be facilitated with the most basic of means. KotaKrat was a small pavilion described as a 'space of kindness'. Fabricated from the simplest of materials, a bunch of plastic crates, it reduced waste while also providing a small enclosure within which to gather for prayer. Located in Indonesia, the first pavilion was used as a mosque, but over time others will be deployed to be used in different forms of devotion. The simple and humble stacked crate makes anuminous environment within which the soul can be focused for worship.

Collective worship, dancing, eating, drinking or just grabbing a coffee on the go, the social public interior is the space that gathers its occupants inside unique environments. Social public interiors always collectivize their occupants, often with the simplest means for the maximum gain and effect.

Shop

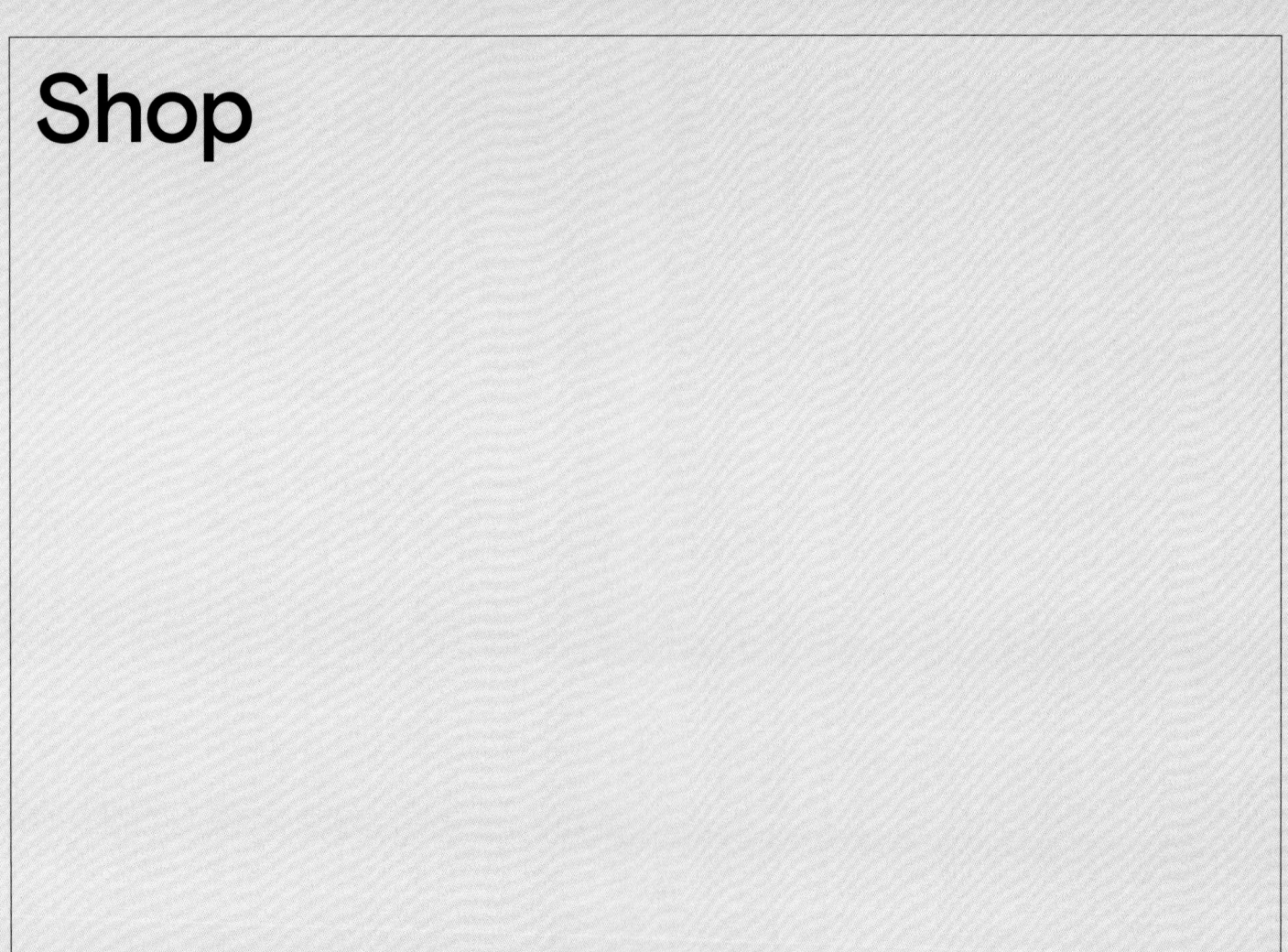

56 *Prada Marfa*, Elmgreen & Dragset, 2005, embodies the desire of acquiring something that is often inaccessible, a symbol of shopping.

On the outskirts of Texas, an incongruous sight appears by the roadside. Standing alone in the landscape is a Prada shop. The one-storey building has two display windows flanking a central door. In the windows were two free-standing plinths with handbags placed upon them. A display wall at the back of the space featured fourteen right-footed shoes in recessed shelving, all of which were selected from the 2005 Prada collection. The back-lit wall and shoes stood out, especially at night. It looks like a shop, but the front door doesn't open. Customers usually pass at speed in their cars; there is no footfall. *Prada Marfa* was designed by Elmgreen & Dragset. They made a jarring intervention into the endless landscape of the desert. The installation is a display case, a vitrine that is inaccessible and completely out of place in its context. It is an absurd feature in the landscape. The artists described it as 'pop architectural land art', an intervention that was designed to fall into disrepair and then melt back into the landscape.

Prada Marfa is an advert captured behind glass. It is one that created a longing and the desire to get inside so much that just before its 'opening' night someone broke down the false door and stole the handbags and the fourteen right-footed shoes. *Prada Marfa* represents numerous aspects of shop culture, but above all the concept of a sophisticated instrument that provokes attraction. *Prada Marfa* was designed to be a condensed emblem of the cultures of shopping. Its goal was the arousal of the need for goods, things that had to be acquired – even if it illegally.

'Shop' is a term that has been around since the twelfth century to describe a place where goods are for sale. It is related to the Old English *scoppa*, a shed made for trade. Shops have numerous types. Ancient Rome had markets, such as those built by

57 The fundamental characteristics of stalls selling goods beneath a roof have changed very little. Trajan's Market, Rome, early second century CE.

58 Goods on sale in markets often overwhelm the enclosure they are displayed within, as at al-Hamidiyah souk, Damascus.

59 The display of goods in a shop often makes for lively dialogue. A medieval street depicted in a fifteenth-century edition of Aristotle's *Ethics*.

the emperor Trajan in the early second century CE, which provided a covered space within which goods were sold. In ancient Greece, the agora was the place for stalls of goods. Bazaars or souks are an ancient form of covered market that are still in existence today, such as Istanbul's Grand Bazaar – the oldest in the world – or al-Hamidiyah souk in Damascus.

We can recognize the elements of their modern-day counterparts in medieval shops. They were often one-roomed spaces with secure storage set deeper into the interior. They usually had a counter set across the open door or archway, upon which goods were displayed and money exchanged for them. In time, this arrangement became more elaborate, the openings were enlarged, decorative goods would be displayed more enticingly and textiles would be hung around the openings to draw the eye in and towards the items. The addition of awnings protected the goods and the sellers from the weather. As in *Prada Marfa*, viewing and enticement was prioritized.

In the seventeenth and eighteenth centuries, the increased sophistication of customers and their choices of where to shop created a competitive market for trade. Forms of display needed to work harder to stand out. These developments were manifest in two types of space: the arcade and the department store. The formal characteristics of the arcade and the store were appropriated from exhibition spaces such as London's Crystal Palace. They utilized the language of large-span structural sheds, glazed top-lit atriums and the convenient circulation of large numbers of people through the space. The combination of these features with displays of commodities of all shapes and sizes from across the world proved to be a forceful precedent for how large-scale retail environments could entice customers into them and get them to consume.

THE PUBLIC INTERIOR | SHOP

European arcades such as Burlington Arcade in London (1819), Galleria Vittorio Emanuele II in Milan (1865), Kaisergalerie in Berlin (1873), GUM in Moscow (1893), or the numerous covered streets in Paris that appeared from 1815 onwards, all relieved customers of worries about the weather. Thus freed from meteorological distractions, visitors were able to wander between stores and focus on buying goods. In parallel, large department stores took elements of the city such as the street and internalized them to form the circulation between counters of products. Previously stores, or *maisons*, were only accessible once an appointment had been made or a bell rung for permission to enter. Instead, department stores were open and free, to entice the visitor into a world of products, entertainments and spectacle.

The department store was a place where goods were displayed in increasingly extravagant and ever-changing interiors. This ensured that customers could experience consumption as amusement as well as necessity. Store design utilized three fundamental principles: variety, novelty and service. Service began as you came through the door, an opening operated by a doorman to assist entrance. Legions of staff were on hand to aid choices. Variety and novelty were manifest in the entertainment of customers and the indulging of their needs and tastes. The aim was to hold customers for as long as possible inside the space in order for them to spend. The Wertheim in Berlin, a reconfigured market hall designed by Alfred Messel in a Gothic style, had huge shop

60

60 Arcades such as Galleria Vittorio Emanuele II, Milan, 1865, provided relief from weather-related intrusions.
61 The arcaded street could also enforce separation as to who might enter these spaces. GUM, Moscow, 1893.
62 (Opposite) Galerie Vivienne, Paris, c. 1880–1900.

THE PUBLIC INTERIOR | SHOP

63 Similar to the arcade, the modern department store prioritized spectacle to seduce guests into consuming its goods. Le Bon Marché, Paris in 1875.

64 This stategy is still employed to ensure that historic department stores survive in the age of online shopping. Le Bon Marché in 2023.

windows to the street, which afforded passers-by tantalizing glimpses into the main hall beyond. Huge over-scaled figures presided in the glass-topped vaulted hall, surrounded by mezzanines laden with more and more goods. Novelty and variety all mixed with good service created the buzz of desire.

The visual splendour of goods was developed alongside other forms of entertainment. In order to attract custom, Le Bon Marché in Paris organized concerts that were often attended by thousands of people. The Grands Magasins Dufayel department store, also in Paris, contained a 3,000-seat theatre as well as a 1,500-person early cinema. Marshall Field & Company store (known as Marshall Field's) in Chicago, which opened in 1902, featured orchestras. The whole interior was often bedecked in freshly cut flowers. On launch days Marshall Field's often refused to sell any goods and instead focused on the heightening of need and desire: attendees could look, they could touch, but they couldn't buy. Store owners and designers realized that the more comfortable their customers, the longer the stay and thus the more they would consume. Wertheim introduced counters selling refreshments. Coffee, cake, beer and chocolate were sold to make a visit feel even more like a day-long excursion. Extra spaces such as parlours, sometimes reserved exclusively for ladies, tea rooms, libraries, reading rooms, even gardens and a palm house in the Wertheim store, were added, alleviating fatigue, yet, even in their moments of repose, keeping customers on the premises and consuming.

All of these features of the early department store are still in evidence in today's modern counterpart. Customers in the Fondaco dei Tedeschi

Marshall Field & Co.
Retail Store

THE PUBLIC INTERIOR | SHOP

65 A souvenir postcard, 1937, demonstrates how important shops were to a city's image. Chicago's first department store, Marshall Field & Company, 1902.
66 Marshall Field's enticed customers to return to the store with changing floral displays, musical recitals and a variety of refreshments.
67 The interior of a department store is always a carefully orchestrated combination of drama and effect. Tiffany mosaic dome, Marshall Field's.
68 Display at Marshall Field's, 1945.

in Venice, which was renovated by OMA in 2016, traverse its internal streets, consuming the fine goods on offer. Cafés, refreshments and bars, along with a rooftop terrace giving visitors views across the city, all relieve the customers of the fatigue of shopping, while keeping them close to the goods on sale in the store. Galleria in Gwanggyo, South Korea, also by OMA, prioritizes the spectacularized qualities of circulation using a loop that offers views across the surrounding city. The department store contains cinemas, performance spaces, cafés and a rooftop viewing garden. The loop around the building was designed to encourage shoppers to see the city and have a dialogue with it while they consumed the goods on offer.

The arcade and the department store were superseded in the twentieth century by their contemporary counterpart – the mall. Lined with buildings distributed around an internal covered street, with places for refreshment and gardens for repose, the mall combined both types of building. The difference was that the shopping mall was out of town and prioritized visits by car. The first mall was the Southdale Center in Minnesota, which opened in 1956. It contained 7,500 square metres (800,000 square feet) of shopping space in a huge shed. Austrian architect Victor Gruen designed the centre to remind people of an idyllic arcaded European city centre, albeit one maintained at a comfortable 24°C (75°F) year-round temperature. Gruen envisaged that Southdale would contain not just stores but also medical centres, schools and houses and would essentially evoke a small city brimming with life around a central city square – mimicking the ideal urban centre it was replacing. Its central 'Garden Court of Perpetual Spring' featured fountains, plants, goldfish, an aviary, works of art, eateries and pavement cafés. The reliance on nature in mall interiors has always been a curious strategy. To incorporate landscape is considered to appease consumers' anxieties and enable them to consume in comfort. Linehouse architecture practice embedded landscape in the structure of CentralWorld shopping centre in Bangkok. Seven floors of retail

69 Contemporary department stores such as Galleria in Gwanggyo, South Korea, by OMA, 2020, utilizes the same strategies such as circulation and focused views as its historic counterparts.
70 Galleria externalizes the movement between floors to offer spectacular views across the city.
71 The central courtyard of the Fondaco dei Tedeschi, Venice, by OMA, 2016, offers respite from shopping in the form of a bar and café.

287

72 The indoor rollercoaster at Nickelodeon Universe Amusement Park in Mall of America in Minnesota takes the fundamental retail strategy of circulating shoppers to almost absurd levels.

73 Movement within an Ikea store takes the form of a prescribed internal street ensuring all customers encounter the merchandise.

74 A bird cage in the Garden Court of the Southdale Center, by Victor Gruen, Edina, Minnesota, 1956.

75 The duty free 'street' in Terminal 1 at Charles de Gaulle airport, Paris, mimics an external street where customers take a carefully managed route.

space was organized around a series of tree-like structures creating what the designers described as 'peace' in the chaos of the city. In the mall, nature can be enlisted in the service of consumption.

From Southdale onwards, the evolution of the mall gathered apace and soon numerous US cities and others around the world had them. Like its forebears, the department store and the arcade, more fantastical elements were added, not just to entice its participants to deliberate over goods but to envelop them in a fully formed fantasy of the city. Beyond the shops and cafés, fountains and gardens, malls started to incorporate more entertainment, with cinemas, theatres and even amusement parks such as in the Mall of America, Minnesota. They even overcame their reliance on the car by integrating public transport infrastructures such as train or subway stations.

Features of the arcade, department store and mall are evident in numerous forms of contemporary commerce-based environments. They are often seen in places where a focused and explicit navigation of consumers through displays of goods is required, usually when proceeding to a further destination. The micro-scaling of these formats has become a prominent feature in train stations and airport terminals. In these spaces, the interior street is often deployed as a non-linear route that provides a mixture of bewilderment and control – a potent combination in commercial spaces. This strategy is epitomized by the journey from security to gate in an airport terminal. A route that now requires the circulation of passengers through a prescribed route in the duty-free shop. This non-linear path was originated in Ikea stores worldwide, where customers undertake a carefully managed route through a series of set-piece rooms. This approach to circulation heightens the desire for goods by delaying consumption: customers see the products in context before being allowed to obtain a trolley and fill it in the second element of the sequence, the 'market'. Learning from the techniques of Marshall Field's in delaying gratification enhances the need to consume.

Like arcades, department stores and malls, market buildings have often prioritized the 'big roof'. Timber and stone structures, such as that of

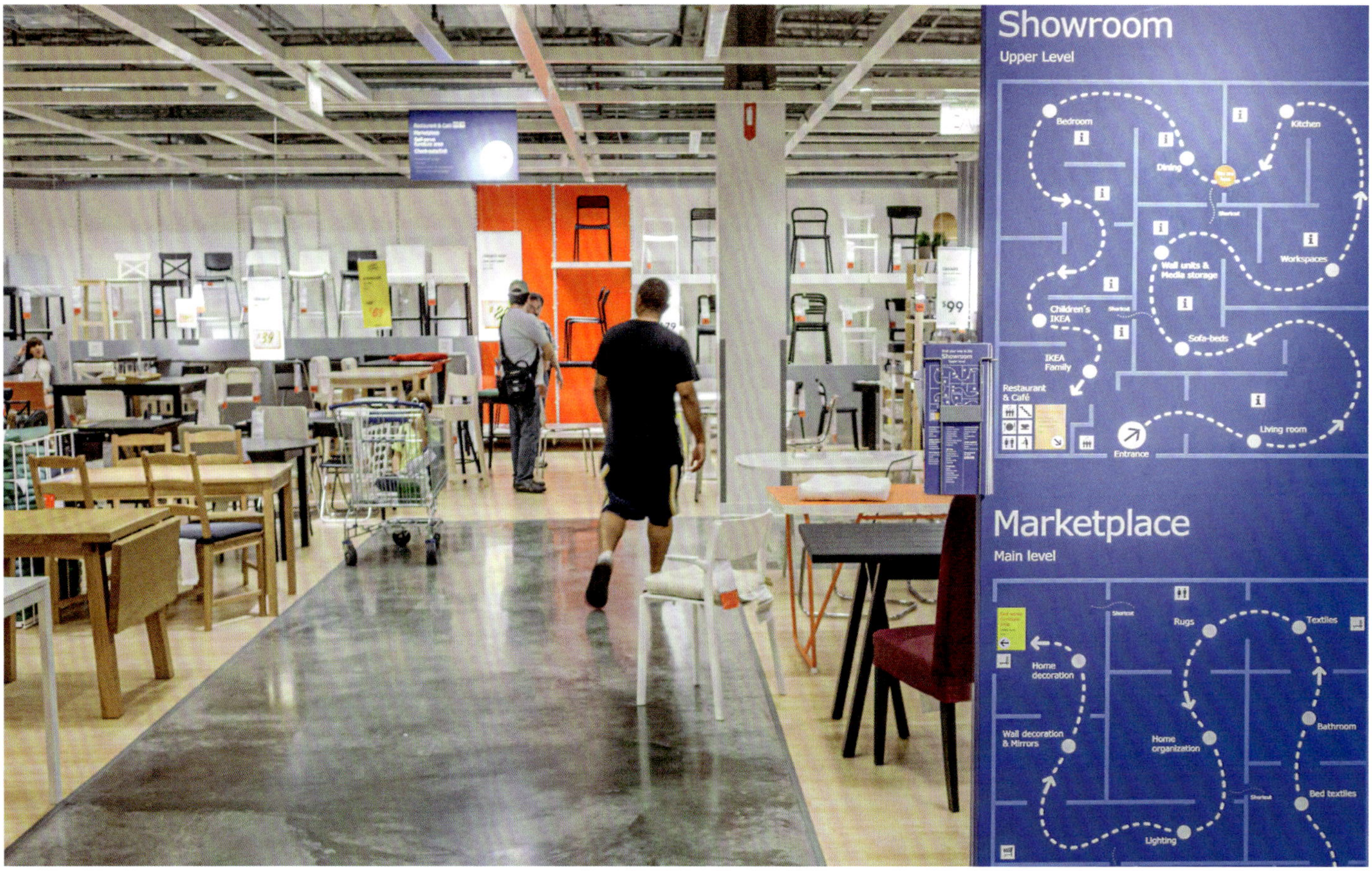
Showroom
Upper Level
Bedroom
Kitchen
Dining
Workspaces
Wall units & Media storage
Children's IKEA
Sofa-beds
IKEA Family
Restaurant & Café
Entrance
Living room
Marketplace
Main level
Rugs
Textiles
Home decoration
Bathroom
Wall decoration & Mirrors
Home organization
Bed textiles
Lighting

73

74

JO MALONE

75

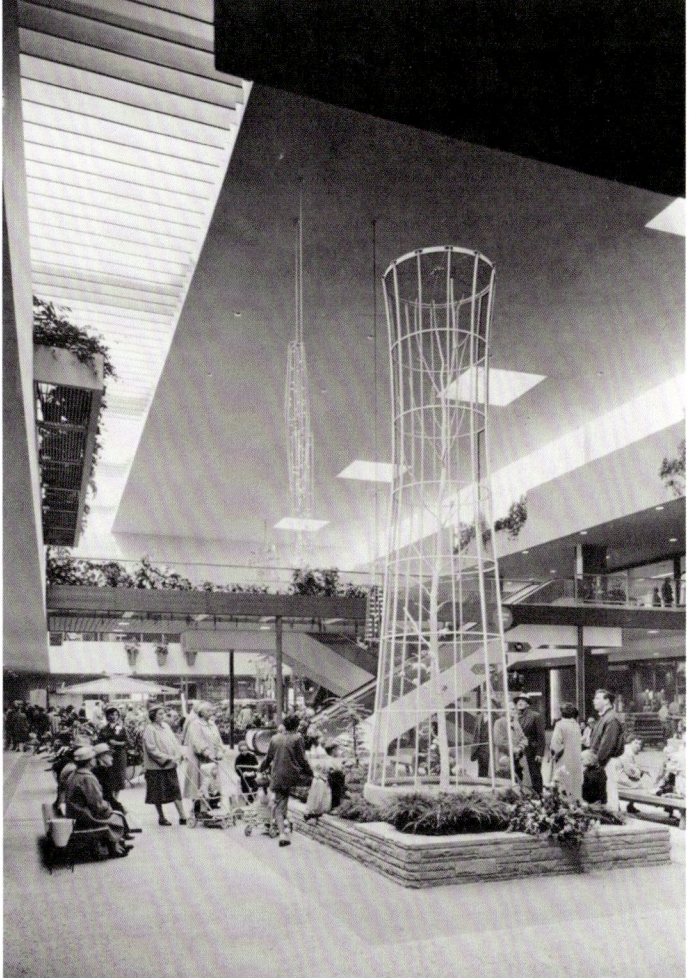

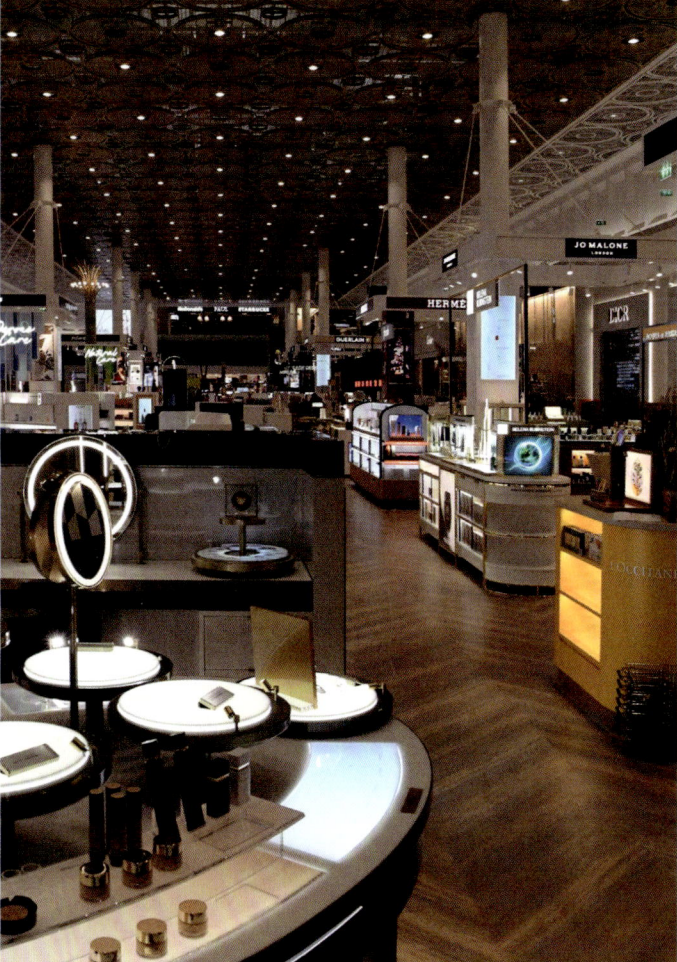

76　The underside of the Encants Vells flea market, Fermín Vázquez Arquitectos, Barcelona, 2013, reflects the eclectic jumble of goods laid out below it.

77　Mercato Rialto in Venice, has remained relatively unchanged in the same location for almost a thousand years.

78　Victor Baltard and Félix Callet's cavernous Les Halles, the central market of Paris from the 1850s until its demolition in 1971–72

the Mercato Rialto in Venice, were superseded by steel and glass. These materials had the capacity to create vast sheds that covered swathes of the expanding city. The extensive Les Halles in Paris, designed by Victor Baltard and Félix Callet in the 1850s, was inspired by the steel and glass of the Crystal Palace. The series of pavilions internalized a number of city streets, incorporating roof lights, illuminating the otherwise cavernous interiors. Its ten sheds occupied an enormous section of the city until it was demolished between 1971 and 1973. Encants Vells is a flea market in Barcelona. Its presence in the city is signalled by a huge reflective roof. It can be seen for miles around, with its underside reflecting the bustling stalls trading discarded and second-hand goods below it. Roofs cover and protect the trading going on underneath them.

Evolving from the outdoor market and introduced in the 1950s, the US 'super market' promoted a hygiene-led efficient self-service experience. The customer could circulate freely through the store and gather the goods they needed. Like its historic equivalents, the covered aisles and rows of goods were positioned enticingly at differing levels and near checkouts in order to seduce the customer into a purchase. Like the arcade and the mall, supermarket climate is highly regulated allowing the consumer to focus only on the goods. Contemporary market halls take this consideration further. In the Netherlands, recognizing that future European regulation would impact upon the sale of fresh and chilled goods in the open air, Rotterdam council commissioned MVRDV to design a new enclosed marketplace in the city. Along with extra housing and parking, the new market would provide a temperate interior climate within which goods could be displayed and sold. Like a historical arcade the designers configured the new space around the enclosing of a huge internal street. Formed by a generous curved arch, eighty market stalls are contained inside the 120-metre (390-foot) long, 40-metre (130-foot) wide 'vault'. Glazed ends not only offer views into and through the market, but also buffered external winds, helping to regulate air flow through the interior. The underside of the huge arch was finished with a giant artwork of fresh market produce, just to remind the shoppers why they were there. Markets across the world rely on similar types of structure albeit on differing scales. Atelier Masomi (now Mariam Issoufou Architects) designed the Dandaji Market in Niger with a series of colourful recycled-steel canopies. The design provided fifty-two enclosed stalls for the permanent market, shading the lots with the canopies and forming stalls with brick enclosures. The market was organized around an ancestral tree that has been an important public space for the community for many years. The public market interior reinforces the relations between food, the city and the interior in which to consume it.

At the turn of the twentieth century, the novelty of arcades and department-store sales strategies started to wane as they strove to outdo each other with increasingly extravagant forms of entertainment. The blunting of the senses through overwhelming stimuli in a climatically sealed box meant that the street and the outside world once again offered some attraction. The specialist

79 An image of a 1950s supermarket demonstrates how little the basic model has evolved.
80 The huge arch of the Markthal by MVRDV, Rotterdam, 2014, encompasses not just stalls and produce but also a car park below it and apartments in the curved roof.
81 Artwork of fruits and flowers lining the inner vault of the Markthal was designed by Arno Coenen to make visitors feel like insects as they stood underneath it.
82 The colourful shade-giving steel canopies of Dandaji Market by Atelier Masomi, Niger, 2018.

boutique emerged on the boulevards and high streets of the city. They relied on specialized knowledge and ranges of particular products for sale.

Boutiques appropriated some of the features of department stores and arcades. The shop window, circulation and methods of display were all deployed as instruments to entice custom. Adolf Loos's Knize tailors, in central Vienna, reacted to the department store in two ways. Instead of prioritizing accessibility, it clearly distinguished the public and private parts of its showroom. The lower-level shop, selling shirts, ties and cufflinks, utilized a carefully choreographed shop-front window display to entice its customers in. Then, it carefully separated the casual consumer from the regular patrons by a stair that defined the privacy of the upper-level salon. This was where the customers were expected to spend time relaxing and selecting garments for fitting. The upper level was accessed via a dogleg stair complete with a mirror through which the ascending customer was viewed by the watchful assistant. Service was then issued appropriately, depending on an assessment of the familiarity and status of the guest. Loos exploited familiarity as a device with which to make its customers feel at ease, with comfortable chairs and rugs deployed in the upper-level space. This further distinguished between the public downstairs and the private faux-domestic salon.

Knize's carefully stage-managed approach is a key feature of the boutique. Because of its smaller scale, the boutique is the purveyor of relationships, primarily between customer and product and how they identify with the brand. Boutiques have always represented a very direct appeal to specific communities and customers.

83 The domestic qualities of the upstairs showroom of Knize by Adolf Loos, Vienna, 1910–13, aimed to relax its customers as they tried on outfits.

84 In contemporary shopping, the brand–customer relationship has evolved into forms of membership represented in environments such as Rapha Cycling's 'clubhouses' by Brinkworth.

85 (Opposite) Shop assistant and punk icon Pamela Rooke outside the Ben Kelly-designed SEX (later Seditionaries with an interior by David Connor), London, 1976.

Fashion boutiques, such as Biba or SEX (later renamed Seditionaries), in London in the 1960s and 1970s were at the epicentre of fashion. Vivienne Westwood and Malcolm McLaren started Let It Rock in the early 70s, selling Teddy Boy clothes and 1950s records. They provocatively renamed the shop SEX and advanced from reselling clothes to designing and making them. SEX inspired punk and provided a meeting place for the Sex Pistols, supplying them with their aesthetic, their name and ultimately providing a springboard to fame and notoriety.

The notion of a 'club' for like-minded souls is evident in many boutiques and stores. Boutiques for sports enthusiasts address customers with very particular needs. After developing a strong online brand ethos, cycling apparel brand Rapha commissioned Brinkworth to design its first physical shops on the high street. The new stores were devised to be 'clubhouses', spaces where the consumption of clothing and accessories was not the central theme, as much of it could be bought online. Instead, clothing could be handled and tried on, but more important was the socialization around good quality coffee, food and watching cycling events on big screen TVs.

Boutiques and shops as indicators or reflections of particular consumers have not always needed to be so niche. Terence Conran's Habitat store, first opening in Fulham in London in 1964, offered utilitarian goods to the middle classes. The interior was designed to portray a very distinct identity, with whitewashed brick walls, quarry-tiled red floors and spot-lit displays of tasteful glass jars and cooking utensils. Just as Let It Rock would do eight years later, Habitat identified a particular

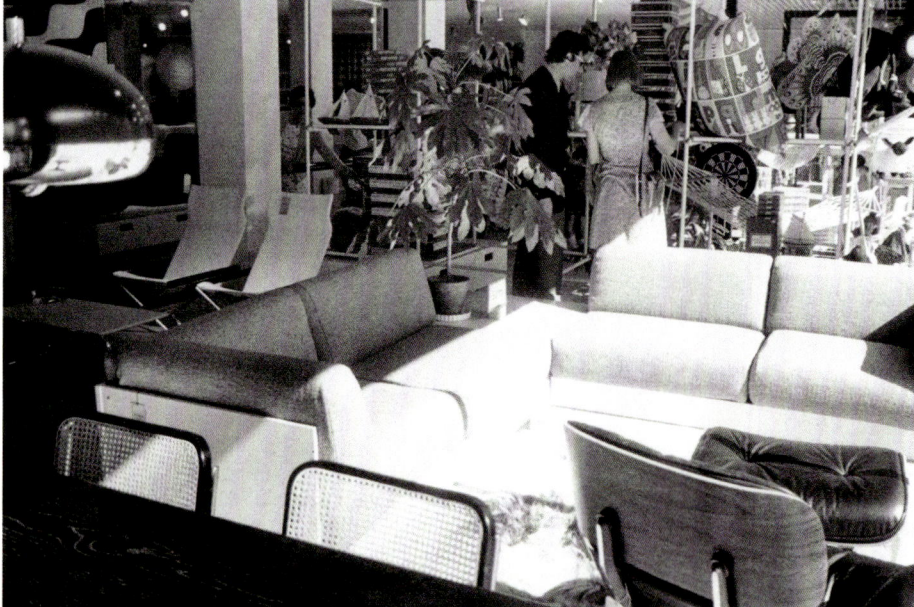
86

87

group of people who wanted to coalesce around an ideal image of their life and then buy into it.

The language and appearance of boutiques and stores on the high street changed significantly in the 1980s when interior design, advertising and marketing began to merge around the notion of brand identity. Marketers started to understand how space, identity and the product could form a seamless relationship, engineered to fashion an experience. In exclusive boutiques selling expensive fashion, the language of the modern white cube art gallery was deployed in order to display artfully placed garments like one-off works of art. Japanese designers such as Rei Kawakubo (Commes des Garçons), Issey Miyake and Michiko Koshino have utilized interior design to create gallery-like spaces where, in some instances, like the Comme des Garçons store in the Axis Building in Tokyo, none of the clothing was actually on display. It was only brought out from behind glass-panelled cupboards upon request. The gallery approach influenced store design in its striving to achieve a seamless cohesion between object, space and identity.

Like its arcaded forebears, the circulation of people among the goods is an enduring feature of boutique design. In Katharine Hamnett's store in London, designed by Foster Associates in 1984, the ultimate form of movement in fashion – the catwalk – was used to move people closer to the goods inside the space. Visitors were led into the reused mechanics garage on Brompton Road via a long glass-floored catwalk. The main two-storey showroom then opened out into one large room with its far wall clad from floor to ceiling in mirror, uniting customers with a reflection of themselves and the goods. Luring customers between levels in store design is notoriously difficult. Eva Jiřičná' s designs for the clothing brand Joseph were dominated by elaborately engineered stairs that connected floors to each other. In New York, Thomas Heatherwick used a fluid steel-ribbon display stair to unify the street and the products in one sinuous element that circulated customers to the upper levels of a Longchamp boutique. Movement is critical in store design. Objects with a close affinity to the human body

86 Customers in a Habitat furniture store, 1973. The chain was founded in 1964 by designer Terence Conran.
87 Michiko Koshino designed by Fern Green Partnership, London, 1990. A store ahead of its time with neoprene-wrapped changing rooms and a resident DJ.
88 A huge mirrored wall reflected customers as they entered the Katharine Hamnett store, by Foster Associates, London, 1987.
89 The perennial difficulty of moving consumers beyond the ground floor was overcome by Thomas Heatherwick's fluid, ribbon-like staircase in Longchamp, New York, 2006.
90 The spectacular steel and glass tensioned stair of Joseph designed by Eva Jiřičná, London, 1988.

such as a garment or shoes can be used to reinforce the link between space, consumer and object. August Endell designed numerous shoe stores for Salamander in Berlin in the early twentieth century. Due to advances in mass production the shoes were moderately priced and provided an alternative to the expensive handmade bespoke norm of shoe purchasing at the time. Endell reinforced this with the prominent display of shoe boxes around the store, defining not just the space but also the availability of the object. The Bally shoe store in Paris, designed by Robert Mallet-Stevens and Francis Jourdain, invited its customers to participate in its carefully choreographed exclusivity.

The dramatic façade used glass and chrome-plated nickel-silver to differentiate the shop from its elegantly ornate 16th arrondissement location. The interior was organized as three rooms: boutique, *grand salon* and *petit salon*. Instead of walls, spaces were demarcated by raised floors and columns. The boutique was for everyone and was the first space, while the *grand salon* was deeper into the room and formed the backdrop of the store. Its entrance was to the side and directly opposite the cash desk, with a circular stained-glass window forming the back wall of the interior. The *petit salon* was for preferred customers and only those who were invited. Contemporary shoe companies such

as Camper utilize similar approaches: in a Milan store Kengo Kuma displayed the shoes in a grid of plywood boxes. Martí Guixé added a personal touch by inviting customers to leave their mark on the interior by writing on the walls of a pop-up shop also in Milan – an approach that was then adopted in Camper stores across the world. Consumers could communicate with the brand; the performance was part of the action of shopping. The boutique became a distillation of the relationship between the customer and the shoes.

The fusion of brand, object and space in retail interiors has become an incredibly important aspect of communicating increasingly sophisticated identities. Apple stores are so seamless in their sleek and elegant combination of product and interior that it is hard to tell where the space and the devices on display begin and end. The Olivetti showroom in Venice by Carlo Scarpa was commissioned by Adriano Olivetti. Scarpa was invited to remodel a small showroom in St Mark's Square. Using an existing central column, he divided the store into two halves. Scarpa inserted a mezzanine which, by returning the visitor to the front of the shop, gave a view of the square from which they had just come. The two levels were linked by an expressive stair formed from a series of stone slabs shaped to appear as though a sculpture of display plinths. At the side of the stair Scarpa placed a typewriter, ensuring that the visitor was drawn to the centre of the space. At the edges of the room, in the shop windows, typewriters were placed on cantilevered shelves, elegantly fashioned from timber and steel. Both Apple and Olivetti are examples of the unification of product and a carefully considered retail strategy and environment.

When reusing buildings to make boutiques, the narratives inherent in the existing can supersede any seamless connections between product and interior. Instead, the space can become a protagonist that enhances the presentation of the product. While living in a squat in Zurich, the brothers Markus and Daniel Freitag started making bags from discarded lorry tarpaulins. As graphic designers and cyclists, they were inspired by the colourful lorries rattling past their

91 The availability of the mass-produced shoe was emphasized with stacked boxes lining the Salamander store in Berlin by August Endell, 1911.
92 Customers were invited to add a personal mark on the walls of Camper stores by Martí Guixé.
93 A tiered, mirror-plated display unit with built-in lighting conveyed exclusivity in the Bally shoe shop by Robert Mallet-Stevens and Francis Jourdain, Paris, c. 1928.

94 The layered stone staircase of Carlo Scarpa's Olivetti showroom, Venice, 1957, mirrors the plinth (right) built explicitly to display one typewriter.

95 Apple stores excel at epitomizing the essence of the products through the design of the display environment.

96 Freitag's ethos of reusing lorry tarpaulins lent an urban language of hazard stripes and raw materials to this store in Kyoto by Torafu Architects, 2019.

97 Atelier Tao+C repurposed a warehouse by inserting two square frameworks to create a new Ziin furniture store in Beijing, 2022.

98 The interior of the store was expressed externally via its wooden extrusions.

99 The reuse of distinctive buildings encourages unusual juxtapositions as in the church repurposed by Merkx + Girod for the Selexyz Dominicanen bookstore, Maastricht, 2007.

apartment and started Freitag by making bags for friends. Now a global brand, the unique recycled processes of Freitag bags is emphasized in their store designs. In Kyoto, the space has a designated 'micro-factory' where customers can finish their products or customize them themselves. In a store in their hometown of Zurich, the stacking of an iconic found object – the shipping container – forms a nine-storey tower advertising the brand. The tower was placed in amongst a tangle of train lines and roads, the very places that inspired the brothers to reuse lorry coverings when they initially formed the company.

Reusing an existing warehouse in Beijing, Atelier Tao+C conceived an interior for the furniture company Ziin as a piece of large-scale furniture. Two carefully crafted elements were rotated 45 degrees to provide circulation and display spaces within the large open warehouse. When reused, existing buildings with particular features can create unique resonances between the old and the new uses. In the Selexyz Dominicanen bookstore in Maastricht, an old church provided a strongly focused space for the organization of the new interior. Merkx + Girod constructed a three-storey bookcase that not only displayed the products but also illuminated the restored painted ceiling of the church. The Twiggy store by Architecten de Vylder Vinck Taillieu (DVVT) in Ghent, Belgium, used the historic existing building in a more playful manner,

94

95

96

THE PUBLIC INTERIOR | SHOP

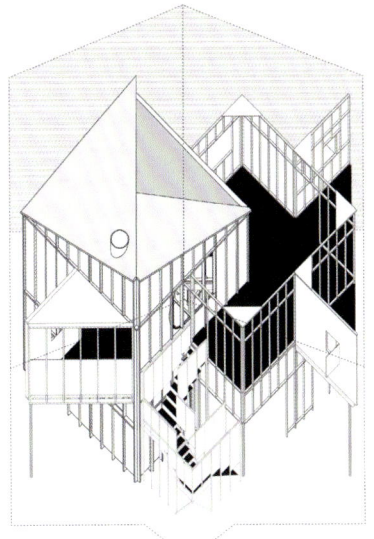 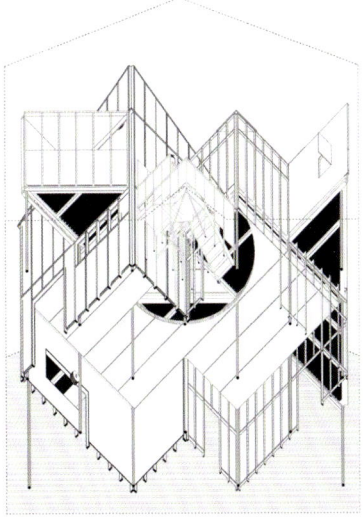 

exposing the various elements of the interior through selective cutting and demolition of the floors and walls. In the main room, a fireplace, once the heart of the room, has been left floating in the air after the flooring was removed around it. Reusing spaces to make shops always creates unique one-offs that are almost impossible to recreate in new-build interiors.

Shop windows are portals into the interior of the store through which stories are relayed via the arrangement of goods and objects. Each window is a distillation of the messages, signs and symbols of desire and curiosity. Austrian-American architect Frederick Kiesler was adept at the design of window displays. He suggested that each display was a drama with a set, characters and a plot. At Saks in New York he would drape garments, such as a fur coat, across a piece of furniture with an accessory such as a glove in order to attract the curiosity of the passing pedestrian. Kiesler understood that the fundamental forces of the window display were twofold: the ability to stop and the invitation to travel beyond the window to seek further delights inside the store. Window displays have always been the scene of innovation and provide the opportunity to charm. In New York in 1954, the Olivetti showroom designed by Studio BBPR explored how the interior could be externalized in order to draw visitors to the store. The designers installed a typewriter

100 Shop windows have to work incredibly hard to attract attention in busy urban environments. Paul Smith store by 6a Architects, London, 2013.
101 Frederick Kiesler, window display design for Saks Fifth Avenue, New York, 1927/28.
102 By removing the floors, DVVT created a memorable interior for Twiggy shop in Ghent, 2011, where objects such as fireplaces became floating sculptures.

outside in the recess between the shop window and the street. A *Life* magazine photographer set up a camera inside the store and took pictures of visitors typing. The ability to stop pedestrians, get them to contemplate the device for sale and then naturally orientate them towards the door of the showroom was innovative – but more importantly enticing.

Windows work hard to soften the distinctions between inside and out. Some, like 6a Architects' shop window vitrines for Paul Smith, offer a glimpse into the inner life of the store. Others, such as Thomas Heatherwick's shop display for Harvey Nichols during the 1997 London Fashion Week, are eye-grabbing extrusions into the street. Heatherwick's display consisted of a twisting faceted tube that raced between the stone columns of the building and slipped seamlessly between the inside and outside of the twelve plate-glass windows of the façade. The installation was in-situ for just two months but garnered huge amounts of attention. Pedestrians

THE PUBLIC INTERIOR | SHOP

103 *Life* photographer Michael Rougier taking pictures of people trying the outdoor typewriter installed by Studio BBPR at Olivetti, New York, 1954.

104 Thomas Heatherwick's wiggling sculpture for Harvey Nichols, London, 1997, united the normally separate windows.

wondered how this structure worked while motorists queried what this sinuous, wriggling sculpture was moving alongside them as they sped past on the busy Knightsbridge street.

More recent developments in physical shop design relate to how digital technologies have enhanced relationships between consumption and fulfilment, experience and brand narratives. Designer Howard Sullivan of YourStudio suggests that this development means that 'we're moving into an era of selling emotions and feelings, not "things". The products are now souvenirs of an experience.'[5] The ongoing relationships between the immaterial and the physical are where the future of shop design lies.

303

THE PUBLIC INTERIOR | SHOP

Work

105 The offices of the BMW Central Building by Zaha Hadid Architects in Leipzig, 2001–05, transcended conventional blue- and white-collar worker divisions.

The BMW Central Building by Zaha Hadid Architects in Leipzig, Germany, opened in 2005. The company has been producing cars on this site since the middle of the twentieth century. The new building was designed to facilitate the construction of 850 cars a day and specifically to integrate the mechanics, engineers, managers, design team and office workers into one connected entity. The flow of parts and people was exemplified in the building, where both the blue- and white-collar workers operated as car bodies passed overhead on their way to the next phase of the production line processes. The project illustrates one of the pervasive legacies of the modern office space. Work environments are designed to increase efficiency and the flow of information, goods, and thus money through the interior in which work takes place. The BMW plant explicitly demonstrates that sense of flow, as it contains the movement of both goods and people.

Work interiors tend to focus on the office, a space that, as design expert Jeremy Myerson pointed out, is an interior that fuses economics, politics and workers in a unique environment.[6] Offices are where many of us spend much of our work time, although the growth in mobile technologies and post-pandemic working cultures has significantly altered what might be considered as spaces to work. These days 'office' is now a considerably ambiguous entity.

It was not until the late nineteenth century, as work began to be routinely performed outside of the home, that a particular place where it was to be undertaken was created. The advent of sole-purpose offices meant that ways of relaying prestige, authority and ambition needed to be devised in order to communicate the new *working* classes. The development of new technologies with which to conduct work, such as the telegraph (1844), the typewriter (1866) and the telephone (1876), further enhanced the separation of the commercial office from the home.

An early bespoke office was the Frank Lloyd Wright-designed Larkin Building, built in Buffalo, New York in 1904. Innovative in numerous ways, it was built for a prosperous soap manufacturer to house its mail order

106 The top-lit central atrium of the Frank Lloyd Wright-designed Larkin Building, Buffalo, USA, 1904.
107 A traditional large open-plan office at a division of North American Aviation, Los Angeles, 1963.
108 The interior space of Google's Zurich headquarters by Evolution Design, 2008, is intended to encourage the initiative, collaboration and improvisation essential to 'knowledge work'.

company. It was situated next to a railroad so that its staff could easily commute. It was arranged around a full-height central atrium, a space employed as an emblem of the ambitions of the company as much as for its organizational qualities. The Larkin Building housed 1,800 office workers who would process over 5,000 customer letters and enquiries a day. The orthogonal brick building was organized around the top-lit 23-metre (75-foot) high atrium with office spaces arranged on each of the floors overlooking the void. In an unusual move the company's managers' offices occupied the ground floor at the base of the atrium where they could be overlooked by the workers. The top floor was where the staff canteen was located, with access to a rooftop terrace. This reversal of the traditional office hierarchies spoke volumes about the company's ethos and the forward thinking of the Larkin family. Air conditioning, the first of its kind, was integrated into the design of the building. There was a classroom, lockers for staff and an adjacent branch of the Buffalo Public Library. It was not all democratic. Any conversations unrelated directly to work were frowned upon on the office floor, and workers were reminded repeatedly of the company's exacting ethos – 'Intelligence, Enthusiasm, Control' – inscribed across the atrium walls. The building was controversially demolished in 1950, but the factory-like efficiencies of its operations lived on. Its success provided a template of ideas that have endured in office design throughout the twentieth century, including concepts that are present in the BMW factory production line that started this chapter.

The early modern office was inspired by the factory floor, with processes of mass production being applied to clerical work. This combination of office and factory was inspired by the work of US engineer Frederick Winslow Taylor, who studied time and

106

THE PUBLIC INTERIOR | WORK

107

108

motion in factory production in order to understand how it could be applied to offices. 'Taylorist' principles were incredibly popular in the early twentieth century with their efficiencies enabling the rationalizing of space as though a machine. Taylorism essentially took the processes of work and divided them into separate parts, each undertaken by a worker trained to perform that duty. Thus, along with specialized office furniture and equipment, and new organizational structures with which to oversee operations, mechanized factory-line production could be put in place to rationalize any type of work. This had the same effect on offices as it did on the factory floor. Workers became more specialized and therefore less widely skilled; instead they were utilized as a component in a mechanized system. It was often one that relied on them processing and dispatching their part of the job quickly and with a minimum of fuss. Early twentieth-century office interiors mirrored these structured processes. The standard endless line of workers or cubicles mirrored the production line of a factory floor. It's an idea that has been difficult to shake off in work interiors.

The opposite of this approach is what has been referred to as 'knowledge work', taking place in the 'networked office'.[7] An early adopter of these types of workspaces were big brands such as Google. The company's Zurich headquarters, built in 2008, relied less on the factory-like efficiencies of its staff and instead encouraged its workers' initiative, collaboration and improvisation, all nurtured in an environment that supported play. This creative workspace contained meeting cabins, 'hot-desk' workstations, slides between floors and sports courts, all installed to encourage knowledge workers to feel unrestricted and thus stimulated in their work. It is a model that is prevalent today.

The Taylorist and 'knowledge worker' approaches have been supplemented by a third type of space, one that emerged in the mid-twentieth century and which combined elements of both practices. Referred to as the 'socially democratic' office, its clearest expression was formulated by the Quickborner team, who pioneered the concept of the *Bürolandschaft* (office

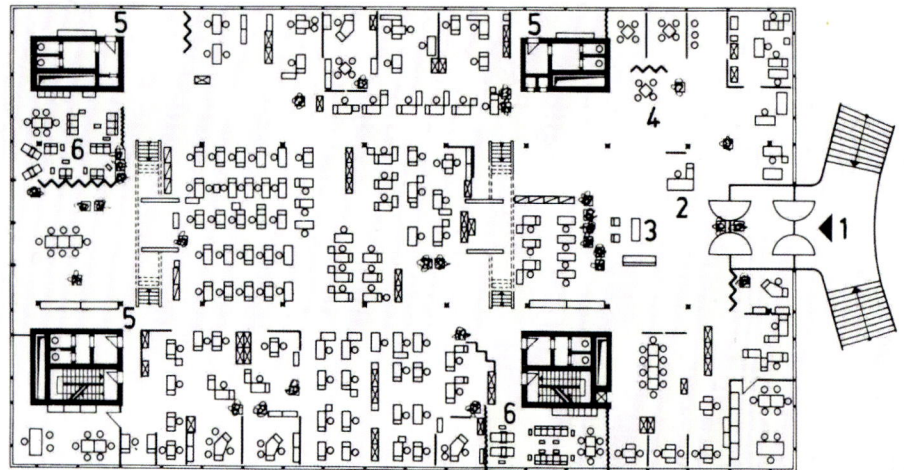

landscape) in the mid-1950s. This was effectively a planning strategy for large corporate structures, often basing their workforces in bespoke deep-plan office buildings. Large North American corporate giants like Seagram and Union Carbide commissioned Modernists such as Mies van der Rohe and Skidmore, Owings & Merrill (SOM) to design these huge structures for thousands of workers. Utilizing *Bürolandschaft* strategies for their workspaces was based on a deep systemic analysis of the flow of work and people in the companies they were designing for.

Before *Bürolandschaft*, office environments were highly structured hierarchical environments. While Modernist architects espoused transparency, honesty and truth to materials, the interiors were anything but. Executive offices were prioritized and given windows around the perimeter of the floor plate. The mostly male executives surrounded the predominantly female secretarial and clerical workforce, who were usually located centrally in windowless ranks of artificially lit desks. *Mad Men*, the HBO television series, portrayed these interiors (and the gender politics of the workplace) in exacting detail.

Bürolandschaft recognized that Taylorist divisions of labour was actually decreasing efficiencies, primarily by disenfranchising the workforce. *Bürolandschaft* strategies encouraged a more human-centred democratic approach to the office interior. It was proven that they increased output due to the improved satisfaction levels of the workers. *Bürolandschaft* appeared unstructured in its organization of floor plates of office furniture, but it was actually a systematically planned layout that encouraged interaction between staff. This was achieved through specific routes through the office and the positioning of the break spaces such as coffee bars and dining areas. To encourage sociability, Quickborner dispensed with specific break times, reversing officially regulated Taylorist break times. Instead, food was available throughout the day and night, allowing workers to freely associate when they wanted to. The breaking down of barriers in the office, creating open and large organizations of tables, chairs

109 Quickborner's systematic analysis of workers and their circulation gave rise to 'office landscaping' as demonstrated in this plan for Boehringer Mannheim, 1960.
110 The set from the HBO series *Mad Men*, designed by Claudette Didul-Mann, forensically recreated mid-twentieth century Manhattan office environments.
111 The sharply defined geometries of Natalie de Blois's workspaces for the Union Carbide Building by SOM, New York, 1960.
112 Natural light was filtered atmospherically to create a calming environment in the reception of D. E. Shaw offices, Steven Holl Architects, New York, 1992.
113 The dynamic interplay between old and new in Google's Los Angeles headquarters housed in the seven-storey former Spruce Goose hangar by ZGF Architects, 2018.

and even strategically placed pot plants, relied on carefully controlled environmental conditions. Low ceilings reduced acoustic variance, and artificial lighting was deployed in the deep plan in order to illuminate each workspace. While also assisting the acoustics of the interior, carpets were used to add a domestic and homely feel to the workspace. At the time it was deemed a radical design initiative. This approach was to remain popular for decades and is still used in some offices.

Reusing existing buildings to make workspaces means that the host building, especially if unusual, can form a part of the narrative of both the workers' and company's identities. Google's headquarters in Los Angeles, designed by ZGF Architects in 2018, made use of a huge 229-metre (750-foot) long hangar space built by Howard Hughes in 1943 to house the 'Spruce Goose', his huge Hercules IV seaplane. The seven-storey twin-shed building was designed to host the workers in a playful landscape of elements distributed around a central street. The reuse of existing buildings to make networked offices is a response to the demands of knowledge-based economies and advances in digital technologies. Steven Holl designed a networked workspace for the D. E. Shaw office, reusing the thirty-ninth and fortieth floors of a New York skyscraper. The office houses scientists, economists, physicists and mathematicians who advise investors via their analysis of the shifts in stocks and shares across global markets. The space needed to accommodate the various time-zone impacted shifts that track global financial markets. Holl devised a calming light-filled environment that reduced and filtered the views across Manhattan and focused views onto the screens. Though locked into an expansive global network, each trading desk was contained in a cellular room.

Due to the advances of mobile technologies, networked spaces are less tethered to a specific building or location. The new work economy has advanced from bricks and mortar to knowledge. In this context, any physical environment now needs to be intelligent and a memorable place to go and work in. Brooks + Scarpa's work on the West Coast of the US, for companies like Reactor Films, XAP Corporation

and Jigsaw Editorial Studios, used existing abandoned warehouses in order to contain new creative, flexible workspaces. They were bold and striking statements on how interiors were communicating a workplace's identity to potential clients. For Reactor, a shipping container was deconstructed to make a bold shop-window statement. Jigsaw saw its black-box editing suite facilities contained inside ping pong ball-encased steel-framed boxes, floating in shallow pools of water. XAP received a series of free-standing sculptural elements within a warehouse in Culver City, Los Angeles. New meeting rooms were located in leaning steel-framed curved walls. These spaces were designed not only to enhance the working lives of the users but also to impress brand identities upon prospective clients.

The shift towards the intangible aspects of knowledge reinforces how work environments need to become statements, places where the narratives of a company and its ethos can be constructed to enable workers and clients to engage with the brand. The networked workspace is scenography; it is transient 'brandscaping'. Olson Sundberg Kundig Allen reworked a machine factory into new offices that had initially been partially renovated. This process left unused building material that the designers used to make the offices, meeting rooms and worker spaces for the advertising

114 Elements such as shipping containers can bestow appropriate 'everyday' properties on interiors where identity is critical. Pallotta TeamWorks headquarters by Clive Wilkinson, Los Angeles, 2002.

115 Using salvaged material, Olson Sundberg Kundig Allen conceived advertising firm Sedgwick Rd's headquarters as an open workspace that reduced traditional hierarchies, Seattle, 2003.

116 Marimekko fabric-covered lampshades provide both light and acoustic baffles over the large concrete table workspace of Mother, Clive Wilkinson, London, 2004.

agency Sedgwick Rd. Scenographic approaches utilize dramatic elements. Pallotta TeamWorks is an LA-based charity fundraising company and it would have been inadvisable to create a slick, glossy workspace for such an organization. Clive Wilkinson Architects used off-the-peg elements, shipping containers and tents to create an environment that was appropriate for the client. These elements had the benefit of being able to be separately environmentally controlled. To heat and cool the whole building would have been a prohibitive cost for such an expansive space. The containers could also anchor the tents which were flexible spaces that could be extendable or retracted, depending on the space needed for meetings or events.

'Stage-set' approaches can be extended to creating distinct elements such as furniture. Mother is an advertising company in London that started with the distinct ethos of being a non-hierarchical company. As its success led to growth in staff numbers, an approach was needed to soften any distinctions between workers. Clive Wilkinson designed a huge concrete table that circulated the entire floor of the East London warehouse office. All of the 200+ staff could be seated at the 76-metre (250-foot) long, 7.5-centimetre (3-inch) thick piece of cast-in-place concrete. In order to offset the harsh echoic qualities of the table, large colourful lampshades were hung from the ceiling, lighting the open-plan space and ameliorating any reverb.

Existing buildings can make memorable workspace environments. A disused fifth- and sixth-floor bowling alley in Tamachi, downtown Tokyo, was chosen to house the new TBWA\HAKUHODO offices. The company was

117 Grass-covered project rooms emerge from the floors of the former bowling alley like hills in a landscape in the TBWA\HAKUHODO offices by Klein Dytham, Tokyo, 2007.
118 The floating interventions in the grand banking hall of Expensify by ZGF Architects, Portland, Oregon, 2017, were designed to be removed when the company's lease expired.
119 The curved timber roof requires minimal supporting structure thus enabling an open interior workspace in Sanno office by Studio Velocity, Okazaki, Japan, 2020.
120 The large expanse of the dish-like roof at Sanno creates a new outdoor workspace for meetings and socializing.
121 Rather than a traditional fixed-seating approach, Kinzo's Amorepacific headquarters in Seoul, 2019, favours an 'event' landscape for occupants to choose the working location that suits them.
122 A WeWork co-working space in Manhattan, New York, 2019.

a new American–Japanese venture. Its first home needed to be a distinct environment. Klein Dytham architecture utilized the deep plan of the two floors to make a linear space in which the flow of workers, their desks and the rooms in which they held meetings all complied with the bowling alley-lane plan. In each of the lanes the floor lifts to make an enclosure, a meeting space for the staff to get some privacy in the new space. To complete the aesthetic, the designers decked the alleys in timber strips with garden furniture laid out in the break-out spaces. Artificial grass on top of the meeting rooms gives the appearance of a small park inside the cavernous floor space. A project for Expensify in Portland, Oregon, used the grand backdrop of the atrium of an early twentieth-century bank building to provide the space for a dramatic new insertion. The bank was designed in 1916, yet its designers opted for a traditional, classical language, undoubtedly designed to communicate reassurance and solidity in its handling of its customer's money. ZGF reworked this power and energy but channelled it in a different fashion. In the main banking hall two new double-height contemporary meeting rooms were cantilevered into the space. Both had open meeting spaces on top of and below them; a hanging chaise longue under one reiterates the informal response to the grandeur of the surrounds.

New-build workspaces exemplify networking, flow, efficiencies and democracy. Amorepacific commissioned David Chipperfield to design its new headquarters in Seoul in 2017; Kinzo was asked to design workspaces for the twenty-first floor of the building. The interior was designed to be a landscape of 'events' that supported all manner of working. Individual rooms for private moments are located alongside expansive open terraces of seats and books for communal talks and presentations. The interior relayed the essences of the networked knowledge-economy workspace. It was a landscape of interaction. Sanno's office in Okazaki, Japan, by Studio Velocity created a similar landscape of opportunities. In a dense residential location, the designers realized that the workspace could be accommodated in one large room that filled much of the site. This left no space for exploration and chance, so they used the new roof as a workspace. The curved timber roof could be used for meetings, taking time out to catch the sun or even just eating lunch. Working and play were combined on top of the ground-floor office.

Networked space is a phenomenon that can be characterized by

119

120

121

122

co-working. Co-working was initiated by software engineer Brad Neuberg when, out of the boredom of working alone, in 2005 he invited colleagues and online friends to come and work together. He initiated this group in a place called Spiral Muse, a feminist collective in San Francisco. This idea has grown into a billion-dollar industry, with 35,000 co-working spaces across the world, a figure which in the US alone is expected to contribute to 30 per cent of all workspaces by 2030.[8] Co-working spaces take social democracy, networking, and the knowledge economy models to a new level of thinking. Interiors are characterized by a series of environments to rent on short- or longer-term leases. These are supported by a range of services such as refreshments and networking opportunities. In the age of work precariousness, exemplified by what is often referred to as the 'gig economy', a flexible approach to contracted staff and how they operate in their fields means that workspaces to house these new forms of operating will be prevalent in the near future and beyond.

Workspace futures are based on the fixed versus nomadic dichotomy and how workers can feel supported and part of a community. The Covid-19 pandemic has significantly challenged these relationships. The fixed office space, with its associated overheads and the time cost of the commute back and forth to it, in relation to the challenges and benefits of staff working from home has created challenges in how work is undertaken.

123 Home to approximately 120 businesses, the B:HIVE is the largest co-working space in New Zealand. BVN with Jasmax, Auckland, 2019.

124 The Wing was a women-focused co-working and social club that was formulated to enable users to relax between business meetings.

125 *Saint Augustine in His Study*, Sandro Botticelli, 1494–95.

Companies need to support their staff and workspaces need to reflect these demands. The Wing was a women-focused co-working space that operated between 2016 and 2022 in New York. Its exponential growth was due to its support of the professional advancement of women. The workspaces are social rooms with a 'little wing' for children. Workspaces that speak to the explicit support of workers means they will come back into the office. Smales Farm in New Zealand re-engineered an office/industrial park into a new hub of small companies and start-ups. This created a village of collaboration with flexible, community-based working. The five-storey B:HIVE building was organized around a central open atrium and 'park' of spaces where meeting rooms, open events and the 'farm' community were intended to overlap with each other. Designed by BVN with Jasmax, the space was created to house the community in a completely flexible, open building.

Saint Augustine in His Study, a painting by Botticelli from 1494–95, demonstrates how work is enabled via furniture. It shows Saint Augustine, patron saint of theologians and printers, sitting in an alcove on a carefully fitted writing desk. The books he needs are close to hand and disused quills litter the floor around his feet, suggesting he has been busy. The relationship between the furniture and the building is fascinating. You wonder what came first, the alcove or the desk? How did Augustine even get behind the furniture in order to write? But what is really important is the curtain. Augustine may choose to close it and secrete himself away or draw it back to watch whatever is in front of him. This simple vignette of working life portrays the centuries of enduring thinking in the design of workplaces, the furnishings that they need and the rooms surrounding them. Workplace furniture has always been rationalized and increasingly ergonomically orientated in the name

123

124

of instrumentalizing the management of work.

Office is derived from *officium*, the Latin word for service, duty and business. *Bureau*, the French term for office, is also closely related to furniture precisely because it derives from the Old French *burel*, a wool covering for a tabletop. Office furniture constitutes the elements that really personify and characterize work. Taylorist approaches prioritized furniture that enabled efficient production. Desks and chairs were designed to aid flow and reduce the worker occupying them to but one element of the machine of production.[9] Desk features such as pigeonholes, roll tops, even legs, were all systematically rationalized and either removed or made thinner to reduce forgotten papers and decrease dust (illness would cost the company money as a worker would be unable to work). Drawers were frowned upon, as this encouraged hoarding and the possible loss or slowing down of the processing of documents. The modern efficiency desk, designed in 1915, epitomized Taylorism. It was little more than a timber top with legs. Chairs were also scrutinized for efficiencies. Fatigue was considered the enemy of profit, so new chairs were invented that were slightly more comfortable. The longer the worker could spend at their desk the more they could work. Technologies such as the typewriter, dictation machines, and latterly the telephone, desktop computer and wireless technologies have all significantly altered office furniture and how the workplace is organized.

Companies such as Hille, Knoll, Steelcase and, most famously, Herman Miller, became the twentieth-century experts in office furniture design. Herman Miller had been in business since 1905, but it was the addition of the designer George Nelson to the company in 1944 that had the most impact on the firm's output. It took three years for Nelson and Robert Propst, head of research, to create a new work environment: the Action Office. Its first iteration, AO-1 released in 1965, was a flop. This was after Nelson's intervention, which ensured it was beautifully designed; but it was too expensive. But AO-2, released in 1968, caught the mood of the time and

126

was a critical success. The system was essentially a kit of parts and could be deployed in a number of ways, both in ranks and in a freer plan reminiscent of *Bürolandschaft*. Primarily, it was considered egalitarian: anyone could have it and thus whole offices could be kitted out in it, ensuring no status differentiations between managers and workers. AO-2 is still in production today. The cubicle has often been the recipient of jokes in the history of office furniture as it represents the exemplar of 'battery-hen' Taylorist approaches to work. In Jacques Tati's 1976 movie *Playtime*, the cubicle represents the absurdities of the modern world through its rigid planning and dehumanization of its workforce. In 'Tativille', the nickname for the city visited by the character Monsieur Hulot, workers are reduced to atoms within the extensive labyrinth of cubicles and glass-walled interiors. But the cubicle doesn't always have to be rigid or inhumane. Studio Autori designed the Catena Media workplace in Serbia using a greenhouse full of vegetation. Rather than treat the occupants as animals in a pen, workers have privacy and a space to concentrate amongst the greenery. Cubicles can also be useful and contain services that need to be tucked away. A bathroom or kitchen, technologies such as copiers and printers, and storage can all be cellularized. In Studio Represent, architecture firm Alder Brisco contained all of these in a timber box akin to a small building.

Office furniture has always had the opportunity to facilitate radical experiments in the creation of workplaces. The multi-purpose micro office by LUO Studio demonstrated how the floors, walls and ceilings of a space can be flexible. Cubicles could be made into movable walls and tables to facilitate all kinds of different working arrangements. The Love Table by Édouard François encouraged

126 Robert Propst and George Nelson's aim for Action Office II, Herman Miller, 1968, was to make a flexible environment in which to encourage spontaneity and idea-sharing.
127 The first iteration of Action Office, 1964, relied on individual pieces of furniture to make workspaces. The second introduced modularity and more flexibility.
128 The Ethosspace system, designed by Bill Stumpf and Jack Kelley for Herman Miller in 1984, is still in production today because of its adaptability to the workspace's changing needs.

THE PUBLIC INTERIOR | WORK

129 In the 1967 satirical silent comedy *Playtime*, by Jacques Tati, Monsieur Hulot gets lost in an office characterized by a maze of incomprehensible cubicles.

130 The necessary separation of meeting and workspaces in the Catena Media offices by Studio Autori, Belgrade, 2017, was offset with plants and soft textures.

131 Meeting and service rooms for Studio Represent were introduced to the former warehouse space in the form of spruce-plywood timber boxes.

132 In offices for Studio Represent, London, 2019, Alder Brisco architects retained and painted white the goods elevator frame, gears and pulley wheel.

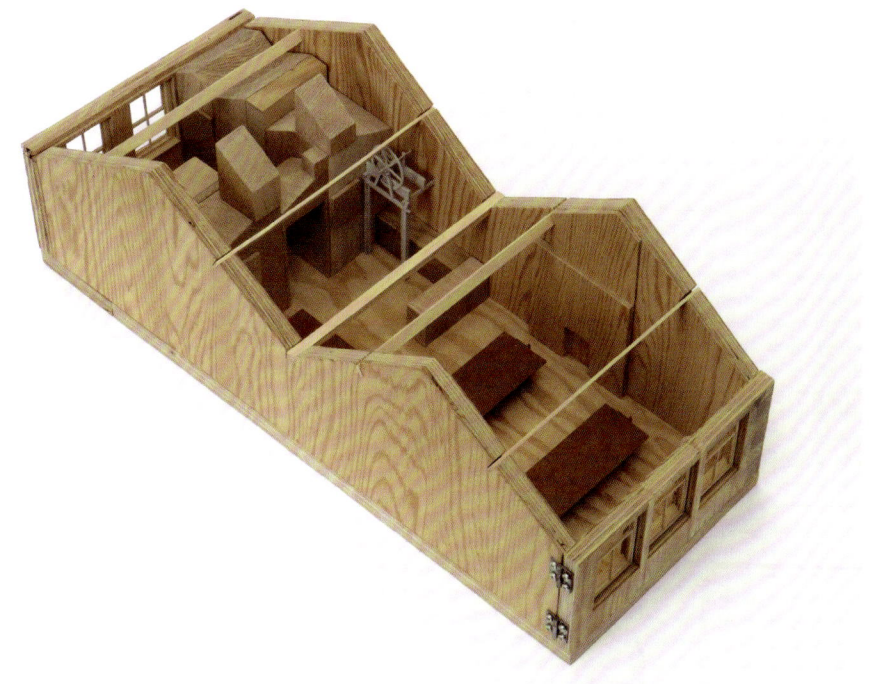

THE PUBLIC INTERIOR | WORK

133 The micro office by LUO Studio, 2019, is composed of several minimal modular units that integrate the basic elements for working: seat, desk, cabinet, lamp and socket.

134 An alternative to the open-plan office, the Love Table by Édouard François is a single piece of furniture that allows individuals to express their personality while remaining part of the collective.

135 (Above and below) Pop Up (Corner Bench) by Liddy Scheffknecht and Armin B. Wagner creates the potential for anyone to set up an office wherever they like.

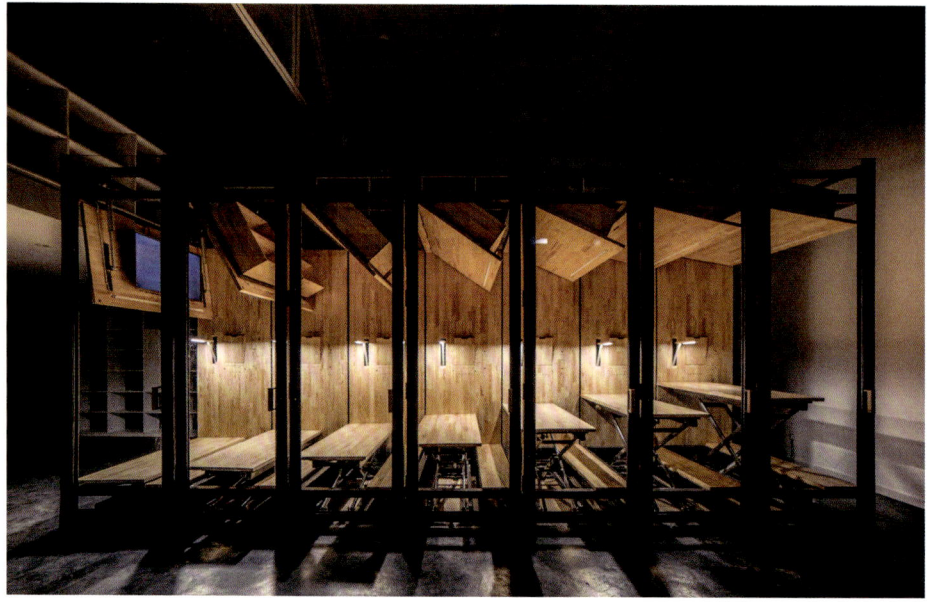

intimacy. The pop-up cardboard office by Liddy Scheffknecht and Armin B. Wagner and the Work at Home office by Studio Makkink & Bey created a portable home-office enclosure. Work furniture always represents the direct connection between the worker and their environment.

Contemporary ways of working do not necessarily reflect Taylorist ideologies or networked or *Bürolandschaft* strategies. Instead, work can be viewed as less structured, even an organic way of developing people and the city. The contemporary language of start-ups, incubators and work hubs are commonplace. When brought together they can invigorate cities and with careful consideration energize regeneration. The textile factory La Laguna was built in 1920 by a German family in Mexico City. Its success in garment production was curtailed in the twenty-first century when economic conditions in the fashion industry changed. The 4,500 square-metre (48,438 square-foot) factory was reinvented to become what its owner described as a 'factory of factories'.[10] Utilizing the building as a space that could be adapted for new uses, La Laguna was reworked to regenerate community as well as undergoing economic reconfiguration. Designated as a trade workshop project after an earthquake in 2017, businesses such as coffee producers, ceramics and architecture studios,

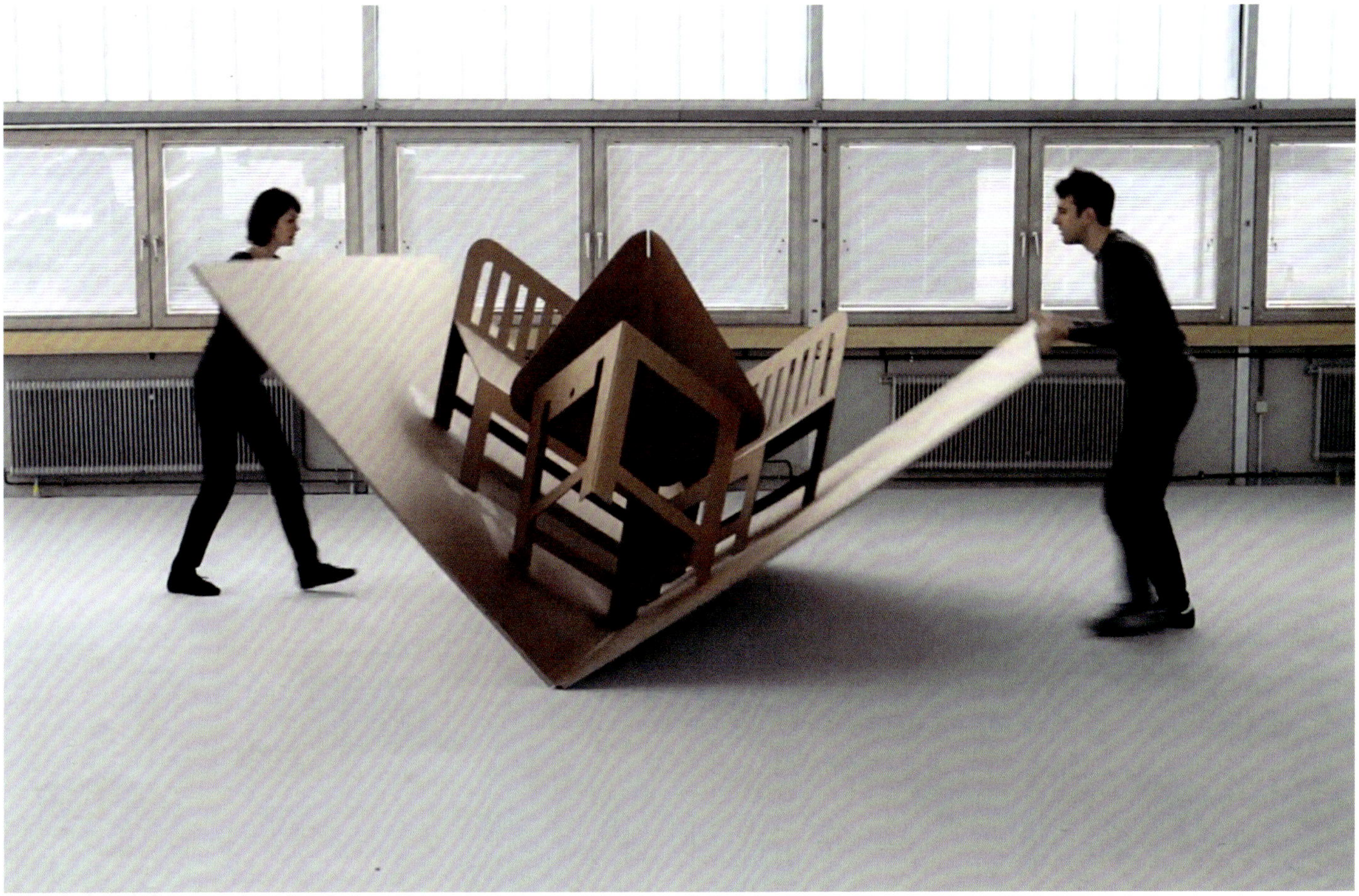

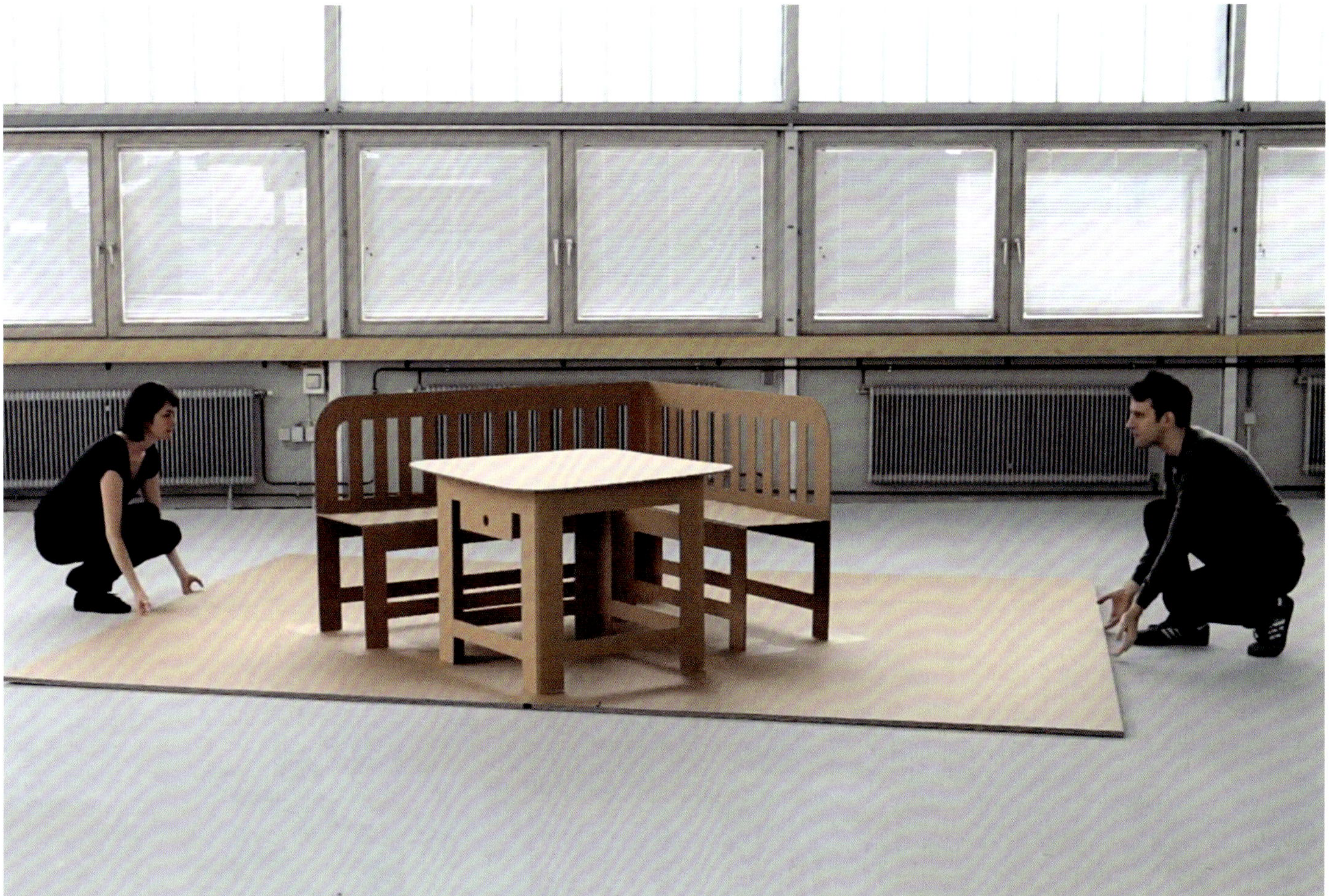

136

136 Studio Makkink & Bey created Work at Home, 2013, a mobile work dormer that could be used anywhere.
137 La Laguna, a 1920s textile factory, was repurposed by Productora to make a new workspace in Mexico City in 2023.
138 Organized around a central courtyard much of the factory machinery was left in situ as a reminder of its past.
139 The factory now houses twenty-five companies ranging from coffee brewers to ceramicists.

137

a bookshop, a film company, offices and a felt textile workshop moved to the surviving building. The building was adapted by Productora, one of the architecture studios that inhabit it, to incorporate these new uses. Central to the project was the retention of the textile factory machinery. Left in situ it provides a constant reminder of the previous histories of the working space but also symbolizes the weaving together of a new one. In a climatically challenged world, as new building becomes more and more challenging this subtle change of use is a model for all new forms of working spaces as they reinhabit obsolete industrial buildings.

THE PUBLIC INTERIOR | WORK

Infrastructures

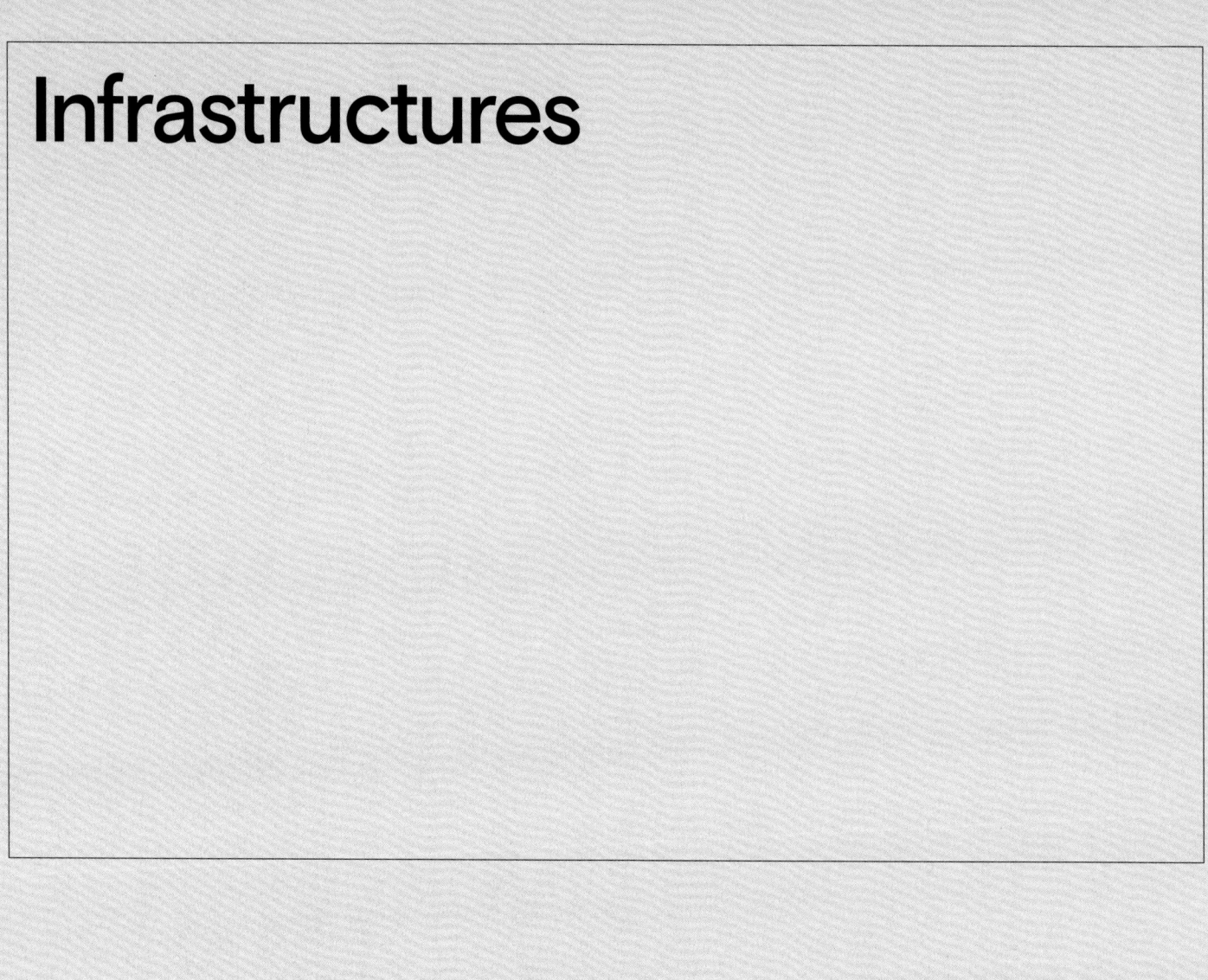

THE PUBLIC INTERIOR | WORK

Infrastructures

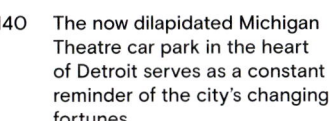

140 The now dilapidated Michigan Theatre car park in the heart of Detroit serves as a constant reminder of the city's changing fortunes.

Detroit's demise is well documented. Its position as the fourth most populous city in the US by the 1950s was primarily due to it being the centre of the nation's car production. This reliance on one industry was ultimately its undoing, as automation, decentralization through distributing factories to the edges of the city and the resulting suburbanization decimated jobs. Rapid depopulation propelled a drop from almost two million to under 650,000 residents in just a few decades. In 2013 the city filed for the largest municipal bankruptcy case in US history.

There is a unique space that illustrates this dramatic shift in fortunes. Without money to run them or a population to enjoy or move around in them, many of the city's cultural institutions and transport infrastructures were either mothballed or completely closed down. The car became the primary way of moving around the city. The Michigan Theatre was constructed in 1925 in the city centre with a seating capacity of over four thousand people. It operated as a popular nightclub until its closure in 1976. As public transport options were reduced, the tenants of the thirteen-storey block above the theatre requested more parking spaces. In response, the owners unsentimentally inserted a car lot into what was once the main auditorium. The theatre's elaborate interior stood out markedly against the rudimentary steel-framed parking lot, creating a remarkable hybrid interior. The ornate plasterwork of the ceiling and proscenium arch was left intact as were fragments of the balconies, foyers and stairs. Like a recombined car made from two vehicle halves welded together, this was a 'cut and shut' interior. The interior embodied the manifestation of the changing fortunes of Detroit. It is a symbol of the city through the combination of theatre and car park, of culture and infrastructure bonding entertainment and mobility via the fight for the survival of Detroit.

Infrastructures chart the fortunes of a city. In a booming prosperous place, networks of trains, buses, trams, cars and bikes are developed to move residents efficiently and quickly between work and home, entertainment and play. Airports are built to transit

141 The Line, a proposed 'linear city' in Saudi Arabia, is projected to house nine million residents and be powered entirely by renewable energy.

142 *Continuous Monument*, a collage by Superstudio, 1969–70, represented total urbanization and a critique of globalization.

people between cities and countries. Grids of power infrastructures supply these systems. Big cities become dynamic agglomerations of transit networks and flows of people, information and goods. As Detroit shows, when a city or country is in decline the reuse of defunct infrastructures becomes of paramount importance. How can these often monumental infrastructures and buildings be repurposed and made to adapt to new uses?

This chapter will explore both new builds and the reclamation of abandoned and outdated infrastructures. Infrastructure design can be understood as interior urbanism. These are interiors that are characterized by large-scale enclosed spaces that are built to make flow, circulation and transit efficient. They might include retail opportunities, food and drink outlets, exhibitions and entertainments. Whatever they contain, infrastructure spaces frequently result in dramatic urban-scaled public (with often contested elements of private) interiors.[11]

Because of its scale and impact, to build new infrastructure often takes a long time and many years of planning ahead. New roads, railway lines and airports are controversial propositions and always consume vast tracts of land as well as displacing people and hungrily consuming resources. Their planning is always long term, therefore speculation is a fundamental aspect of infrastructure design. Testing and experimenting, forging new ways of thinking, proposing sometimes radical ways of inhabiting and moving around a city and country is part of the DNA of infrastructure. Sometimes, what might be viewed as fanciful is actually built. In 2021, construction began on The Line, a linear city in Saudi Arabia. It was designed to stretch from Tabuk to the Red Sea, a 170-kilometre (106-mile) long passage. It was conceived to accommodate nine million people in a continuous reflective horizontal block, 200 metres (656 feet) wide and 500 metres (1,640 feet) tall, making it the longest and third-tallest building ever constructed. The Line would have no cars or traditional streets, instead it was designed to have pedestrian levels and two underground levels for transport, including a train that could travel the length of the line in twenty minutes at 510 kilometres (317 miles) per hour. An underground marina with a canal large enough for cruise ships was also part of the masterplan, along with a plant that could produce 20,000 cubic metres (710,000 cubic feet) of concrete daily, needed for the project. Over 100,000 workers are on site preparing the ground. The project is expected to consume over 20 per cent of the world's annual steel production until its planned completion in around 2045.[12]

Approximately fifty years before The Line broke ground, collages of a never-ending gridded oblong 'plinth' cutting across deserts and surrounding cities such as Manhattan appeared. *Continuous Monument* by Superstudio was a critique of bombastic Modernism

142

and the capitalist structures that supported it. *Continuous Monument* was a warning against overdevelopment. Superstudio's Adolfo Natalini, Gian Piero Frassinelli, Cristiano Toraldo di Francia and Roberto Magris were part of a left-wing political group that made the collages to provoke reactions to the excesses of design that they considered were leading to an impending environmental and social crisis. The grid of the monument was designed to keep inhabitants inside and away from destroying the countryside and ultimately the planet. The monument represented their concerns through the portrayal of a dystopian never-ending Modernist box. Frassinelli, the last surviving member of the studio, noted in 2021 that it was upsetting to see their idealistic work misinterpreted and instead influencing The Line's construction – arguably now realizing the dystopian ideal that they had set out to critique.[13]

All monolithic infrastructures such as The Line or *Continuous Monument* order and organize systems and features of the city usually through the design of large urban interiorizing elements. Almost two hundred years before the expected completion of The Line and just four years after the 1851 Crystal Palace, Joseph Paxton proposed the Great Victorian Way. It consisted of a 16-kilometre (10-mile) loop covering much of central and west London under a glass and steel roof. The loop incorporated streets, shops, railway stations and two crossings of the River Thames. It was given planning permission but ultimately abandoned on the grounds of cost. After the Great Stink of 1858, when a smelly and polluted River Thames made the city unbearable, funds were diverted for a different infrastructural project: Joseph Bazalgette's sewering of the city, which redirected effluent to downstream processing plants. Just over one hundred years after the Great Victorian Way, French designer Yona Friedman designed the Spatial City (*Ville spatiale*), a roof that hovered above the city of Paris, uniting disparate elements under one huge infrastructure. A 60 × 40-metre (197 × 131-foot) grid of columns supported a series of 6 × 6-metre (20 × 20-foot) modules that could be adjusted by the inhabitants to

143

144

create environments for housing or workspaces. Though monumental in scale and appearing to be a fixed grid, at the heart of the Spatial City was the desire to allow its users to construct their own interior spaces. Guidelines for this were to be issued via manuals and data collected via a computer program called Flatwriter, which in 1967 was radically ahead of its time. The project was a provocation, posing the question of how can cities flourish while not diminishing themselves or their environs through demolition or unwarranted expansion into the countryside? Both the Great Victorian Way and Spatial City covered their respective cities with large roofs, interiorizing them and facilitating the movement of goods and people unfettered by any external influences, such as the weather. From The Line to the Spatial City, *Continuous Monument* and the Great Victorian Way, all infrastructures have in common the predilection to enclose and interiorize, whether countryside, desert or parts of the city in order to question living and mobility and their impacts upon the city.

Spaces for transport are critical to how cities and countries can operate. The development of the railway initiated one of the most profound impacts on nineteenth-century cities across the world. Once the first line opened in 1825, in northern Britain between Stockton and Darlington, it spread with increasing rapidity. From the 1830s onwards, lines were started in France, Germany, Ireland, Italy and Russia. The first American line, opening in 1830, was between Baltimore and Ohio. The first railways in India from 1843 were between Mumbai (then known as Bombay) and Thane. In 1876 the Woosung Road line opened in Shanghai. By the 1840s, railways linked all of Britain and the US had laid over 4,828 kilometres (3,000 miles) of track. This linked cities and countries together, unified nations and integrated economies by distributing products and people more efficiently and forging quicker communications through mail and news delivery. These all required infrastructure to support and define their journeys. This led to the evolution of a new public interior: the train station.

One of the first train stations in the world was that of Heighington, built in

143 Joseph Paxton's proposed Great Victorian Way, London, 1855, was intended to circulate people amongst shops and houses while keeping out the smog and cold.
144 Yona Friedman's Spatial City, 1967, conceptualized an elevated city that did not impact too heavily on the land and could be configured by its occupants.
145 The 'funnel' on the western concourse of King's Cross station by John McAslan + Partners, London, 2012.
146 King's Cross in the early 1900s.

1827 on the Stockton and Darlington railway line in the UK. Subsequent advanced capacities in steel and glass production, evolved from the 1851 Crystal Palace project, progressed both economies of scale in output alongside the potential for greater structural spanning capabilities. In station design this meant bigger and better termini that were able to handle more trains, more passengers and more goods. King's Cross in London, by Lewis Cubitt, was originally conceived as a smaller timber construction. This idea was superseded due to the aforementioned advances in steel which were utilized to enable two huge vaults to span the numerous railway lines of the terminus. The column-free sheds of steel and glass could accommodate many platforms and train engines, increasing movement and the circulation of people and goods. In 2012 the nearly two-hundred-year-old King's Cross station was adapted by John McAslan + Partners to accommodate the huge growth of train passengers since it was built in 1852. Retaining Cubitt's façade, a new single-span roof was inserted alongside the building creating a large new concourse on its western flank. This new roof, the largest single-span structure in Europe, is supported by sixteen steel columns, fanning out from a base to form a tree-like lattice construction, and encloses the entrance to the underground as well as the ubiquitous shops and cafés.

The new roof created a new city square and a public concourse for the building, showing how good infrastructure can be adapted to accommodate changes in the way the city grows and how it moves.

The development of large interior spaces through which thousands of travelling citizens could be efficiently processed gave rise to the idea that stations should represent the celebration of the visual power of arriving and entering a city. Oppositions between engineering and building, between advanced glass and steel construction and more traditional architectural styles were exemplified in stations such as London's St Pancras. The train shed was an exemplar of modern design, a huge steel and iron vaulted structure designed by the engineer in chief to the Midland Railway company William Henry Barlow (who had been the assistant to Joseph Paxton on the Crystal Palace). Stripped back and expressing its structural integrity, the 74-metre (243-foot) span was the biggest single interior constructed at that time. However, the front of the building was given over to the Midland Grand Hotel, designed in a traditional Gothic style in 1865 by George Gilbert Scott. It was an eclectic Victorian design, very much of its time. The public spaces such as the stairs were highly decorated and each room was finished in a range of materials and surfaces, with gold leaf on the walls.

It was serviced by over three hundred servants bringing chamber pots, tubs and the hot water to fill them for its travel-weary guests. The jarring contrast between highly engineered, refined shed and the extravagantly decorated hotel were, and still are, palpable.

Two of the greatest public infrastructure interiors of the nineteenth century were both built in relation to the advances in importance of the railways, both were in New York. Grand Central Station, built in 1913, and Pennsylvania (Penn) Station, in 1910, were termini that beautifully demonstrated their purpose as places of arrival and departure. Grand Central has forty-four platforms, serving sixty-seven tracks, forty-three of which are public – still the greatest number of platforms of any station in the world. Penn Station was smaller but no less a statement of how to arrive or depart a city. It contained eleven platforms serving twenty-one tracks. Like Grand Central it was also built in a Beaux Art style, yet Penn Station was considered a grander entrance to the city, an accolade which didn't save it from demolition in the 1960s. Both original stations' concourses were filled with restaurants, shops and spaces in which to linger, consume and watch the city pass by. Waiting rooms contained smoking lounges, newspaper stands and bars and shops selling chocolates and flowers. Grand Central housed the famous oyster bar, still a feature today. Both buildings expressed a particular approach to infrastructure and the public interior but only one has survived and flourished. Grand Central was woven into the surrounding network of streets while Penn Station was a bombastic terminus of epic, Roman-temple proportions. Covered in eighty-four Doric columns and 14,000 cubic metres (0.5 million cubic feet) of pink granite, its waiting room was modelled on St Peter's Basilica in Rome. Underused and compromised by several unsympathetic alterations, its demolition had one positive. It galvanized support for modern historic preservation in the US to stop the demise of any other beautiful buildings in the city.

In contrast, Grand Central's longevity is partly due to its adaptability. Its main concourses, such as the Vanderbilt Hall, were adapted to house everything from squash tournaments to design exhibitions. Its upper levels once housed CBS television studios and later the Vanderbilt Tennis club, owned, until recently, by a certain Donald Trump. Even the office of John W. Campbell, a railroad executive, was transformed

147 The grand staircase of the Midland Grand Hotel (now the St Pancras Renaissance London) designed by George Gilbert Scott in 1865.
148 The neoclassical barrel-vaulted main waiting room of Penn Station, New York, c. 1910.
149 The Beaux Art main hall of Grand Central Station, New York, 1913, topped by an elliptical barrel vault with a mural of 2,500 stars.
150 The Guastavino interlocking terracotta-tiled vault of Grand Central's oyster bar, New York.

150

into a discreet cocktail lounge. Like all good infrastructure, Grand Central has adapted its interior to the ever-changing needs of its users and the city, thereby maintaining its position as an important transport hub.

Infrastructure projects not only remind us how public transport is valued amid the challenges of climate change, but also how important they are as urban interiors in their own right. The Hauptbahnhof in Berlin is an enormous transit hub, where trains cross each other at various levels surrounded by shops, bars, restaurants and all kinds of amenities. Not only is travel facilitated, but its role as a public square is paramount to the life of the city. The primacy of the roof as a covering for the expanse of operations undertaken beneath it is an enduring infrastructure design strategy. In central Jiaxing, China, MAD Architects have designed a huge underground train terminal that utilizes the ground floor as a roof to cover the six tracks of the station. Expected to be used by up to six million people annually, MAD built a full-scale replica of the original 1907 station building to form the north entrance to the terminus interior. The contrast between the old building and the new modern station is deliberate not just as a potent reminder of the history of the city, but also to demonstrate a significant shift in the scale of the growth and use of contemporary infrastructure. Public interiors of transit

151

152

153

are always enclosures where both aimless drift and direct movement are encouraged and where connection, ambience and control are facilitated.

Metro and underground transit spaces are always focused on speed and direction. Since the opening of the first underground in London in 1863, cities have developed subterranean systems that move passengers efficiently beneath the city. Traditionally, stations fall into two broad categories: cut and cover, meaning they are close to the surface, and deeper tunnelling systems that require digging with a tunnel boring machine (TBM). Opened in 1935, the Moscow Metro is undoubtedly one of the most efficient, cost-effective and beautiful underground systems, as well as one of top four busiest in the world (Shanghai, Tokyo and Seoul are the others). Stations were deemed as 'palaces of the people'; they were elaborately decorated, often with Soviet socialist classicism, in order to reflect the preoccupations and concerns of Soviet life and its leaders. It was built in consultation with engineers of the London Underground, a situation which ironically resulted in strained British–Soviet relations when several were considered *too* knowledgeable about Russian life and were tried as spies and deported. The first stations were cut and cover. Later additions were tunnelled with the proviso of becoming useful shelters in the advent

151 Berlin Hauptbahnhof, the largest railway intersection in Europe, by GMP, 2006, forms a cross shape with railway lines, platforms and the metro overlaying each other.
152 Jiaxing Train Station in China by MAD Architects, 2021, consists of six underground train tracks with the ground level given over to 1,500 hundred trees and a lawn.
153 A replica of the original 1907 station, positioned as the north entrance to the new terminus, is a stark reminder of the scale of growth in travel during the twenty-first century.
154 Elektrozavodskaya metro station, Moscow, 1944, designed by Vladimir Shchuko and Vladimir Gelfreich with twelve bas reliefs by Georgy Motovilov.

of any nuclear strike. Station decoration themes included scenes of everyday life, sport and athleticism, industry and latterly heroic war efforts, all of which ensured that travellers received daily doses of ideology as they moved through the stations. Deeper stations meant huge escalators, fitted with speakers, relaying news and information to commuters as they journeyed up and down. The stations' decoration was evaluated on three principles: aesthetics, technology and ideology. The stations were beautiful essays on Russian lives.

Subterranean infrastructures rely on iconography and symbolism to express place and, like the Moscow Metro stations, have lent themselves to forms of elaborate expression.

The Paris Métro entrances are iconic, each one signalling the delights of the spaces below them. In Milan in 1964, Franco Albini and Franca Helg, with Dutch graphic designer Bob Noorda, developed a complete interior language for the city's red line. It combined structure, materials and graphics in such a way as to make the journey underneath the city a refined and fluid experience. A simple palette of shell-figured granite, rubber flooring, steel-framed panels organizing signage, and maps, along with the selection of carefully considered accessories such as benches and clocks, created a coherent and refined spatial language. Unlike Moscow, instead of portraying heroic narratives of the people and the city, the most expressive detail was

155

155 The stimulating interior of Università metro station, Naples, redesigned by Karim Rashid in 2011, was based on energizing and increasing the mobility of its users.
156 An iconic art nouveau sign by Hector Guimard marking a Paris Métro stop.
157 The red line of the Milan Metro, designed by Franco Albini and Franca Helg in 1964, features the expressive use of a handrail as a wayfinder.
158 A three-storey barrel vault announces the entrance to Jahad Metro Plaza by Mohammad Khavarian Architecture Studio, Tehran, 2023.
159 In light of protests against the oppression of women that started at subway stations, the entrance is also conceived as a democratic open public space.

a tubular red steel handrail. It formed a continuous route-map that, through touch, led travellers from the train, through the stations, to the street and out to the city.

Expressive and sometimes theatrical motifs still abound in contemporary underground stations, where artifice is combined with pragmatism in order to celebrate the act of passing through the city's infrastructures. Karim Rashid's design for a Naples underground station choreographs the movement of the passengers through a series of colourful chambers before they get to the platform. The ticket hall, the first chamber, is lined with coloured tiles and backlit lenticular artwork, making it change as the passengers move through the space. The hall is filled with over-scaled pastiches of Renato Bertelli's *Continuous Profile (Head of Mussolini)* sculpture. A blue mirrored ceiling encloses the descent to the platforms, where the trains, rushing through the station, provide further stimulation for travellers. Specific materials and textures can provide the motifs or identity for making infrastructural landmarks. The Jahad Metro Plaza was constructed above an existing metro station, located at a busy, unprepossessing road intersection in Tehran. Workshops and labourers were employed to supply 300,000 bricks from surrounding rural areas formed into a series of interconnecting arches across the site. Bricks were cheap and well suited to the climate as they were cleanable in relation to the pollution levels of the road-side site. A triple-height arch provides a welcome entrance as well as a performance space for waiting travellers to enjoy a show. Arches connected to this provide sheltered spaces to escape the sun, with some inhabited by street vendors. The application of the arcuated construction, a Persian vernacular, reinvested the junction with a civic landmark as well as an upgrade on its infrastructure.

Because of the increase of affordable air travel, airport terminals are a building type that has developed exponentially in scale and organization throughout the late twentieth and early twenty-first centuries. The airport is a hub of overlapping transit services. Its users have to be processed safely

156

157

158

159

160 Encased moving walkways link the surrounds of the circular *aérogare* designed by Paul Andreu in 1966, Charles de Gaulle airport, Paris.

161 The flowing sculptural interior of the TWA Flight Center by Eero Saarinen, John F. Kennedy airport, New York, 1956–62.

and efficiently through them, usually while being exposed to a maximum of opportunities to indulge in retail or consume food and drink. It is the terminus experience – the clarity of organization and the ability to represent the dynamism of travel – that has become the critical factor in their design.

A unique, innovative exemplar is Charles de Gaulle airport on the outskirts of Paris built in 1966. It was originally named Roissy, or also known as Paris North, and was designed by Paul Andreu. Terminal 1 was designed as a ten-storey circular *aérogare* with a number of satellites projecting from it. The satellites were for the planes to dock while the circulation of passengers took place in the main circular building. The original masterplan had five *aérogares* after Andreu's design, but only one was ever built.

The building was positioned directly above a motorway and the vertical processing of car passengers from the autoroute into the terminal was intended to be seamless. Once they had alighted from their car and after checking in, dropping off baggage, security screening and so on, passengers would move through the centre of the domed building via a series of moving walkways encased in glass. There were plans to make the journey between car and plane so seamless that the designers envisaged drive-in check-ins – now a normal process albeit undertaken via mobile technologies such as a phone. While striking, the formal quality of the *aérogare* precluded easy expansion when cheap tickets made air travel increasingly accessible throughout the 1970s and 1980s. Still in use today, the one *aérogare* has now been joined by a series of other orthogonal and less seamless terminals, making the airport one of the busiest in Europe.

The TWA Flight Center of New York's John F. Kennedy airport, designed by Eero Saarinen between 1956 and 1962, like Charles de Gaulle, was an iconic form of a building that was quickly

161

superseded by the increasing popularity of air travel. It took the form of a huge wing-shaped roof atop four Y-shaped structural supports. Underneath the roof was an expansive, fluid three-storey urban interior, filled with stairs, baggage carousels and circulation for passengers. Though Trans World Airlines closed the terminal in 2002, its status as a landmark building meant it was not demolished. Its redesignation as a hotel has ensured that many of its original features have been preserved.

Both airports characterized air travel through the assignation of forms to symbolize circulation and movement. Charles de Gaulle represented circulation through its willingness to integrate the car into its structure. TWA took a much more expressive approach through the provision of a large, expansive sculptural roof that represented flight. Ultimately, both formal responses compromised the buildings' futures as it was not possible to add to or extend them. Both are now icons of a certain period of air travel.

In a fluid and ever-changing context, the easily extendable and flexible shed has become the airport typology of choice. Stansted, designed by Foster Associates and built in 1991 to the northeast of London, set a new benchmark for airport design with its clarity and simplicity. Passengers arrived by road and rail into a large and, when first opened, uncluttered box. Travellers could see straight through to their waiting plane. The building was organized around a series

162

163

of tree-like structural columns. These contained services and supported the roof sections. The repeatable roof pattern could be added to endlessly, a possible answer to the issues of future expansion. Unfortunately, this clarity of thought has been undermined by the increasingly complex routines of air-travel security and the growth of the shopping and refreshment needs of its customers. Stansted is now less clear than ever. The huge transport interchange that is Schiphol airport in the Netherlands has handled interchange and infrastructure in a very different manner. Ever-expanding passenger numbers and the requirement to provide differing revenue streams, such as through retail and hospitality, has meant that the airport has drawn inspiration from the shopping mall, the lobbies of the great hotels, even museums. Schiphol is one of a handful of airports that incorporate an art gallery. Situated between lounges two and three a pavilion containing a dozen Dutch master portraits on loan from Amsterdam's Rijksmuseum is open twenty-four hours a day. It is a small interior of art and contemplation set amongst a sea of commerce that transits fliers across the globe.

Air travel is considered to be a major contributor, via carbon emissions, to climate change. It therefore seems paradoxical that when building airport infrastructure an ultra-sustainable approach is pursued. Most contemporary airport designs prioritize sustainability while giving precedence to efficiencies in the movements of passengers between the city and the plane. Beijing's Daxing airport is one of the largest in the world. Its unique starfish-shaped prongs, each facilitating aircraft docking piers, were designed to minimize the journeys between security and gate. Designed by Zaha Hadid Architects, the centre of the building contains a large naturally lit courtyard. The airport is powered by solar energy with extensive heat and water management systems put in place. The lounges within airports are the 'domestic' spaces within the public interior of the airport. These range from the soothing to the shrill. Minimal spaces designed to calm the traveller before they board their flight, like the Avianca lounge at Bogotá's

162 The uncluttered departure area of London's Stansted airport, designed by Foster Associates, 1991, was organized by modular tree-like structures holding up the large roof.
163 In Schiphol Airport, the Netherlands, a Rijksmuseum satellite by Benthem Crouwel architects, 2003, presents passengers with a selection of old masters before take-off.
164 The LATAM VIP lounge at Arturo Merino Benítez International Airport, Chile, by Grupo Arquitectos and Kriskadecor aims to reconnect travellers with tranquillity and relaxation.
165 Avianca lounge at El Dorado airport, Bogotá, by Francesc Rifé studio, 2018.

El Dorado airport by Francesc Rifé studio, rely on the use of soothing lights and materials to steady the nerves of the anxious passenger. Other methods stimulate the senses and prepare the traveller for adventure. The business lounge by Nefa Architects at Nizhny Novgorod airport in Russia, is like a miniature symbol of the city in its use of steel and concrete. A lack of natural light and view is counterpointed with shafts of illuminated columns. Grupo Arquitectos used light differently in the bar of the VIP lounge for LATAM Airlines in Santiago de Chile's airport, designing a huge structure that filtered light onto the waiting travellers below. Lounges prepare their occupants for departure in all manner of ways.

This chapter has documented infrastructures that chart the fortunes of a city when it is prosperous. Trains and stations, airports, buses, trams, cars and bikes are developed to move residents efficiently and quickly through the city and the country. What happens when infrastructures become obsolete? Their reuse is of paramount importance. Reanimating certain types of derelict infrastructures can make meaningful connections to the past and retain a city's identity through its heritage. With vast tracts of land, often appealing to developers, airports can be very valuable for reuse. Tempelhof airport is just fifteen minutes by bike from Berlin city centre. Adapted from a previous airport that opened in 1923, Albert Speer redesigned it as part of Hitler's

166 Beijing's Daxing airport by Zaha Hadid Architects, 2014–19, was designed to accommodate up to 100 million passengers per year.

167 (Opposite) Illuminated columns of light provide a relaxing environment in the VIP lounge by Nefa Architects at Strigino airport, Nizhny Novgorod, Russia, 2016.

168 (Opposite) Reusing obsolete infrastructures makes for compelling new interiors. Tate Modern's Turbine Hall, a power station transformed into an art gallery by Herzog & de Meuron, London, 2000.
169 Temporary rooms with beds are set up in an emergency shelter for refugees in the former hangar of Tempelhof airport.
170 The turbine hall of Battersea Power Station, London, reused for shops and apartments.

'Germania' project, which aimed to make Berlin a new world capital. Closed in 2008, from 2009 it was reopened as a public park. Berliners could escape the city and use the runway to rollerblade, ride bikes and barbecue in the green spaces in between. In a 2014 national referendum plans to redevelop the park were rejected and prospective developers sent packing. Instead, the airport hangars now house Syrian, Afghan and Iraqi refugees. The reuse of the building reappropriated its fascist roots.

Buildings such as train stations, underground lines, steel works or redundant power stations can be reanimated and reused by breathing new life into them. Battersea and Bankside power stations in London were two enormous buildings supplying the city with electricity. Bankside 'B' was designed by Giles Gilbert Scott. When fully operational, in just one hour it consumed almost seventy tons of oil and extracted ten million gallons of water for cooling from the adjacent River Thames. It was closed in 1981 and left redundant for many years until, in 1994, it was reinvented as the Tate Modern gallery by Herzog & de Meuron. The designers utilized the building's awesome scale and physical presence, creating a vast new public interior in the turbine hall from where the enormous generators had been removed. Battersea Power Station has also been reanimated but, as an indication of differing motivations, it contains expensive housing and exclusive retail opportunities within its huge walls and underneath its four iconic chimneys. The reuse of infrastructures charts not just the fortunes of a city but also serves its impulses and demands.

The reclamation of transport infrastructure is resistance to the loss of legacy and the embodied energies of a place. It provides the opportunity to create atmosphere and presence

171

172

171 The first electrified urban terminal in the world, the Gare d'Orsay, Paris, opened in 1900.
172 In 1986 the former station reopened as Musée d'Orsay, exhibiting nineteenth-century art in the cavernous main shed redesigned by Gae Aulenti.
173 Main hall of the former Hamburger Bahnhof station in Berlin in use as a railway museum in 1984.
174 The Hamburger Bahnhof now Nationalgalerie der Gegenwart designed by Josef Paul Kleihues, 1986.

that new builds just cannot convey. Cultural venues such as galleries are often suited to reworked infrastructure precisely for two reasons: the existing spaces provide flexibility and narratives that can be a source of inspiration. Musée d'Orsay was inserted into a 1900 train station on the left bank of the River Seine in Paris. With no space to lengthen platforms to accommodate new trains, the station closed in 1939, yet it was listed as a *Monument historique* in 1973 and thus was protected from demolition. Gae Aulenti was commissioned to undertake the interior design, creating an urban interior landscape within the cavernous train shed. This incorporated a public square that enabled larger elements to be displayed and also a set of rooms for paintings and objects that shouldn't be overwhelmed by the scale of the former station. Similarly, the Hamburger Bahnhof in Berlin was built in the middle of the nineteenth century but was deemed redundant at the start of the twentieth. In 1986 a new museum of contemporary art was placed in the station. Designed by Josef Paul Kleihues, the new museum celebrated the structural clarity of the main train shed, adding two new wings either side to accommodate a collection of twentieth-century artists. In both projects the huge train sheds provided ample space for the installation of both small- and large-scale artworks.

Reclaiming infrastructure for art galleries is not the only way forwards to make new and innovative urban-scaled interiors. Braaksma & Roos and Civic Architects, working with Mecanoo, transformed a locomotive shed in Tilburg, the Netherlands, to create a new library. LocHal was named after the huge shed in which it was situated. With a height of 15 metres (50 feet) and measuring 60 × 90 metres (200 × 295 feet), a series of flexible spaces for browsing books, meeting, eating and drinking were distributed throughout the shed space. Relics of the building were incorporated into its new use: tracks provided the lines for movable 'locomotive' tables; an old oil pit became a sunken workspace. Like all reanimated industrial projects, the narratives of work and making form a meaningful post-industrial backdrop for the new leisure spaces.

175 Transport infrastructure such as train sheds can provide large open spaces for reuse. LocHal public library by Mecanoo in Tilburg, the Netherlands, 2018.

176 TanArt Community renovation by Nomos Architects, Xi'an, China, is an open gallery in a coal-burning station made obsolete by new energy sources.

177 The old cooling towers of the Orlando Power Station, 1951, turned into a bungee jumping attraction, Soweto, South Africa.

178 Blast furnace no. 2 illuminated at night in Landschaftspark Duisburg-Nord, Germany, a public park encompassing a disused steelworks.

Deindustrialization across the world has left a legacy of 'difficult' buildings to repurpose. Often dirty, dangerous and, because of their robust structural qualities, physically difficult to rework. Steel works, coal mines and gasometers all form the post-industrial landscape of cities and countries. Changes in energy use from fossil fuels to renewables means that large-scale power infrastructures are becoming increasingly redundant, and their repurposing, as opposed to their demolition, is important and progressively welcomed in the search for unusual heritage-rich spaces. The Xi'an Shiyou power station in China was closed in 2014, obsoleted before it was fully operational. Its large spaces are well-suited for events and exhibitions and the renovation by Nomos Architects was intended to regenerate the surrounding area by accommodating creative communities. The robust concrete structure of the building was left intact in order to form a powerful backdrop for the new uses.

The demolition of obsolete infrastructures can be so difficult, dirty and dangerous that new and unique responses to the infrastructure are found which completely transform them. One of the forerunners of showing how reworking redundant infrastructures can be done successfully was in the Ruhr region in north-western Germany that incorporates the towns and cities of Essen, Duisburg and Oberhausen. The International Building Exhibition Emscher Park was a huge infrastructural project from 1989 to 1999 that redeveloped numerous industrial sites of the region to make one large park, work and culture space. 800 square kilometres (300 square miles) of park link various sites together, creating the potential for over two million inhabitants to cycle, climb the old blast furnaces, visit design museums in old coal mines, watch films in the open-air cinema and scuba dive in the water-cooling tanks of the steel works. At night the Duisburg steel plant is lit as though a huge stage set accommodating concerts that utilize the decayed infrastructure as a backdrop. Cranes, gantries and towers provide excellent infrastructures for unique reuses; in Duisburg they become virtually scenographic. The formal qualities of the buildings can often provide the inspiration for their reuse. Wunderland

Kalkar is an amusement park located in a nuclear power plant in Germany. The plant was built but never operational and stood empty until bought and repurposed. The most striking moment is the 58-metre (190-foot) high vertical swing placed in the complex's cooling tower. Similarly, in the Soweto Towers just outside of Johannesburg in South Africa, a huge mass of infrastructure is reused for leisure. The Orlando Power Station was constructed in 1935 with two cooling towers added in 1951. It was decommissioned in 1998 and its towers decorated with murals to represent the changing nature of Soweto and the country. The main building collapsed in 2014, but the towers were retained and used for bungee jumping, climbing and BASE jumping. Their vivid decoration makes them stand out as iconic landmarks and reminders of the post-industrial shift to leisure. No matter what the infrastructure, demolition is often not a viable option, but reanimation for the future is.

The early 2020s and the Covid-19 pandemic focused minds on the futures of cities and their infrastructures. Climatic challenges and social justice initiatives are forcing a rethink and a move away from the car and towards healthier forms of transit. One of these is the bike. Bike-riding infrastructure such as safety lanes, rental systems, storage and servicing has numerous benefits for cities. Riding reduces carbon emissions, congestion and frees up space usually dominated by motor vehicles. It makes people healthier,

THE PUBLIC INTERIOR | INFRASTRUCTURES

179 The painted cooling tower and attached tents signal the complete change of use from nuclear power station SNR-300 to Wunderland Kalkar amusement park.

180 The vast interior of the cooling tower provided a startling location for a swing ride and climbing walls.

181 Cycling infrastructure, such as the Hague Cycle Park by Silo and Studio Marsman, signals how bikes are becoming increasingly more important than cars in urban planning.

enables more equitable systems of movement and increases air quality by ensuring fewer cars on the road. Protected cycle lanes, hangars and service-station infrastructures support these changes. The Netherlands, where cycling has formed an integral part of transit culture for a long time, has developed a number of infrastructures to enhance and uplift the experience of cycling. Near Amsterdam Centraal Station, 9 metres (30 feet) underneath the canals and connected directly to the metro is a storage park that can secure 7,000 bikes. Next to the Hague's central train station, Silo in conjunction with Studio Marsman, completed a garage for 8,000 bikes. Cyclists ride directly into an underground garage via sloping escalators. Once inside, cyclists are met with a light and graphically vibrant interior. The space was conceived as a museum of the city, to be viewed from a moving bike. The walls of the garage were designed as an abstracted version of the façades of the city, backlit to provide the rider with a taster as they zip around the track in search of a slot to park their bike. The cycle garages are located at transit hubs such as stations and form seamless connections between different modes of transport thereby unifying all forms of city infrastructures and encouraging bike use.

Whether new build or reused, city-scaled infrastructures create interior spaces that are formulated to efficiently transport users while impacting upon their senses as they enter or move around a city.

Culture

182 Kurt Schwitters' *Merzbau* in Hanover, 1933. The installation, was destroyed by a bomb in 1943.

183 André Malraux's 'museum without walls' invokes a process of creating an ideal collection of works drawn from the universal world of art.

Merz was the word the artist Kurt Schwitters used to describe collages he made from found objects. *Merzbau* was the name given to *Merz* formed into dynamic spatial sculptures. He produced a number of *Merzbau* works in Hanover, in Norway and one in Britain between 1923 and 1948. Hanover's was demolished by a bomb in 1943, Norway's was subsumed by fire and the *Merzbau* in the Lake District in the UK was left unfinished after his death in 1948. It was rescued and completed when one wall was removed and installed in Newcastle University, where it still resides today. The most complete *Merzbau* was in Hanover. It filled the studio anteroom and balcony of his house. Schwitters set out to create a display that rendered fluid the relationship between artwork, frame, composition, material and its audience. He salvaged waste from the streets of the city to be embedded into the columns of *Merz* in his home. Visitors were invited into the *Merzbau* and were free to touch, play and even to listen to it, returning to bring more objects for Schwitters to add to it. Gradually columns took over the house, growing through the floors and walls of the studio.

Also in the mid-twentieth century, André Malraux was creating the *Musée imaginaire* – the museum without walls. Malraux conceived the museum as a collection of curated photographic images. His argument was that the role of the museum was always to transform the objects it housed. The photographic image meant objects were freed of their context to then be reused in all manner of different places. Malraux's proposition to dissolve walls anticipated a prototype of the interactive museum, a space requiring the viewer to engage and consume culture. The imaginary museum is the books, postcards and souvenirs that accompany exhibitions. It anticipated how art could be interpreted in numerous ways via various mobile and digital technologies and platforms. Both the *Merzbau* and the imaginary museum challenged notions of how an object was curated and then how it was viewed. Both questioned the relationship between the visitor and the object. Both could be immersive and all encompassing.

184 Uffizi Gallery, Florence, built by Giorgio Vasari in the sixteenth century, pictured after its 2012 restoration.
185 'Bauhaus: 1919–1928' at MoMA, New York, curated by Alfred H. Barr Jr and Herbert Bayer, 1938–39, marked the beginning of a new 'white wall' exhibition aesthetic.
186 Piero Antonio Martini, after Johann Heinrich Ramberg, *Exposition au Salon du Louvre en 1787*.
187 Opening of the First International Dada Fair, Berlin, 1920. Standing, left to right: Raoul Hausmann, Otto Burchard, Johannes Baader, Wieland and Margarete Herzfelde, George Grosz, John Heartfield. Sitting: Hannah Höch and Otto Schmalhausen.

All of these considerations impact on the design of the cultural public interior.

Cultural public interiors can relay their contents in temporary or permanent ways. They may be placed inside buildings that have been custom made for them, or they can inhabit a reused building. The latter can give the contents a 'charged' dimension, especially when the contrast between the new and the old is at its most provocative. This approach means that the building can also become an exhibit.

One of the most prominent cultural public interiors is the museum. A museum is an institution that collects and presents artefacts, but it is not a neutral container. Instead, it must always be understood as a complex weave of different cultures, messages, stakeholders, histories and narratives.[14] Much like libraries, public museums evolved from the requirements of rich patrons to house their collections. One of the most famous examples is the Uffizi Gallery in Florence, built by Giorgio Vasari in the sixteenth century for the Medici family. Housing collections of objects for people to learn from gathered pace in the eighteenth and nineteenth centuries. Museum interiors were designed with traditional display methods such as cabinets and vitrines.

Museums and galleries are not always custom-built to house a specific collection of art and objects. The autonomous exhibition, characterized by the temporary or white-walled display space, emerged in the twentieth century. Modern exhibitions prioritized the judgement of the curator and designer of the space. The adoption of the white-wall approach was initiated by Alfred H. Barr Jr, the director of New York's Museum of Modern Art (MoMA). Instead of traditional floor-to-ceiling approaches, Barr hung art at eye level only and with space between to reveal the neutral white background. Barr's famous exhibition 'Bauhaus: 1919–1928', exhibited in MoMA in 1938, exemplified the new white-wall aesthetic. It conveyed an experimental quality in narrating the links between images.

Autonomous and freed from the specificities of the museum site, exhibitions of art can create strong messages. In the middle of the nineteenth century the 'Salon des Refusés' ('exhibition of rejects') tested the power and authority of the Académie des Beaux-Arts in Paris. Entries to the Academy's 1863 Salon were severely restricted and objections by the rejected artists were so vociferous that Napoleon III decreed that the refused pieces would be shown at the opposite end to those selected in the Palais de l'Industrie on the Champs-Élysees. This was a significant

THE PUBLIC INTERIOR | CULTURE

186

187

moment. The emperor had challenged the authority of the Academy and let the general public decide on the merits of the submitted work.

Three exhibitions between 1920 and 1940 exemplify the political dimensions of objects, site and their curation. In 1920, artists of the Dada movement held their first international fair in Berlin. Attracting considerable attention, the exhibition was located in two rooms of a gallery on the ground floor of an apartment building owned by Dr Otto Burchard, a dealer in art and antiques. Covering the walls with posters, collages and photomontages the exhibition drew controversy for its aggressive and sometimes inflammatory response to politics in the country. A mannequin of a Prussian officer suspended from the ceiling of one of the rooms was considered inflammatory enough that five of the group were charged with insulting the German army. Twentieth-century German politics was further laid bare in the infamous exhibition 'Degenerate Art' held in Munich in 1937. On the eve of the Second World War, the German government's antipathy to modernity was expressed in the curation and display of work that was claimed to explicitly link modern art with social degeneracy and political subversion. 650 confiscated works by 112 artists were displayed in rooms with stickers proclaiming the price paid for them, the museum they were from and the statement that it was paid for with taxes from working German people. Two *Merz* paintings by Kurt Schwitters were mocked for their 'trash-can material' aesthetic. Tellingly though, the exhibition was seen by three times as many people as the 'Day of German Art' exhibit of Nazi-approved art, which opened at the same time in Munich and was personally curated by Adolf Hitler. Meanwhile, in Paris Frederick Kiesler designed the 'City in Space' exhibition in 1925. It was an installation at the Exposition Internationale des Arts Décoratifs et Industriels Modernes. The exhibition was an adaptation of his previous work of a transportable framework for the International Exhibition of New Theatre Techniques in Vienna. Kiesler developed the frame system to house models of buildings, paintings, set designs and costumes.

188

189

The system he designed was one of the first instances that encouraged interaction between viewer and the work. It asked the viewer to move panels and adjust the walls of the exhibition and enabled them to reconfigure how they wanted to interpret and thus understand the work. All three exhibitions demonstrated the power of curatorial strategies to relay very specific narratives and intentions – however odious.

The opposite to the white-wall approach of exhibiting objects, consists in using the location (such as a unique or interesting building) to evoke a site-specific narrative and response. Carlo Scarpa's design for the Castelvecchio in Verona is one of the greatest examples of the interweaving of a historic building with a museum collection. Scarpa used the former castle as an instrument of storytelling, an exhibit of importance in the narrative of the city. He treated the Castelvecchio as an archaeological dig, uncovering the layers of the building's history and exposing them by carefully placing exhibits at the most evocative junctions of old and new. His treatment of the statue of Cangrande I highlighted this approach. It was placed at the point of the building where the layers of history were at their densest. He exposed the end of the castle barracks where they touched the city walls leading to the bridge and placed the famous statue atop a new concrete plinth. Cangrande I, an important relic in Verona's history, acted as a hinge for the whole of the museum, occupying a place that the visitor would see and connect with in various ways as they circulated throughout the museum.

Treating buildings as artefacts relies on them having interesting stories to tell. The site of the Anno Museum in Hamar, Norway, consists of a series of buildings constructed on top of one another, making the site a compaction of layers of archaeology: a palimpsest. Added buildings were a series of simple rural barns. These were retained for the new museum in order to house the archaeological finds that were being extracted from beneath them. For the museum's Storhamarlåven (Storhamar barn), built on the site of the former bishop's palace, Sverre Fehn added what he described as a 'suspended museum', a series of walkways with rooms displaying the finds. Andrea Bruno's renovation of Rivoli Castle,

188 Frederick Kiesler's 'City in Space' exhibition design and city model, Paris, 1925.
189 A visitor viewing the confiscated subversive material in the 'Degenerate Art' exhibition, Munich, 1937.
190 Museo di Castelvecchio, Verona, restored by Carlo Scarpa in 1973.
191 Scarpa repositioned the imperious statue of Cangrande I, representing Verona's ruling family, at the building's most historic site to demonstrate its importance.

190

191

set on a hillside just outside Turin, explored the storytelling of a succession of very different buildings many of which were unfinished. A new museum was placed in two buildings: one designed by Filippo Juvarra for the House of Savoy, which was only half completed before the family were deposed and the project abandoned; and a long gallery wing that pre-dated Juvarra's building. Bruno's work focused on arresting the decay of both buildings and attempted to stitch them together in a coherent fashion. The chronologically disparate building components formed the central aspect of the life of the Savoys and the building.

Underneath the tracks of Milan's railway system, roughly a kilometre from the central station terminus, is Binario 21. This secret platform was initially constructed to load and transport sacks of mail across the country. It did this with a platform that raised the train carriages to the tracks above. Between 1943 and 1945 it was used to transport Jewish inmates from the San Vittore Prison. In two

192

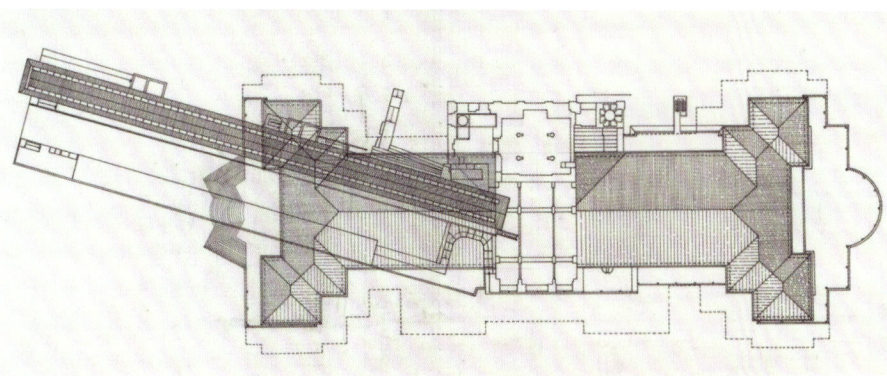

194

193

years over 1,200 people were loaded onto carriages and elevated to the lines above to be transported to their deaths in concentration camps. From 2013 onwards, the Shoah Memorial by Morpurgo de Curtis architects has been opened in this space. The dissonance between the history of the site and the still in-use station, with the rumble of trains permanently overhead, is relayed via a series of powerful spatial elements. The Wall of Indifference greets visitors, bluntly communicating the attitudes implicit in this aspect of Italian history. A boxcar, on the platform where it was lined up for the prisoners, is stepped through and frames an illuminated wall listing the 1,200 names of the deported. A space of reflection, a steel enclosure for contemplation, affords the visitor some respite from the overhead noise of commuter trains. A library of books and texts visibly externalizes the continued learning from history. The resonance between the existing building, the new elements and the narrative encapsulated in the environment provides the visitor with a harrowing yet unforgettable memory of this sad and dark part of Italian history.

Old factories and warehouses can create dramatic backdrops for exhibits. The Centrale Montemartini museum in Rome was formerly a thermoelectric power station, which opened in 1902, adjacent to the River Tiber, on which it was reliant for its supply of water. Converted into a museum in 1997, the enormous turbines and engines

192 Storhamarlåven, part of the Anno Museum in Hamar, was a new museum built on top of significant archaeological ruins in Norway.

193 Maurizio Cattelan's *Novecento*, 1997, a solemnly hanging taxidermized horse, is juxtaposed significantly with the ornate room of Rivoli Castle, Turin.

194 Andrea Bruno's plan for the restoration of Rivoli Castle, attempted to unite the half-built Filippo Juvarra house and an older long gallery.

195 The unequivocal message of the Wall of Indifference at the entrance to the Shoah Memorial, Morpurgo de Curtis, Milan, 2019–22.

now hold Roman archaeological finds, arranged beguilingly among the modern machinery. The Grain Silo complex, a set of buildings in the port of Cape Town, was abandoned in 2001 due to its obsolescence through the use of shipping containers. Thomas Heatherwick was commissioned to preserve the buildings and create spaces for the new Zeitz Museum of Contemporary Art Africa (MOCAA). The approach to the renovation was to slice the silos to create a very unusual atrium while maintaining the buildings' form. An industrial building's polluted past does not mean that it will not be reused; contamination might form a part of the new narrative. The small island of Inujima, in the Seto Inland Sea in Japan, was the site of a copper refinery. Its remote location was partly due to the toxic nature of producing copper. There were six thousand workers on the small island until the refinery closed in 1919, and today there are just fifty-seven official residents. Hiroshi Sambuichi was commissioned to redesign the refinery to become Seirensho Art Museum. This was organized as a journey through the ruins, utilizing the raw materials of the island: wind, light and water. Sambuichi described these as the 'moving materials', site specific elements extracted to make the story of the interior and its location intimately entwined.

Like Inujima, the Ningbo Museum, by Wang Shu in Zhejiang, China, extracted and then absorbed the materials on site, in this case the remnants of demolished villages and government buildings, incorporating them into the new construction. It was an act that created a continuity of action and appearance. The old construction technique of *wapan* was resurrected by local craftspeople. This involved assembling materials left on the site in order to quickly make the new building. This gave the craftspeople

a free hand in what material and stones they chose and how they deployed them. This approach was used to create a sense of continuity between the past and the present and was also a subtle commentary on the irrational demolition of the village underneath the building.

Site-specificity can be used to interrogate the role of the host building in which an exhibition is installed. *Mural* and *Para-Site* by Diller + Scofidio – the former in the Whitney Museum, the latter at MoMA in New York – did just that. *Mural* consisted of a robotic drill mounted on a track and guided by a computerized system moving across the white wall of the gallery and randomly drilling half-inch holes. Installed for the duration of a 2003 show entitled 'Scanning: The Aberrant Architectures of Diller + Scofidio', the drill perforated the wall to the point

196 Seirensho Art Museum, Hiroshi Sambuichi, with Yukinori Yanagi's installation *Solar Rock* on the island of Inujima, Japan, 2008.
197 Ancient statues on display in the former power station now Centrale Montemartini museum, Rome, 1997.
198 The sliced-open former grain silos of the Zeitz MOCAA interior by Thomas Heatherwick, Cape Town, 2017.
199 Section through Zeitz MOCAA detailing how eight of the silos were carved out to provide a monumental light-filled atrium between the galley spaces.

200 The track-mounted drill of Diller + Scofidio's *Mural*, 2003, cruised through the galleries of the Whitney Museum, New York, drilling holes until the walls became unstable.

201 *Para-Site* by Diller + Scofidio, 1989, 'invaded' MoMA and turned visitors into the exhibits through surveillance.

202 Wang Shu's Ningbo Museum, Zhejiang, China, 2008, advanced continuity through the incorporation of excavated material into the walls of the museum.

of collapse. Its actions and its noises were a deliberate riposte to the white walls of the gallery. *Para-Site* critiqued the supremacy of sight and it 'infested' MoMA through a series of installations in prominent areas of the building. The designers considered them to be spaces that legitimized the institution's authority. The revolving doors of the entrance, the elevators moving between the gallery floors and the doors to the famous sculpture court were filmed, with live feeds relayed to the rooms of the main gallery. The visitors therefore became the exhibits.

Contemporary developments in curating and museum display are manifest in new approaches to exhibits that have been removed from their context. Post-colonial and decolonial strategies and the restitution of illegally extracted objects are now at the forefront of museum and exhibition thinking across the world. Echoing Malraux's 'museums without walls' approach, art historian and anthropologist Alice Procter established tours of London museums and galleries under the title Uncomfortable Art Tours. Procter unofficially guides visitors around the objects of numerous London museums that have very complex stories. In her book *The Whole Picture*, she documents numerous displayed objects that have been extracted from differing contexts in somewhat dubious circumstances.[15] These include objects such as seven *mokomokai* (tattooed and preserved heads of Maori) held in storage by the British Museum. They were the subject of a 2008 request for restitution back to New Zealand, which was refused. In essence, all museums pose the question: where do the cultural

200

THE PUBLIC INTERIOR | CULTURE

artefacts of the world belong? Who owns the cultures that these artefacts represent? And how might their stories be told?

A museum project in Lagos directly addresses some of these questions. The John Randle Centre for Yoruba Culture and History was designed to be strikingly different to the reverential hushed tones of its European counterparts. Its designer Seun Oduwole and curator Will Rea described it as performative and full of colour, light and noise, 'a theatre of living memory'.[16] External walls of earth and gold lattice represent Yoruba cultures. Inside, the galleries commence with an animated calabash (a gourd of cultural significance) that explores myths and religions alongside deities such as Shango, god of thunder. The building is opposite an outdoor swimming pool, which was a significant gathering place for young Lagosians. The museum takes its name from John Randle, a Sierra Leonean doctor who built the pool when colonial rulers refused to do so. The museum and the pool were redeveloped and opened together in 2024. The imperative to repatriate and reconstitute museum objects can also

203

involve virtual strategies. The Milele Museum is Africa's first virtual museum dedicated to African knowledge and practices but not narrated by Western scholars and institutions. In 2023 the museum collaborated with Looty to create a VR treasure hunt. Looty is a collective founded by artists Chidi Nwaubani and Ahmed Abokor and named after Queen Victoria's Pekinese dog that was taken from the sacking of the Old Summer Palace near Beijing in 1860. The collaboration with Milele tasked users to activate heritage points by virtually repatriating Nigerian, Kenyan and Rwandan objects from Western collections.[17] A new archiving strategy that does not need permission to repatriate, but instead requires a smartphone; just like Malraux's *Musée imaginaire* the collection is built up of objects set free from their contexts.

Public interiors of culture also include libraries and archives, places where knowledge is stored and cultivated. In 2006 the artist Theaster Gates purchased an abandoned two-storey property in Greater Grand Crossing, a downtown area of south Chicago. As well as purchasing the building, Gates started to acquire crisis-discarded collections: a 60,000-piece glass-slide archive from the University of Chicago; 8,000 LPs from the closed down Dr Wax record store; and stock from the Prairie Avenue bookstore and the Johnson Library collection, including publications documenting decades of black lifestyle and achievements. Gates acquired more buildings in the vicinity of the house transforming the Dorchester area into a series of places of knowledge and culture. Describing himself as an 'un-real' estate developer, the purchases and renovations were largely financed by the artworks Gates made from the acquired collections and salvaged materials reused from the building sites. He used both to reflect upon and communicate cultures of black lives and histories.

Public libraries emerged to demonstrate how knowledge could be accessed by all. The Bibliothèque Sainte-Geneviève, designed 1842–50, and the Bibliothèque nationale de France (BnF), designed 1858–68, both by Henri Labrouste, utilized advances in iron construction tested in the Crystal Palace to realize great open halls that meant books and readers could be distributed freely underneath the large roofs. The BnF's stacks of books and desks organized under nine porcelain-panelled top-lit domes is still open today. Resonances when reusing an existing building for a cultural public

203 The John Randle Centre for Yoruba Culture and History, by Seun Oduwole and Ralph Appelbaum Associates, Lagos, Nigeria, translated Yoruba storytelling and nature into built form.

204 Theaster Gates' *Dorchester Projects*, Chicago, 2012, rehouses abandoned archives and discarded collections to reflect upon the erasure of black cultures.

interior provides a source of narrative for the acquisition of knowledge. Klaus Block's new library for the parish church in Müncheberg, Germany, transformed an existing building with an extraordinary past life. Block adapted the church to maintain a space for the reduced size of the congregation, but in the nave he inserted a tall timber-clad ship-like library. The new dual-purpose community space could accommodate religious services while the library kept the building in use all throughout the week.

In an age of information, the reach of digital and mobile technologies means that libraries and archives have had to be very clear as to what they contain outside as well as within their actual walls. Learning is something that must be embedded at a young age, but it is not always easy in different parts of the world. A square in the Cicendo district of Bandung, Indonesia, had a stage upon which the local community would gather and interact. Not wishing to take this away, but keen to engage the local children in reading, SHAU created a 'pocket' library, elevated above the stage, helping to shade the platform and also to encourage kids upstairs to read. In order to make the interior a cool environment, but to avoid using expensive air conditioning, the steel frame was clad in a simple yet abundant and cheap product: used ice-cream tubs. When the bottoms were cut open, they would let air pass through but keep the rain out. SHAU also realized that this cladding made a pattern like a binary code. The mayor was invited to contribute a message to be displayed on the tubs. 'Books are the windows to the world' can now be read on the façade cladding in binary.

In China, *hutongs* are narrow alleys formed by rows of traditional courtyard dwellings. They have been subject to demolition during extensive urban regeneration. Once owned and lived in by over a dozen families, no. 8 Cha'er Hutong is one such courtyard home located just a mile from Tiananmen Square in Beijing. ZAO retained and reused the building by inserting a small timber children's library. Kids drop into the library, pick up a book, stay and read before being picked up by their parents. They may climb onto the roof and play among the leaves of a large

205 Advances in iron construction helped realize the open halls of Henri Labrouste's reading room in the Bibliothèque nationale de France, Paris.
206 The ship-like library element by Klaus Block, 1998, in the nave of St Mary's Church, Müncheberg, Germany.

207 (Above and below) The Courtyard Children's Library by ZAO, Beijing, 2016, inserted into the traditional residence no. 8 Cha'er Hutong, celebrates the old building as well as the tree in the centre of the courtyard.

208 SHAU's microlibrary in Bandung, Indonesia, 2016, utilized ice-cream containers to create a façade with a message for the children using it.

209 Shared Lady Beetle, a micro movable library, by LUO Studio, 2019.

ash tree on the site, or just hang out with the other kids and make friends. Knowledge is acquired through playing. If you cannot get to a library, it might be able to come to you. LUO Studio responded to the mass of dumped free-share bicycles in China by creating a mobile library for children. The reclaimed bike has a new element on its back, playfully arranged in the shape of a beetle that opens its wings to reveal the books inside.

Whether small or large, public culture interiors are all required to do at least one thing, that is inspire the acquisition of knowledge within its users. It is this knowledge that can give young users confidence. The METI Handmade School in Radrapur in Bangladesh, designed by Anna Heringer and Eike Roswag, was constructed as a two-storey building with three classroom 'caves' on the ground floor for the children to discover and explore either individually or as a group. The open upper-floor bamboo construction was designed to be open and airy, full of light and breeze among the treetops of the surrounding landscape. Places of culture can also protect. The SOS Children's Village in Tadjoura, Djibouti, was designed to give orphaned and in-need children a safe and calming space for them to live, feel secure and to grow again. In what is one of the hottest places on earth, Urko Sanchez Architects created fifteen houses designed with thermal comfort in mind. Natural ventilation corridors with wind catchers draw the flow of air into the interior spaces. Cultural spaces are interiors for knowledge and confidence,

210

210 The *trompe l'oeil* stage set of the Teatro Olimpico, Vicenza, Italy, was designed by Vincenzo Scamozzi with Andrea Palladio in 1580–85 and is still used as a theatre today.

211 Traditional techniques such as working with earth and bamboo were used for the construction of METI Handmade School by Anna Heringer and Eike Roswag, Radrupar, Bangladesh, 2007.

212 Urko Sanchez Architects arranged fifteen houses as though a traditional walled city to provide a safe enclosure for the SOS Children's Village, Tadjoura, Djibouti, 2020.

213 The ground floor's thick walls and numerous openings encourage natural ventilation and cooling in order to ensure the right environment within which children can focus on their studying in the METI School.

spaces for their users to develop and grow.

Culture can be performed. The Teatro Olimpico in Vicenza, Italy, features the oldest surviving stage scenery in the world. It set the standard for European Renaissance theatres with its auditorium and stage framed by a proscenium arch. Its impressiveness has endured because of the dynamic illusory spectacle of the seven perspectively altered streetscapes set deep into the backstage. Performance has particular cultural implications. The Great Mosque of Djenné in Mali is the largest mud-built structure in the world. The site has been inhabited since 250 BCE and the current building dates from 1907. Every year, the *Crépissage* (plastering) takes place in April, a one-day festival that maintains and fortifies the building for another year before the rainy seasons come. It is not just building maintenance but a cultural festival that starts at 4 a.m. and continues until the building is re-covered in a new skin of mud. Teams from the town compete to undertake their section in the quickest time. Participants are covered in *banco*, which is a mixture of clay, rice bran, butter, baobab powder and water. Contestants and mud become one as the day is spent scrambling up ladders and smearing the substance on top of last year's efforts. The *Crépissage* is a festival of the culture of the town celebrated through material and is a

211

212

213

THE PUBLIC INTERIOR | CULTURE

214 The Great Mosque of Djenné, Mali, is the largest mud-built structure in the world.
215 Thousands of people gather each year to replaster the walls of the mosque in an activity known as the *Crépissage* (plastering).
216 The rebuilding of the Ise Jingu shrine depicted in a woodblock print by Utagawa Kuniyoshi, 1849.

THE PUBLIC INTERIOR | CULTURE

symbol of the cohesion of the community. A similar celebration is the remaking of the Ise Jingu shrine in Japan. For over 1,300 years it has been torn down every 20 years and identically rebuilt. This process is called *Shikinen Sengu* and it reifies the tradition of passing Japanese culture to the next generation. Unlike the speed of the *Crépissage*, the ceremony takes eight years to prepare.

Performance is not always so reverent. Michael Landy's *Break Down* consisted of an installation in a disused C&A clothing store in the centre of London's main shopping area on Oxford Street. In a performance that lasted two weeks he destroyed all 7,227 of his possessions. Standing on a central platform overseeing operations, materials were dismantled by an army of helpers who placed wood, paper, metal, plastic in yellow trays to be passed along the production line and shredded. The production line displayed the objects to curious passers-by as they visited the performance and watched the artist dispose of all his worldly possessions. Even his car was granulated. In a disused consumer emporium, Landy used the location to make a comment on his own consumerism albeit via the dispossession of his own goods.

Performative interiors exemplify the body in space through the association of the narratives being relayed and the people involved. This approach questions traditional relationships between audience and actor. In these experiences, the boundaries between set, performance, actor and audience are completely limitless. In collaboration with Ward Shelley, Alex Schweder constructs elaborate environments that rely on both artists to inhabit the structure for a period of time. They are challenging and designed in such a way that both must negotiate their occupancy of the space in relation to each other. *In Orbit* was a huge timber wheel installed inside a decommissioned power plant in Brooklyn, New York. Both artists lived in and on the wheel for ten days: Schweder in the lower inside level, Shelley on the upper outside. Incorporated within the structure were two kitchen units with sinks, comfortable chairs and a bed for each occupant. In order to access the items of furniture, both artists had to negotiate the move and decide which way to 'walk' the wheel. They would do this until the piece

217 Michael Landy's *Break Down*, the destruction of all his possessions in a disused department store in London in 2001, questioned consumerism.
218 The 1867 Paris Exposition featured more than 50,000 exhibitors in the elliptical building designed by Gustave Eiffel.
219 World's fairs have become enormous demonstrations of wealth, power and sometimes imperial ambitions. Gallery of Machines, Paris Exposition, 1889.

of furniture they required came to their position. Visitors came and watched the performance for the duration of the event. The performance was about relationships and negotiation, but also about care. Schweder was responsible for Shelley's balance atop the wheel, only moving when agreed and taking care not to destabilize his position. Performative culture can include the site in which an activity takes place as the central attraction of the show. Jinyun County in Zhejiang Province, China, has been shaped by the manual mining of natural stone. Beijing architect Xu Tiantian of DnA_Design and Architecture was commissioned to develop strategies for new uses of nine of the more than three thousand small abandoned quarries. The first nine pits were adapted with circulation in the form of bridges and stairs taking visitors to numerous stages placed in the crevasses of the quarries. Each space relies on the power of the site to create a dramatic backdrop for performances.

Since the Great Exhibition of 1851, expositions and world's fairs have been a dominant force in the *performing* of a nation's 'message'. Hosting spectacular events demonstrates the wealth and power of nations. Theme is an important element of the spectacle. The Great Exhibition and the subsequent Paris Exposition of 1855 were both distributed into categories of industrial, fine arts and agricultural. The Paris Exposition of 1867 was spatially sophisticated and held in a huge elliptical hall designed by Gustave Eiffel. Frédéric Le Play was the commissioner of the exhibition and he organized it around seven categories distributed in concentric rings. The orbital pavilion was known as the Palais Omnibus. The first category was entitled 'The History of Labour', showing ancient tools; then the gallery of fine arts; and further corridors for furniture, textiles and material. The next range of galleries was the machine halls. On the outside were restaurants. Each nation was

allocated a 'wedge' that cut across the rings from the centre to the outside. Visitors could either traverse the different nations or move from inside to out, savouring one nation's arts, power and technological innovation along with their national dish. Exhibits, objects and machines were set into lifelike contexts. Craftspeople and workers demonstrated their skills to passers-by; agricultural workers were presented in *tableaux vivants* of the place in which they would normally work.

The New York World's Fair of 1939 featured 'The City of Light', a huge diorama designed by Walter Dorwin Teague for the Consolidated Edison company. It presented the illusion of watching the city through a twenty-four hour cycle with four thousand replica buildings including the Empire State Building at 6.7 metres (22 feet) to represent its 102 storeys. The Dutch pavilion by MVRDV at Expo 2000 in Hanover performed nationhood through the enclosure of six landscapes, stacked one on top of another in a high-rise pavilion. It required the visitor to descend through each one, exploring differing themes of space and how it was used thoughtfully throughout the country. The British Seed Cathedral by Thomas Heatherwick at Expo 2010 in Shanghai, preserved the world's plant species. The pavilion was formed from 60,000 metal rods, 7.5-metres (25 feet) long, that protruded outside the pavilion to give the appearance of a fibre-optic lamp. All demonstrated innovative nationhood identities.

The legacy that Expos and games leave behind after they have finished has become an increasingly important strategy for the future of large-scale events. Invited by Lebanon's then president Fouad Chehab, Oscar Niemeyer designed the enormous Rashid Karami International Fair in Tripoli in 1964. Never completed due to civil war, military occupation and sectarian troubles the building has languished in disrepair for decades.

220 For ten days in 2014 Alex Schweder and Ward Shelley lived on *In Orbit*, a large wheel movable only through cooperation.
221 (Opposite) A former quarry in Zhejiang, China, reused by DnA_ Design and Architecture in 2022 as a public performance space.

222

223

THE PUBLIC INTERIOR | CULTURE

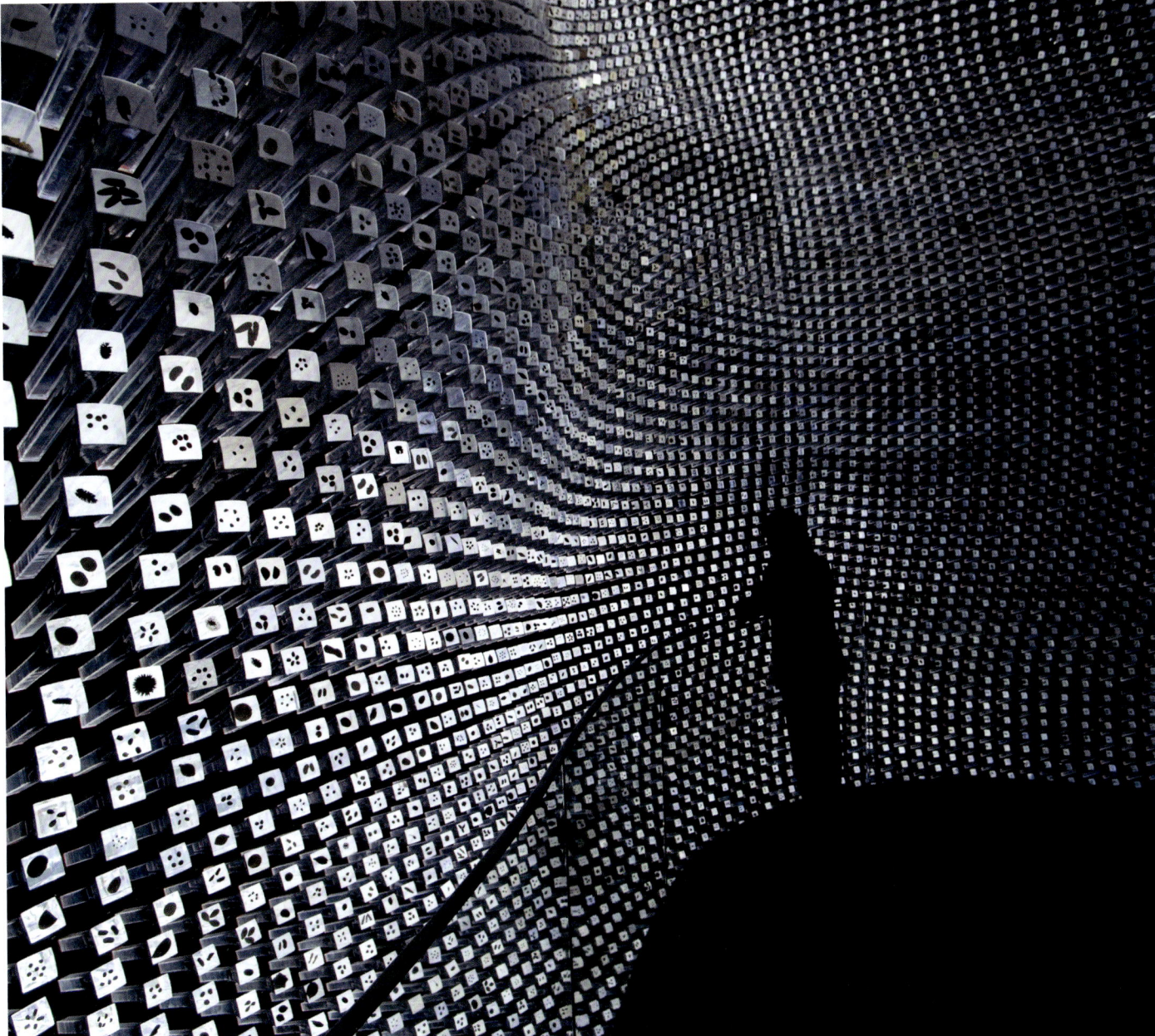

222 Man working atop a replica of the Empire State Building in Consolidated Edison's diorama at the World's Fair, New York, 1939.

223 The Dutch pavilion by MVRDV at Expo 2000 in Hanover was a six-level stacked hi-rise of stereotypical tulips, windmills and dykes as a performance of nationhood.

224 The UK's Seed Cathedral by Thomas Heatherwick at Expo 2010 in Shanghai preserved plant species.

Subsiding tensions in the city meant new plans were put in place to revive several iconic disused structures in the exhibition centre. The guest house of the enormous derelict fair pavilion has been reused by East Architecture Studio to become a furniture-making facility, training new carpenters and designers. The guest house had been used as a prison by Syrian occupiers, but once cleaned out the designers set about making the building usable for trainees and Minjara, a local furniture making company. The site of the fair is crumbling and decaying, but its huge expanse means families go to picnic there. As an official public space for the city it is still contested and sealed off; plans to reuse it are on hold for economic reasons.

From the Palais Omnibus to *tableaux vivants*, to reused derelict world's fair sites, the 'theatres' of pavilions and expositions speak to the desires of immersion – one of the fundamental principles of a visit to an exhibition. All Expos and pavilions perform a new approach to nationhood, one that aims to connect rather than divide. This is an enduring form of knowledge and the transmission of culture.

225

225 In 2018 East Architecture Studio reused the guest house of Oscar Niemeyer's derelict pavilion for the Rashid Karami International Fair in Tripoli as a furniture-making facility.
226 (Opposite) The structure now exhibits the work of local craftspeople and artisans. The interventions in the structure are all reversible.

Notes

Introduction

1. In May 2021, the Environment Protection Agency (EPA) stated that Americans spent 93 per cent of their time indoors: 87 per cent in buildings, 6 per cent in cars For Europeans, the proportion of time spent indoors was 90 per cent. The global average is between 90 and 98 percent.
2. Charles Rice, *The Emergence of the Interior: Architecture, Modernity, Domesticity* (Abingdon: Routledge, 2007), 2.

The Room

1. Do Ho Suh, quoted in Lucy Ives, 'Do Ho Suh's Translucent Architectures', *Frieze*, 229 (21 September 2022), https://www.frieze.com/article/do-ho-suh-translucent-architectures.
2. Jo Tonna, 'The Poetics of Arab-Islamic Architecture', *Muqarnas*, 7 (1990), 187, as cited in Rem Koolhaas and Irma Boom, *Wall: Elements of Architecture* (Venice: Marsilio, 2014), 36.
3. Mario Praz, *An Illustrated History of Interior Decoration: From Pompeii to Art Nouveau* (London: Thames & Hudson, 1982), 20–21.
4. Adolf Loos, *Ornament and Crime* (London: Penguin Classics, 2019). Loos gave a lecture with this title at the Akademischer Verband für Literatur und Musik in Vienna in 1910. It was first published in German in 1929.
5. Charles-Édouard Jeanneret (Le Corbusier), *Decorative Art of Today*, trans. James Dunnett (Cambridge, MA: MIT Press, 1987), 90.
6. See Anne Massey, *Interior Design of the 20th Century* (London: Thames & Hudson, 1990), 124, and also Joel Sanders, 'Curtain Wars', *Harvard Design Magazine*, Winter/Spring 2002, 18.
7. Robin Evans, 'The Developed Surface: An Enquiry into The Brief Life of an Eighteenth-Century Drawing Technique', in *Translations from Drawing to Building and Other Essays* (London: AA Publications, 1997), 209.
8. Ibid.
9. Diane Fuss, *The Sense of an Interior: Four Rooms and the Writers That Shaped Them* (Abingdon: Routledge, 2004), 200.
10. Mark Girouard, *Life in the English Country House* (London: Penguin, 1980), 30.
11. Witold Rybczynski, *Now I Sit Me Down: From Klismos to Plastic Chair: A Natural History* (New York: Farrar, Straus and Giroux, 2016), 163.
12. Michelle Perrot, *The Bedroom: An Intimate History* (New Haven: Yale University Press, 2018), 15.
13. Justin McGuirk, 'The Porous Interior: Privacy and Performance at Home', in Eszter Steierhoffer and Justin McGuirk Justin, eds, *Home Futures* (London: Design Museum Publishing, 2018), 258.

The Private Interior

1. UNESCO, 'Majlis, a cultural and social space', https://ich.unesco.org/en/RL/majlis-a-cultural-and-social-space-01076, accessed May 2024.
2. See Sherry McKay, 'The "Salon de la Princesse": "Rococo" Design, Ornamented Bodies and the Public Sphere', *RACAR*, 21/1–2 (1994), 76.
3. Eszter Steierhoffer, 'Introduction', in Eszter Steierhoffer and Justin McGuirk Justin, eds, *Home Futures* (London: Design Museum Publishing, 2018), 10.
4. Ashley Simone, ed., *Allan Wexler: Absurd Thinking: Between Art and Design* (Zürich: Lars Müller, 2017), 174.
5. Robert Kerr, *The Gentlemen's House, or How to Plan English Residences* (London: John Murray, 1865), 204.
6. Christine Frederick, *The New Housekeeping* (New York: Doubleday, 1913) [online facsimile], http://nationalhumanitiescenter.org/pds/gilded/progress/text4/frederick.pdf, accessed January 2024.
7. The Kitchen Sisters, *Hidden Kitchens How Russia's Shared Kitchens Helped Shape Soviet Politics* [podcast], NPR (20 May 2014), https://www.npr.org/sections/thesalt/2014/05/20/314054405/how-russias-shared-kitchens-helped-shape-soviet-politics?t=1592411834532.
8. Sasha Archibald, 'Womanhouse Revisited', *The Believer*, 103 (1 November 2013), https://www.thebeliever.net/womanhouse-revisited/, accessed September 2023.
9. Katie White, 'James McNeill Whistler's "The Peacock Room" Is a Glittering Masterpiece With a Dark History', Artnet (10 October 2024), https://news.artnet.com/art-world/how-james-mcneill-whistlers-peacock-room-2545955, accessed November 2024.
10. Lawrence Wright, *Clean and Decent The History of the Bathroom and the WC* (Abingdon: Routledge, 1960), 56.
11. Beatriz Colomina and Mark Wigley, 'Toilet Architecture: An Essay About the Most Psychosexually Charged Room in a Building', *PIN-UP*, 23 (Fall/Winter 2017/18), https://archive.pinupmagazine.org/articles/toilet-modern-architecture, accessed July 2024.
12. Barbara Penner, *Bathroom* (London: Reaktion Books, 2013), 10.

13 Ibid.
14 The University of Kansas, 'Explore KU and the design-build of a smart home' [video], YouTube (22 January 2018), https://www.youtube.com/watch?v=PZOzl7CvyBY, accessed March 2024.
15 Emily Anthes, *The Great Indoors: The Surprising Science of How Buildings Shape our Behaviour, Health and Happiness* (New York: Scientific American Books, 2020), 173.
16 Michelle Perrot, *The Bedroom: An Intimate History* (New Haven and London: Yale University Press, 2018), 301.
17 Edwin Heathcote, *The Meaning of Home* (London: Frances Lincoln, 2012), 73.
18 Kerr, *The Gentlemen's House*, 115.
19 Elsie de Wolfe, *The House in Good Taste* (New York, 1913; repr. Jefferson Publications, 2015), 58.
20 Marcel Proust, quoted in Diane Fuss, *The Sense of an Interior: Four Rooms and the Writers That Shaped Them* (Abingdon: Routledge, 2004), 153.
21 Anthes, *The Great Indoors*, 166.

The Public Interior

1 'Alchoholic Architecture', Bompas & Parr, https://bompasandparr.com/case-study/alcoholic-architecture/, accessed December 2024.
2 Otto Riewold, *New Hotel Design* (London and New York: Laurence King/Watson Guptill, 2002), 7.
3 Conrad Hilton, quoted in Franziska Bollerey, 'Beyond the Lobby Setting the Stage for Modernity', in Tom Avermaete and Anne Massey, *Hotel Lobbies and Lounges: The Architecture of Professional Hospitality* (Abingdon: Routledge, 2013), 10.
4 For a very good explanation of clubs see Nigel Coates, 'New Clubs at Large', *AA Files*, 1 (Winter 1981–82), 4.
5 The author in conversation with Howard Sullivan in February 2024.
6 Jeremy Myerson, 'The Evolution of Workspace Design: From the Machine to the Network', in Graeme Brooker and Lois Weinthal, eds, *The Handbook of Interior Architecture and Design* (London: Bloomsbury, 2013), 213.
7 Ibid., 217.
8 Dominic Catacora, 'Coworking by the Numbers', Allwork.Space (12 September 2024), https://allwork.space/2024/09/coworking-by-the-numbers-2024-data-and-trends-that-offer-insights-into-the-future-of-flex/, accessed December 2024.
9 Adrian Forty, *Objects of Desire: Design and Society since 1750* (London: Thames & Hudson, 1986), 125.
10 Juan-Carlos Cano, 'Laguna Mexico', *Architectural Review* (July/August 2023), 62–72.
11 For a fuller explanation of the infrastructural public interior see Mark Pimlott, *The Public Interior as Idea and Project* (Prinsenbeek: Jap Sam Books, 2016).
12 Andrew Hammond, 'Neom "uses one fifth of world's steel"', *AGBI* (15 October 2024), https://www.agbi.com/giga-projects/2024/10/neom-uses-one-fifth-of-worlds-steel/, accessed November 2024.
13 Oliver Wainwright, 'Nine million people in a city 170 km long; will the world ever be ready for a linear metropolis?', *Guardian* (8 September 2022), https://www.theguardian.com/artanddesign/2022/sep/08/nine-million-people-in-a-city-170km-long-will-the-world-ever-be-ready-for-a-linear-metropolis, accessed September 2022.
14 Christopher Grunenberg, 'The Modern Art Museum', in Emma Barker, ed., *Contemporary Cultures of Display* (New Haven: Yale University Press, 1999), 48.
15 Alice Procter, *The Whole Picture* (London: Cassell, 2020).
16 Saeed Kamali Dehghan, 'Nigeria Welcomes a Museum Like No Other', *Guardian* (30 April 2024), https://www.theguardian.com/global-development/2024/apr/30/john-randle-centre-yoruba-culture-lagos-nigeria, accessed May 2024.
17 'Collaboration with Milele Museum', Looty, https://www.looty.art/works/milele, accessed January 2024.

Further Reading

Aben, Rob and de Wit, Saskia, *The Enclosed Garden: History and Development of the Hortus Conclusus and its Reintroduction into the Present-day Urban Landscape* (Rotterdam: 010 Publishers, 1999).

Banham, Joanna, ed., *Encyclopedia of Interior Design*, 2 vols (London and Chicago: Fitzroy Dearborn Publishers, 1997).

Blakemore, Robbie G., *History of Interior Design Furniture: From Ancient Egypt to Nineteenth-Century Europe* (New York: Van Nostrand Reinhold, 1997).

Bourriaud, Nicolas, *Postproduction* (London: Sternberg Press, 2010).

Brooker, Graeme, *Key Interiors Since 1900* (London: Laurence King, 2013).

Brooker, Graeme, *Adaptation Strategies for Interior Architecture and Design* (London: Bloomsbury, 2016).

Casson, Hugh, ed., *Inscape: The Design of Interiors* (London: Architectural Press, 1968).

Diller, Elizabeth and Ricardo Scofidio, *Flesh* (Triangle Architectural Publishing, 1994).

Evans, Robin, *Translations from Drawing to Building and Other Essays* (London: AA Publications, 1997).

Flanders, Judith, *The Making of Home* (London: Atlantic Books, 2014).

Forty, Adrian, *Objects of Desire: Design and Society since 1750* (London: Thames & Hudson, 1986).

Frye, David, *Walls: A History of Civilization in Blood and Brick* (London: Faber & Faber, 2018).

Fuss, Diane, *The Sense of an Interior: Four Rooms and the Writers That Shaped Them* (Abingdon: Routledge, 2004).

Girouard, Mark, *Life in the English Country House* (London: Penguin, 1980).

Harris, John, *Moving Rooms: The Trade in Architectural Salvages* (New Haven: Yale University Press, 2007).

Heathcote, Edwin, *The Meaning of Home* (London: Frances Lincoln, 2012).

Hollis, Edward, *The Memory Palace: A Book of Lost Interiors* (London: Portobello Books, 2013).

Kerr, Robert, *The Gentlemen's House, or How to Plan English Residences* (London: John Murray, 1865).

Koolhaas, Rem, et al., eds, *Elements* (Venice: Marsilio, 2014).

McCarter, Robert, *The Space Within: Interior Experience as the Origin of Architecture* (London: Reaktion Books, 2016).

McKeon, Michael, *The Secret History of Domesticity: Public, Private and the Division of Knowledge* (Baltimore: John Hopkins University Press, 2005).

Massey, Anne, *Interior Design of the 20th Century* (London: Thames & Hudson, 1990).

Muthesius, Stefan, *The Poetic Home: Designing the 19th-Century Domestic Interior* (London: Thames & Hudson, 2009).

Parissien, Steven, *Interiors: The Home since 1700* (London: Laurence King, 2009).

Pennell, Sara, *The Birth of the English Kitchen, 1600–1850* (London: Bloomsbury, 2016).

Penner, Barbara, *Bathroom* (London: Reaktion Books, 2013).

Perrot, Michelle, ed., *A History of Private Life*, vol. iv (Cambridge, MA, and London: Belknap Press, 1990).

Perrot, Michelle, *The Bedroom: An Intimate History* (New Haven and London: Yale University Press, 2018).

Pimlott, Mark, *The Public Interior as Idea and Project* (Prinsenbeek: Jap Sam Books, 2016).

Praz, Mario, *An Illustrated History of Interior Decoration: From Pompeii to Art Nouveau* (London: Thames & Hudson, 1982).

Rice, Charles, *The Emergence of the Interior: Architecture, Modernity, Domesticity* (Abingdon: Routledge, 2007).

Rybczynski, Witold, *Now I Sit Me Down: From Klismos to Plastic Chair: A Natural History* (New York: Farrar, Straus and Giroux, 2016).

Sample, Hilary, *Maintenance Architecture* (Cambridge, MA: MIT Press, 2016).

Sarti, Raffaella, *Europe at Home: Family and Material Culture 1500–1800* (New Haven: Yale University Press, 2002).

Scott, Fred, *On Altering Architecture* (Abingdon: Routledge, 2007).

Sensual City Studio, *A History of Thresholds: Life, Death and Rebirth* (Berlin: Jovis, 2018).

Simone, Ashley, ed., *Allan Wexler: Absurd Thinking: Between Art and Design* (Zürich: Lars Müller, 2017).

Sparke, Penny, *The Modern Interior* (London: Reaktion Books, 2008).

Thornton, Peter, *The Italian Renaissance Interior 1400–1600* (London: Weidenfeld & Nicolson, 1991).

Thornton, Peter, *Authentic Decor: The Domestic Interior 1620–1920* (London: Weidenfeld & Nicolson, 1993).

Wharton, Edith and Ogden Codman Jr, *The Decoration of Houses* (New York, 1897; facs. edn, New York: The Mount Press and Rizzoli, 2007).

Acknowledgments

This book is dedicated to the memory of David Crow. David was a designer, academic and writer and a colleague from my time at Manchester Metropolitan University who became a firm friend and a mentor for my own journey as an educator. David's unwavering calm and unique insight into any situation or problem was a help to so many. His unique understanding and human sensibility will live on in the WhatsApp group 'WWDD' (What Would David Do), a source of assistance when any of its members reach out for answers to particular problems or thoughts.

Numerous people have played a part in making this book a reality, all deserve huge thanks. Billy Norwich, who introduced the project to me. Rebecca Sandell, once of Pew Literary, and Barnabas Calder, who helped it along the way. To Augusta Pownall and Emma Barton who, along with Yasmin Garcha, Jane Cutter, Rachel Hughes, Frank Gallaugher, Yasmin Gapper and Lucas Dietrich at Thames & Hudson, not only believed in the project but have gently and persuasively wrestled me and it into this reality. Thanks to Astrid Stavro for her beautiful design work. Huge thanks to numerous colleagues who have offered astute advice as they heard me road-test some of these ideas in various talks and conferences around the world, including a well-deserved Ed Hollis 'discussion' in Berlin. To my RCA Interior Design and School of Architecture colleagues – Gem, Tania, Steve, Pierre, Ella, Amelia, Gae, Ian, Jim, Simon, Kazuma, Kevin, Sylwia, Patrick, Adrian, Sandra, Beth, Godo', Dubravka, Mark, Christina, David, Thandi, Taz, Alice, Kimberley, Josh, Sam and Ines – thanks for your help and support. To Jesper Authen for research help when it was needed. To Greg Shannon for all the pep talks. To all the students I have taught in the time it has taken to write this book I would like to say thanks for your sometimes willing and more often unknowing support. My work with so many great colleagues in twenty years of Interior Educators and United in Design has been inspirational. Finally, thanks to my mum and Les but most of all to Claire and Mr Osgood for their fortitude when things in 'the loft' were heating up.

Author Biography

Graeme Brooker is an interior designer with extensive experience in practice, education and research. He is Professor and Head of Interior Design at the Royal College of Art in London. He has taught at institutions in the US, Europe and Asia and is the author of numerous books on the histories, theories and processes of the interior.

Sources of Illustrations

a = above
b = below
c = centre
l = left
r = right

p. 2 Photo © Timothy Hursley. © Keith Haring Foundation
p. 5 **al** Leopold von Ungern / Alamy Stock Photo; **bl** Photo Tate, London. © Succession Marcel Duchamp / ADAGP, Paris and DACS, London 2025; **ac** Photo Karen Warren / Houston Chronicle via Getty Images; **bc** Photo The Museum of Modern Art, New York /Scala, Florence. © Ettore Sottsass DACS, London 2025; **r** Universal Images Group North America LLC / Alamy Stock Photo
p. 6 **al** © Rene Burri / Magnum Photos; **bl** Dylan Perrenoud; **c** © Allan Wexler; **ar** Dir. Kubrick, Warner Bros. / Hawk Films / Peregrine / Producers Circle; **br** Photo Antonia Reeve. The Hill House, National Trust for Scotland
p. 7 **al** Adam Scull / Shutterstock; **bl** Hulton Archive/ Getty Images; **ac** ymgerman / Shutterstock; **bc** Daniele Mattioli; **r** © C. Toraldo di Francia | Superstudio, Archivio Filottrano

Introduction

1 Photo Bas Princen. Courtesy Studio Anne Holtrop
2 © Aga Khan Trust for Culture / Rajesh Vora
3 Photo © Schnepp Renou. Courtesy Kinzo
4 Leonard Stern. Courtesy *The New York Times*
5 James McDonald
6 Photo © Wen Studio. Courtesy Atelier tao+c
7 Photo James Morris. Courtesy David Connor and Kate Darby

The Room

1 © Qingjun Huang
2 The National Gallery, London
3 Courtesy the artist and Lehmann Maupin, New York, Seoul, and London. © Do Ho Suh
4 © Aljan Gharem
5 The Africa Image Library / Alamy Stock Photo
6 Photo Wang Ziling. Courtesy DnA_Design and Architecture
7 DnA_Design and Architecture
8 Richard Buchbinder / Alamy Stock Photo
9 Photo Anna Sara. Courtesy Decolonizing Architecture Art Research
10 Courtesy Toyo Ito & Associates, Architects
11 Shigeru Ohno
12 Helen Dixon / Alamy Stock Photo
13 Ronald Rael and Virginia San Fratello / Rael San Fratello
14 Les Archives Digitales / Alamy Stock Photo
15 Joana Kruse / Alamy Stock Photo
16 Nikreates / Alamy Stock Photo
17 Gerry O'Leary
18 Ayhan Altun / Alamy Stock Photo
19 Inside Outside
20 Inside Outside
21 Photo Bas Princen. Courtesy OFFICE Kersten Geers David Van Severen
22 Mondadori Portfolio / Electa / Marco Covi / Bridgeman Images
23 Leopold von Ungern / Alamy Stock Photo
24 Alex Ramsay / Alamy Stock Photo
25 Shutterstock/ Kiev.Victor
26 Iwan Baan
27 Imago / Alamy Stock Photo
28 M_AA / iStock
29 Gary Cook / Alamy Stock Photo
30 Photo courtesy the artist. © Mary Griep
31 Photo The Museum of Modern Art, New York / Scala, Florence. © DACS 2025
32 Bridgeman Images
33 Photo James Wang. Courtesy Mariam Issoufou Architects

34	Photo James Wang. Courtesy Mariam Issoufou Architects
35	mauritius images GmbH / Alamy Stock Photo
36	Photo Andrew Dunkley & Marcus Leith / Tate London Courtesy the artist; neugerriemschneider, Berlin; Tanya Bonakdar Gallery, New York / Los Angeles © 2003 Olafur Eliasson
37	Penta Springs Limited / Alamy Stock Photo
38	Adrià Goula
39	Petr Bonek / Alamy Stock Photo
40	robertharding / Alamy Stock Photo
41	ONLY FRANCE / Alamy Stock Photo
42	Image courtesy White Cube. © Tracey Emin. All rights reserved, DACS / Artimage 2025.
43	akg-images / Werner Forman
44	Richard Maschmeyer/ Robert Harding
45	Juergen Ritterbach / Alamy Stock Photo
46	Baarssen Fokke / Alamy Stock Photo
47	Photo schranimage. Courtesy Studio Zhu-Pei
48	Photo schranimage. Courtesy Studio Zhu-Pei
49	Scala, Florence – courtesy of the Ministero Beni e Att. Culturali e del Turismo
50	Scala, Florence – courtesy of the Ministero Beni e Att. Culturali e del Turismo
51	Scala, Florence
52	Architecture2000 / Alamy Stock Photo
53	Courtesy World Monuments Fund
54	Andreas von Einsiedel / Alamy Stock Photo
55	Suzuki Kaku / Alamy Stock Photo
56	HOH architecten and Paulien Bremmer
57	Photo Chao Zhang. Courtesy Studio 10
58	Youssef Haidar Architect
59	Photo Kang Wei. Courtesy One Take Architects. ©Li Hao
60	Rasmus Hjortshøj
61	Karen Warren / Houston Chronicle via Getty Images
62	*The Modern Builder's Assistant: or a Concise Epitome of the Whole System of Architecture.* William Halfpenny, John Halfpenny, Thomas Lightoler, Robert Morris, 1742. Published by James Rivington and J. Fletcher (London). Robert Sayer (British, Sunderland 1725–1794 Bath). Getty Research Institute
63	Photo 12 / Alamy Stock Photo
64	Photo 12 / Alamy Stock Photo
65	Gianni Dagli Orti / Shutterstock
66	Science History Images / Alamy Stock Photo
67	Photo NPL – DeA Picture Library / M. Borchi / Bridgeman Images
68	Photo Ettore Bellini. Courtesy Querini Stampalia Foundation, Venice
69	Paul Bird / Shutterstock
70	DeAgostini / Getty Images
71	Mohammed Ashkanani. Courtesy Babnimnim Design Studio
72	*Extraordinario libro di architettura*, Sebastiano Serlio, 1560. Published by Giovanni Battista & Marchio Sessa, Venice. Lessing J. Rosenwald Collection, Library of Congress, Rare Book and Special Collections Division
73	Photo The Art Institute of Chicago / Art Resource, NY / Scala, Florence. © Kochi Prefecture, Ishimoto Yasuhiro Photo Center
74	akg-images / Album / sfgp
75	Schloß Schönbrunn Kultur-und Betriebsges.m.b.H. / Photo Edgar Knaack
76	Photo Yuya Miki. Courtesy 2m26
77	Walter Godfrey, *The site of Beaufort House, in Survey of London: Volume 4, Chelsea, Pt II*, 1913, London
78	Eric de Mare / RIBA Collections
79	Bridgendboy / iStock
80	Courtesy the Ministry of Culture – Vittoriano and Palazzo Venezia
81	Courtesy the Ministry of Culture – Vittoriano and Palazzo Venezia
82	Rural Urban Framework
83	Brian Jannsen / Alamy Stock Photo
84	Hulton Archive/Getty Images
85	Vito Arcomano / Alamy Stock Photo
86	Universal Images Group North America LLC / Alamy Stock Photo
87	The National Gallery of Art, Washington, Mark J. Millard Architectural Collection
88	The National Trust Photolibrary / Alamy Stock Photo
89	Andreas Billman
90	B.O'Kane / Alamy Stock Photo
91	*In English Homes: The Internal Character Furniture and Adornments of Some of the Most Notable Houses of England Historically Depicted from Photographs Specially Taken* (Vol 1), Charles Latham, 1904.
92	Courtesy the artist and Lehmann Maupin, New York, Seoul, and London. © Do Ho Suh
93	GI1570Z993 / iStock
94	DeAgostini / Getty Images
95	The Metropolitan Museum of Art, New York, Harris Brisbane Dick Fund, 1963
96	The Metropolitan Museum of Art, New York, Rogers Fund, 1907
97	National Museum of Antiquities, Leiden
98	Ian Dagnall / Alamy Stock Photo
99	Photo Lubna Hammoud. © Dunne & Raby
100	Formafantasma
101	Studio Rolf.fr i.c.w.
102	Imagekontaainer / Knölke / www.imagekontainer.com
103	Studio Rolf.fr i.c.w.
104	Photo Theo Tennant. Courtesy Retrouvius
105	Photo PHX India. Courtesy S+PS Architects
106	Photo Adrià Goula. Courtesy Flores & Prats
107	Photo Agostino Osio. Courtesy Fondazione Prada
108	Flores & Prats
109	Ricardo Bofill Taller de Arquitectura
110	The Metropolitan Museum of Art, New York, Harris Brisbane Dick Fund, 1941
111	James Anderson, Alinari Archives, Florence
112	Guy Bell / Alamy Stock Photo
113	Photo Tate, London. © Succession Marcel Duchamp / ADAGP, Paris and DACS, London 2025
114	View Pictures / Universal Images Group via Getty Images
115	Peter Aaron / OTTO
116	Photo Martin Rand. Courtesy Brooks + Scarpa
117	Photo Zhao Liqun. Courtesy PAO
118	Dir. Michael Gordon, Arwin Productions / Avernus Productions
119	Konrad Zelazowski / Alamy Stock Photo
120	Photo Laurian Ghinitoiu. Courtesy MAS Architecture
121	Photo Sergei Mikhailovich Prokudin-Gorski. Prokudin-Gorskii Collection, Library of Congress Prints and Photographs Division Washington, D.C. (LC-P87-80x)
122	Library of Congress Prints and Photographs Division Washington, D.C. (Illus. in DK854.T87 1872, part 3, pl. 45, no. 211 [Case Z])
123	Detail Heritage / Alamy Stock Photo
124	*Regole generali di architettura*, Sebastiono Serlio, 1537. Published by Francesco Marcolini da Forli, Venice. Columbia University Libraries
125	Aurelio Amendola / Archivio Aurelio Amendola / Mondadori Portfolio via Getty Images
126	Stephen Dorey - Bygone Images / Alamy Stock Photo

127	National Trust Images / Andreas von Einsiedel
128	GM Pictures / Shutterstock
129	Pacific Press Service / Alamy Stock Photo
130	TAO Images Limited / Alamy Stock Photo
131	Photo Antoin Sevruguin. The Myron Bement Smith Collection, FSA A.04. National Museum of Asian Art Archives. Smithsonian Institution, Washington, D.C. Gift of Katherine Dennis Smith
132	Photo Austin Seymour Masterson. UTSA Special Collections
133	Stephen Barnes / Medical / Alamy Stock Photo
134	Mary Evans / Grenville Collins Postcard Collection
135	Mary Evans / Grenville Collins Postcard Collection
136	Jonathan Player / New York Times / Redux / eyevine
137	Library of Congress, Prints & Photographs Division (HABSIL-1030)
138	Courtesy Mondanock Building
139	Library of Congress, Prints & Photographs Division (HABS IN-253)
141	Unknown Photographer. Peter Smithson and Alison Margaret. House of the Future, Daily Mail Ideal Homes Exhibition, London, England: interior view looking down from the viewing platform, March 1956. Canadian Centre for Architecture (DR1995:0042)
142	Photo Murray Fredericks. Courtesy CPlusC Architects
143	Photo Murray Fredericks. Courtesy CPlusC Architects

The Private Interior

1	Photo José Hevia. Courtesy TAKK
2	Iwan Baan
3	Photo Sue Barr. Courtesy Jencks Foundation at The Cosmic House
4	akg-images / arkivi
5	Photo James Morris. Courtesy David Connor and Kate Darby
6	Shinkenchiku-sha Co., Ltd
7	Simone Padovani / Awakening / Getty Images for Bolton&Quinn
8	akg-images / Duits Collection
9	Dinodia Photos / Alamy Stock Photo
10	Andreas von Einsiedel / Alamy Stock Photo
11	Universal Images Group North America LLC / DeAgostini / Alamy Stock Photo
12	Hemis / Alamy Stock Photo
13	Penta Springs Limited / Alamy Stock Photo
14	James Caulfield
15	Johan Dehlin
16	Koji Taki
17	Courtesy Toyo Ito & Associates, Architects
18	Bravo Images / Alamy Stock Photo
19	Collection Artedia / Bridgeman Images
20	Estate of Evelyn Hofer / Getty Images
21	SuperStock / Eye Ubiquitous
22	*The House in Good Taste*, Elsie de Wolfe, 1913. Published by The Century Co. New York
23	James McDonald
24	GABRIELE CROPPI / Scala, Florence
25	© Rene Burri / Magnum Photos
26	Hemis / Alamy Stock Photo
27	Courtesy Fondazione Achille Castiglioni
28	Courtesy Shinichi Ogawa & Associates
29	Photo José Hevia. Courtesy David Kohn Architects
30	© John G. Zimmerman Archive
31	Diller Scofidio + Ren
32	Richard Powers
33	Peter Stackpole / The LIFE Picture Collection / Shutterstock
34	Library of Congress Prints and Photographs Division Washington, D.C. (HABS PA,26-OHPY.V,1—48)
35	Adam Štěch
36	Carla De Benedetti / www.cdbstudio.com
37	Carla De Benedetti / www.cdbstudio.com
38	George Cserna
39	Richard Powers
40	Jacques Schumacher
41	Heritage Foundation of Pakistan
42	travelbild-asia / Alamy Stock Photo
43	Brendon Carlin
44	Toshiyuki Yano
45	© Allan Wexler
46l	Photo Martin Zwaan. Courtesy the artist
46c	Photo Bart Van Dijk. Courtesy the artist
46r	Photo Martin Zwaan. Courtesy the artist
47	David Wall / Alamy Stock Photo
48	imageBROKER.com GmbH & Co. KG / Alamy Stock Photo
49	Tuul and Bruno Morandi / Alamy Stock Photo
50	Photo Henry Bedford Lemere. Historic England Archive
51	Wellcome Collection
52	Harris & Ewing photograph collection, Library of Congress Prints and Photographs Division, Washington, D.C. (LC-H25-91369-A)
53	The Museum of Modern Art, New York / Scala, Florence
54	Frank and Lillian Gilbreth Library of Management Research and Professional papers. Courtesy of Purdue University Libraries, Karnes Archives and Special Collections (0655-3, Folder 2, Box: 71, Folder: 2)
55	Frank and Lillian Gilbreth Library of Management Research and Professional papers. Courtesy of Purdue University Libraries, Karnes Archives and Special Collections (0655-6, Folder 11, Box: 164, Folder: 11)
56	Howard Sochurek / The LIFE Picture Collection / Shutterstock
57	Unknown photographer, Canadian Centre for Architecture (PH1998:0013:022:004)
58	DeAgostini Picture Library/ Scala, Florence
59	Tomio Ohashi
60	Photo The Museum of Modern Art, New York / Scala, Florence. © Ettore Sottsass DACS, London 2025
61	© Ignazia Favata – Studio Joe Colombo
62	California Institute of the Arts Library & Institute Archives
63	Photo José Hevia. Courtesy Aixopluc
64	Photo Yohei Sasakura. Courtesy Atelier Luke
65	Freer Gallery of Art, National Museum of Asian Art, Smithsonian. Gift of Charles Lang Freer (F1904.61)
66	Amber Gray Photography. Courtesy the artist and DC Moore Gallery
67	Dylan Perrenoud
68	Daici Ano
69	Maximum Film / Alamy Stock Photo
70	Basilica di Santa Maria delle Grazie, Milan
71	Pictorial Press Ltd / Alamy Stock Photo
72	Angelo Hornak / Alamy Stock Photo
73	Angelo Hornak / Alamy Stock Photo
74	Photo Robin Hill. Courtesy Fendi and Lukas Gschwandtner
75	Chronicle / Alamy Stock Photo
76	Ivan Terestchenko
77	© Sarah Wigglesworth
78	RBA Köln, Marion Mennicken
79	Everett Collection Inc / Alamy Stock Photo
80	© Verner Panton Design AG
81	Photo David Zildicky. Courtesy Muzeum města Brna
82	Courtesy David Connor Design
83	Courtesy David Connor Design
84	Photo Jose Campos. Courtesy Studio Marshall Blecher
85	Sergio Pirrone
86	Andreas von Einsiedel / Alamy Stock Photo
87	Richard Bryant / Arcaid Images
88	Photo Yash R Jain. Courtesy RAIN

89	César Béjar Studio	132	Bridgeman Images	9	Photo Koji Fujii / Nacasa & Partners. Courtesy Kengo Kuma
90	Alastair Carew-Cox. All rights reserved 2024 / Bridgeman Images	133	Werner Forman / Universal Images Group / Getty Images	10	Photo David Hugo Cabo. Courtesy Pan-Projects
91	Fine Art Images / Heritage Images via Getty Images	134	Country Life / Future Publishing Ltd	11	Picture Kitchen / Alamy Stock Photo
92	Everett / Shutterstock	135	GrandPalaisRmn / Christophe Fouin	12	Gottscho-Schleisner Collection, Library of Congress Prints and Photographs Division, Washington D.C. (LC-G612-35851)
93	© Ignazia Favata – Studio Joe Colombo	136	Ariadne Van Zandbergen / Alamy Stock Photo		
94	Archivio Ugo La Pietra, Milano	137	Byron Company, Museum of the City of New York (93.1.1.18271)	13	Chronicle / Alamy Stock Photo
95	Courtesy Domat Ltd.	138	Look and Learn / Bridgeman Images	14	APA-PictureDesk / Alamy Stock Photo
96	Courtesy Domat Ltd.				
97	Photo © Deidi von Schaewen	139	BEAUMONT Frédéric / Alamy Stock Photo	15	piemags /POL24 / Alamy Stock Photo
98	yannick luthy / Alamy Stock Photo	140	Photo Pavel Štecha. Courtesy Prague Museum	16	Photo Dirk Weiblen. Courtesy Lukstudio
99	Izzet Keribar / Getty Images	141	Ivan Terestchenko		
100	Mike Goldwater / Alamy Stock Photo	142	Hubmann Bass Architekten	17	Photo Yousub Song. Courtesy Workment
101	DeAgostini/Getty Images	143	Heritage Images / Getty Images	18	Teki Design
102	Roger-Viollet / TopFoto	144	Photo Antonia Reeve. The Hill House, National Trust for Scotland	19	14sd / Fourteen Stones Design
103	SPK / Alamy Stock Photo			20	14sd / Fourteen Stones Design
104	Heritage Image Partnership Ltd / Alamy Stock Photo	145	Photo Matevi Paternoster. Courtesy Plečnik House / Museum and Galleries of Ljubljana	21	Historic England Archive
105	Dir. Kubrick, Warner Bros. / Hawk Films / Peregrine / Producers Circle			22	ORCH Chemollo / RIBA Collections
		146	By kind concession of the State Property Agency, Carlo Mollino Fund preserved at the Polytechnic of Turin, Gabetti Library Archives Section	23	La Construction Moderne No. 31, 1934
106	United Archives GmbH / Alamy Stock Photo			24	Paul Warchol
107	Courtesy Jeroen Offerman			25	Photo Gareth Gardner. Courtesy Morag Myerscough
108	Richard Powers			26	Courtesy Yinka Ilori
109	Photo Jannes Linders. © DACS 2025	147	Matěj Činčera	27	SUPERFLEX
110	Manuel Bougot	148	Manuel Bougot	28	Photo Andrew Meredith. Courtesy Landini Associates
111	Canadian Centre for Architecture (DR1995:0037), © CCA	149	Therese Bonney		
		150	© Estate of David Hicks	29	Diller Scofidio + Ren
		151	Photo Filippo Bamberghi. Courtesy Studio Harry Thaler	30	Courtesy Enter Projects
112	Courtesy of the RISD Museum, Providence, RI. © The Estate of R. Buckminster Fuller			31	Riddle Stagg-VIEW / Alamy Stock Photo
		152	Photo Paul Warchol. Courtesy LOT-EK	32	Nicholas Calcott
113	ONB / Wien 197.319-B (Glasbadewanne Otto Wagner)			33	Seokgyu Hong
		153	Photo Punto Dos Studio / Andrés Villota. Courtesy Mestizo Estudio Arquitectura	34	Seokgyu Hong
114	Peter Aaron / OTTO			35	Denis Guzzo
115	Photo © Deidi von Schaewen			36	J Marshall – Tribaleye Images / Alamy Stock Photo
116	Architectural Press Archive / RIBA Collections	154	Photo Rei Moon. Courtesy Studiomama		
				37	Pascal Chevallier
117	Allan Grant / The LIFE Picture Collection / Shutterstock	155	Courtesy dot Architects	38	David Giral / Alamy Stock Photo
		156	Photo José Hevia. Courtesy TAKK	39	Courtesy Park Hyatt Tokyo
118	Photo Chris Gascoigne. Courtesy Simon Conder			40	Alastair Philip Wiper-VIEW / Alamy Stock Photo
		157	Fuse Project		
119	Pino Guidolotti – CISA A. Palladio	158	Fuse Project	41	Richard Bryant/Arcaid Images
		159	© 2008 Reversible Destiny Foundation. Reproduced with permission of the Reversible Destiny Foundation	42	Werner Dieterich / Alamy Stock Photo
120	Tuomas Uusheimo				
121	Katinka Bester			43	Photo © Wen Studio. Courtesy Atelier tao+c
122	Future Publishing Ltd				
123	FAT Architecture			44	Amit Geron
124	Alex Schweder	**The Public Interior**		45	Photo © Tsing Lim@AGENT PAY. Courtesy Lissoni & Partners
125	Photo Donald Woodman. © 2025 Judy Chicago / Artists Rights Society (ARS), New York / DACS, London				
		1	Library of Congress Prints and Photographs Division, Washington D.C.	46	Rasmus Hjortshøj
				47	© Edmund Sumner / VIEW
		2	Iwan Baan	48	Pedro Pegenaute
126	Photo Courtesy Saatchi Collection, London. © Terence Koh	3	Photo www.tdm.space. Courtesy Robert Storey Studio	49	Gruppo 9999 / Elettra Fiumi
				50	Konstantin Grcici
127	*The Bathroom: Criteria for Design*, Alexander Kira, 1966. Published by Center for Housing and Environmental Studies, Cornell University	4	John Warburton-Lee Photography / Alamy Stock Photo	51	Archivio Ugo La Pietra, Milano
				52	Photo © Timothy Hursley. © Keith Haring Foundation
		5	Photo Hufton+Crow. Courtesy Zaha Hadid Architects	53	Adam Scull / Shutterstock
128	Courtesy Professor Joe Colistra			54	© Ben Kelly Design
129	Dir. Mahnaz Afzali, Iranian Independents	6	Photo Marcus Peel. Courtesy Bompas & Parr	55	PSA Studio
				56	Associated Press / Alamy Stock Photo
130	Photo Bruce Damonte. Courtesy WORKac	7	Courtesy Raffles Hotel Singapore		
131	Batlab Architects	8	John Esperanza / Alamy Stock Photo	57	Vito Arcomano / Alamy Stock Photo

58	Lebrecht Music & Arts / Alamy Stock Photo	94	Marco Introini	139	Photo Camila Cossio. Courtesy Productora
59	Bridgeman Images	95	ymgerman / Shutterstock	140	NurPhoto SRL / Alamy Stock Photo
60	Scala, Florence/Mauro Ranzani	96	Photo Daici Ano. Courtesy Torafu Architects	141	NEOM
61	Alexander Cimbal / Alamy Stock Photo	97	Atelier tao+c	142	© C. Toraldo di Francia | Superstudio, Archivio Filottrano
62	Musée Carnavalet / Roger Viollet via Getty Images	98	Photo © Wen Studio. Courtesy Atelier tao+c	143	Victoria and Albert Museum, London
63	Svintage Archive / Alamy Stock Photo	99	Photo Roos Aldershoff (www.roosaldershoff.com) Courtesy Merkx & Girod	144	Photo GrandPalaisRmn / image ville de Paris. © DACS 2025
64	Shutterstock/ Andrei Antipov	100	Photo David Grandorge. Courtesy 6a Architects	145	View Pictures / Universal Images Group via Getty Images
65	Nextrecord Archives / Getty Images	101	© 2024 Austrian Friedrich and Lillian Kiesler Private Foundation, Vienna	146	KGPA Ltd / Alamy Stock Photo
66	FAY 2018 / Alamy Stock Photo			147	Jon Arnold Images Ltd / Alamy Stock Photo
67	Skimage / Alamy Stock Photo	102	Architecten de Vylder Vinck Taillieu	148	RICOWde / Getty Images
68	Hedrich Blessing Collection/ Chicago History Museum/Getty Images	103	Peter Stackpole / The LIFE Picture Collection / Shutterstock	149	Hagley Museum and Library / Bridgeman Images
69	Photo Hong Sung Jun. Courtesy OMA	104	Steve Speller	150	Michael Freeman / Alamy Stock Photo
70	Photo Hong Sung Jun. Courtesy OMA	105	View Pictures / Universal Images Group via Getty Images	151	Marcus Bredt
71	A. Astes / Alamy Stock Photo	106	The Frank Lloyd Wright Foundation	152	Photo CreatAR Images. Courtesy MAD Architects
72	Alvis Upitis / Alamy Stock Photo	107	Hulton Archive / Getty Images	153	Photo ArchExist. Courtesy MAD Architects
73	Jeffrey Isaac Greenberg 18+ / Alamy Stock Photo	108	Phoro Peter Wuermli. Courtesy Evolution Design	154	Chan Srithaweeporn / Getty Images
74	Victor Gruen Papers, American Heritage Center, University of Wyoming	109	Combine Consulting, Hamburg	155	Photo Iwan Baan. Courtesy Karim Rashid Studio
		110	Eric Laignel		
		111	© Ezra Stoller / Esto	156	Owen Franken / Getty Images
75	ERIC PIERMONT / AFP via Getty Images	112	Photo Paul Warchol. Courtesy Steven Holl Architects	157	Fulget
76	Inigo Bujedo Aguirre / View Pictures / Universal Images Group via Getty Images	113	Photo Connie Zhou. Courtesy Google	158	Mohammad Hassan Ettefagh
				159	Mohammad Hassan Ettefagh
		114	Photo Benny Chan, Fotoworks. Courtesy Clive Wilkinson	160	Image courtesy Sprüth Magers. Andreas Gursky / DACS, 2025
77	Awakening / Getty Images	115	Tim Bies / Olson Kundig	161	World of Triss / Alamy Stock Photo
78	Library of Congress Prints and Photographs Division Washington, D.C. (Unprocessed in PR 13 CN 2010:100, P80.4155)	116	Photo Adrian Wilson. Courtesy Clive Wilkinson	162	Martin Charles / RIBA Collections
		117	Photo Kozo Takayama. Courtesy Klein Dytham	163	Photo Jannes Linders. Courtesy Benthem Crouwel Architects
		118	Garrett Rowland	164	Photo Aryeh Kornfeld. Courtesy Kriskadecor
79	Alison Hoblyn / Alamy Stock Photo	119	Studio Velocity	165	Photo David Zarzoso. Courtesy Francesc Rifé Studio
		120	Studio Velocity		
80	Photo © Daria Scagliola & Stijn Brakkee. Courtesy MVRDV	121	Photo © Schnepp Renou. Courtesy Kinzo	166	Photo Hufton + Crow. Courtesy Zaha Hadid Architects
81	Photo © Daria Scagliola & Stijn Brakkee. Courtesy MVRDV	122	David 'Dee' Delgado / Bloomberg via Getty Images	167	Courtesy Nefa Architects
				168	Peter Scaife / RIBA Collections
82	Photo Maurice Ascani. Courtesy Mariam Issoufou Architects	123	B:HIVE, Smales Farm, New Zealand	169	Sueddeutsche Zeitung Photo / Alamy Stock Photo
		124	Tory Williams	170	Dave Porter / Alamy Stock Photo
83	brandstaetter images / Getty Images	125	Scala, Florence – courtesy of the Ministero Beni e Att. Culturali e del Turismo	171	GrandPalaisRmn / Patrice Schmidt
84	FRENCH+TYE	126	Herman Miller	172	GrandPalaisRmn / J. Derenne
85	Sheila Rock	127	Herman Miller	173	Günter Peters / ullstein bild via Getty Images
86	Evening Standard / Hulton Archive / Getty Images	128	Herman Miller		
		129	Allstar Picture Library Limited / Alamy Stock Photo	174	Henry Herrmann / ullstein bild via Getty Image
87	Photo Alan Williams. Courtesy David Fern	130	Photo Relja Ivanić. Courtesy Studio Autori	175	Photo Ossip Architectuurfotografie. Courtesy Mecanoo
88	Richard Bryant / Arcaid Images	131	Thom Brisco		
89	Nick Leroux	132	Photo Agnese Sanvito. Courtesy Brisco Loran	176	Photo Studio Ten, Tan Xiao. Courtesy NOMOS Architects
90	View Pictures / Universal Images Group via Getty Images	133	Photo © Jin Weiqi. LUO Studio	177	Mmo / Alto Press via ZUMA Press / Alamy Stock Photo
91	Jahrbuch des Deutschen Werkbundes. Die Kunst in Industrie und Handel, 1913	134	Photo Paul Raftery. Courtesy Édouard François		
				178	imageBROKER / Shutterstock
		135	Photo courtesy the artists. © DACS, London 2025	179	imageBROKER.com GmbH & Co. KG / Alamy Stock Photo
92	Imagekontaainer / Knölke / www.imagekontainer.com	136	Studio Makkink & Bey		
		137	Photo Camila Cossio. Courtesy Productora		
93	© The Regents of the University of California, The Bancroft Library, University of California, Berkeley. This work is made available under a Creative Commons Attribution 4.0 license	138	Photo Camila Cossio. Courtesy Productora	180	Jasper Juinen / Bloomberg via Getty Images

181	Photo Mike Bink. Courtesy Silo		Washington, D.C. (LOT 13418, no. 327)
182	Scala, Florence / bpk, Bildagentur fuer Kunst, Kultur und Geschichte, Berlin	220	Double Cyclops
183	Maurice Jarnoux/Paris Match via Getty Images	221	Photo Wang Ziling. Courtesy DnA_Design and Architecture
184	Scala, Florence	222	Margaret Bourke-White / The LIFE Picture Collection / Shutterstock
185	The Museum of Modern Art, New York / Scala, Florence	223	Joop van Reeken
186	The Metropolitan Museum of Art, New York, The Elisha Whittelsey Collection, The Elisha Whittelsey Fund, 1949	224	Daniele Mattioli
		225	Photo Charles Kettaneh. Courtesy EAST Architecture Studio
188	© 2025 Austrian Frederick and Lillian Kiesler Private Foundation, Vienna	226	Aga Khan Trust for Culture / Cemal Emden
189	Sueddeutsche Zeitung Photo / Alamy Stock Photo		
190	RIBA Collections		
191	Federico Puggioni		
192	Jan Haug – Anno Domkirkeodden		
193	Photo Castello di Rivoli Museo d'Arte Contemporanea, Rivoli, Torino. © Maurizio Cattelan		
194	Università Iuav di Venezia, Archivio Progetti, Fondo Andrea Bruno		
195	Photo Mateo Piazza. Courtesy Morpurgo de Curtis		
196	Iwan Baan		
197	Stefano Ravera / Alamy Stock Photo		
198	© Hufton+Crow		
199	Heatherwick Studio		
200	Diller, Scofidio and Ren		
201	Diller, Scofidio and Ren		
202	Iwan Baan		
203	SI.SA Architects / Ademola Olaniran		
204	Photo Sara Pooley. Courtesy White Cube. © Theaster Gates		
205	Hemis / Alamy Stock Photo		
206	Ulrich Schwarz		
207a	Photo Su Shengliang. Courtesy ZAO / standardarchitecture		
207b	Photo Wang Ziling. Courtesy ZAO / standardarchitecture		
208	Photo Sanrok Stufio. Courtesy SHAU		
209	Photo Jin Weiqi. Courtesy LUO Studio		
210	Scala, Florence / Luciano Romano		
211	Photo BKS Inan. Courtesy Studio Anna Heringer		
212	Photo Javier Callejas. Courtesy Urko Sanchez Architects		
213	Photo BKS Inan. Courtesy Courtesy Studio Anna Heringer		
214	J. Enrique Molina / Alamy Stock Photo		
215	OUSMANE MAKAVELI / AFP via Getty Images		
216	Museum of Fine Arts, Boston. All rights reserved / Bridgeman Images		
217	Photo Parisa Taghizadeh. Courtesy Artangel		
218	Fine Art Images / Heritage Images via Getty Images		
219	Library of Congress Prints and Photographs Division		

Index

Page numbers in *italics* refer to illustrations

14sd/Fourteen stones design 254, *255*
2m26 75, *75*
2050 Coffee 254–55, *254*
6a Architects 302, *302*

A

Ab anbar (water reservoir) 107, *108*
Abildgaard, Nicolai Abraham *91*
Action Office 315–16, *316*, *317*
Adam and the Ants 184
Adam, Robert and James 252, *253*
Aftimos, Youssef 60
Afzali, Mahnaz
    The Ladies Room 220, *220*
A House for Essex 153, *156*, *157*
Aixopluc *172*, *173*
Ajanta Caves 32, 56, *56*
Al-Azhar Mosque *40*
Albini, Franco 333, *335*
Alcoholic Architecture 249, *249*
Alder Brisco architects 316, *319*
al-Hamidiyah souk 278, *278*
Almost Cube House 184, *187*
American Bar 256, *257*
American National Exhibition 167–68
AMO 271
Amorepacific 10, 312, *313*
Andreu, Paul 336, *336*
Anno Museum 354, *356*
Antonello da Messina
    Saint Jerome in his Study 20, *21*
Apple 298, *300*
Arakawa, Shusaku 237, *239*
Arcgency 270
Arch of Constantine 102, *103*
Architecten de Vylder Vinck Taillieu (DVVT) 300, *302*
art deco 60
art nouveau 190, 334
Arts and Crafts 87, *87*, 113
Atelier Luke *171*, *173*
Atelier Masomi *see* Mariam Issoufou Architects
Atelier Peter Fong 254, *254*
Atelier Tao+C *12*, 268, *268*, 300, *301*
Atrium 29, 109, 244, 267, 278, 306, 312, 314, 357, *359*
Aulenti, Gae 344, *345*
Avianca lounge, El Dorado airport 338–39, *339*
Avon Tyrrell 87

B

B:HIVE building 314, *314*
Baader, Johannes 353
Babnimnim Design Studio 71, *71*
Bach, Anna and Eugeni 48
    Mies Missing Materiality 48
badawi 26
Bait ur Rouf Jame mosque 10
Balac, Luka 261
Bally shoe store 297, *299*
Baltard, Victor 291, *291*
banco 142, 368
Bang Bang nightclub 271, *273*
banjiha 64, *65*
Bao House 235, *236*
Barcelona Pavilion 40, *41*, 48, *48*
Barjeel 108
Barr Jr, Alfred H. 352
Barragán, Luis 144, *144*
Batlab Architects 223, *223*
Battersea Power Station 343, *343*
'Bauhaus: 1919–1928' exhibition 352, *352*
Bayer, Herbert 352
Beaufort House 75, *75*
Beaux Art 330
Bedouin 26, *28*, 29, 90
Beecher, Catherine 165
Beetle Under the Leaf, The 152, *154*
Béhar, Yves 237, *238*
Behrens, Peter 183, *184*
Beit Beirut Museum 60, *60*
Beijing Daxing International Airport 246, 338, *340*
Beijing Tea House 250, *250*
Béjar, César 188
Benthem Crouwel architects 338, *338*
Bergl, Johann Wenzel 74
Berlin Hauptbahnhof 331, *332*
Bernini, Gian Lorenzo 82
Bester, Willie 197
Bibliothèque nationale de France (BnF) 362–63, *364*
Bijvoet, Bernard 141
Biosleave House 238–39, *239*
Blecher, Marshall 184, *187*
Block, Klaus 363, *365*
BMW Central Building 305, *305*
Boffrand, Germain 140, *141*
Bofill, Ricardo 98, *102*
Bompas & Parr 249, *249*, 256
Bonvicini, Monica 203
    Don't Miss a Sec. 205
Borromini, Francesco 82, *83*
Botticelli, Sandro
    Saint Augustine in His Study 314, *315*
Braaksma & Roos 345, *346*
Bremmer, Paulien 58, *59*
Brinkworth 294, *294*
British Coffee House 252, *253*
British Seed Cathedral 244, 373, *377*
Brooks + Scarpa 105, *105*, 309–10
Brown, Randy 153
Bruggink, Rolf 93, *94*
Bruno, Andrea 148, 354, *356*
Buckminster Fuller 204–07, *207*
Bugatti, Carlo 229, *230*
Burchard, Otto 353, *353*
Bürolandschaft 307, *308*, 316, *320*

C

Cabanon 204, *205*
Caffè Bongo 257, *258*
Cahir Castle *70*
Callet, Félix 291, *291*
Camper store 298, *299*
Capsule Hotel and Bookstore *13*, 267–68, *268*
caravanserai 70, 107, 263, *264*
Carmody Groarke Studio 261
Carrer Avinyó 145, *149*
Carrier, Willis 114
Casa das Canoas 151, *152*
Casa Devalle 230, *232*
Casa Lazzari 152, *155*
Casa Los Tigres 189–90, *191*
Casa Luis Barragán 144, *144*
Castiglioni, Achille 144, *147*
Catena Media office 316, *318*
'Cathedral to Seeds' *see* British Seed Cathedral
Cattelan, Maurizio
    Novecento 356
Cave of Hands *see* Cueva de las Manos
Centerprise Bookstore 103
Centrale Montemartini museum 356–57, *358*
César Béjar Studio *191*
Chand Baori 40, *40*
Chareau, Pierre 141
Charles de Gaulle airport 289, 336–37, *336*
chashitsu 249
Château de Blois *81*
Château de Chambord 81–82, *81*
Château de Groussay 146
Chefferie 136, *136*
Chicago, Judy 169
    Menstruation Bathroom 215, *216*
Chrysler Building 251, *252*
Chulah Cookstove 159, *159*
Cisternerne (Fredriksberg Museums) 62, *63*
'City in Space' exhibition 353–54, *354*
Civic Architects 345, *346*
Clive Wilkinson Architects *310*, 311, *311*
Coates, Nigel 257, *258*
Coenen, Arno 292
Colectivo Chopeke 30
Collage House 97, *97*
Colombo, Joe 121, *170*, 171, 193, *193*
Commes des Garçons 296
Concrete Tent 28–29, *28*
Conisbrough Castle 109, *109*
Connor, David *14*, 131, 184, *186*, 294
Conran, Terence 294
Conversation Pieces 177, *177*
Coppola, Sofia
    Lost in Translation 264
Cosmic House 129
Cosmopolitan hotel 264, *265*
Counterspace 103
Courtyard Children's Library 363–64, *366*
Courvoisier Bar, Selfridges 258, *259*
CplusC Architects *122*, 123, *123*
Crace, Frederick 180
Cramer, Stuart 114
Crate House 161, *161*, 162
Crocker, Templeton 231–32
Croft Lodge Studio *14*, 131
Crystal Palace 58, 84, 243–44, *243*, 278, 291, 327, 329, 362
CS Studio Architects 197
Cubitt, Lewis 329, *329*
Cueva de las Manos (Cave of Hands) 49, *49*

D

DAAR *see* Decolonizing Art Architecture Research
Dabbagh, Sumaya 32, *33*
Dada 352, 353
da Montefeltro, Federico 144
Dandaji Market 292, *293*

Dar Al Jinaa cultural centre 33–34, *35*
Darby, Kate *14*, *131*
David Kohn Architects 145, *149*
Da Vinci, Leonardo
    Last Supper 178
Day After House, The *127*, 235–36, *237*
Deanery Garden 87, *87*
de Blois, Natalie *308*
Decolonizing Art Architecture Research (DAAR) 28, *28*
'Degenerate Art' exhibition 353, *354*
D. E. Shaw office *309*
Design Miami 183
de Wolfe, Elsie 142, *143*, 226, *227*
Didul-Mann, Claudette *308*
dikengyuan residence 38, *40*
Diller + Scofidio 260, *260*
    Mural 358, *360*
    Para-Site 358, *360*, *361*
    The Withdrawing Room 150, *151*
Diller, Elizabeth 150
diwan 136, *137*
DnA_Design and Architecture 26, *27*, 372, *375*
dolmen 30, *30*
doma 159–61, *160*, 171
DOMAT *194*, 195, *195*
Dot Architects 235, *236*
Drivier, Léon-Ernest 257
Dry Bar 104, *104*
Duchamp, Marcel 103
    Fountain 104
Dunand, Jean 231–32, *233*
Dunne & Raby *92*, 92
DVVT *see* Architecten de Vylder Vinck Taillieu
Dymaxion bathroom 207, *207*

E

E-1027 231, *233*
East Architecture Studio 377, *378*, *379*
East London Dining 260
Edison, Thomas 118
Eert Mangwon *254*, 254
Egyptian revival 230
Eiffel, Gustave 372, *373*
El Hallak, Mona 61
Eliasson, Olafur
    The weather project 47, *47*
Elmgreen & Dragset
    Prada Marfa 277, *277*
Emin, Tracey
    Everyone I Have Ever Slept With 1963-1995 50, *50*
Empire State Building 373, *376*
Encants Vells *290*, 291
Endell, August 297, *298*
enfilade 73–74, *74*, 79, *79*, 180, *180*
engawa 134–136, *135*, 159
Enter Projects Asia 260, *261*
Escoffier, Auguste 263
Esmaili, Yasaman 45
Evans, Robin 63, 75
Evolution Design *307*
Expensify 312, *312*

F

Fallingwater 151, *154*
Faraday chair *92*, 92
FAT (Fashion Architecture Taste) 155, *156*, 157, 212
    Bathroom Sweet 212–15, *215*
Favata, Ignazia 193
Fehn, Sverre 354
Fellini, Federico 257
Fendi 182
Fermín Vázquez Arquitectos *290*, 291
First International Dada Fair 353, *353*
Flores & Prats Architects 98, *98*, *100-01*
Flower, Cyril 229
Fondaco dei Tedeschi 283–85, *287*
Fondazione Prada 99
Fondazione Querini Stampalia 69, *69*
Fontana, Carlo
    Templum Vaticanum et Ipsius Origo 83
Formafantasma *92*, 93
Foster + Partners (previously known as Foster Associates) 296, *297*, 337, *338*
Francesc Rifé studio *339*, 339
François, Édouard 316, *320*
Frankfurt Kitchen 121, 166, *167*, 168
Frazier, Susan
    Nurturant Kitchen 169–71, *171*
Frederick, Christine 165–66
    Household Engineering 165, *166*
Freitag bags 300, *300*
Freitag, Markus and Daniel 298
Frey, Albert 151, *153*
Friedman, Yona 327, *328*
Fujimoto, Sou 38, *39*, *128*
Fuseproject 238
Fuss, Diane 63
fusuma 35, 37, *37*, 71, 73

G

Galerie Vivienne *281*
Galleria 285, *286*
Galleria Vittorio Emanuele II 279, *280*
garderobe 202, *202*
Gates, Theaster
    Dorchester Projects 362, *363*
Gelfreich, Vladimir 333
Gesamtkunstwerk 184, 190
Gharem, Ajlan
    Paradise Has Many Gates 25, *25*
Ghiberti, Lorenzo 71
Gilbreth, Lillian Moller 166–67, *167*
Gins, Madeline 237, *239*
Ginzburg, Moisei 168–69
GMP 333
Google 123, *307*, 307, *309*, 309
Grand Central Station *330*, 330, *331*
Graves, Michael *129*
Gray, Eileen 231, 232, *233*
Grcic, Konstantin 271, *272*
Great Bath of Mohenjo-daro 201, *200*
Great Bed of Ware 224, *224*
Great Mosque of Djenné 368, *370*
Great Stupa at Sanchi 56, 68, *69*
Great Victorian Way 327, *328*
Great Wall of China 25
Gribaudo, Ezio 145

Griep, Mary *41*

Grosz, George *353*
Gruen, Victor 285, *289*
Grupo Arquitectos *339*, 339
Gruppo 9999 272
Gschwandtner, Lukas
    Modern Triclinium 182
Guimard, Hector 335
Guixé, Martí *93*, 298, *299*
    Stop Discrimination of Cheap Furniture 94
GUM, Moscow 279, *280*

H

Habitat furniture store 294–96, *296*
Haçienda, The 104, 271–72, *274*
Haidar, Youssef 60, *60*
Hamburger Bahnhof 345, *345*
Hamnett, Katharine 296
Hardwick Hall 84, *84*
Harem 58, 92, *92*
Haring, Keith *274*
Harper, Paula 169
Harry Thaler Studio 233, *234*
Harumi Apartments 160, *160*
Harvey Nichols department store 302–03, *303*
Hatshepsut Mortuary Temple 51, *51*
Hausmann, Raoul 353
Hauteville House 57
Hayward, Luke 171
Heartfield, John 353
Heatherwick, Thomas 244, 296, *297*, 302, *303*, 357, *359*, 373, *376*
Hefer, Porky 212, *213*
Helg, Franca 333, *335*
Heringer, Anna 367, *369*
Herzfelde, Wieland and Margarete 353
Herzog & de Meuron *342*, 343
Hicks, David 233, *234*
Hikma Community Complex 44
Hill House 137–38, *138*, 230, *231*
Hill, Oliver 212, *214*
Hilton, Conrad 263
Hippodrome, London 118
Hitchcock, Alfred
    Psycho 203
Höch, Hannah 353
Hodgetts, Vickie
    Nurturant Kitchen 169–71, *171*
Hoffmann, Josef 191, *192*, 192
HOH architecten 58, *59*
Horta, Victor *190*, 191
Hôtel de Soubise 140–41, *141*
House in Takaya *160*, 161
House NA 38, *38*, *128*
House of the Future 121, *121*, 206, *207*
Huang, Qingjun 19, *19*
Hubmann Vass Architekten 230
Hyatt Regency 267, *267*

I

Ideal Home Exhibition 121
Ikea 288, *289*
Ilori, Yinka 258, *259*
industrial 98, 102, 104, 117, 165, 197, 204, 267, 272, 314, 322, 346, 357, 372

industrialization 165, 168, 243
Inside Outside 34, 35
Institute for Smart Cities 218, 219
Irving House 142–43, 143
Isaacs, Ken and Jo 148, 150
Ise Jingu shrine 371, 371
'Italy: The New Domestic Landscape' (1972) 121, 171, 193
Ito, Toyo 138, 139
    Pao: Dwellings for the Tokyo Nomad Woman 29, 29

J

Jacober, Aldo 273
Jacobsen, Arne 265, 266
Jaffa Hotel 267, 268
jagli 135–36, 135
Jahad Metro Plaza 334, 335
jali 35
Jan Henrik Jansen 184, 187
Jeckyll, Thomas 175–76, 175
Jekyll, Gertrude 87
Jencks, Charles 129
Jencks, Penelope 129
Jiaxing Train Station 331–32, 332
Jingdezhen Imperial Kiln Museum 53–54, 53
Jiřičná, Eva 296, 297
John McAslan + Partners 329, 329
John Randle Centre for Yoruba Culture and History 361, 362
Johnson, Philip 11, 259–60
Jones, Robert 180
Joon-ho, Bong
    Parasite 64, 65
Jourdain, Francis 297, 299
Jungle House 122, 123, 123
Juvara, Romano 152, 155
Juvarra, Filippo 355

K

Kalkin, Adam 104, 105
kamado 159
kamara 224
Kamara, Mariam Issoufou 45
kang 113, 115
Karla Caves 31, 32, 32
Karnak Temple Complex 51
Katsura Imperial Villa 35, 37, 73, 73
Kaufman apartment 210, 212
Kawakubo, Rei 296
Kelly, Ben 103, 104, 272, 274, 294, 295
Kerr, Robert 164, 226
Khrushchev, Nikita 168, 168
kibitka 108–09, 109
Kiesler, Frederick 301, 302, 353, 354
King's Cross station 329, 329
Kingsley, Mark 195
Kinzo 10, 312, 313
Kira, Alexander 217, 218
Kircher, Athanasius 68
Kitchen Practical, The 167
Kleihues, Josef Paul 345, 345
Klein Dytham 312, 312
Klimt, Gustav 191, 192
klismos 90, 91
Knize 293, 294
Koffee Mameya Kakeru 254, 255

Koh, Terence
    Untitled (Medusa) 215, 217
Konchi-in temple 37, 37
korsi 113, 115
Koshino, Michiko 296, 296
KotaKrat 275, 275
kotatsu 113, 114
Kozah, Fouad 60
Kubrick, Stanley
    The Shining 203, 203
Kuma, Kengo 105, 177, 250, 250, 298
Kunitomo, Eiichi 254
Kuniyoshi, Utagawa 371
Kurokawa, Kisho 170, 171

L

LAB Design Studio 264, 265
Labrouste, Henri 362, 364
La Fábrica 98, 102
Lagerfeld, Karl 153, 157
La Laguna 320–22, 322–23
La Maison du Café 257, 257
LAND Arquitectos 184, 187
Landini Associates 259
Landschaftspark 347
Landy, Michael
    Break Down 371, 372
Lantian Village Project 80, 80
Lanyon Quoit 30
Lapidus, Morris 251, 252
La Pietra, Ugo 193, 193, 271, 273
Lari, Yasmeen 159
Larkin Building 305–06, 306
Lascaux Caves 49, 49
LATAM VIP lounge, Arturo Merino Benitez International Airport 339, 339
Le Bon Marché 282, 283, 283
Le Corbusier 47, 204, 204, 205
Lee, Ang
    Eat Drink Man Woman 178, 179
Leigh, Janet 203
Les Halles 291, 291
Lethaby, William 87
Library House 145, 148
Lightoler, Thomas 63, 64
Linehouse Architecture 285
Lisagor, Solomon 169
Lissoni & Partners 267, 269
Living Structure 148, 150, 150, 152
LocHal public library 345–46, 346
Loewy House 151, 153
Loewy, Raymond 151
Loos, Adolf 47, 48, 226, 228, 229, 230, 256, 257, 293, 294
Loos, Lina 229
Losch, Tilly 210
Loseley House 110–13, 112
LOT-EK 234, 235
Love Table 316–20, 320
Lukstudio 254, 254
LUO Studio 316, 320, 367, 367
Lutyens, Edwin 87, 87, 97

M

Ma, Maggie 195
McDonald's 258–59, 259
machiya 171

McKim, Mead & White 136, 137
Mackintosh, Charles Rennie 137, 138, 139, 230, 250, 251
McLaren, Malcolm 294
MAD Architects 331, 332
Mad Men 308, 308
Maekawa, Kunio 160, 160
Mahlangu, Esther 208, 210
Maison à Bordeaux 34, 35
Maison de Verre 141, 141
majlis 128, 134–36, 134
Mallet-Stevens, Robert 228–29, 297, 299
Mall of America 288, 288
Malraux, André 351, 351
Mamluki Lancet Mosque 71, 71
Mansfield, Jayne 210, 211
marble
    cipollino 47
    giallo antico 52
    green Alpine 48
    pavonazzetto 52
Mariam Issoufou Architects 44, 45, 292, 293
Marina Tabassum Architects 10
Markthal 292, 292
Marshall Field & Company 283, 284, 285
Martini, Piero Antonio
    Exposition au Salon du Louvre en 1787 353
MAS Architecture 107, 108
mashrabiya 86, 87
Mecanoo 345, 346
medieval 74, 80, 83, 91, 102, 201, 202, 203, 226, 236, 278, 279
Memphis design group 153, 157
Meneguzzo, Giobatta 152
Mercato Rialto 291, 291
Merkx + Girod 300, 301
Merzbau 351, 351
Messel, Alfred 279
Mestizo Estudio Arquitectura 234, 235
Metcalfe House 136, 137
METI Handmade School 367, 369
Michelangelo 42, 42–43
Michigan Theatre car park 325, 325
microlibrary 363, 367
micro office 316, 320
Middle Ages 30–31, 109–10, 224; *see also* medieval
Midland Grand Hotel 329, 330
Mies van der Rohe 40, 41, 48, 183, 185, 252, 259, 308
mihrab 11, 33, 33
Milam Building 116, 117
Milan Design Week 177
Milan Expo 177
Milan Metro 333–34, 335
Miller, Herman 315, 317
Mimi Calpe 188, 188
Minikitchen 171, 171
minka 159
MIT Media Lab 237, 238
Miyake, Issey 296
Miyamoto, Katsuhiro 133, 133
Modernism 37, 47, 153, 326–27
modularity 148, 150, 152, 170, 171–72, 195, 317, 320, 338, 339
Mohamed Abdulkhaliq Gargash Mosque 32, 33
Mohammad Khavarian Architecture Studio 334, 335
Mollino, Carlo 230–31, 232

MoMA *see* Museum of Modern Art
Monadnock Building 120, *120*
Monastery of Anba Hatre 31, *31*
Monroe, Marilyn 203, *203*
Morpurgo de Curtis 356, *357*
Morris, William *112*, 113
Morton Loft 234, *235*
Moscow Metro 332–33, *333*
Mother 311, *311*
Motovilov, Georgiy *333*
Movement Café 258, *258*
Muhammad, prophet 32–33
mural 56, *330*, 331, *347*
Musée d'Orsay *344*, 345
Musée imaginaire 351, 362
Museion 233, *234*
Museo di Castelvecchio 354, *355*
Museum of Modern Art, New York (MoMA) 121, 193, 352, *352*, 358, 360, *361*
MVRDV 292, *292*, 373, *376*
Myerscough, Morag 258, *258*
Myerson, Jeremy 305

N

Nagaya House 75, *75*
Nakagin Capsule Tower 170, *171*
Nakatsuka, Junko *171*
Naples Metro 334, *334*
Nash, John 179, *180*, *181*
Nash, Paul 210, *211*
Natoire, Charles-Joseph 140
Nefa Architects 339, *341*
Nelson, George 315, *316*
Nendo 177, *177*
neoclassical 330
Neri & Hu 212, *213*, 270, *271*
New Century Global Center 45, *45*
Newgrange 67, *67*
Nickelodeon Universe Amusement Park 288
Nieby Crofters Cottage 184, *187*
Niemeyer, Oscar 151, *152*, 377, *378*
Nike 245
Ningbo Museum 357–58, *361*
Nixon, Richard 168, *168*
Nomos Architects 346, *346*

O

Oduwole, Seun 361, *362*
Offerman, Jeroen 203
  The Portable Psycho Shower Scene Stage Set Party, Part I–V 203
Office Kersten Geers David Van Severen 33–35, *35*
O'Kelly, Michael J. 67
Olivetti 298, *300*, 301, *302*
Olson Kundig (previously known as Olson Sundberg Kundig Allen) 310, *310*
OMA 34, *35*, 98, 285, *286*, *287*
ondol 113, *113*
One Take Architects 61
  Internal Theater 61
open plan 148, 150–52, 154, 220, 236, 306, 311, 320
Ore Streams 92–93, *93*

Ori 237, *238*
Orlando Power Station 347, *347*
Osterley Park 225, *225*

P

Palace of Tranquil Longevity 56, *57*
Palace of Versailles 202, 225, *225*
Palais Stoclet 191–92, *192*
Palazzo Barberini *82*, 83
Palazzo Davanzati 110, *111*
Palazzo del Te 55, *55*
Palazzo Ducale 54, *55*, *144*
Palazzo Venezia 76, *78*, *79*
Palladio, Andrea 37, *368*
Palladium 271, *274*
Pallotta TeamWorks *310*, 311
Pan- Projects 250, *251*
Pantheon 52, *52*
Panton, Verner 184, *184*
pao 29–30, *29*
PAO *see* People's Architecture Office
Paris Exposition, 1867 372–73, *373*
Paris Métro 333, *335*
Park Hyatt Tokyo 264, *265*
Pawson, John 267, *268*
Paxton, Joseph 327, *328*
Penn Station 330, *330*
People's Architecture Office (PAO) 105, *105*
Perry, Charles
  Eclipse 267
Perry, Grayson 156, *157*
Peruzzi, Baldassare 37
Peter Behrens House 183, 185
Pharaoh Nynetjer 90, *91*
Pillow Talk 107, *107*
Pirroni, Marco 184, *186*
Plečnik, Jože 230, *231*
Pompeii 200, 226
Ponti, Gio 152, *154*
pop-up office 320, *321*
portcullis 70, *70*
Portman, John 267, *267*
Portrait Pavilion 58, *59*
post-industrial 272, 346
Praz, Mario 47
Productora 322, *322*, 323
Propst, Robert 315, *316*
Proust, Marcel 63, 64, 232, 264
PSA Studio 275
Push Button House 104, *105*

Q

qibla 33
Quickborner 307–09, *309*
Qur'an 33, 40, 92

R

Rael, Ronald 30
Rael San Fratello 30
Raffles Hotel 249, *249*
RAIN studio 190, *190*
Ralph Appelbaum Associates 362
Ranalli, George 153, *156*
Rapha Cycling 294, *294*

Rare Architects 268, *270*
Rashid Karami International Fair pavilion 373, *378–79*
Rashid, Karim *334*
Raumplan 47
Reactor 105, *105*, 309
readymade 103–05
Reagan, Ronald and Nancy 192
recycling 53, *93*, 108, 234, 261, 292, 300
Repton, Humphry 180
Restaurant Moes 261, *263*
Retrouvius 96, 97
Reyers, Zeger 162, *162*
Rietveld, Gerrit 37, *38*
Rijksmuseum, Schiphol Airport 338, *338*
RISD Student Success Center 220, *221*
Ritz, César 263
Ritz, Paris 263, *264*
Rivoli Castle 354–55, *356*
Rizzatto, Paolo 273
Robert Storey Studio 245
Robie House 183, *184*
Robinson, W. Heath 197
Rodin, Auguste 257
Rookery Building 120, *120*
Rossetti, Dante Gabriel 251
Roswag, Eike 367, *369*
Rotating Kitchen 161–62, *162*
Rotor
  Ex Limbo 98, *99*
Rougier, Michael 302
Royal Pavilion, Brighton 179–80, *180*
Royalton Hotel 265–66, *266*
Royal Victoria Hospital, Belfast 117, *117*
Rudolph, Paul 207, *209*
Ruhs, Kris 228
Rural Urban Framework 80, *80*

S

S+PS Architects 97, *97*
Saarinen, Eero 336, *337*
Saint Gall monastery 31, *31*
Saint Mark's Basilica 40, *41*
St Mary's Church, Müncheberg 365
St Pancras Renaissance London 330
Saks Fifth Avenue 301, *302*
Sala Beckett 98, *98*
Salamander shoe store 297, *298*
Sambuichi, Hiroshi 61, *62*, *63*, 357, *358*
San (a people of southern Africa) 25, *26*
Sancaklar Mosque 33, *33*
San Fratello, Virginia 30
Sanno 312–13, *313*
Santa Maria Assunta cathedral 102–03, *103*
SAS Royal Hotel 265, *266*
Scamozzi, Vincenzo 368
Scarpa, Carlo 69, *69*, 210, *212*, 298, *300*, 354, *355*
Schapiro, Miriam 169, *171*
Scheffknecht, Liddy 320, *321*
Schmalhausen, Otto 353
Schönbrunn Palace 74, *74*
Schrager, Ian 265
Schröder House 37–38, *38*
Schütte-Lihotzky, Margarete 166, *167*
Schweder, Alex

In Orbit 371–72, *374*
Plumbing Us 215, *216*
Schwitters, Kurt 351, *351*, 353
Scofidio, Ricardo 150
Scott, George Gilbert 329, *330*
Seagram Building 11, 259–60, *260*
Sedgwick Rd *310*, 311
Seirensho Art Museum 357, *358*
Selexyz Dominicanen bookstore 300, *301*
Selfridges, London 258, *259*
Serlio, Sebastiano 70, 109–10
    Extraordinary Book of Doors 70–71, *72*
    Five Books on Architecture 110–11
Serpentine Pavilion 103, *103*
SEX 294, *295*
sgabello 90, *91*
Shah Abbas I 264
Shangri-La Shougang Park hotel 267, *269*
Shared Lady Beetle 367, *367*
SHAU architecture 363, *367*
Shchuko, Vladimir 333
Sheesh Mahal 58, *58*
Shelley, Ward
    In Orbit 371–72, *374*
Shinichi Ogawa & Associates 145, *148*
Shoah Memorial 355–56, *357*
Shröder House 37–38, *38*
Shu, Wang 357, *361*
Siclis, Charles 257, *257*
Silo 349, *349*
Simic, Stefana 134, *134*
Simon Conder Associates 210, *212*
Sissay, Lemn 258
Sistine Chapel 42–43, *43*–45
Skidmore, Owings & Merrill (SOM) 308–09
Smart Mobile Disco 271, *272*
Smith, Paul 302
Smithson, Alison and Peter 121, *121*, 206, *207*
Smithsonian Institute 175
Smuts, Carin 197
Soane, John 188, *189*
soffitto 43
SOM *see* Skidmore, Owings & Merrill
SOS Children's Village 367, *369*
Sottsass, Ettore 121
    Preliminary Project for Microenvironment 170, 71
Southdale Center 285, *289*
Sozzani, Franca 228, *229*
Space Electronic 271, *272*
Spatial City 327–28, *328*
Speculum Romanae Magnificentiae 103
spolia 102–04
Stansted airport 337–38, *338*
Starck, Philippe 265, *266*
Starsis *262*, 263
step well 40, *40*
Steven Holl Architects 309, *309*
Stimmung 47
Stokesay Court 118–19, *119*
Strigino airport 339, *341*
Strutt, William 114
Stucki, Hermann 143
Studio 10 58, *59*
Studio 54 271, *274*
Studio Anne Holtrop *9*
Studio Autori 316, *318*

Studio BBPR 301, *302*
Studio Chahar 44, *45*
Studio East Dining 261, *261*
Studio Makkink & Bey 320, *322*
Studiomama 235, *236*
Studio Marsman 349, *349*
Studio Represent 316, *319*
Studio Velocity 312, *313*
Studio Zhu-Pei 53, *53*
Sugawara, Seizo 232
Suh, Do Ho 21–22
    Home Within Home Within Home Within Home Within Home 22, *23*
    Rubbing/Loving Project: Seoul Home 89, *89*
Sullivan, Howard 303
Sultan Han caravanserai 70, *70*
SUPERFLEX
    Flooded McDonald's 258, *259*
Superstudio
    Continuous Monument 326–27, *327*, 328
Superuse 261, *263*
Suppose Design Office 160, *161*
Surrey House 230
sustainable 38, 104, 123, 254, 260
Suwŏlok *262*, 263
Swan, Joseph 118
Sylvester, Charles 114

T

TAKK *127*, 235, *237*
TanArt Community 346, *346*
tatami 73, 90, *90*, 113, 133, 135, 171, 250, *250*
Tate Modern 47, *47*, *342*, 343
Tati, Jacques
    Playtime 316, *318*
Taylor, Frederick Winslow 165–66, 306, *307*, 315
TBWA\HAKUHODO 311, *312*
Teahouse Ø 250, *251*
Teatro Olimpico 368, *368*
Teeter-Totter Wall 30–31, *30*
Teki Design 254, *254*
Telematic House 193, *193*
Tempelhof airport 339–43, *343*
Temple of Edfu 51
Temple of Horus 73, *74*
Temporary Museum (Lake) 9
tepee 25
Terrace House 171–73, *173*
The Krane 268, *270*
The Line 326–28, *326*
The Nest 210–12, *213*
The Vyne 75, *76*
thinnai 134–36, *136*
Thorpe, John 74–75
Times Square 259
tokonoma 73
Tomb of Meresankh III *50*
Topkapi Palace 92, *92*
Torafu Architects 300
Total Furnishing Unit 121, 193, *193*
Town Hall Hotel 268, *270*
Trajan's Market 278, *278*
trompe l'oeil 54–55, *368*
Tsodilo Hills rock paintings 49, *49*
Tubular Baitasi 105, *105*
tulou 79–80, *80*
Turrell, James 63, *63*

TWA Flight Center, John F. Kennedy airport 336–37, *337*
Twiggy store 300–01, *302*
'Type F' unit apartment 169

U

Uffizi Gallery 352, *352*
Union Carbide Building 308
Urko Sanchez Architects 367, *369*

V

Vally, Sumayya 103, *103*
Van Kannel, Theophilus 120, *121*
Vasari, Giorgio 352, *352*
Vatican Palace 83, *83*
vedika 68, *69*
Vélez, Simón 134, *134*
Venice Biennale 134
Veronese, Paolo *36*, 37
Victorian 87, 166, 201, 256, 327–29
Vigo, Nanda 152, *154*
Villa Barbaro *36*, 37
Villa Cavrois 228, *228*, 229
Villa Farnesina 37
Villa Müller 47, *48*, 226–28, *228*
Villa Ottolenghi 210, *212*
Villa Savoye 204, *204*
Villa Tugendhat 183, *185*

W

Wagemans, Niek 94
Wagner, Armin B. 320, *321*
Wagner, Otto 207, *208*
Wall of Indifference 356, *357*
Waterhouse at South Bund hotel 212, *213*, 270, *271*
Waterston, Darren
    Filthy Lucre 176, *176*
Welles, Orson
    Citizen Kane 178, *179*
Weltsch, Robin 169
    Nurturant Kitchen 169–71, *171*
Westwood, Vivienne 294
Wexler, Allan 161, *161*
Whistler, James McNeill 175–76
    Art and Money; or, The Story of the Room 175, *175*
White House 192
White U 138–39, *139*
Whitney Museum 63, 358, *360*
Wigglesworth, Sarah 180–82
    The Disorder of the Dining Table 182, *183*
Wightwick Manor 112, *113*
Wilder, Billy
    The Seven Year Itch 203, *203*
Willis, George 117
Willow Tea Rooms 250–51, *251*
Womanhouse 169–71, *171*, 215, *216*
WORKac 220, *221*
Work at Home 320, *322*
Workment 254, *254*
Wright, Frank Lloyd 136–37, *137*, 151, *154*, 183, *184*, 305, *306*
Wunderland Kalkar 346–47, *348*

Y

Yanagi, Yukinori
    Solar Rock 358
YourStudio 303
yurt 19, *19*, 25, 29, 109
Yusuf, Ali ibn 76

Z

Zaha Hadid Architects *247*, 305, *305*,
    338, *340*
ZAO 363, *366*
Zárraga, Ángel 257
Zein-o-Din caravanserai *264*
Zeitz Museum of Contemporary Art
    Africa (MOCAA) 357, *259*
zellij 141
Zenkai House 133–34, *133*
Zepeda, Fernando Sánchez 188, *191*
Zero Waste Bistro 261, *261*
ZGF Architects 309, *309*, 312, *312*
zidaka 12, 143, *143*
Ziin furniture store 300, *301*

On the cover (clockwise from top): *Museum of the Moon*, Luke Jerram, Old Royal Naval College, London, 2022. Imageplotter Travel / Alamy Stock Photo; Elektrozavodskaya metro station, Vladimir Shchuko and Vladimir Gelfreich, Moscow, 1944. Chan Srithaweeporn / Getty Images; Jingdezhen Imperial Kiln Museum, Studio Zhu-Pei, China, 2020. Photo schranimage. Courtesy Studio Zhu-Pei.

First published in the United Kingdom in 2025
by Thames & Hudson Ltd, 6–24 Britannia Street,
London WC1X 9JD

First published in the United States of America in 2025
by Thames & Hudson Inc., 500 Fifth Avenue, New York,
New York 10110

The Story of the Interior © 2025 Thames & Hudson Ltd,
London

Text © 2025 Graeme Brooker

All Rights Reserved. No part of this publication may be reproduced or transmitted in any form or by any means, electronic or mechanical, including photocopy, recording or any other information storage and retrieval system, without prior permission in writing from the publisher.

EU Authorized Representative: Interart S.A.R.L.
19 rue Charles Auray, 93500 Pantin, Paris, France
productsafety@thameshudson.co.uk
interart.fr

A CIP catalogue record for this book is available from
the British Library

Library of Congress Control Number 2025934787

ISBN 978-0-500-02759-2
01

Printed and bound in China by C&C Offset Printing Co. Ltd

Be the first to know about our new releases, exclusive content and author events by visiting
thamesandhudson.com
thamesandhudsonusa.com
thamesandhudson.com.au